EMPIRE'S MOBIUS STRIP

EMPIRE'S MOBIUS STRIP

HISTORICAL ECHOES IN ITALY'S CRISIS OF MIGRATION AND DETENTION

STEPHANIE MALIA HOM

CORNELL UNIVERSITY PRESS
Ithaca and London

First published 2019 by Cornell University Press

Library of Congress Cataloging-in-Publication Data

Names: Hom, Stephanie Malia, author.
   Title: Empire's Mobius strip : historical echoes in Italy's crisis of migration and detention / Stephanie M. Hom.
Description: Ithaca : Cornell University Press, 2019. | Includes bibliographical references and index.
   Identifiers: LCCN 2018060525 (print) | LCCN 2019000660 (ebook) | ISBN 9781501739910 (pdf) | ISBN 9781501739927 (ret) | ISBN 9781501739897 | ISBN 9781501739897 (cloth) | ISBN 9781501739903 (pbk.)
   Subjects: LCSH: Lampedusa Island (Italy)—Emigration and immigration. | Refugees—Italy—Lampedusa Island. | Alien detention centers—Italy—Lampedusa Island. | Libya—Emigration and immigration. | Lampedusa Island (Italy)—History. | Libya—History.
Classification: LCC JV8139.L36 (ebook) | LCC JV8139. L36 H66 2019 (print) | DDC 304.8/45—dc23
LC record available at https://lccn.loc.gov/2018060525

CONTENTS

ILLUSTRATIONS

Figures

Maps

EMPIRE'S MOBIUS STRIP

Introduction

> And call by his own name his people Romans.
> For these I set no limits, world or time,
> but make the gift of empire without end.
>
> —Virgil, *The Aeneid*

Italian empire, by conventional definition, was a short-lived affair. It lasted just eight years, bookended by Italy's invasion of Ethiopia in 1935 and the fall of the Fascist regime in 1943. Its relative brevity has led, in part, to its omission from studies of modern European imperialisms even though Italy's colonial projects in East Africa and Libya stood among the most brutal and bloody of the last century.

Empire was anything but short-lived for the hundreds of thousands of Italians who carried out Italy's imperial ambitions. Nor was it brief for the many more people who became subjects of those ambitions and have since remained subjugated to that power decades after Italian empire officially ended. Empire creates a ripple effect across time and space, and in the words of Ann Stoler, "saturates the subsoil of people's lives and persists, sometimes subjacently, over a longer durée."[1] The ongoing ripple effects have been called imperial formations, that is, "polities of dislocation, processes of dispersion, appropriation and displacement . . . dependent upon moving categories and populations . . . [and] on material and discursive postponements and deferrals."[2] These are uneasy, messy constellations always in the process of becoming and unraveling.

Some imperial formations are more explicit than others. In the context of modern Italy, take, for example, the Via dei Fori Imperiali in Rome (figure 1). Built between 1924 and 1932, this street physically and symbolically linked the foremost sign of Italy's ancient empire, the Roman Colosseum, with the nerve

FIGURE 1.   View of the Via dei Fori Imperiali and Colosseum, Rome. Photograph courtesy of Shutterstock, 2017.

center of its new Fascist empire, Piazza Venezia. Mussolini ordered the demolition of one of Rome's most densely populated neighborhoods to make way for this imperial artery, evicting and displacing thousands of residents, appropriating their homes, bulldozing churches, razing gardens, demolishing medieval and Renaissance structures, and destroying untold numbers of archaeological ruins, the debris of the Roman Empire. The road still stands, and each day thousands of tourists shamble along this vector of Italy's empires, appropriating the space anew.

The Via dei Fori Imperiali is a clear example of an imperial formation materialized in brick and cobblestone.[3] Its existence is owed to a discrete constellation of dispersion and dislocation that arose at a particular historical moment in a particular cultural context: Fascist Italy. In fact, it was at the terminus of this road, from the balcony of a palazzo in Piazza Venezia, that Mussolini famously issued his proclamation of Italian empire on May 9, 1936. "L'Italia ha finalmente il suo impero," he said. "Dopo quindici secoli, la riapparizione dell'impero sui colli fatali di Roma." (Italy finally has its empire . . . after fifteen centuries, the reappearance of empire on the fated hills of Rome.)[4] Concretized in roadwork and by rhetoric, Italy's new Fascist empire symbolically and physically appropriated the empire of ancient Rome along the Via dei Fori Imperiali.

Other imperial formations are harder to pinpoint. Sometimes they require adjusting one's critical lens to recognize deeper, subtler constellations that arise over time. For example, take the controversial "nomad emergency decree" issued in 2008 by then prime minister Silvio Berlusconi's government. This decree pronounced "nomads" a threat to public order and security, by which it meant the Roma specifically (who are pejoratively called gypsies). Some of these Roma were Italian citizens. Others had migrated from European Union (EU) countries and had the legal right to reside in Italy. Still others came from elsewhere such as the Balkans.

By declaring a state of nomad emergency, the decree empowered municipalities including Rome, Naples, and Milan to intervene with force. Bulldozers and excavators arrived with little notice at the entrances of Romani settlements known as *campi nomadi* (nomad camps) and quickly went to work demolishing them. When the bulldozers were finished, all that remained of these communities were crumpled walls and scattered two-by-fours. Thousands of Roma were dispossessed and displaced in the process. This act of forced dislocation has a name in Italian: *sgombero*. It is roughly translated as "eviction" but carries connotations of evacuation, clearing, vacating, and loss as well.[5] The Roma who lost their homes by *sgombero* either relocated to other camps or became sequestered in government-built villages scattered along the urban periphery.

Yet the Roma were not the first "nomads" who presented a threat to the Italian state. Italian colonial officials considered *il grande nomadismo* (the great nomadism) of Bedouin tribes in Libya a clear and present danger, so much so they declared a state of emergency against them in 1930. This nomad emergency decree paved the way for the forced dispossession and displacement of more than one hundred thousand Bedouin from their homelands. Not only that, the decree also provided the juridical pretense for imprisoning them in Italian-built concentration camps along the desolate Cyrenaican coast. Nomadism was thought to be so threatening that it could be countered only by immobilization. The squalid conditions of these camps made for deathly living among the barbed wire, frayed tents, famine, intractable diseases, and endless dust and wind. In the span of just five years, 1929–33, at least forty thousand Libyan Bedouins died in these Italian-built concentration camps. Some historians put the death toll closer to seventy thousand. It was a genocide that remains little known outside Libya today. If mentioned at all, the camps are but footnotes in studies of European imperialisms. More often than not, they are simply absent, unknown, and long repressed by the myth of Italians as good colonizers.

When we expand our analytic frame, the bonds between what were once seen as distinct constellations are revealed. In this example, the nomad emergencies that manifested almost a century apart are connected by the practices and the logics rooted in Italy's imperial ambitions. The one finds direct resonance in the other. Practically, Italian functionaries took the same actions to neutralize the threat of nomadism: they dispossessed, dislocated, and immobilized Bedouin and Roma in concentration camps and government-built villages, respectively. Logically, what links the Roma of today with the Bedouin of yesterday was the threat their nomadism allegedly posed to Italian sovereignty. It was deemed an utmost danger to public safety under the auspices of which racist and xenophobic violence—even genocide—could be carried out in the name of the state. Suffice it to say, the nomad emergencies declared in Italy and Libya almost a century apart signal the surfacing of an imperial formation in all of its messy, uneasy, violent becoming and unraveling. The camps and villages linked to nomadism are hardly imperial debris but rather live sites of this formation as it stretches out across time and folds back on itself: empire's Mobius strip.

∞

This study examines, historically and anthropologically, the imperial formations that have shaped modern Italy. It traces the ways in which Italy's neglected colonial history, particularly in Libya, has been cited and expanded in its current crisis of migration and detention. To be more precise, Italy's disavowed colonial past not only becomes expressed by this crisis but also emerges with amplified force. I take up the task set forth by anthropologists and historians of empire who have called for a reimagining of how imperial formations organize contemporary practices structured in dominance as well as how they demarcate and particularize histories of the present.[6] My study grapples with the messy ways that Italy's empire organizes itself across time and space, and how that organization violently produces exclusionary spaces and marginalized subjects, and, at the same time, generates the very structural conditions for inclusion within the Italian state and related civic projects.

I contend that mobility—and specifically, the control of mobility—forges lasting connections between Italy's imperial formations. Mobility regimes operate unevenly between times and spaces, between macro- and microscales, and between political and economic spheres to create powerful sovereignties that stratify and subjugate over the longue durée. Empire rests on these connections: the power over movement equates to power over people. What is at stake in *Empire's Mobius Strip* is a deeper and more complicated understanding of the unacknowledged historical forces that drive those who move by choice and those who are moved by force. My aim is to account for mobility as the crucial connective tissue between the politics of difference exercised by empire and to position Italy—long the site of contested mobilities—as the critical site for the study of contemporary European imperialisms in the Mediterranean.

The power over people names the driving force of empire. Ample scholarship has been dedicated to understanding how this force operates.[7] For example, myriad histories of imperialism have chronicled the vexed, violent operations of imperialist expansion across Africa and Asia in the late nineteenth and early twentieth centuries. Others, too, have documented the rise of a market empire in the United States and Europe and a civilizing mission retooled toward consumption. Likewise, theorists of empire have detailed the emergence of a new form of global sovereignty based on decentralized and de-territorialized networks of power, the apotheosis of late capitalism. All, directly or indirectly, acknowledge the primacy of mobility to the imperial exercise of power. These scholars together constitute a chorus—to which I add my voice—that gives a catholic sense of empire's alchemy, that is, the means by which this force has come to transfuse, deleteriously, the lives of so many.

Our voices have taken on new urgency in this second decade of the twenty-first century—a moment when the "threat" of unsanctioned mobilities has incited upsurges in xenophobia, racism, and isolationism that historically have portended hardline authoritarianism. In Italy, the United States, and elsewhere, attempts to control mobility have led to unspeakable traumas: families separated at borders, discriminatory travel bans, human rights violations, and endless detention, to name just a few. At last count, more than sixty-eight million people have been forcibly displaced in 2018 as a result of conflict or persecution, the highest level ever on record, according to the UN Refugee Agency.[8] Almost thirteen million of them are under eighteen years old. The study of empire and mobility is more crucial now than ever.

When mobility comes by way of force, not choice, people are shunted into an existence of temporary permanence. They are buffeted, inter alia, between makeshift camps, overcrowded detention centers, traffickers' houses, cramped vehicles, and waiting zones—each one a space that localizes what Michel Agier has called an "indefinite temporality" and "permanent precariousness."[9] Yet everyday life forges ahead in these purportedly temporary spaces. For example, generations have been raised in the world's largest refugee camp at Dadaab in northeastern Kenya. It has existed for more than twenty-five years, and in 2018 remains home to more than five hundred thousand people. Dadaab contains the rudiments of urban life: markets, coffee shops, restaurants, video stores, mobile phone shops, a fitness center, even its own newspaper, *The Refugee*. It is hardly a transitory place. Tents have become mud brick houses. Children graduate from school. Tens of thousands of people spend their entire lives there. Even if one is able to leave the camp's permanent precariousness and resettle elsewhere, one is still connected to family and friends who remain.[10] In this way, ties of kinship and community sustain the condition of temporary permanence even for those who have left the camp. It haunts from afar, in conversations and memories, as a reminder of the chronic precariousness linked to unsanctioned mobilities.

The same goes for those who have passed through migrant detention centers in Italy that were once named for the condition itself: Centri di Permanenza Temporanea (Centers of Temporary Permanence), known by their abbreviation, CPT. The people who were detained in CPTs describe their experiences in the same words used by those living in Dadaab: uncertainty, survival, insecurity, limbo, interminable waiting. "Temporary permanence" is itself an oxymoron. Semantically, the two terms cancel each other out and in doing so create a condition of absolute suspension, according to Marco Rovelli. He writes, "Il *centro* in cui vige questa assoluta sospensione di senso si pone dunque come (non) luogo di deprivazione, di svuotamento. Uno svuotamento tanto da un punto di vista esistenziale . . . quanto da un punto di vista giuridico." (The center in which this absolute suspension of sense is enforced therefore is set as a non-place of deprivation, of evacuation. An emptying as much from an existential point of view . . . as from a legal point of view.)[11] Sites like the CPTs in Italy or the Dadaab refugee camp institutionalize this suspension. For those moved by force, suspension gives way to life in perpetual limbo. Temporary permanence becomes the shorthand for empire's power over people through the control of mobility.

Limbo takes topological form in the figure of the Mobius strip, this book's guiding metaphor. The strip appears as an infinite loop. It looks like a smooth ribbon with a single twist that endlessly reverses inside and outside. It is suspension made manifest. Its essential geometric quality is that it cannot be oriented. In fact, the Mobius strip disorients in that it has no clear front or back, up or down, inside or outside much in the same way imperial formations disorient those caught up within them. Imperial formations constitute the practice of empire, and they suppress through dislocations, dispersions, displacements, deferrals, appropriations, and postponements—that is, they govern through movement of all sorts.[12] They are slippery, messy, and difficult to orient. They also span past and present, and are ongoing. The essays in this book mirror the Mobius strip by tracing out Italian imperial formations across time and space. They show how empire's power over people does not belong to a superseded era but rather resides very much with us. The divide between those who move by choice and those who move by force grows wider and starker. Empire expands its reach while tightening its grip.

Specifically, I train my lens on the moving categories and populations that structure Italian imperial formations to illustrate how they were controlled in colonial Libya, and how those controls resurface, both explicitly and subjacently, among the exclusionary spaces and discriminatory practices of Italy's current migration and detention crisis. My analysis focuses on key sites, past and present, in which these formations accrete: carceral islands, migrant detention centers, concentration camps, agricultural villages, "equipped villages," and refugee camps. I privilege the built environment as an especially legible context in which to analyze these operations precisely because it is where the imperial finds fixture in physical form. The island, the camp, and the village are fitting metonyms that signify the points at which Italy's empire touches down in space.

I use the term "colonial" and its variants to describe attitudes and actions that affect the forced takeover of physical and psychic territories. One need only think of the nineteenth-century European scramble for Africa or exercises of internal colonization in places like the Pontine Marshes south of Rome. I expand the term "empire" and its variants to include mobility-generated disparity as that which subtends the hierarchical relations, unequal rule, and inequitable treatment that have long defined the study of empires. At sites like the island, the camp, and the village, empire operates unevenly and contentiously between times, spaces, scales, and spheres to reinforce gradations of sovereignty that oppress those less powerful. It is hardly solid but rather built on mobility.

On a literary note, the study of Italy's empire lends itself toward fulfilling Jupiter's erstwhile promise in book 1 of *The Aeneid*, arguably the founding narrative of Italy itself. The Roman god foretells of Rome's ascendance from the ruins of Troy and its lot of refugees, and bestows on Aeneas "the gift of empire without end." Just as Jupiter set no limits to the Roman Empire, there are seemingly "no limits, world or time" to modern Italy's imperial formations and the refigured expanses of its imperial terrains.[13] *Empire's Mobius Strip* seeks, in its own way, to bring new perspective and meaning to this empire without end.

Mobile Lives

Mobility is both a key colonial concern and chief organizing principle of our time. The freedom of movement—of people, objects, and ideas—has become a "scarce and unequally distributed commodity" in our era of intensified circuits of globalized exchange, de-territorialized imaginaries, and techno-scientific value systems.[14] It discriminates and subjugates by fortifying the hierarchical relations between those who move by choice, like tourists, and those who are moved by force, like refugees.

Accelerated mobilities have cemented the power and privilege of a ruling class of global elites today. For the people belonging to this class, life has been shaped positively by mobility in all of its corporeal, material, imaginative, communicative, and virtual modalities.[15] These "mobiles," as Anthony Elliott and John Urry have called them, move seamlessly across borders of all sorts. They speed through customs with the right visas and passports. They inhabit airport lounges and luxury hotels. They use digital technologies to keep in touch with home and work. They shop for everything online. Theirs is a mobile life of intricate negotiation—it centers on figuring out how to be in different places simultaneously (for example, telecommuting), how to accumulate and expend network capital (for example, elite frequent flyer programs), and how to deal with the psychic fallout of a fragmented life all the while espousing mobility-generated ideals like flexibility, adaptability, liquidity, and instant transformation. For this class of elites, "mobility is both ideology and utopia of the twenty-first century."[16]

At the same time, accelerated mobilities have debilitated a vastly larger class of people today. These people do not move seamlessly across borders. In fact, they experience quite the opposite. Their movements are blocked, detoured, interrupted, extended, and deferred at every turn. They are detained on islands, interned in camps, and shuffled between villages. These "mobiles" have been given many different names, including refugees, asylum seekers, economic migrants, stateless people, *sans-papiers*, displaced persons, *clandestini*, evacuees, disaster victims, and more. No matter the label, the intent behind every one of these categorizations is the same. It isolates and alienates this immense underclass of mobiles into what Michel Agier has called an indistinct set of undesirables.[17]

At no other time in modern history have so many "undesirables" been on the move. Wars, famine, and climate change have led to the highest levels of forcible displacement on record. So unprecedented is this scale of movement that the news media, international development agencies, academics, and politicians of every ilk have labeled it a crisis. As Mayanthi Fernando and Cristiana

Giordano note: "This so-called crisis has turned immigration, asylum, border control, and state sovereignty into interconnected problems, making migration not only a political event but also a media spectacle."[18]

To put it another way, this great mobile underclass has become ensnared in what Achille Mbembe describes as the "new moment of global mobility" wherein "a patchwork of overlapping and incomplete rights to rule emerges, inextricably superimposed and tangled, in which different de facto juridical instances are geographically interwoven and plural allegiances, asymmetrical suzerainties, and enclaves abound."[19] No entity has authorized the movements of this underclass. They do not have the proper visas and passports. They do not inhabit airport lounges or luxury hotels. They do not possess the digital technologies required to gain access to globalized flows of goods and services. And yet theirs, too, is a mobile life of intricate negotiation. It also centers on figuring out how to be in different places simultaneously (for example, one's home and host countries), how to accumulate and expend network capital (for example, wiring money to bribe traffickers), and how to deal with the physical and emotional fallout of a life shattered that was often not of their own choice.

Nowhere did I witness this disparity between the mobile lives of "undesirables" and those of global elites more clearly than on the island of Lampedusa. This tiny limestone shelf, just five miles long, sits in the center of the Mediterranean Sea at the southernmost border of Europe. On the one hand, the island has become synonymous with humanitarian emergency as the destination for hundreds of thousands of migrants making the dangerous crossing from Africa to Europe. Dramatic scenes of rescue off its shores register among the most iconic images of Italy's migration crisis today. On the other hand, Lampedusa serves as a destination for tens of thousands of luxury tourists who are drawn to its sunshine and pristine beaches. Boutique hotels, seafood restaurants, and a modernized airport aimed at these tourists run up against the coast guard ships, emergency field offices, and detention facilities intended for migrants. It is the scene of two mobile classes resigned to two very different fates.

How was I to understand, much less reconcile, this disparity between tourists and migrants? It made me question the politics of difference operating on the island and led me to ask how differential mobilities might produce hierarchical relations and inequitable treatment in new and unforeseen ways. Such unequal dynamics instinctively turned my thoughts to the work of empire and its practices structured in dominance. I wondered what links might exist between the mobility-generated inequality on Lampedusa and the imperial formations that have long been active in the Mediterranean.

My experience on Lampedusa opened up a broader set of questions that orient *Empire's Mobius Strip*: What dynamics are at work between human mobility expanding on a global scale and imperial formations persisting over time? How does mobility-generated disparity change or deepen historical understandings of empire in Italy and elsewhere? How do attempts to control unsanctioned mobilities mutate practices of exclusion and discrimination? Where are these practices localized? Who occupies these marginal spaces? What do we see when we put these spaces together? What do we lose sight of? And what does this all mean on the ground for those who move by choice and those who are moved by force?

Migration and Detention in Italy

Anthropologists have published a number of innovative, multisited ethnographies over the past decade that have perspicaciously explored the intricate and intimate negotiations of daily life among this mobile underclass in Europe, especially along the continent's porous Mediterranean borders.[20] These works have also detailed the extreme measures that nation-states and supranational unions have taken to control the unsanctioned movements of this class. For one, they have criminalized "undesirables" by marking them as illegal, irregular, or clandestine and passed laws against them. Once so labeled, a person crosses over the threshold into the illegality industry. Entrée is almost always a one-way ticket, for "illegal" is a classification that once attached becomes almost impossible to remove, like a stain or an accusation. In his study of West African migrants in Spain, Ruben Andersson has shown that people labeled as "illegal immigrants" come to accept this categorization only ex post facto, that is, after they have been caught up in the multibillion-dollar illegality industry, often for years. Indeed, some of the migrants interviewed in Andersson's study considered themselves *aventuriers* (adventurers) at the start of their journeys to Europe. At first, theirs were quests undertaken for self-realization as well as financial gain until they were pushed "below-board" into illegality. Then their quests transformed into struggles for survival and finding a way home.[21]

On a vocabulary note, the terms "migrant" and "migration" encompass countless nuances and declensions that are elided by the very act of labeling—an act that in itself might be considered colonial in the way that it flattens and reifies difference of all kinds. I remain conscientious that every instance of naming can be considered a political act, and when I engage the terms "migrant" and "migration" in the essays that follow, I deliberately call attention to the weighty histories that each term carries within itself.

For many of this mobile underclass, labels like "illegal immigrant" or "asylum seeker" have little meaning until they are forced to identify—or more precisely, to be recognized—as such before the law. Personhood and legality are often at odds. In her ethnography of migrant mental health care in Italy, Cristiana Giordano illustrates this disconnect using the legal documents that interpellate migrant subjects, texts that prompt her informants to ask: "Who does the law want me to be?"[22] Only by submitting to legal categorization, followed by the state recognizing and approving that categorization, can one gain access to what Hannah Arendt has famously called "the right to have rights."[23] In such a way, the Italian state maintains a powerful border regime that exercises a monopoly over movements and legalities in a concerted effort to keep "undesirables" out no matter what their label, migrant or otherwise.

Yet Italy remains one of the most important destination countries for millions of migrants to Europe, an altogether profound shift from a century ago when it was the source country for millions of emigrants, the largest voluntary out-movement in recorded history.[24] Its crisis of migration and detention testifies to the intense struggles within Italy, and Europe more broadly, of coming to terms with the human consequences of an increasingly borderless, mobile, and globalized world.

Italy is a compelling site in which to study these struggles, for it has always been defined by the power and politics of mobility. Pilgrims, merchants, tourists, emigrants, colonists, repatriates, and immigrants have been coming and going to and from the Italian peninsula and its islands for centuries. Italy's geographical location at the margins of Europe but also at the center of a crucial space of transit, the Mediterranean, has created a constitutive tension between inclusion and exclusion that characterizes Italian mobilities writ large.[25] Since Italian Unification in 1861, the sense of belonging to a homeland beset with deep traditions and strong ties to the local has existed in parallel with the movements of Italians outward to the Americas and elsewhere, and after the 1970s, the movements of migrants inward seeking to make Italy their home. Italian diasporas have played a critical role in shaping modern Italian history by simultaneously transgressing and reinforcing territorial and psychic borders.[26] Surprisingly, these diasporas also galvanized Italy's imperial ambitions.

Unlike the colonial trajectories of Britain or France, the Italian colonies were born out of fear. Italy was bankrupt after Unification, and abject poverty drove millions of Italians to leave home at the very moment Italy became a nation-state. To stem this "hemorrhage" of newly minted Italian citizens, policymakers set about redirecting this flow of emigrants into colonies overseas. As I wrote with Ruth Ben-Ghiat, "Italian imperialism must be seen as an attempt to provide a 'national' outlet for the millions on the move to North and South America, the Antipodes, and France and the French colonies."[27] Italian empire was conceived not out of some grand lust for power or shrewd geopolitical wrangling or nostalgia to re-create the Roman Empire, but rather out of the very pragmatic fear that the new Italian nation-state would altogether lose its citizenry through emigration. From the outset, Italy's imperial project was predicated on the control of mobility.

Italian Colonialism

Italy's official tenure as a colonizing power lasted approximately fifty years, from 1890 to 1943. In chronological order, Italian forces occupied Eritrea (1890); a small concession in Tianjin, China (1900); Libya (1911–12); Rhodes and the Dodecanese Islands in Greece (1911–12); Somalia (1927); Ethiopia (1936); and Albania (1939). Some places, such as Eritrea, bear the lasting residues of Italian colonialism by dint of the many years under Italian rule. In Asmara, for example, one finds Italian-built cinemas, cafés, markets, and service stations still standing; the city is filled with exemplars of modern Italian architecture. In other places, such as Rhodes, folklore carries the vestiges of Italian colonization as in the dictum *una faccia, una razza* (one face, one race; in Greek, *mia fatsa, mia ratsa*), which signifies the shared Mediterranean kinship between Italians and Greeks. Still others, such as Albania, bear the imprint of Italy's colonial presence in its Fascist-era buildings, such as those in central Tirana. Albania's geographic proximity also left it open to Italy's linguistic and cultural influences, which turned out to be lifelines to the outside world under Enver Hoxha's dictatorship. So strong were these affinities that when the regime fell in the early 1990s, Italy became the prime destination for Albanian migrants. Their mass arrivals marked the beginning of Italy's current crisis of migration and detention, as I explain in the first essay of this book.

A sense of belatedness haunted Italian colonialism too, but not in the way that Ali Behdad, Renato Rosaldo, and others have described in other colonial contexts. This was not imperialist nostalgia but rather frustration with "a late start at colonization with respect to other Europeans."[28] Added to this displeasure was also shame—in 1896, Italian troops had been resoundingly defeated at the Battle of Adwa by Ethiopian forces. It was the most significant defeat of any European army on African soil. Mia Fuller writes, "Italian aspirations crumbled under the ridicule of what many Italians perceived as the most ignominious loss possible."[29] Adwa would act as both scar and shadow on all Italian colonial endeavors thereafter.

The defeat raised doubts among Italian policymakers at the turn of the nineteenth century as to the wisdom and prudence of colonial expansion. Their vacillation comes as no surprise insofar as ambivalence, according to Homi Bhabha, underpins colonial discourse.[30] We find a telling example of this ambivalence in the nicknames given to Libya. On the one hand, Libya was magnanimously referred to as Italy's *quarta sponda* (fourth shore), the geography that would bring full circle Italy's domination of the Mediterranean. Implicit in that nickname, too, was the fact that Libya was once ruled by the Roman Empire, from which Italian colonizers saw themselves as direct descendants, poised to take up Rome's imperial mantle. On the other hand, Libya was popularly known as *lo scatolone di sabbia* (the giant sandbox), a wasteland unworthy of Italy's attention much less its colonizing energies. These nicknames demonstrate how Libya vacillated in the Italian cultural imagination between having enormous value and having no worth at all, the expected ambivalence of colonial enterprise.

I focus my attention on Libya in the essays that follow as the through line for the historical echoes that subtend Italy's crisis of migration and detention. Its proximity to Italy and inherent *romanità* (Romanness) mobilized constellations of displacement, dispossession, appropriation, and dislocation in service to Italian imperial ambitions. What made Italian colonial Libya unique was that those ambitions were also always oriented to a distant imperial past, Rome. "Italians' colonization of Libya was justified as a return; they were merely taking back what was already theirs," adds Fuller. "In terms of imaginative geographies taking Libya bridged the historical gap between Italy and its own Roman heritage."[31] *Romanità* tempered almost all that Italian colonizers did in Libya particularly under the Fascist regime (1922–43), which advanced Mussolini's desire to found a new empire, or in his words, a Third Rome. An example of this *romanità* in the built environment was the aforementioned concentration camps erected in Cyrenaica. These were modeled on the *castrum* (military camp) of the Roman Legion and functioned as a moving threshold of empire in space, as I detail in the second essay of this book. Spotlighting Libya also returns ancient Rome, the original model of empire in the West, to the forefront of studies on modern European imperialisms. I hope that future studies will widen the scope to include other imperial orbits such as the Ethiopian empire (Abyssinia) and the Crusaders and Venetians in Rhodes to better amplify and enrich the ways in which mobility forms the connective tissue between Italian imperial formations.

An equally important geography, the Mediterranean, bridges Italy and Libya. Much more than just a sea, as Fernand Braudel has written, the Mediterranean is a rich repository of cultural crossings, creolizations, and uneven historical memories.[32] It is also an unstable realm with fluid, porous borders that invites cultural misprision and personal metamorphosis. As early as the eighteenth century, Italian travel writers documented the destabilizing effects of their movements in and across the Mediterranean. To Italians living along coastlines as late as the nineteenth century, the Mediterranean was a "sea of fear" notorious for piracy, kidnapping, and slavery by way of the Barbary Coast. For pro-colonial advocates in Italy in the early twentieth century, the Mediterranean was *mare nostrum* (our sea), the name by which it was known during the Roman Empire. Throughout the Italian occupation of Libya, colonial officials engaged the discursively fluid idea of *mediterraneità* (Mediterraneanness) to justify not only their territorial invasion but also the expansion of Italy's colonial state apparatus. For example, *mediterraneità* proved the rationale that guided urban planning and residential architecture. *Mediterraneità* also became a key pillar of Italian criminal anthropology and racial theories in which the Mediterranean figured as the *Ursprung* of all European races. Not least Libya's *mediterraneità* justified its "natural" place as an Italian colony, restored to Rome's dominion once more.

Today, the Mediterranean still serves as the copula between Italy and Libya, but this middle sea now serves as the viaduct for hundreds of thousands of migrants arriving at the doorstep of Europe in unstoppable waves from the global south. Braudel described the Sahara as the "second face of the Mediterranean."[33] The sea cannot be imagined without its desert counterpoint. Libya has emerged as the unstable realm that haunts Italy's current crisis of migration and detention. It is the infernal *préterrain* of the Mediterranean crossing where people disappear into human traffickers' warehouses, suffer with heat and illness on overcrowded camions, endure unthinkable forms of abuse, or are simply left to die in the desert—Libya is the black hole on the journey to Europe. Many of the men and women who traverse this former colony seeking to enter Italy are themselves often from the ex–colonial territories that once made up Italian East Africa (Eritrea, Somalia, and Ethiopia). These migrants are the people for whom Italian empire continues to saturate, directly and violently, the subsoil of their lives, and for this reason, too, Libya is a key interpretive locus for Italy's empire.

Empire's Mobius Strip builds on the growing body of scholarship addressing Italy's disavowed colonial history and its contemporary repercussions. Despite the pioneering work by Italian historians such as Angelo Del Boca and Nicola Labanca as well as interventions in the burgeoning field of Italian postcolonial studies, Italy's colonial project remains a markedly neglected one.[34] This disregard is the result of several factors. For one, Italy did not undergo any real process of decolonization but rather existed in what Pamela Ballinger has called an "extended colonial twilight." She has shown that Italian farmers in Libya, for example, continued to work their lands into the 1960s, almost two decades after Italy officially relinquished its colonies.[35] Italy's "long decolonization" was also mitigated by the fact that no singular figurehead like Frantz Fanon or Gayatri Spivak emerged to speak out and back against the Italian colonial enterprise. Silent for years, the voice of the subaltern is only now beginning to emerge in Italy through the genre of Italophone literature.[36] The myth of Italians as "good colonizers," or *brava gente*, also figures in the lack of sustained critical interrogation of Italian colonialism.[37] As *brava gente*, Italians could imagine their colonial experiences as positive and productive, not grave or gruesome like those of the French or British. Instead, the myth of *Italiani brava gente* helped repress deeds so painful, such as the genocide of Bedouin in concentration camps or the three-day massacre of thirty thousand Ethiopians in Addis Ababa, that it created a long-standing blind spot in both the Italian cultural imagination and Italian historiography, which, in turn, ensured Italian empire's elision from a broader set of imperial histories. My study calls up and critiques these tacit expressions of colonial disavowal by setting them in dialogue with Italy's contemporary crisis of migration and detention.

Method and Plan of the Work

Empire's Mobius Strip renounces neat categories, linear chronologies, textual symmetries, fixed territories, and even disciplinary certainties. It is messy and uneven like the imperial formations it attempts to articulate. It limns the fraught borders where the control of mobility becomes exercised and politicized in the context of migration and colonialism, where the lines of inclusion and exclusion are ever more sharply drawn and increasingly blurred at the same time.

Its form has followed its content. My study is an example of long-form academic writing in which novella-like essays, instead of chapters, make up its composition. Figuratively speaking, these essays give room for imperial formations to breathe. They give space to the ways in which imperial formations at different times and in different places surface, submerge, entangle, disappear, resurface, and infinitely loop back on themselves like a Mobius strip. When the essays are read in concert with one another, Italy's empire comes into focus.

My methodology combines ethnographic reportage with archival research. Over the course of the past decade, I conducted extended field visits to Italy's carceral islands, ex–concentration camps, migration detention centers, "equipped villages," nomad camps, former refugee camps, and other sites I identified as expressions of Italy's colonial past in the present. Not all of them made it into this book. Places like the newly opened "Libia" metro stop in Rome, the ruins of the Mostra Triennale d'Oltremare colonial exhibition in Naples, the Graziani monument in Affile, and the Piana delle Orme *bonifica* museum in Latina all deserve sustained critical attention.

My archival research centered on the colonial records housed in the Archivio Storico del Ministero dell'Africa Italiana (Historical Archive of the Ministry of Italian Africa) and the Archivio Centrale dello Stato (Central State Archives), both in Rome, and the documents available at the Istituto Agronomico per l'Oltremare (Overseas Agricultural Institute) in Florence. While these archival materials anchor my present study, there is still much research to be done in the way of personal and regional archives, oral history, and resources available in Libya.

This last point is a notable lacuna, for I was unable to visit Libya during the course of my research for this book. It was difficult to travel there under Muammar Qaddafi's regime and became even more so when the country descended into civil war after his demise in 2011. I have made it a point whenever possible in this study to incorporate the scholarship on Italian colonialism by Libyan academics as well as that of Italian scholars who have done fieldwork and archival research there. The Libyan Studies Center in Tripoli has been at the center of scholarly efforts to document the everyday consequences of Italian occupation including gathering an extensive collection of oral histories. These voices, when they become fully accessible, deserve the space to be heard in future scholarship, the witness and the archive in one.

Each essay in *Empire's Mobius Strip* sets into relief a space from Italy's colonial past in Libya (for example, a concentration camp) against one from its present crisis of migration and detention (for example, a migrant detention center) that I see as being controlled by forceful mobility regimes. In the juxtaposition of these spaces, imperial formations are rendered explicit, and I contend that they coalesce around three metonymical sites: the island, the camp, and the village. I draw these terms from the spaces themselves—for instance, the islands where Libyan and Italian prisoners were detained, the camps where Bedouin were interned, the villages where colonial settlers relocated, and so on. At all of these sites, the control of mobility was paramount.

Essay one, "The Island," illustrates the ways in which the current spaces of migration and detention on the island of Lampedusa intersect with those of Italy's carceral archipelago in the nineteenth and twentieth centuries. Lampedusa has become the symbolic geography of the migration crisis in contemporary Italy, if not Europe in general, and its detention center one of the most notorious. It is the watery frontier of Fortress Europe. The controls employed here against mobile Others, migrants, who are believed to threaten the Italian state find direct historical precedent on the islands of Ponza and Ustica, where Bedouin leaders were forcibly deported from Libya—beginning in 1911 and continuing for two decades—to make way for the Italian colonial regime. This essay weaves together historical and ethnographical accounts to show how Italy's empire emerges from the linkages between its colonial enterprise and current migration and detention crisis, and also from Lampedusa's history as a penal colony for internal exiles, a base for U.S. military imperialism, and a luxury tourism destination.

Essay two, "The Camp," illuminates the links between what I have identified as the alpha and the omega of the camp in the modern Italian context: the concentration camps of Italian colonial Libya (1929–33) and the Centro di Identificazione e Espulsione (Center of Identification and Expulsion), known as Ponte Galeria, a migrant detention center outside Rome. This essay draws on archival evidence, ethnographic fieldwork, and translated Libyan oral histories to show how the Italian state forced the containment within camps of mobile Others, Bedouin, who were considered to be threats to state power. It provides a long overdue English-language account of the camps in Libya to complement those already published in Italian and Arabic, and adds to them by showing how the Italian colonial regime succeeded in immobilizing the Bedouin population only by weaponizing mobility itself. This essay also shows that Ponte Galeria is the heir to these camps. Documenting the inside story of Ponte Galeria offers a rare glimpse into the day-to-day life of the center, which is often the last stop for migrants before being forced out of the country. It also offers a close-up view of the legal and medical apparatuses that underpin the migration and detention crisis in Italy. Many of the detainees are victims of human trafficking as well as systemic violence and abuse, and still they are called "guests" and "welcomed" into the center. I argue that the camp is the darkest space that manifests empire, arising from the threat of unsanctioned mobilities more so than racially charged grounds.

Essay three, "The Village," compares what are known as the *villaggi attrez-zati* (equipped villages) constructed for Roma today with the mass creation of *villaggi agricoli* (agricultural villages) for Italian farmers in Libya in the late 1930s. The former are state-funded trailer parks that have been built along municipal peripheries in the past two decades, where thousands of Roma have been resettled after their homes were destroyed by government bulldozers as part of the nomad emergency decree. My field visits to the village called La Barbuta near Rome reveal a mobility regime of reclamation at work: the destruction of camps and construction of villages were done in the name of reclaiming the land for public health and safety. I compare these current villages with the ones built for Italy's ambitious project of demographic colonization in Libya in 1938 known as the Ventimila because a parallel discourse of reclamation was also at work there. Twenty thousand Italian farmers were sent to reclaim the land in the mountains east of Benghazi and to make it safe, healthy, and productive. My archival research shows that many of the agricultural villages in Libya were actually built by the Bedouin survivors of the aforementioned concentration camps. After the camps closed in 1933, not only were these Bedouin forced into hard labor but they were also sedentarized into a different exclusionary space: the *villaggio musulmano* (Muslim village). Both the village and the camp surface again during Italy's "long decolonization" as Italian repatriates from Libya, along with exiles from Istria, were sequestered into national refugee camps and, later, government-built villages. This essay sheds light on the imperial formations elicited by the form of the village, and the ways in which the Italian state harnesses the inscriptions of race, ethnicity, and nationality implicit in these formations to put its stamp on its subjects. That stamp is the recognition or the refusal of citizenship, and the ultimate exercise in dominance of Italy's empire.

The coda transplants empire's Mobius strip into the context of the United States. A story similar to that of Italy's islands, camps, and villages easily could have been written about the United States at sites such as Manzanar, Fort Sill, Guantánamo, and many others. Empire and mobility, again, exist as insidious bedfellows. To recognize and interrupt these imperial formations is a necessary and urgent task in every context, and not least our moral duty, so that the freedom of movement can actually exist in reality as a fundamental human right for all.

The Island

And the cage of Lampedusa has become an infernal machine . . .

The cage of Lampedusa today has become the shame of our democracy.

—Fabrizio Gatti

What material form do ruins of empire take when we turn to shattered peoples and scarred places rather than to their evocations and enchantments?

—Ann Laura Stoler

It is hard to think of Lampedusa as a place that holds the promise of salvation. Flat-topped and windswept, this tiny island is a mesa of scrub and limestone set in the middle of the Mediterranean. In the fall and winter, the marine haze merges sea and sky into a pale, silvery curtain, one indistinguishable from the other. In the spring, the winds blow alternately warm from Africa or clay-cold from the north, and the sea surrounds the isle in a halo of brilliant turquoise. It has only one town, close to the center of which lies a graveyard of boats (figure 2). It is a sepulcher of brightly colored wood, frayed ropes, and rusting hulls covered by a fine mixture of dirt and sea salt. These are the remains of hundreds of old fishing boats known as *pescherecci*, which carried tens of thousands of migrants from North African shores across the liquid plateau of the sea to a long-dreamt-of life in Italy. The *pescherecci* appear to have been abandoned in a hurry. As if frozen in the time of emergency, they were left pell-mell in the tense and frantic moments of rescue. Shoes were scattered on the decks of splintered wood and sun-cracked rubber. Crumpled blankets stained with engine oil were discarded in a corner. A faded life jacket. Unopened bottles of water. What must have once been valuable possessions were abandoned instantly at the prospect of salvation. And those who actually made it to these rocky shores, like the survivors of a plane crash, bore

FIGURE 2.   The graveyard of migrant boats on Lampedusa. Photograph by the author, 2013.

impossibly good fortune. Most have withstood harrowing desert crossings, debilitating illnesses, constant hunger, enduring poverty, unthinkable abuses at the hands of traffickers, and even the sea itself. Those who arrive on Lampedusa are already shattered and scarred by death and loss, but they survived. Many are not so lucky.

I saw this boneyard on my first visit to Lampedusa in March 2013. Each boat carried the scars of its traumatic journey. Some had prayers painted in Arabic. Others gave the boat's name and port of origin. Many were spray-painted with a date and the code "C.C. 808" in a rough red scrawl. This code delineated the agency that recovered the boat—the naval unit C.C. 808 Petracca—and the moment when the boat and its survivors were quite literally fished out of the sea. Migrant arrivals on Lampedusa are commonly called *sbarchi* (landings); however, residents are quick to point out that rare is the case of a boat actually landing on shore. One hotel owner told me that it was more accurate to call them *recuperi* (recoveries) because each arrival involved a complex, quasi-theatrical rescue operation. He described how sirens sound in the harbor, then a coast guard flotilla motors out to sea and brings back sea-soaked migrants huddled against their gunwales. White vans whisk these people off to the nearby migrant detention center, a place misleadingly classified as a "welcome center."[1] It is a coordinated dance between ships and skiffs, *carabinieri* and coast guards, social workers and boat migrants that repeats itself again and again on the proscenium of Lampedusa—a Sisyphean passion play of a political and humanitarian crisis inextricably linked to the massive waves of migrants arriving, unannounced, from the global south.[2]

The island has become an unqualified signifier of globalized mobilities today in two contradistinct senses. It is a destination of luxury tourism in Italy, on the one hand, complete with boutique hotels, gourmet restaurants, and a beach, Isola dei Conigli (Rabbit Island), ranked as the best in the world in 2013.[3] On the other hand, Lampedusa has become more famously synonymous with the humanitarian emergencies that have arisen from the fraught collisions between the mass movements of people and the politics of migration. Both are big businesses. The island has emerged as the symbolic geography of the migration crisis in contemporary Italy, if not Europe in general—a crisis brought forth as millions of people engage mobility as the strategy to ameliorate their stations in life. Yet the perceptions of emergency and crisis here do not emerge spontaneously.

Lampedusa has long been tied up in the histories of modern empire: it was an enclave in the crosshairs of Napoleon's march across the Mediterranean and Egypt and a potential territory for the British Empire. Its miniscule population has ebbed and flowed for centuries, migrating with fishing seasons, military directives, and social obligations on nearby islands. The island has always been caught in the tides of transit across the Mediterranean, as well as in the tides of empires, and it is important to see the island in the context of these multidirectional movements. Too often the perception of today's migration crisis as unidirectional, from northern Africa to southern Europe, eclipses the omnidirectional networks that have characterized Lampedusa historically. By positioning Lampedusa within these longer histories of movement and empire, it becomes clear that direct antecedents exist for the techniques of containment and spaces of exclusion present on the island today.

This essay explores the layered histories of Lampedusa, and in particular, the ways in which the movements occasioned by Italy's nation-making and colonial projects in the early twentieth century have lent their peculiar texture to the country's crisis of migration and detention in the twenty-first. The island is the scene of an imperial palimpsest, a critical node for what Ann Stoler and Carole McGranahan have called imperial formations, or "polities of dislocation, processes of dispersion, appropriation, and displacement [that are] dependent both on moving categories and populations."[4] Lampedusa entwines a number of imperial strands, among them the colonial empire of Italy, the military empire of the United States, and the global economic empire of neo-liberalism, all of which come under scrutiny in this essay.

Its "islandness," too, needs to be taken into account. Islands are often outposts that mark imperial borders, but their porousness renders them flashpoints of conflict surrounding who should be included in or excluded from empire as well as to why and how.[5] Islands are alluring objects to think with, for they are defined paradoxically by their insularity and their connections to elsewhere. They have always been connected by an intricate skein of commercial and transit networks, especially in the Mediterranean.[6] The interdisciplinary field of island studies has made great strides to critically map the ways in which islands emerge as sites of political and cultural contestation, powerful imaginaries, and "forces in the making of new social relations and knowledges" via the contrapuntal relations between land and sea.[7] While these studies underscore the remarkable diversity of islands, the through line in all of them emphasizes the fact that islands are multivalent. Godfrey Baldacchino refines this notion of insular multivalence, noting that some islands exist as "endotopias" (an interior space that protects residents from the outside, like a sanctuary), while others can be defined as "exotopias" (an outside space excised from society, like a quarantine).[8]

Lampedusa is the rare island where sanctuary and quarantine visibly collide. In the space of just a few miles, the clash takes shape in the tourists seeking sanctuary and the migrants being quarantined within intimate proximity of one another. This island is a living laboratory, not only for Darwinian natural selection but also where the mobility regime of temporary permanence contributes to the evolution of different subjectivities. The space of the island throws into relief the "unnatural" selection of people who are deemed "fit" for moral-political inclusion within state and society, as well as those who are excluded from it, often by the very same means. "Illegal immigration" has proved an especially attractive object of study for it hinges on such notions of inclusion and exclusion, and a number of scholars have taken this to task, tracing the limits of the law and the state on Lampedusa, a seemingly bounded, finite space. My aim here is to unpack the historical forces that have given rise to these limits: Lampedusa is not wholly circumscribed by the present crisis of migration and detention but rather located in a much wider network of imperial formations.

These formations, too, exist on moving grounds. The pages that follow weave together an account of Lampedusa's contemporary crisis with that of its imperial histories in the modern era. I employ a sort of analytic enjambment, an asymmetrical crosscutting between past and present, to render a picture of Italy's empire that is both historically deep and ethnographically present, which at the same time attempts to capture the unevenness of imperial formations, or in the words of Edward Said, the very contradictory energies of empire itself.[9] The mobility regime of temporary permanence spatializes empire on Lampedusa, and as the oxymoron of its name suggests, this regime brokers in paradox. Many scholars have argued that the "temporary permanence" of Lampedusa stakes out the island as a space of exception, a limbo that exists both inside and outside of the law, a biopolitical limit that collapses distinctions in the sense of Giorgio Agamben's camp.[10] Yes, temporary permanence certainly marks such a limit; however, it also marks empire's broader power over people through the control of mobility. Once the crossing of the indeterminate boundary of Lampedusa takes place—one might think of the island as something like an event horizon—it sets into motion a process by which the fluidity of one's mobility becomes inscribed within, and thus controlled by, the increasingly hardline politics of the Italian state and the sharpening lines of inequality intrinsic to neoliberalism. This movement from fluid to rigid works in concert with what Ruben Andersson has described as the increasing abstraction of the "migrant" as a subjective category the further she becomes imbricated within the illegality industry.[11]

Thus, the mobility regime of temporary permanence on Lampedusa marks a chiasmus—a simultaneous crossing—from fluidity to rigidity and from actuality to abstraction. And to state the obvious more clearly, the mobility regime of temporary permanence marks an accelerating compartmentalization, petrification, and essentialization of people who are perceived to be threats to the Italian state owing to their unsanctioned mobilities. What is happening on Lampedusa, then, can be seen as a renewed Manichean division of the world into those who move by choice and those who are moved by force—not unlike the black-and-white categories described by Frantz Fanon in the era of European colonial imperialism—a rigidity that takes shape among the flows and liquidity said to characterize our globalized age.

Destination Nowhere

I often heard a common refrain on my field visits to Lampedusa: while the island is politically Italian, it is geologically African. The Pelagian Sea is shallow here, and an underwater plateau connects the island to North Africa. Its limestone, flora, and fauna more closely resemble those of Tunisia, just seventy miles away, than those of Sicily, its administrative unit, more than one hundred miles to the north. Lampedusa connects Italy and Africa in many ways, geologically and geographically as well as historically and politically. It feels like both and yet neither at all. It is quite literally a place between—a middle place in the middle sea.

The island is only five miles long with a single town at its southeastern end. It is surrounded by bays and inlets with strange-sounding names that trip up the tongue: Cala Giutgia, Punta Javuta, Rutta n'ammurati, Cala Sponze. Its few streets lattice the main pedestrian drag, Via Roma, where the evening *passeggiata* (stroll) takes place and local gossip changes lips. As the undisputed center of island life, Via Roma sits atop a hill and commands a view of the *porto vecchio* (old port) to the southeast and the *porto nuovo* (new port) to the northwest. The former, quite smaller than the latter, provides anchorage for fishing boats and sightseeing excursions. The entrance to the new port, on the contrary, is guarded by the hulking boats of the coast guard, *carabinieri* (police), and *guardia di finanza* (finance guard). This is where the *sbarchi* happen. This is the island's watery stage.

Most tourists arrive in Lampedusa at the airport, a mile-long scar etched atop a limestone bluff not far from Via Roma. It is one of the newest constructions on the island, having been renovated and expanded at a cost of $21.4 million in 2012.[12] The terminal is designed to serve 350,000 passengers per year. On the opposite end of town at the new port, migrants rescued from *pescherecchi* are greeted by barbed-wire fences, surveillance cameras, and soldiers as they are whisked off to the migrant detention center. Put another way, two opposite mobile classes collide on Lampedusa: tourists and migrants. Rarely do they come into such close contact in a singular place. The mobility of one class is sanctioned, even celebrated, by the Italian state with millions of euros spent to aid, even increase, their movements to and around Lampedusa. The mobility of the Other is criminalized and constrained, yet still with millions of euros spent to restrict, even arrest, their movements to and around Lampedusa. Two mobile classes, two very different fates.

For many migrants, the journey to Lampedusa begins in sub-Saharan Africa, in some of the most violent and inhospitable places on earth: the Sahel, Darfur, Liberia, the Horn of Africa. These are well-publicized sites of the international crisis imaginary, and as such, exist first and foremost as sites of military and humanitarian intervention. Rumors of Lampedusa circulate in all of these places. Some call it Lampa-Lampa Island. The dilapidated fishing boats used to transport migrants are sometimes known as "lampa-lampas." Indeed, the paths to Lampa Lampa are many, and they are often circuitous and tragic.[13]

There are myriad narratives of such migrant journeys to the island, and they are being given the critical attention and documentation they deserve thanks to the work of organizations such as the Rome-based Archivio di Memorie Migranti (Archive of Migrants' Memories), journals such as *Scritture*

Migranti, and the participatory video/documentary cooperative ZaLab, also in Rome.[14] Films such as Gianfranco Rosi's *Fuocoammare* (Fire at sea, 2016) and Andrea Segre and Dagmawi Yimer's *Come un uomo sulla terra* (Like a man on earth, 2008) and books such as Angela Lanza's *La storia di uno è la storia di tutti* (The story of one is the story of all, 2014) provide testimonies of the journey and its afterlife in Italy and elsewhere. Innovative, multisited ethnographies such as Hans Lucht's *Darkness before Daybreak* (2012) and in-depth journalistic accounts such as Fabrizio Gatti's famous *Bilal* (2006) also fill out the context of these travels. I surrender to them the critical task of bearing witness to the journeys to Lampedusa in all of their dolorous detail. I choose instead to provide only the briefest of sketches, not least because I have known only second- and thirdhand accounts of the journey, but also my unwillingness to reproduce the narratives of suffering that too often unwittingly create a victimology as a result.[15]

The Journey to the Cage

The routes to Italy begin in sub-Saharan Africa and head north across the Sahara, entering Libya from the southwest or the southeast depending on one's point of departure. Those traveling from western Africa typically travel through Mali and Niger, while others from the Horn of Africa travel across Sudan and Darfur. It is important to note that these journeys across the Sahara are often multidirectional: some people travel for seasonal work in Libya with plans to return home within a few months (for example, this has been the pattern for decades among many Nigerians working in the oil sector), others plan to stay long-term in Libya, and still others intend to risk the crossing to Lampedusa. No matter what the intention or route, by all accounts these journeys are intensely traumatic.

They also cost a lot of money. People pay up to $200 for a single space atop a camion for passage across the Sahara.[16] These are hulking beasts of machines, staggeringly overloaded with goods and people. Sometimes land cruisers and pickup trucks are used as transport, and there is evidence that airtight shipping containers of the sort used to transport gasoline have also been used in trans-Saharan trafficking.[17] According to one asylum seeker from Darfur now living in Italy, "Probably more people have died in the desert than by boat, but of course there are no statistics."[18] The camions are usually crammed so tightly that people have to stand for days, not to mention urinate and defecate in situ.[19] A driver who takes 150 people on board at $200 each will make $30,000 in just one trip. Often it is more. Fabrizio Gatti adds that the authorities on each side of the border expect bribes and typically earn far more than the drivers. In

Dirkou alone, he writes, they receive about $2 million each month, all of it paid in cash.[20]

Certain places along the way are notoriously accursed: Agadez, Dirkou, Ajdabiya, Kufra. Their names conjure both fear and dread. For those who cross into Libya via Sudan it is the town of Kufra that is the most terrifying. An oasis district at the edge of the Sahara—which Italians once mercilessly bombarded with poison gas in 1930—Kufra has become synonymous with imprisonment, torture, barbarism, and despair.[21] Migrants who arrive here are taken into custody almost instantly by Libyan "authorities" and confined in detention centers. According to Human Rights Watch, there is only one government-run detention center in the region; however, there are many more "informal" centers, often no more than a run-down house, set up by traffickers themselves. These traffickers have very close relationships with Libyan officials, all of them fully complicit in this modern-day slave trade. Things are so awful that there is a saying among the Ethiopian immigrants in Rome: "If someone kills your father, do not take revenge: leave him in the prison at Kufra without any money."[22] More than anything else, these detention centers are centers of business, where untoward profits are made on the perpetual exchange of human flesh.[23] It is in this trafficking—the literal exchange of being sold and resold—that people are flattened into the abstract category of migrant, and as Ruben Andersson so eloquently put it, they come to accept and embody "illegal immigrant" as a lived-in category.[24] The control of mobility—of who can move where, when, and how—permeates the action in all of these places.

These places are also inextricably tied to Lampedusa. The island cannot be imagined apart from the Sahara, or what Fernand Braudel has described as the "second face of the Mediterranean."[25] For those who are lucky (and moneyed) enough to have made their way out of the agonizing cycle of waiting, trafficking, and imprisonment to arrive on the Libyan coast, there is still the matter of finding a boat to Lampedusa. The most common point of departure is the coastal town of Zuwarah, just thirty-seven miles southeast of the Tunisian border, and it is there that one finds a *scafista* (trafficker) to secure one's passage across the sea.[26] Another town, Zliten, east of Tripoli, is also a frequent site of embarkation. These cities offer the shortest distances between Italy and Libya, and migrants tend to converge here in anticipation of the crossing.[27] Before anything, money must change hands among migrants, *scafisti*, and whatever other middlemen might also be involved. Since the early 2000s, the going rate for a single crossing has held steady between $1,000 and $1,500.[28] If the crossing fails, however, and the boat and its passengers return to Libya, these migrants will most often be imprisoned and forced to bribe their way out once again.

For a period of time during the mid and late 2000s—most notably after the signing of the Italy-Libya Friendship Pact in 2008—if a migrant boat got close to Lampedusa, Italian authorities would push it back to Libya (an act known as *respingimento*) without so much as conducting a health and welfare check.[29] For those on board, the dream of Italy slipped out of reach like a whisper. The principle of nonrefoulement is a binding obligation under both international human rights law and international refugee law whereby governments cannot return migrants to places where they would face inhuman or degrading treatment. By any small measure of imagination, Libya's prisons and informal detention centers would certainly qualify as such places. The interdiction of *pescherecci* in international waters and subsequent refoulement of boat migrants to Libya violates a number of human rights ensured by the Geneva Convention as well as EU law. David Forgacs describes these violations as "one of the most dismal episodes in recent Italian history."[30] The Italian government, especially under ex–prime minister Silvio Berlusconi, has come under intense scrutiny for these *respingimenti* from the UNHCR and other supranational organizations and has been pressured to change its policies. In 2012, Italy was even condemned by the European Court of Human Rights for its interdiction and refoulement of boat migrants back to Libya.[31]

Whether because of unforgiving seas or militant border patrols, the Mediterranean passage is known to be perilous, yet the number of people making the crossing continues to grow. An estimated 432,761 people made the journey from North Africa to Europe by way of the Mediterranean in 2015, according to the International Organization for Migration (IOM), with more than 121,000 passing through Italy, many via Lampedusa.[32] In 2016, that number decreased somewhat to 358,156. In comparison, however, the total number of Mediterranean crossings in 2013 was estimated to be only 63,000. The Italian state, the EU, and international aid organizations debate these statistics no end, but all agree that they are likely to be underestimates given the difficulty of tracking the number of deaths at sea. It is even more difficult to gather statistics on the people who died while crossing the Sahara desert en route to Libya and Italy or in detention centers along the way.[33] What is apparent, however, is that pervasive political instability, changing climatic conditions, natural disasters, endemic poverty, an ongoing demographic boom in much of sub-Saharan Africa, and as of 2017, the mass exodus of Syrian refugees will ensure that migrations to Italy and Europe continue to increase as will the *sbarchi* (landings) on Lampedusa.

A restaurant owner on the island, V., told me that "Where is the train station?" is the first question that many migrants ask on arrival. "They know they have arrived in Europe," she added. "But had no idea they are on an island." Instead, they have arrived at the southern frontier of Fortress Europe. They have arrived at the cage.

Welcome to Temporary Permanence

On Lampedusa, the topography of immigration pivots on the so-called Centro di Primo Soccorso e Accoglienza (Center of First Aid and Welcome). I attempted to find it on my first visit to the island. It was not easy. There were no signs or flags, nor was it marked on any map. Local residents knew where it was but seemed reluctant to point the way. "Non è molto distante" (It's not very far), they said. "È vicinissimo." (It's very close.) One only needs to go "verso il campo sportivo e giri a sinistra" (toward the soccer pitch and turn left). The center sits at the end of a shallow valley not far from the center of town in a zone called Contrada Imbriacola. The bluffs on either side are scattered with cacti and flora that are typical of the Mediterranean maquis. A single road leads into and out of the valley. In fact, this road is what gives away the center's position because it looks unlike any other road on the island. Its poured concrete is smooth and level. New streetlamps evenly stud a metal guardrail. This expensive road ends at a cul-de-sac and metal gate covered in translucent plastic obstructing the view onto one of the most infamous migrant detention centers in Italy. A barbed-wire-and-chain-link fence surrounds the entire complex. Uniformed guards loiter with machine guns near the entrance. The center's relative isolation is striking on an island where all other buildings sit so close together. It is a space of exclusion par excellence. The center exists on the margin of an already marginal place.[34] It localizes Italy's outside edge there on Lampedusa, the limen between Europe and Africa.

Many Italians still refer to the center by its former abbreviation, CPT, which stands for Centro di Permanenza Temporanea (Center of Temporary Permanence). In 1998, the Turco-Napolitano law (Legge 40/1998) established migrant detention centers throughout the country.[35] The name was changed by additional legislation in 2009, which not only further criminalized immigration—it was now a crime for anyone to render aid to any "illegal immigrant"—but also divided CPTs into three categories: Centri di Primo Soccorso e Accoglienza (Centers of First Aid and Welcome), Centri di Accoglienza Richiedenti Asilo (Centers of Assistance for Asylum-Seekers), and Centri di Identificazione e Espulsione (Centers of Identification and Expulsion). For decades, these detention centers have been repeatedly charged with abysmal conditions and human rights abuses so much so that they have become colloquially known as *lager*.

Lampedusa's CPT has undergone numerous iterations that manifest both the temporary permanence of its nomenclature and the imaginary of crisis that sustains it. The center as such spatializes, according to Paola Zaccaria, "a type of apartheid that follows a policy of 'preemptive' seclusion-exclusion . . . out of considerations labeled 'crime prevention.'"[36] Fabrizio Gatti, who spent a week undercover in Lampedusa's CPT as a Kurdish refugee named Bilal, also frames this apartheid in terms of its metaphysical stakes:[37]

Davanti a questo cancello finiscono i nobili sentimenti dell'umanità. Quel sentir comune che ci unisce come individui liberi di pensare. Che non fa differenze tra gli uomini e le donne. E dimentica cosa sono. Amici o nemici. Connazionali o stranieri. Cittadini o clandestini . . . Oltre questo cancello entrano in scena gli accordi di Stato. Le menzogne dei loro governi. Il tradimento dei loro parlamentari. Grazie a questo cancello verde non siamo più individui. Ma siamo quello che siamo.

The noble sentiments of humanity end in front of this gate. That common feeling that unites us as individuals free to think, that does not differentiate between men and women, and forgets what they are. Friends or enemies. Compatriots or foreigners. Citizens or *clandestini*. . . . Beyond this gate, State agreements enter the scene. The lies of their governments. The betrayal of their MPs. Thanks to this green gate we are no longer individuals. But we are what we are.

For both Gatti and Zaccaria, the migrants who pass through the gates of the CPT are simultaneously inscribed into a rigid, exclusionary schema while being stripped of any individual agency. They are counted, photographed, labeled, and given numbers, systematized as if in a prison or a camp. They huddle and wait for hours on the cold ground. If the dorms are full, they sleep outside uncovered, if insomnia allows for it. After registration, they are given a small kit with toiletries, a set of clothes, and a phone card.[38] Nonetheless, Zaccaria sums it up best: "The migrant desperately trying to reach Southern Europe's shores has, in the eyes of many politicians, no value: he or she is 'refuse' (in the double sense of the world), a nonrecyclable shell to be disposed of, a life that can disappear together with the worn-out vessel he or she embarked on without anybody claiming it."[39] It is no surprise, then, to hear migrants in the CPT declare that they are not treated as humans but rather feel like animals. They are, as Alessandro Dal Lago has shown, effectively *non-persone* (nonpeople).[40]

The mobility regime of temporary permanence marks out a limbo of space and time, and the CPT is the site where this suspended existence takes place. Not only does it suspend, but it also collapses the distinctions between person and nonperson, human and animal.[41] One's potential for mobility is the very prerequisite for immobilization in the center. The migrants who arrive on Lampedusa begin their journey into abstraction and categorization at the gates of the CPT. It is here that they first come into contact with the Italian state and its deep complicity with the illegality industry. It is also here that those arriving on Lampedusa begin to inhabit the category of "illegal immigrant." The chiasmatic movement from actual to abstract, and fluid to rigid begins here at the CPT on the island. Thomas Claviez writes that this regime of temporary permanence captures "the form of our special existence in and experience of such a [globalized] world" and "to conceive of such places as 'centers,' moreover, might just add a dose of supplemental irony—or, uncanniness, if read against Agamben's camp."[42] The CPT is a localizing dislocation where mobile subjects are immobilized as well as unmade. It is a space of unraveling, of coming undone, and also of recalibration.

No one stays on Lampedusa for very long. All migrants are relocated to other detention centers throughout Italy within roughly one week's time. It is, after all, only a "welcome center." One resident, Giacomo, said that before the CPT was built and the numbers of arrivals were relatively low, residents would meet the *sbarchi* and willingly give food and drink to those who were rescued, sometimes even hosting them in their homes or buying them ferry tickets to Porto Empedocle (Sicily). Migrants were not yet classified as clandestine or irregular or illegal. They were simply "persone in movimento" (people in movement). But then, Giacomo added: "Si è deciso di fare un centro . . . un altro tipo di politica al livello europeo e nazionale, e sono stati CPT che poi di fatti erano anche quelli dei carceri. Ed è finito così l'incontro." (It was [then] decided to make a center . . . another type of politics at the European and national level, and there were CPT that then, in fact, were also those of prisons. And like that the encounter was finished.)[43] The moment migrants were put into place, quite literally, was the moment their abstraction into the rigid category of "illegal immigration" began.

The CPT on Lampedusa has twice risen from the ashes. It opened in 2007 to hold approximately eight hundred people but has contained up to three thousand at times. Before this, migrants arriving on Lampedusa were detained and processed at an ad hoc facility near the airport. In February 2009, the center partially burned down in a fire set during an attempted revolt.[44] A group of detainees went on a hunger strike to protest forced repatriations, overcrowd-ing, and abusive treatment and then gathered up mattresses and started them on fire. The fire destroyed the center's warehouse and damaged several other buildings. The CPT reopened two years later in February 2011 to accommo-date, in the words of right-wing politician Roberto Maroni, then minister of interior, the "biblical exodus" from North Africa stemming from the Arab Spring.[45] In September 2011, it dramatically burned down again, this time al-most completely. Similar to the previous blaze, this one was also set by de-tainees, revolting against confinement and repatriation. Yet once again, the CPT was rebuilt and reopened at reduced capacity in July 2012. Its destruc-tion never seems final. The regime of temporary permanence—much like the state of exception—has become the permanent rule of this space. And it, too, has become mobile.

New migrant detention centers financed primarily with Italian funds have been constructed in Libya. The 2008 Italy-Libya Friendship Pact provided Libya with nearly $5 billion over twenty-five years to improve Libyan infrastructure, paid in part as reparations for "i danni inflitti alla Libia da parte dell'Italia du-rante il periodo coloniale" (the damages inflicted on Libya by Italy during the colonial period), in the words of ex–prime minister Silvio Berlusconi.[46] While this statement appeared to signal a volte-face in Italian politics—it was not only an admission of the country's dark colonial past in Libya but also an attempt to reconcile that past with contemporary statecraft—in actuality, the accord masked an alternative agenda. The treaty promised favorable business condi-tions for Italian companies investing in Libya, particularly those seeking to ac-cess the country's vast oil and gas reserves. More importantly, it specified that Italy and Libya would cooperate in the "battle" against illegal immigration by strengthening Libyan border controls, that is, by creating additional detention centers.

Even before this pact, Italy had already funneled millions of dollars into Libya under the rubric of stemming the flow of migration through the exter-nalization of asylum processing.[47] In the early 2000s, the creation of "transit processing centers" in third-party countries outside the EU had gained favor among many policymakers. In 2003 alone, Human Rights Watch documented that Italy "had provided training and equipment to stem illegal immigration and financed the construction of a reception center for undocumented mi-grants in Libya" and spent more than $6.2 million in Libya to do so.[48] In a separate report, Human Rights Watch identified sixteen of these centers in Libya, with at least one of them, Ajdabiya, built on the same site where the Italian colonial administration had imprisoned tens of thousands of Bedouin in a concentration camp between 1929 and 1933 (detailed in essay two).[49] The parallels were not lost on the Libyan intellectual Abi Elkafi, who lodged a protest against these new camps with Libya's ambassador in Rome: "How can you forget the concentration camps built by Italian colonists in Libya into which they deported your great family, the Obeidats? The reason I write to you are the atrocious new concentration camps set up on Libya's soil on behalf of the Berlusconi government."[50] Yet there is little recourse for protest in Libya, nor are there any protections for migrants and refugees there since the country is not party to main refugee conventions or human rights law treaties. Since the fall of Muammar Qaddafi's regime in 2011, the weak central government has relied on local militias to manage detention centers. Organizations such as the UNHCR have had very little access, often facing intimidation and persecution.[51] Detainees who have suffered in both Italian and Libyan centers testify that the ones in Libya are much worse—sites of unthinkable brutality and indescribable sadism. In 2017, Dr. Joanne Liu, president of Médecins Sans Frontières (Doctors Without Borders), visited various detention facilities in Libya and described them as "the incarnation of human cruelty at its extreme."[52]

Thus, the temporary permanence spatialized by the Lampedusa CPT reaches across the Mediterranean to materialize once again in Libyan migrant detention centers. These connections mark an imperial formation folding back on itself in space, empire's Mobius strip. For example, the concentration camp at Ajdabiya, where Italians immobilized thousands of mobile subjects (Bedouin) in the name of colonial power in 1930, links up to the informal prisons where traffickers immobilize thousands of different but equally abject mobile subjects (migrants) in the 2000s. Likewise, these carceral houses connect to the CPT on Lampedusa via the migrants who traverse between them. And Lampedusa reconnects back to Libya as migrants are pushed back from Italy and returned to Ajdabiya, only to be immobilized once again, not in an informal trafficker's prison this time but rather a different circle of hell: a government-run migrant detention center built with Italian money.

In symbolism and practice, then, Lampedusa cuts across geographies and temporalities. It is a layered site that Joseph Pugliese has described as a "crisis heterotopia." Drawing on the work of Michel Foucault, Pugliese expertly details how the island is a space that simultaneously accommodates violent and contradictory differences (for example, vacation resorts and prisons, tourists and imprisoned refugees). His analysis shows how Lampedusa expresses a transnational biopolitical economy that stretches across centuries and is "inscribed by overlapping racialogical histories of whiteness, colonialism, and empire, and attendant anxieties about securing a nation's borders."[53] Pugliese's study gives an excellent overview of the historical circumstances and the biopolitical stakes that circumscribe Lampedusa; however, there is even greater historical depth to the crisis heterotopia that he describes, which demands a further accounting upon which I now train my lens.

The Island as Imperial Palimpsest

Before the migration crisis and the tourism boom today, Italians since the mid-twentieth century have associated the word "Lampedusa" with the celebrated author Giuseppe Tomasi di Lampedusa. In 1956 he wrote *Il Gattopardo* (The leopard), a historical novel about the decadent life of a minor aristocratic family in Sicily dealing with ambivalence and compromise in the face of the Italian Risorgimento. It is widely considered one of the most important novels of modern Italian literature, praised for its literary realism and its ability to capture the dawning extinction of one way of life amid the birth of the modern Italian nation-state. The work is cursorily based on Tomasi di Lampedusa's family, noble and in decline. They were the princes of Lampedusa for centuries, having been given the title by the Spanish Habsburgs in the seventeenth century, although they rarely, if ever, visited the island. Many others have visited the island in the meantime, coming and going over centuries.

A Sea of Fear and the Possibility of a "Second Malta"

Long a way station for sailors and pirates, Lampedusa has remained largely uninhabited throughout its history. Its livelihood has always been intertwined with that of Sicily to the north, Malta to the east, and Tunisia and Libya to the south. The ancient Greeks knew it as Lopadussa, and the Romans used it as a place to produce a fermented fish sauce called *garum*.[54] Corsairs found refuge in its shallow harbors, and its location at the center of a "sea of fear" was seen as a detractor rather than an advantage; for until the early nineteenth century, Mediterranean coastlines were famously plundered, with scores of people kidnapped and sold into slavery.[55] The majority were Christians taken captive by corsairs and enslaved at Muslim hands along the Barbary Coast. The white slave trade peaked in the years between 1580 and 1680 with Algiers its epicenter. Historians estimate the city had a steady population of around twenty-five thousand white slaves on average by the early seventeenth century, followed by Tunis, with seven thousand.[56] This is not to say that Muslims were never enslaved in Europe; on the contrary, Salvatore Bono argues that at least thirty thousand Muslim slaves were held captive in Italian city-states for most of the sixteenth and seventeenth centuries.[57] Robert Davis adds that during this era across the Mediterranean there were approximately one hundred thousand "faith slaves"—Christian and Muslim—at any given time.[58] Some tried to escape. There are accounts of Christian fugitives fleeing the Maghreb on ramshackle caïques, such as the story of two Maltese slaves, Giuseppe Mifsud and Giuseppe Darmanin, who escaped from Tripoli in 1761 and sailed to Lampedusa.[59] Their route was the very same one traveled by many migrants on *pescherecci* today. Yet Lampedusa was hardly a safe haven during that era: more than one thousand of the island's inhabitants were kidnapped by the infamous Ottoman corsair, Turgut Reis, and sold into slavery in 1553, causing the island's desertion for centuries to follow.[60]

As a fraught crossroads belonging to neither Europe nor Africa, Lampedusa, Roger Stritmatter and Lynne Kositsky note, "was the staging ground for a number of historic confrontations, both real and imaginary, between Christian crusaders and Muslim warriors during centuries of conflict for control of the Mediterranean basin," and argue that for this reason, among others, it was the setting for Shakespeare's *The Tempest* (1623).[61] Although the remote island of the play remains unnamed, Lampedusa is named explicitly as the site of the climactic battle between Christians and Muslims in Ludovico Ariosto's well-known epic poem, *Orlando Furioso* (1516), with which Shakespeare was sure to have been familiar. Stritmatter and Kositsky painstakingly trace the Lampedusan imprint of Ariosto's poem on Shakespeare's play and show how both stage the island as "a theater for chivalry, a stage for the climactic showdown between honorable protagonists of Christendom and Islam."[62] Certainly in the literary imagination of Ariosto and likely also that of Shakespeare, as well as in the historical fact of faith slavery, Lampedusa was the historical site of vexed encounters between Europe and Africa, Christian and Muslim, Orient and Occident—a position not unlike the one that the island currently occupies in the European imaginary of crisis.

Half-hearted attempts at colonization were made by the Maltese and the British in the late eighteenth and early nineteenth centuries but were quickly scrapped. For a variety of reasons, the era of piracy had largely ended in the Mediterranean by 1800, and slavery as a trade shifted its tide across the Atlantic and more explicitly from faith to race.[63] In 1802, the British civil commissioner in Malta, Alexander Ball, became interested in using Lampedusa as a military base since Malta's wartime neutrality would not allow for the berth of British warships there. Ball argued the cost to outfit a garrison and fortify this "second Malta" would be negligible.[64] His proposal fell on deaf ears but he pressed on as the memory was still fresh of Malta being the first strike in Napoleon's campaign to take over Egypt and Syria. Malta fell to Napoleon in 1798 and remained under French rule for two years until naval forces from

Britain and the Kingdom of the Two Sicilies blockaded the island and caused French troops to surrender. Although Malta was now under British dominion, fears abounded that Sicily—its valued trading partner—would fall to France, and this anxiety compelled Ball's persistence. Desmond Gregory lays out the complicated history behind Ball's resolution to acquire Lampedusa, which was ultimately quashed with the publication of Charles Pasley's damning 1810 report, *Essay on Military Policy*. Pasley directly contradicted Ball's assertion that the island was a fertile, sustainable place: "Such therefore is Lampedusa; a place without resource, without strength, and to sum up everything without a harbor; a place in short, completely insignificant, worthless and contemptible."[65]

One year later, Alexander Fernandez, then deputy commissary-general to the British Admiralty in Malta, made a futile attempt to colonize Lampedusa himself; he had hoped to grow crops and raise cattle there as an alternative food supply for Malta. However, this too failed due to excessive cost and lack of political will.[66] Problems mounted for Fernandez, including an outbreak of the plague on Malta in May 1813 and the forced quarantine of the yellow-fever-ridden HMS *Partridge* on Lampedusa.[67] Upon learning the reasons for the quarantine, more than 120 inhabitants panicked and fled the island on small boats. According to Thomas Zerafa, "Like today's boat people, they spent the next few days without food and water, plying the waters between Malta and Lampedusa, undecided whether to return to that island or to land in plague-ridden Malta."[68] By 1843, the island's population had dwindled to just twenty-four people.[69]

The island was not inhabited en masse again until it became a colony of the Kingdom of the Two Sicilies. The Bourbons made settling Lampedusa a priority, and colonization was well under way just a few years later. Some seven hundred inhabitants lived on the island by 1847, according to Bernardo Maria Sanvisente, the Bourbon knight and captain leading the effort.[70] Most of these settlers came from various regions of Sicily. They built much of the island's infrastructure during the first four years of their tenure; Sanvisente detailed the construction of roads, houses, cisterns, warehouses, facilities for oil and pasta production, the customs office, and the cemetery, among others.[71] He also reported the island to be a fertile place for agriculture: "tutto si è mostrato in ottima vegetazione . . . i seminati si sostengono con poche acque . . . terreno buono." (All is shown to be in optimum vegetation. . . . The plantings sustain themselves with little water . . . good soil.)[72] However, Sanvisente later admitted that on the ground, "la coltivazione non si portò a seconda dei desideri" (the cultivation did not deliver as desired).[73] So invested was the Bourbon regime in the success of the island that King Ferdinand II and his second wife, Maria Theresa of Austria, made an unannounced visit to Lampedusa on June 23, 1847. Sanvisente was ecstatic and praised the largesse of the royal couple in encouraging agricultural productivity as well as blessing marriages among the settlers.[74] He ends his description of the island on a positive note, proclaiming the continued expansion of the island's prosperity.

Yet history would prove otherwise. Just one year later, the Kingdom of the Two Sicilies would be caught up in the revolutions of 1848 and the Sicilian revolution in particular, which began in Palermo and quickly spread. Lampedusa was all but forgotten. Sanvisente left in 1854, and by 1860 the island was bankrupt.[75] Nonetheless, the newly unified Italian state found a different use for Lampedusa, one that haunts the island to this day: prison.

Italian Unification, the Southern Question, and the Institution of Domicilio Coatto

With the Risorgimento primarily a northern—and specifically Piedmontese—invention, the fiercest opposition to a unified Italian political state occurred in the South. Resistance strategies included brigandage and organized crime, which continued in the years before and after Unification in 1861. For many in the South, the Risorgimento represented yet another colonial project on par with centuries of others, from the Greeks, Romans, Vandals, Ostrogoths, Byzantines, Normans, Arabs, Bourbons, and, from the mid-nineteenth century onward, Italians. Under the draconian Pica law, passed in 1863, resistance to the Italian state was criminalized and punished by incarceration, forced labor, and sometimes death. This law, writes Roberto Martucci, legalized a state of exception, which suspended all civil and legal rights for southerners, including the immediate execution of anyone found to have "insulted" the Italian flag or the figure of the king.[76] As many scholars have shown, the South emerged as the Other against which the modern Italian state could be imagined during and after the Risorgimento.[77] It was a terra incognita of filth, poverty, and backwardness that was yet to be discovered as well as a place to be cleaned, colonized, and civilized. Such stereotypes featured prominently in both historical and contemporary debates on the *questione meridionale* (southern question), the term that names this Otherizing discourse.

In the decades after Unification, northerners descended on the South in a variety of scientific and civilizing missions in hopes of resolving the *questione meridionale*. Touring Club Italiano president Luigi Vittorio Bertarelli came with bicycle tourists. Positivist anthropologists, led by Cesare Lombroso, looked to the South for physiognomic proof of "born criminals" who, among other things, stood in opposition to "normal" Italian citizen-subjects. Politicians including Leopoldo Franchetti, Sidney Sonnino, and Pasquale Villari traveled there to compare the region's social and economic conditions with those elsewhere in Italy. So dismayed by what he saw, statesman Luigi Carlo Farini in an 1860 letter to Count Camillo Benso di Cavour famously declared, "Che barbarie! Altro che Italia! Questa è Affrica!" (What barbarity! Other than Italy! This is Africa!)[78]

The conflation of Africa and the Italian South marks the emergence of race as a pivotal node in the broader discourse of Italian nationhood and, thus, Italy's claims to modernity. Not only did *meridionalismo* (southernness) and race exist in a mutually constitutive relationship, but a great deal of scholarship has shown how this discursive constellation links up to parallel ideological projects that constructed Italianness by way of difference. Racial, colonial, emigratory, exilic, and criminalizing discourses all situated the locus of the modern Italian state—its subjects and its sovereignty—on a holdfast of inclusion and exclusion, localization and dislocalization, the licit and the illicit, the exception and the rule.[79] And the consequences of these historical discourses are still very much present in contemporary Italy in places like nomad camps and migrant detention centers, as the following essays will show.

Since the mid-nineteenth century, Lampedusa's establishment as a carceral island has tied it intimately to the Otherizing discourses that emerged in concert with Italian Unification and, more broadly, the sovereignty of the Italian state. It was a holding space for those who rebelled against state power and the punitive site of *domicilio coatto* (forced domicile).[80] It was also part of a larger carceral archipelago that took shape during the 1870s, which included the islands of Elba, Favignana, Giglio, Ischia, Lìpari, Pantelleria, Ponza, Ustica, and Ventotene, among others (map 1).[81] The first census of Lampedusa, taken in 1862, documented 918 inhabitants living on the island, but more importantly it revealed rich networks of interisland migration linked to seasonal fishing movements.[82] There was a particularly strong link with the island of Ustica, located some thirty miles north of Palermo and hundreds of miles away from Lampedusa. Of the island's 918 residents, 196 of them were *usticesi.* There were also seventy-seven people from Pantelleria, and a handful of others from Favignana, Lìpari, Marettimo, Malta, and various cities within Sicily.[83] Fishing and growing seasons dictated the frequent movements between the islands. Men would move either by themselves or with their families to fish for sardines on Lampedusa, to fish for tuna on Favignana, or to gather capers or *uva passa* (muscat grape raisins) on Pantelleria. Parish records show that single fishermen sometimes married and started families with local women.[84]

Lampedusa's inhabitants also had close ties to northern Africa, and in particular, the nearby Tunisian cities of Mahdia, Sfax, and Sousse, then still under

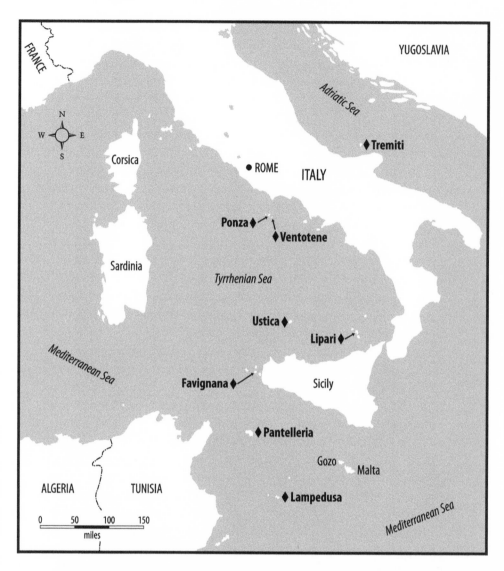

MAP 1. The southern islands of Italy's carceral archipelago, early twentieth century.

Ottoman rule. Travel was commonplace between them as was the exchange of goods and capital. These centuries-old movements across the Pelagian Sea had little regard for the artificial borders set by the new Italian nation-state in 1861. The 1860s marked the beginning of the vast waves of emigration from Italy to the Americas and beyond, and many of Lampedusa's inhabitants crossed the Atlantic to favored destinations such as New York and New Orleans.[85] Therefore it was within this context of frequent and multidirectional movements between islands, across the Mediterranean, and beyond the Atlantic that the first *domiciliati coatti* (prisoners) arrived on Lampedusa on September 8, 1872.

The system of *domicilio coatto* came into force in 1871, and it spread quickly across Italy's new carceral archipelago. Lampedusa initially received forty-seven prisoners, just a small fraction of the almost 1,300 prisoners nationwide.[86] By January 1879, this number had grown to more than 3,000 *coatti* across Italy, and 214 prisoners on Lampedusa, the majority of them from Naples and surrounds.[87] Like the prisoners on Italy's other carceral islands, prisoners on Lampedusa were held in a building near the center of town in large rooms called *cameroni*. They were relatively free to move about the island during the day, but they had to be back in the *cameroni* by the sunset curfew. Those who were sent to the penal colonies were considered severe threats to public order that could be handled only by extreme isolation. The laws that established *domicilio coatto* made this clear. The aforementioned Pica law (1863, n. 1409) that criminalized antistate sentiments also established a state of emergency couched in the rhetoric of public order and security. It was presented as a "mezzo eccezionale e temporaneo di difesa" (temporary and exceptional measure of defense) against the brigandage of the South, sanctioning violent means of repression—Article 2 of the law might be described as a license to kill brigands—as well as creating the colonies of the *domicilio coatto*.[88]

Under the rubric of emergency and crisis, the Pica law and the laws that followed it authorized and perfected various techniques of repression and exclusion on Italy's own citizens who were perceived to threaten Italian state power. These were internal Others—southerners—marginalized from the state in both law and geography who represented the direct historical precedents for the repression and exclusion of migrants in Italy today. Put another way, the *coatti* on Lampedusa in 1872 had much in common with the migrants who are detained in the island's Center of Temporary Permanence in the 2000s.

Giuseppe Damiani, the former director of Lampedusa's penal colony, offers an intriguing glimpse into the life of the *coatti* on the island at the turn of the twentieth century.[89] His 1905 report offers a "pittura fedele della vita di una colonia di coatti" (a faithful picture of the life of a colony of *coatti*) and describes the intimate existence between prisoners and islanders on Lampedusa. Damiani managed approximately 350 prisoners, several companies of police and army troops, and a budget of 100,000 *lire* per year (roughly $500,000 today when adjusted for inflation).[90] The penal colony was unquestionably a boon to the local economy, which had previously depended on fishing and subsistence agriculture, and Damiani noted that "in massima niuno v'ha che

desideri il loro allontanamento, che sarebbe la rovina economica dell'isola"
(by and large no one has a desire for their departure, which would be the economic ruin of the island).[91] Most of the *coatti* slept in the *cameroni*, although
some lived with their families in small houses around town. Prisoners were
frequently transferred from island to island, and like the seasonal fishing migrations, movements among Lampedusa, Pantelleria, and Ustica were common. The wife of one *coatto* followed her husband around these carceral
islands for eight years. She finally became so fed up with this life on the move
that she settled in Palermo while he remained under arrest.[92]

The daily life of the *coatto* can best be described as one of temporary permanence in which the prisoner never knew exactly how long he would remain
on the island, or whether his sentence would be commuted, or whether he
would succumb to illness or disease or become the victim of internecine violence. It was a limbo, an existence of suspension. Although charged with forced
labor, very few detainees actually did any work, according to Damiani. Instead,
he writes that *coatti* passed the time betting, playing, and cheating at cards,
with the favorite game being *la zecchinetta* (lansquenet) as well as drinking ex-
cessively.[93] Illicit activities also abounded, from money-lending schemes to
sexual favors, almost all of which were controlled by members of the *camorra*
(mafia) on the island. Most *coatti* remained suspect of Italian state power and
indifferent in its face; however, the isolation of Lampedusa broke even some
of the toughest men. Some *coatti* committed crimes just to leave the island
and be returned to prisons on the Italian mainland, a strategy similarly employed today by some migrants in detention centers who wish to remain in
Italy.[94] Others, such as the anarchist Errico Malatesta, planned their escape
from the island. In April 1899, after eight months on Lampedusa, Malatesta
walked off into the island's countryside just hours before he was to be transferred to Lìpari and simply disappeared. Days later he resurfaced in Tunis, his
escape having been orchestrated by anarchist colleagues in Tunisia, France,
and England.[95]

After Malatesta's successful prison break, Lampedusa transformed from
being the most lax of Italy's carceral islands to among its most severe. The
mobility regime of temporary permanence moved toward increasing rigidity
on the island, especially in relation to Italian political prisoners. By 1911, the
hardening of the system would reach across the Mediterranean once again
toward Italy's newest colony: Libya. The repression and exclusion tested out
on Italian *coatti* in the carceral isles would be displaced onto Libyans who
were deemed threats to Italy's burgeoning colonial regime. In spite of the
debates about colonialism at the time, which were heated and constant, the
Libyan deportations marked the moment in which Italy's colonizing project

reached its tipping point—the interests of the Italian state and the colonies had become inseparable and the process of colonization unstoppable.

Deportations, Italy's Colonial Empire, and Clandestine Italians in Libya

When Italian troops invaded Tripolitania in October 1911, a key strategy to secure the city was to arrest and deport anyone believed to oppose the occupation. Many were arrested indiscriminately and sent en masse to the carceral islands of the *domicilio coatto*. According to a Libyan history of the resistance, 594 people were deported to Italy on October 26, 1911, shortly after Ottoman soldiers and local fighters handed an embarrassing defeat to Italian troops at the Battle of Shara al-Shatt. Italian records log a higher number: 2,975. Most were taken to the Tremiti Islands off the Gargano peninsula in Puglia and to the small volcanic island of Ustica, north of Palermo. The remaining prisoners were scattered among Favignana, Ponza, and Gaeta.[96] The deportations were meant to be only "una misura di carattere transitorio e temporaneo" (a measure of transitory and temporary character), according to a 1914 memo from the Ministry of the Interior to the Ministry of the Colonies.[97] Despite these provisory claims, many never returned home. "To this day," claims Habib el-Hesnawi's history of the Libyan jihad against Italians, "the fate of most of them is still unknown."[98]

While the system of *domicilio coatto* and its techniques of repression and exclusion set the clear precedent for the Libyan deportations, a parallel model of a carceral island was first tested in the late 1880s and 1890s in the Italian colonial context. In 1887, the fledgling Italian colonial administration in Eritrea set up a prison on the island of Nokra (also known as Nakura) in the Dahlak archipelago just off the coast of Massawa. It operated continuously from 1887 to 1941.[99] Nokra was a desolate and barren carbonate shelf, and its climate was often described as infernal, with perpetual drought and 120°F temperatures. There was a single brick building for guards. Prisoners slept either in tents or in slapdash *tukuls* (huts). Nokra housed 1,800 detainees at its maximum, many of them tribal leaders who resisted Italian occupation in East Africa. Historians describe the conditions at Nokra as inhuman—prisoners chained up in shackles every night, a single well of brackish water often blocked up, the decapitation or hanging of anyone caught trying to escape.[100] One prisoner, Jacob Gabrie Leul, who was incarcerated on Nokra for almost two years (July 1938–June 1940), testified for the UN War Crimes Commission that "there were deaths every day from sunstroke. They used to force us to work. . . . The prisoners were forced to carry stones, wood, build houses, and do other hard labor. . . . The supply of drinking water was insufficient. Some of the prisoners tried to dig for water, or they drank sea water on the beach, the result being they fell sick and died."[101] Similar testimonies by other prisoners emphasize the island's unbearable heat. Ato Qänna was imprisoned on Nokra in 1937, and he described the heat, the limited water rations, chronic illnesses, and constant abuse. According to him, the commander in charge often barked threats at the prisoners, telling them that they would all die on Nokra, "perché siete pigri, perché non amate l'Italia e perché siete disonesti" (because you're lazy, because you don't love Italy, and because you're dishonest).[102] As a carceral island, Nokra had conditions that were clearly much harsher than those on Lampedusa, Ustica, Ponza, or any of the others. Those imprisoned here were not Italian citizens but rather colonial subjects who were punished and subjugated by any means deemed necessary by colonial officials. The violence of incarceration amplified the violence of colonization and vice versa. The one metastasized the other.

While Nokra was the first of Italy's carceral islands in the colonies, the Italian state also experimented with moving the *domicilio coatto* and its most hardened Italian prisoners to colonial shores. In 1898, a small penal colony was established in Assab, a port city in southern Eritrea. Incidentally, Assab was the place where Italy's colonial project first began when the Rubattino shipping company purchased rights to the city's bay in 1869 (the Italian state took over these rights in 1881 and declared Eritrea its first colony in 1890). The purpose of this penal colony was to house recidivist *coatti* and to subject them to such severe forms of discipline so as to instill "un salutare terrore agli altri condannati al domicilio coatto che restano nel continente e di troncare le fila di criminose associazioni" (a salutary terror to the others condemned to *domicilio coatto* that remain on the continent and to break the ranks of criminal associations).[103] Then prime minister Francesco Crispi also took a personal interest in deporting "subversives" (especially anarchists) to Africa, sending a number of telegrams expressing his support for the Assab colony.[104] On June 26, 1898, a ship (coincidently named the *Rubattino*) arrived in the port city with 196 *coatti*, 60 *carabinieri*, 27 guards, 1 doctor, and a handful of administrators. It was the first carceral experiment to take place in an Italian colony.[105] However, the experiment was short-lived, lasting only eight months owing to the region's inhospitable conditions, lack of arable land, incessant illness and disease, and generally unhealthy environment.[106] While the *domicilio coatto* in Assab did not work out in practice, the idea of penal colonies built on Italian colonial soil still appealed to many bureaucrats. For example, Ferdinando Caputo, the vice director of prisons in 1899, argued that "mobile penal colonies" would be indispensable to successful colonization:[107]

Colonie penitenziarie mobili, coi baraccamenti trasportabili e leggieri, avrebbero il primo compito vitalissimo delle arterie stradali e della ferrovia protratte alla frontiera; e, concorse così al compimento d'un'opera, che *è indispensabile per assicurare il possesso del territorio coloniale*, tornare indietro e procedere bonificando e coltivando, sostituite, man mano, le Colonie penitenziarie, dall'iniziativa privata.

Mobile penal colonies, with light and transportable barracks, would have the first vital task [of building] arterial roads and railways running along the frontier; and, to have contributed as such to the completion of a work, which *is indispensable to ensure the possession of the colonial territory*, [will] resume and carry on reclaiming and cultivating, substituting, gradually, the penal colonies with private enterprise.

Caputo was right, in a way. Penal colonies would become indispensable to Italy's colonizing project but not in the way he had envisioned. Instead, the mass deportations of indigenous leadership, especially from Libya after 1911, mobilized Italy's already existing penal colonies into the service of colonization. An entirely new group of prisoners was sequestered in Italy's carceral archipelago alongside the Italian *coatti*, and with them, the inherent violence of colonization arrived on Italy's domestic shores at islands such as Ustica.

Lush and volcanic, Ustica is the opposite of Lampedusa. Wildflowers cover its steep, black hillsides. A pine forest runs along the spine of a now extinct crater's edge, its cool shade a respite from the summer heat. The island bears the nickname the "black pearl" of the Mediterranean, and it was here that the first wave of Libyan deportees, a group of 920 men, arrived in Italy on October 29, 1911, only three weeks after Italian troops invaded Tripoli. They came on a steamship called the *Rumania*.[108] An archival photo of the arrival shows more than a hundred men dressed in white tunics huddled together on Ustica's rocky harbor beach, Cala Santa Maria (figure 3). More are being ferried to shore by a convoy of dinghies. Soldiers with bayonets stand guard while a man in charge stands with hands on hips overseeing the proceedings. The photograph haunts the viewer with the very prosaicness of the business of subjugation at hand.

There were two waves of deportations on Ustica. The first, and the lesser organized, lasted from October 1911 to June 1912. The second lasted from 1915 until 1934, when the last of the rebels in Cyrenaica were "pacified" and Libya was unified into a singular colony. Libyan prisoners were known as either *deportati* (deportees) or *relegati* (relegated) compared with the domestic prisoners, *coatti*. Discipline intensified on the island after the Fascist regime came into power in 1922, and a new class of political prisoners opposed to fascism was

FIGURE 3. The first wave of Libyan deportees, sitting in foreground, arrived on the island of Ustica on October 29, 1911. Photograph reproduced by permission from Centro Studi e Documentazione Isola di Ustica.

also sent into exile: the *confinati* (confined).[109] By the early 1930s, Libyan *deportati*, "regular" *coatti*, and political *confinati* all lived together on Ustica and outnumbered the local inhabitants.

The first wave of deportations was a disaster, even by admission of the penal colony director, Antonino Cutrera, who described the treatment of Libyan deportees "ammonticchiati nei cameroni dei coatti in maniera non confacente né all'umano rispetto, né alla nostra dignità" (piled up in the *cameroni* of the *coatti* in a manner not suited neither to human respect nor to our dignity).[110] The journalist Paolo Valera visited Ustica in January 1912 and wrote a scathing article for the socialist newspaper *Avanti!* (soon to be edited by a young and still left-wing Benito Mussolini, who had just served a five-month jail term for protesting the Italian invasion of Tripoli).[111] Valera was not one to soft-pedal the situation:

> È senza dubbio la colonia dei prigionieri di Stato più spaventosa che io abbia visitata. Si odora l'aria infetta a dieci minuti dalla spiaggia. Si impallidisce come quando si è alle porte di un lazzaretto. Più il piroscafo si avvicina e più la gente diventa silenziosa. Pare avviata al sacrificio . . .

L'accampamento di tutto questo esercito di prigionieri di guerra è senza dubbio antiumano.

It is undoubtedly the most frightening colony of state prisoners that I have ever visited. It smells of infected air ten minutes from the beach. One blanches as if at the gates of a lazar house. The closer the steamer approaches, and the more the people become silent. It seems the beginning of a sacrifice. . . . The camp of all this army of prisoners of war is, without a doubt, anti-human.

Photographs, archival records, and oral histories confirm the fast-moving ruination that characterized this first wave of deportations. The conditions within the *cameroni* were deplorable: deportees slept on piles of straw, the sick and the healthy heaped atop one another like firewood. There was not enough space or food. They were forbidden to go outside save for an hour or two each day and always supervised by armed guards. In their first weeks on the island, a cholera epidemic swept through the *cameroni*, the overcrowded conditions ripe for the fast spread of disease. A makeshift hospital was set up on the outskirts of town to treat the dozens of *deportati* who fell ill. However, so many of them died that Cutrera found it necessary to construct a separate Muslim cemetery, which still exists today adjacent to the Catholic cemetery on the north side of the island. Between October 1911 and June 1912, 132 Libyan deportees were buried there, mostly by other *deportati* who tried their best to adhere to Islamic burial customs.[112] The majority died from cholera and the others from a host of other maladies, including tuberculosis, dysentery, syphilis, internal bleeding, bronchitis, nephritis, meningitis, and pneumonia.[113]

Both authorities and residents were so petrified by the unrelenting spread of death and disease that they instituted a series of sanitary measures that were meant to stay transmission but more often ended up harming the *deportati* by causing new ailments and turning them into humiliating spectacles. One measure was the forced bath at the Cala Santa Maria. It was a frigid, overcast November morning in 1911 when gendarmes mustered all Libyan deportees out of the *cameroni* and marched them down to the harbor beach. The *deportati* were commanded to strip naked, given a bar of soap, and forced to scrub themselves in the gelid waters. Archival photographs show a mass of nude bodies waist-deep in the sea, many of them with arms pulled in close as if to keep warm or in defense against oncoming waves. A crowd made up of guards and curious onlookers surrounded them.[114] When the bath was finished, the deportees got dressed in the uniforms of the *coatti* and were marched back to the *cameroni*. Shivering and wet, many caught pneumonia and bronchitis afterward, adding more patients to the island's already overburdened infirmary.

Another measure was the public burning of the Libyans' *barracani* (barra-cans), the strong camlet-type fabric used for outer garments, in the town's central square. Residents were transfixed by this spectacle of fire. Its intention was primarily symbolic: to reassure the public that the administration was taking all measures necessary to cleanse the island of disease. The first wave of Libyan *deportati* endured this life of sickness, squalor, and humiliation until May 1912, when most of them were repatriated to Libya. The remainder left Ustica for Libya the following month.

From 1913 to 1915, Libyan *deportati* were sent primarily to the island of Ponza, southwest of Rome in the Tyrrhenian Sea. Passenger lists of deportees show they were charged with crimes such as *spionaggio* (espionage) and *atti ostili* (hostile acts).[115] They were to be treated, according to a 1913 memo from the Ministry of the Interior to the Ministry of the Colonies, by the same conventions as applied to the prisoners of *domicilio coatto*.[116] As on Ustica, the deportees on Ponza were housed in *cameroni* that were located inside a large building on Via Roma (now a defunct school), just up the hill from the port. A blue door with a small sign that reads "Centro Polivalente: 'I Cameroni' dei Confinati" (Multipurpose center: "The *Cameroni*" of the prisoners) marks the entrance today. The interior is cold and dark. High, arched ceilings trap the rising heat, leaving little warmth on the ground. There are few windows, just barred slits far above anyone's view. The Libyan deportees were segregated from the population of *coatti* here and sequestered in seventeen *camerette* (small

FIGURE 4. A Libyan deportee stands in the *cameroni* (carceral dormitory) on the island of Ponza circa 1938. Photograph reproduced by permission from the Archivio Storico Diplomatico, Ministero degli Affari Esteri e della Cooperazione Internazionale, Rome.

rooms) within the complex (figure 4). As of January 30, 1914, there were 99 *deportati* incarcerated on Ponza along with 128 *coatti*. A 1914 report by Officer Romeo Nappi, a *consigliere coloniale* (colonial adviser), described the conditions there:[117]

> Dalla visita fatta alle diciassette camerette del dormitorio commune, il sottoscritto ha provato un senso di nausea e di disgusto per il pessimo stato in cui sono tenuti i materiali letterecci . . . gli arabi vivono in un ozio forzato che ne deprime il fisico e li rende neghittosi e trascurati nella nettezza personale . . . abituati alla vita nomade, pochissimo osservanti dei più precetti d'igiene e di pulizia personale.
>
> From the visit made to the seventeen *camerette* of the common dormitory [*cameroni*], the author experienced a sense of nausea and disgust for the poor state in which the bedding was kept. . . . The Arabs live in a forced idleness that depresses the body and makes them neglectful and neglected in personal cleanliness. . . . Accustomed to the nomadic life, [they are] hardly observant of the precepts of hygiene and personal cleanliness.

Nappi also argued that the maritime climate on Ponza was unsuitable for the Libyan prisoners and suggested moving them to an island closer to Libya: Lampedusa. It would save time and money, he wrote, and would perhaps be a more desirable place of residence for the *deportati*. Nappi was dispatched to Lampedusa in February 1915 to determine whether it had adequate facilities to serve a large group of Libyan deportees. Even though Lampedusa had served as a penal colony since 1872, his answer was an unequivocal no. In fact, Nappi painted a rather bleak picture of Lampedusa in 1915:[118]

> Lampedusa è un'isola completamente mancante di parte montuosa, battuta da continui e violenti venti . . . mancando a Lampedusa qualsiasi produzione agricola . . . manca completamente a Lampedusa acqua sorgiva . . . La assoluta mancanza di campagna in Lampedusa renderebbe impossibile di poter occupare gli arabi in lavori agricoli . . . Concludendo: sotto niuno aspetto sembra attuabile la proposta di trasferire da Ponza a Lampedusa la Colonia di deportati arabi.
>
> Lampedusa is an island completely devoid of mountainous parts, battered by continuous and violent winds. . . . Lampedusa is lacking in any agricultural production. . . . Lampedusa completely lacks spring water. . . . The absolute lack of countryside in Lampedusa would render impossible the ability to engage the Arabs in agricultural work. . . .

In conclusion: under no aspect does the proposal to transfer the colony
of deported Arabs from Ponza to Lampedusa seem feasible.

While Nappi found Lampedusa to be untenable, many of the Libyan deportees
on Ponza were soon transferred to Ustica. The second wave of *deportati* there
was much better organized than the first. By June 1915, there were 778 Libyan deportees on Ustica, and by January 1916 that number had increased to
1,400.[119] *Coatti* and *deportati* together outnumbered the local populace. The
majority of the Libyans were conscripted into forced agricultural labor on the
island so as to avoid the *ozio forzato* (forced idleness) that became such a problem on Ponza. By the 1920s, there were so many *deportati* on Ustica that administrators looked for alternative sites of confinement on the islands
Favignana and Ventotene.[120] What is more, the second wave of deportees came
from an altogether different demographic, that of the so-called *capi notabili*
(notable leaders). In particular, they were Sanusi leaders of Islamic religious
and study centers known as *zawiyas* (pl. *zavie*, sing. *zavia* in Italian) and came
from Benghazi and surrounds, the region where Libyan rebels waged a protracted guerilla war against Italian colonizers throughout the 1920s and early
1930s. By removing local leadership through deportation, the Italian administration created a power vacuum through which it could strong-arm its policies onto the local populace.

The *capi notabili* had money and often brought their wives, children, and
servants with them to Ustica. They did not stay in the *cameroni* but rather
rented small villas on the outskirts of town and were free to circulate about
the island.[121] By the late 1920s, many of the *capi notabili* had become fast friends
with the six hundred antifascist political prisoners, *confinati*, also exiled to the
island. There are many stories and photographs of Libyan *deportati* hosting
confinati for tea or of them taking long walks together. Among these political
confinati were the famed political cartoonist Giuseppe Scalarini, the socialist
leader Nello Rosselli, and the communist philosopher Antonio Gramsci (who
lived on Ustica for only forty-four days before being transferred to Turi prison
near Bari). Scalarini thought he would be greeted by other political prisoners
when he arrived on Ustica but found instead a passel of Libyan deportees:
"Sugli scogli stavano accoccolati degli arabi, avvolti nei bianchi mantelli: erano
libici, confinati perché non volevano saperne della civiltà italiana." (On the
rocky shores, Arabs were curled up, wrapped in white cloaks: they were Libyans, confined because they did not want to hear of Italian civilization.)[122] Many
of the *confinati*, Scalarini and Gramsci among them, organized conferences, a
library, sporting activities, and other educational opportunities, including a
first-of-its-kind Scuola Italo-Araba di Ustica (Italo-Arab School of Ustica).[123]

None of these activities, however, could quell the Libyan deportees' pain and anger at being forcibly expulsed from their homeland. In personal letters and official grievances, many of the *deportati* adamantly protested both their confinement and their treatment by the Italians. Many fell quite ill. Some were driven to depression, others to madness. One such prisoner was Abdullah Belaon bu Hamed. Imprisoned on Ustica, Belaon bu Hamed began to present strange medical symptoms in January 1932.[124] He was feverish and vomiting, and suffering from chronic enterocolitis, prostatic inflammation, and sudden loss of vision. He was hospitalized in Palermo for six months, yet his condition only worsened. In August, either a government functionary or Belaon bu Hamed himself requested repatriation to Libya so that he could return home to die. However, upon receiving the request, General Rodolfo Graziani, then governor of Cyrenaica, declared the stricken Belaon bu Hamed an "elemento politicamente pericoloso ed avverso all'azione del Governo italiano" (a politically dangerous element and hostile to Italian government policy) and refused him repatriation.[125] Instead, the sick man was declared a danger to himself and subsequently confined to a psychiatric hospital in Palermo in December 1932. Doctors found no discernible causes of madness and transferred him to a private medical clinic one month later. There, he was found to suffer from syphilis and began a lengthy course of treatment. In March 1933, no longer at the feverish edge of death, he was sent back to Ustica.[126]

Such movements of prisoners between penal and medical institutions were common. Many of the prisoners died. A few returned to Libya. Most ended up back in the decrepit *cameroni* of Ustica and Ponza for years. A rare series of photographs housed in the historical archive of the Italian Ministry of Foreign Affairs provides a glimpse into Ponza's carceral landscape in 1938. It shows the stark white *cameroni*, a military guard formed in the name of *pubblica sicurezza* (public safety), and a bacteriology lab for experiments. Some photos show the Libyan prisoners learning Italian, others sitting with heads bowed during recreation time, and still others taking a *passeggiata ginnastica* (exercise stroll), yet another forced march.

Indeed, the years spent on Ustica and Ponza were hard times. Colonial officials practiced constant brutality under the smokescreen of protecting public safety. Many *deportati* were held without definitive sentences too, their hard time infinite. Without temporal limits, according to one memo, prisoners could better experience their punishments. They would fully sense the value of discipline: "Sono maggiormente in grado di sentire tutto il valore delle sanzioni punitive ed il disagio che ad essi deriva dal non conoscere preventivamente sino a quando dovrà protrarsi la durata della relegazione." (They are better able to feel the value of punitive sanctions and the discomfort that comes from not knowing in advance how long the duration of confinement will continue.)[127] Put another way, the forced deportations to Italy's carceral islands were limited in space but unlimited in time. Inasmuch as Italian colonial tenure in Libya was predicated on the control of mobility, these deportations to the carceral islands paved the way for other spaces and practices of immobilization that would culminate in the horrors of the camp.

Italy's defeat in World War II, its loss of the colonies, and the protracted, incomplete process of decolonization shifted the constellation of imperial formations between Italy and Libya yet again. With the end of the war, the profitable business of incarceration ended on Lampedusa, Ustica, Ponza, and the rest of Italy's carceral archipelago (save the island of Gorgona off the Tuscan coast, which is still used as a prison farm today). The rigid categorizations circumscribed by the mobility regime of temporary permanence—coatto, deportato, confinato—were slowly forgotten, purged from institutional memory and preserved mostly in the realm of personal memoirs.

After the war, there was also the matter of repatriating settlers and citizens from Italy's colonies and possessions. Many Italians who had been born and raised overseas found themselves relocated to a homeland that they had never before visited and much less understood. Pamela Ballinger estimates roughly two hundred thousand Italian rimpatriati (repatriates) "returned" to Italy in the 1940s and 1950s from Africa and the Aegean.[128] Although they did not technically meet the definition of a refugee set forth in the 1951 Geneva Convention, these rimpatriati—caught in a limbo between an unfamiliar homeland and a home to which they could never return—eventually acquired the juridical status of profughi nazionali (national refugees), which entitled them to assistance from the Italian state including accommodation in refugee camps throughout Italy.[129] Chillingly, many of these camps, such as Fossoli and Servigliano, originally functioned as concentration camps under the Fascist regime and had been repurposed to accommodate the flows of refugees, as detailed in essay three of this book.

Some national refugees tried to return to Libya clandestinely. The Sicilian city of Siracusa was a common departure point for these "clandestine Italians," who traveled secretly in small fishing boats back to the Libyan coastline. If they were caught returning to Libya, clandestine Italians faced arrest, jail time, and deportation back to Italy. In the spring of 1947, for example, the British Military Administration, which had taken over operations in Tripolitania and Cyrenaica (the French Military Administration took over the desert province of Fezzan), interdicted and deported 140 Italians seeking entry to Libya on a ship called the Endeavor.[130] This act of forced return in the 1940s hauntingly presages the respingimenti of boat migrants in the mid-2000s. Put another way, the figure of the Italian refugee turned *clandestino* in Libya in the late 1940s and 1950s is not only a reversal of the *clandestino* turned refugee arriving in Italy from Libya today but also its direct historical antecedent. Ballinger put it best: "This history underscores the very recent reversal of flows across the Mediterranean in the Italian case. It is an irony lost on almost all Italians that not so long ago *they* constituted the 'illegals' in those Libyan spaces within which the Italian state sought at the beginning of the 21st century to immobilize potential immigrants to the peninsula; bilateral agreements with the Qaddafi regime facilitated the removal of migrants from Italian locales such as Lampedusa to Libyan detention centers or, alternatively, the preventive detention of migrants in Libya."[131]

The Empire of Pax Americana

The decolonization of Libya, like the rest of Italy's colonies, was slow and protracted. The British and French Military Administrations, charged with managing Libya until an independent government could be established, relied heavily on the economic, social, and institutional structures set up by the colonial regime, often keeping the same Italian staff in place.[132] In 1970, approximately twenty thousand Italians were still living in Libya when Qaddafi issued a blanket decree of expulsion. Under the aegis of regaining the wealth stolen from Libyans by foreign oppressors, Qaddafi declared October 7, 1970, the "Day of Vengeance" and expelled all Italians and Jews in the country, some fifty-seven thousand total.[133] The expulsion was sudden, yet completed in mere months. According to Angelo Del Boca, these unwilling *rimpatriati* found themselves living in refugee camps throughout Italy, newly dispossessed and greatly traumatized by the experience.[134]

At the same time that Qaddafi was consolidating his power in Libya with acts like the Day of Vengeance, the United States set up a small coast guard base on the western end of Lampedusa in 1972 (before this, the United States operated Wheelus Air Base in Libya from 1945 to 1970). Its primary purpose was to house a Loran-C transmitter station, a system of terrestrial radio navigation that has since been replaced by satellite-driven GPS. Loran (short for long-range navigation) depended on a series of low-frequency radio beacons fixed across the globe, and ships and aircraft would triangulate both their position and speed in relation to the fixed radio signals.

The Lampedusa station was part of the Mediterranean Sea Loran-C chain; however, many of the island's residents remain convinced that the United States set up the base to spy on Qaddafi. This may be because the early history of the base is often forgotten in the wake of a calamitous chain of events in 1986, which intertwined the United States, Libya, and Italy in a violent, geopolitical quagmire. These events began on April 5 of that year with a terrorist bombing at a West German discotheque, La Belle, often frequented by U.S. soldiers. Three people were killed and more than 220 were injured, a large portion of them American.[135] Intercepted telex transmissions between Tripoli and the Libyan embassy in Berlin proved that Qaddafi had masterminded the attack. The explosive was even said to have been brought into West Berlin in a diplomatic pouch, and the attack carried out by non-Libyan nationals who worked in the Libyan embassy. La Belle, along with the Lockerbie bombing in 1988, earned Libya the moniker "state sponsor of terrorism."

Ten days after the disco bombing, U.S. president Ronald Reagan ordered a retaliatory airstrike on targets in Tripoli and Benghazi. Squadrons of fighter jets from the U.S. Air Force, Navy, and Marines carried out the bombardments. They launched the attack at 2 a.m. on April 15, 1986, aiming at airfields and army training facilities, as well as Qaddafi's private residence in the Bab al 'Aziiziiyah military compound. There were both civilian and military casualties. Qaddafi narrowly escaped being a casualty himself because three days before the bombings, the Libyan leader had been forewarned that the United States had requested permission to use Italian airspace for the impending sorties into Libya. It was later revealed that the warning to Qaddafi came from then Italian prime minister Bettino Craxi. According to Giulio Andreotti, then minister of foreign affairs, as well as Abdul Rahman Shalgam, Libya's ambassador to Italy at the time, Craxi sent a friend to the Libyan embassy in Rome to warn of the assault. Craxi apparently believed that such immediate retaliation on the part of the United States was a grave error in international relations.[136] When Qaddafi launched two Scud missiles at Lampedusa just fourteen hours after the American raid, Craxi was infuriated. The missiles fell short of the island, landing in the sea, but their ostensible target was the U.S.-run Loran base on the island's western end. Regardless, Craxi was irate that Qaddafi had "repaid" his magnanimous warning by firing on Italy. The next morning he drafted options for retaliation (airstrikes, ground invasion), none of which were ever carried out. On second thought, Craxi began to doubt the veracity of information about the Scud missiles, which was allegedly provided by American sources. Instead, he chose diplomacy over military action, sending a very harsh message to Qaddafi but never forgiving the betrayal.

On Lampedusa, local reaction was a mix of fear and anger, which manifested in an immediate call to either close the Loran base or turn it over to Italian management. Before this, residents had never given much thought to the base, said ex-mayor Giovanni Fragapane.[137] They also believed this was a matter to be resolved solely between the United States and Libya (Craxi's involvement would come to light years later). As a result, security around the base was tightened, an armory added, and the Loran station was recommissioned as a NATO (North Atlantic Treaty Organization) base, even though it was still operated by U.S. forces. In 1994, the base was shut down and handed over to Italian military control.

If once proof of U.S. military empire during the Cold War and its influence in the Mediterranean, today the Loran base is a deserted ruin. Abandoned, everything is left open and exposed to the elements. The metal fences topped with barbed wire are no longer locked up tight but rather rusted and cut. A stray dog greets anyone who approaches the central bunker, where almost every window is broken and every door falling off its hinges. Expensive radio equipment disintegrates in an uncovered storehouse. This is the end of the island, the end of Europe, the end of a Cold War empire. There is nothing here but for the ever-present swirl and caw of seagulls, alternately circling above and nesting below, and the incessant wind eroding this imperial blight like sandstone in the desert.

Yet just as the demise of the Loran base seemed entirely ensured, the base was reopened in the summer of 2011—this time as an improvised migrant detention center (figure 5). While the reopening was only temporary, to accommodate the thousands of migrants fleeing the Maghreb during the Arab Spring, the Loran station, with its dilapidated buildings and lack of running water, was hardly an adequate facility for any type of reception. Fearing physical and sexual assault, women and unaccompanied minors were transferred here from the main CPT. One social worker, Maria Billè, described the scene as one of prolonged suffering: "La loro permanenza nell'isola è stata un calvario," she said. "I minori sono stati abbandonati per settimane senza potere uscire dalle strutture o ricevere visite . . . avevano affrontato tutti viaggi drammatici e rischiosissimi ed esprimevano evidenti segni di sofferenza e disagio psicologico." (Their stay on the island has been an ordeal. The minors were abandoned for weeks without being able to leave the structures or receive visits. . . . They had all faced dramatic and dangerous journeys and expressed obvious signs of suffering and psychological distress.)[138]

Physical conditions were dire: exposed bedrooms, dirty foam mattresses spread haphazardly on the ground, reused paper sheets (if any at all), lack of food, and feculent toilets. Many women and minors were held here for weeks, with little idea of how long they would stay or even where they might go in the future. They were inscribed into the regime of temporary permanence while simultaneously installed into the ever-hardening category of "illegal immigrant." So intense was the stress at the ex–Loran base that, when coupled with the threat of deportation, many would choose death over repatriation.

Figure 5. Graffiti in Arabic etched inside the ex-Loran station turned migrant detention center on Lampedusa registers the presence of one man who was detained there: Abdeldaem Saudi from Al-Qasreen, Tunisia. Photograph by the author, 2014.

Sadly, many of the minors demonstrated this through incidents of self-harm, like swallowing razor blades and auto-laceration.[139] And so the swirl and caw of seagulls was now silenced and replaced, in part, with prayers and sobs in the night.

The Tourism of Emergency

With the Loran base temporarily back in operation and the island overwhelmed by *sbarchi*, the business of migration was booming in 2011. There were inexorable profits to be made off this industry of unsanctioned mobilities. On the contrary, Lampedusa's other mobility-based industry, tourism, suffered dramatically. Reservations plummeted, and the 2011 season was shaping up to be disastrous. To counter, Italy's Ministry of Tourism intervened with subsidized airfares, free hotel rooms, and slickly produced commercials featuring the island's natural landscape.[140] In such a way, a third imperial strand—the empire of globalization, of which migration and tourism are interrelated parts—flexed its neoliberal power on Lampedusa vis-à-vis the modern Italian state.[141] Ironically, it was the aforementioned Scud missile incident in 1986 that put Lampedusa on the tourist map. The international media coverage of the event showed not only the military base but also a sleepy fishing village surrounded by sandy beaches and alluring aquamarine hues of the Mediterranean. Almost overnight, the island transformed into a tourist destination.

Over the years, tourist numbers have increased in manifold, with roughly 176,000 passengers traveling through the Lampedusa airport in 2010 alone.[142] Most are Italian, arriving on commercial airlines and seasonal charter flights. For tourists, Rabbit Beach is the island's central attraction. Located roughly a mile west of town, this shallow cove of pristine sugar sand and beryl-blue water sits in the middle of a protected nature reserve. The endangered loggerhead sea turtle breeds here as do many seabirds. Tourists sunbathe nearby but take care not to disturb the environment. In addition to this beach, tourists frequent other ones closer to town or take boat excursions around the island. Evenings are marked by a slow *passeggiata* down Via Roma and relaxed dinners that last for hours. Touristic infrastructure has also been strictly regulated on Lampedusa. Accommodation consists almost exclusively of midsize family-run hotels, B&Bs, or rental apartments. One hotel owner told me that locals had rejected the development of a *villaggio turistico* (holiday village) à la Club Med in order to maintain the island's intimate character. Despite the dip in tourist numbers in 2011, this same hotel owner was optimistic for the 2013 season thanks to TripAdvisor's proclamation of Rabbit Beach as the best in the world. The migration crisis had been bad for business, he said.

Yet a new type of tourism has sprung up on Lampedusa, a tourism that stems directly from the island's association with migration and its place within the international crisis imaginary. Since 2011, the Italian section of Amnesty International has organized a weeklong summer camp on Lampedusa focused on human rights. It was inspired by the "comportamento dei lampedusani, che mai trasformano le difficoltà in sentimenti xenofobi, ma accolgono le persone che arrivano dal mare" (comportment of the Lampedusans, who never transform difficulties into xenophobic sentiments, but welcome people who arrive from the sea).[143] The first session in 2011 enrolled forty-three people, most of them young, aspiring activists. The next year, 2012, there were seventy participants. In addition to lectures and seminars, these participants chose to make a physical statement against violations of human rights associated with the boat migrations from Libya to Italy. They proved a stark sight: a flash mob dressed in black and standing in the water at Rabbit Beach. They held up signs and spelled out "SOS" in the sand with their bodies. Around them, tourists continued to swim or watch from under their beach umbrellas.

In 2013, Amnesty International Italy not only organized another summer camp focused on human rights and migration but also sponsored an even bigger Festa del turismo responsabile e dei diritti umani (Festival of Sustainable Tourism and Human Rights). The weeklong event raised awareness about the interrelated flows of tourism and migration to the island with presentations by a variety of nonprofit organizations. One of the event's stated goals was to work with local residents to create an action plan to resolve the island's quotidian emergencies related to migration. By engaging the term "emergency," the festival evokes Lampedusa's association with political and humanitarian crises. Or, to put it another way, tourist imaginary meets crisis imaginary here in these Amnesty-organized vacations. Lampedusa again proves the fulcrum where the globalized mobilities of tourism and migration meet, and the festival attempted to reorient this constellation toward more affirmative possibilities, especially in the wake of the dramatic increase in the *flussi* (flows) of immigration that peaked in 2011.

Flows of Crisis: 2011 and Beyond

The *flussi* left an indelible mark on the collective memory of the island. At the time, tens of thousands of people were fleeing North Africa and the upheaval of the Arab Spring on boats headed to the rocky shores of Lampedusa. The numbers tell a gripping story—hundreds, sometimes thousands, of migrants were rescued each day, more than fifty thousand in the first six months of 2011 alone. Roughly half embarked from Tunisia and the other half from Libya. There was literally nowhere to house all of these people on Lampedusa. Video footage shows the island's streets packed with cold and weary people, mostly men. Some huddled together for warmth. Others took pictures on their cell phones. Still others used a lorry as shelter, sleeping underneath it while covered up with plastic tarps. In August 2011, the Italian government officially declared the situation a humanitarian emergency.

V., the restaurant owner, remembers there being three distinct waves of *flussi*. She told me that the first wave started right around Valentine's Day. Migrants who came in this wave were all *persone colte* (cultured people), she said, among them university professors, students, and other professionals. She remembered that many were perfectly quadrilingual (Arabic, Italian, French, English) and were very polite. To her surprise, the first thing that many of them wanted was not food but rather toiletries. At one of the few supermarkets on the island, V. helped many migrants purchase these products at a low cost. They paid her in cash, either in euros or dollars.

A waiter from Agrigento who has worked ten seasons on Lampedusa also remembers the *flussi* of 2011 as such. In one of our conversations, he said that being Italian, and especially being from Sicily, helps one understand the plight of the boat migrants. "L'Italia è una crocevia tra l'Occidente e l'Oriente, e sopratutto la Sicilia," he noted. (Italy is a crossroads between Occident and Orient, and above all, Sicily.) Since Italy was once a country of emigration, he added, Italians were predisposed to understanding—and having more empathy for—a migrant's situation.

However, one person who showed little empathy for migrants was ex–prime minister Silvio Berlusconi. In addition to masterminding the 2008 Friendship Pact with Libya and sanctioning the refoulement of boat migrants, Berlusconi landed in Lampedusa in March 2011 during the first wave of the *flussi*. He announced that he had a plan to clear (*sgombrare*) the island of migrants within three days following his visit, that is, to relocate them to other detention centers throughout Italy. Berlusconi then joked that his plan would include buying up all of the fishing trawlers in Tunisia just so that migrants could not use them. Within the next two days, he proudly proclaimed that "Lampedusa sarà abitata solamente dai lampedusani" (Lampedusa will be inhabited only by Lampedusans).[144]

Yet Berlusconi's promises proved empty insofar as the third wave of the *flussi* that arrived around August 2011 was among the largest yet. According to many residents, it was certainly the most violent. V., the restaurant owner, said the migrants of the third wave were predominantly *briganti* (brigands) who had been released en masse from Tunisian prisons and then crossed to

Lampedusa. She noted these migrants spoke only Arabic and were not at all polite. Instances of theft and burglary increased during this wave. Tensions between migrants and locals escalated throughout the month and culminated in several days of what news reports described as urban guerrilla warfare.

The clashes began with the devastating fire at the CPT set in protest by detainees in September 2011. Violent outbursts swept across the island. D., the proprietor of a rental apartment block, remembers an incident in which a group of migrants took gas tanks from the local gas station and threatened to blow them up. They held lighters to the tanks, he said; however, the police could not legally make the first move to arrest them. Residents allegedly threw rocks at the migrants, and once a single rock was thrown in return, the police took action. The backlash was not limited to migrants. Bernardino De Rubeis, the mayor of Lampedusa at the time, was assaulted by three locals who accused him of being too soft on migration. "Siamo in presenza di uno scenario da guerra" (We are in the presence of a war scenario), he said, and to defend himself, he was ready to use the baseball bat he kept in his office.[145]

As the clashes grew more intense, additional law enforcement was brought in from Sicily. Fifty policemen appropriated the block of rental apartments owned by D. as living quarters. They participated in what many were calling a *caccia al uomo* (manhunt), or the roundup of migrants who had once been in the CPT. Put differently, the recourse to martial law normalized the situation on Lampedusa. Italian state power flexed its full force. And once more, unsanctioned mobile subjects—made visible by an impromptu release from their prescribed holding space, the CPT—were labeled as dangerous to society and coercively immobilized yet again. Within days of the police reinforcements arriving on the island, almost all migrants had been apprehended and transferred to detention centers elsewhere in Italy.

The depth of the chaos in those days was perhaps best described by Gino Strada, founder of Emergency, a Milan-based nongovernmental organization that provides medical treatment to civilian victims of war. He attributed the violent clashes on Lampedusa to an insidious negligence—both political and ethical—of the Italian state and called for Italian citizens to reinsert humanity into this imaginary of crisis:[146]

> Quello che sta succedendo a Lampedusa è figlio di una politica criminale che da molti anni i governi di questo paese stanno attuando nei confronti dei migranti . . . La tensione e la violenza delle ultime ore . . . sono l'inevitabile conseguenza della politica di un governo che tratta gli stranieri come criminali, come problema di ordine pubblico, come

bestie . . . Confidiamo che i cittadini italiani abbiamo la ragionevolezza e l'umanità che finora è mancata al governo, quell'umanità che permette di capire che gli "stranieri," i "clandestini," i "migranti stagionali" sono, prima che qualsiasi altra cosa, semplicemente "persone," esseri umani. E come tali devono essere trattati.

What is happening on Lampedusa is the product of a criminal policy that for many years the governments of this country have been implementing against migrants. . . . The tension and violence of the last few hours [on Lampedusa] . . . are the inevitable consequence of the policy of a government that treats foreigners as criminals, as a matter of public order, like animals. . . . We trust that Italian citizens have the reason and humanity that until now has been lacking in the government, that humanity that allows us to understand that "foreigners," "clandestini," "seasonal workers" are, before any other thing, simply "people," human beings. And that they should be treated as such.

Memories of 2011 are still palpable among the residents of Lampedusa. Talk of the *flussi* punctuates conversations. The island's former mayor, Giusy Nicolini, remembers how "Lampedusa intera, non il Centro Imbriacola o Loran, divenne un immenso campo profughi, un unico Centro di identificazione e espulsione" (Lampedusa as a whole, not just the Center [CPT] or the Loran base, became an immense refugee camp, a singular Center of Identification and Expulsion).[147] Sadly, these memories are being quickly supplanted by tragedies of an even greater scale, in particular the shipwreck of October 3, 2013. In this grisly incident, 366 people burned and then drowned as their boat caught fire and capsized a little more than half a mile from Rabbit Beach, the same beach that was voted the most beautiful in the world that very same year. Most of the victims hailed from Eritrea, once Italy's *colonia primogenita* (first-born colony). For days after the shipwreck, the coast guard recovered bodies. Hundreds of them lined the walls of Lampedusa's new port in makeshift body bags like the scene of a battlefield. Journalists and television crews descended on the island and filed story after story about the tragedy. Àine O'Healy notes, "This televised spectacle of death was matched by the televised performance of grief and outrage . . . [and] reinforc[ed] the island's status as a signifier of large scale humanitarian crisis and as a flashpoint in discussions about the increasing securitization and militarization of the Mediterranean."[148]

There remains a sense of urgency linked to Lampedusa as the number of migrants attempting to cross the Mediterranean continues to grow. More than ever, the island localizes the idea of emergency and the imaginary of crisis at Europe's southern border. Historically, Lampedusa has been a space of containment for the subjects that threaten Italian state sovereignty, and the same is the case today but now amplified in scale. Here the mobility regime of temporary permanence gives rise to bureaucracy intent on immobilization. It presses hundreds of thousands of people into strict legal and medical grammars.

The crossings here are many and multidirectional: sea to land, Libya to Italy, individual to migrant, person to nonperson, actual to abstract, fluid to rigid. The fluidity of mobility—marked by the eponymous term *flussi* (flows)—meets stoppage in the form of Italian state power, which co-opts those who are subject to it into the abstract category of "illegal immigrant." To enter these grammars compels a type of naturalization, as Ruben Andersson has shown, an acknowledgment of one's illicit status before the law and the reluctant acceptance of *clandestino* as a lived-in category. Migrants arriving on Lampedusa not only become conscripted into the apparatus of the Italian state but also live out the very categories, identifications, and classifications that define that process of conscription. And this is little different from the world of European colonial imperialism described by Frantz Fanon. For him, "the colonial world is a compartmentalized world . . . a Manichean world. . . . The colonist is not content with physically limiting the space of the colonized" but plants deep the seeds of alienation.[149] Categorization creates forms of specialized knowledge, and such knowledge precipitates hierarchies, judgments, and strategies of domestication, that is, the ability to tame incomprehension and, with it, the threat of Otherness.[150] Thus, the many discrete categories of migrants in play on Lampedusa (*clandestino*, refugee, *sbarcato*, asylum seeker, et cetera) each carry the weight of specific political histories and the categories linked to them (for example, *coatto*, *deportato*, *confinato*), but also together mark an accelerating compartmentalization, petrification, and essentialization of people who are perceived to be threats to the Italian state because of their unsanctioned mobilities.

To their credit, many activist groups on Lampedusa and elsewhere in Italy have worked tirelessly to resist this movement. For example, Askavusa, a cultural association based on Lampedusa, has plans to open a museum dedicated to migration and serves as a clearinghouse for migrants returning to the island to look for traces of loved ones. The Archivio di Memorie Migranti (Archive of Migrant Memories) in Rome began work on its Lampedusa Project in 2012, which proposes the creation of a document center on the island that would act as a repository for migrant narratives. In February 2014, a number of grassroots organizations drafted and signed the Carta di Lampedusa (Charter of Lampedusa), which recognizes, among other things, mobility-generated inequality as being distinctly linked to stratifying operations that

FIGURE 6. Porta di Lampedusa—Porta d'Europa (The Gate of Lampedusa—The Gate of Europe) by artist Mimmo Paladino. Photograph by the author, 2013.

can be described only as colonial: "Le politiche migratorie sono oggi tra i meccanismi principali attraverso cui si ridefiniscono le divisoni di classe e riemergono i rapporti e le asimmetrie coloniali tra gli Stati." (Migration policies are today the principal mechanisms through which class divisions redefine themselves, and [through which] colonial relationships and asymmetries re-emerge between states.)[151] What the charter implicitly describes are the imperial formations that constitute Italy's empire.

Yet on Lampedusa, the call to reinsert humanity into the humanitarian crisis has been answered perhaps most effectively by the most sophisticated of human faculties: art. At the southeastern end of the island, not far from the old port and the end of the airport runway, there stands a colossal monolith overlooking the sea. Called La porta di Lampedusa—la porta d'Europa (The Gate of Lampedusa—The Gate of Europe), the sculpture was created by artist Mimmo Paladino and erected in June 2008 (figure 6). It is meant to memorialize the many who never arrived on the island, that is, the untold numbers of migrants who were forever lost at sea. The monolith is the color of desert sand and stands alone on a desolate bluff. It cuts a stark figure against the island's backdrop of infinite sea and sky. Sixteen feet high with a doorway cut in its middle, the sculpture consists of galvanized iron borders and special ceramic panels that both absorb and reflect light. From one view, the doorway faces the town, and from the opposite, Africa. A closer look reveals that worn-out shoes, broken bowls, and boat parts as well as two-dimensional hands, numbers, and faces have been fired directly into the ceramic. Much in the same way that a local resident, Luciano, collects the flotsam of wrecked *pescherecci* and hangs it up on a wooden fence, so too does this sculpture materialize the literal and figurative remnants of those lost at sea.[152] "Ho provato a spiegare qualcosa che avesse a che fare con un esodo forzato, qualcosa di comprensibile a tutti i popoli" (I tried to explain something that would have had to do with a forced exodus, something comprehensible to all people), said the artist Paladino in an interview with *La Repubblica*. "Per questo ho voluto la porta il più lontano possibile dal centro abitato e il più vicino possibile all'acqua e quindi all'Africa." (That's why I wanted the Gate as far away from the town as possible and as close as possible to the water, and therefore, to Africa.)[153] Several residents of Lampedusa pointed me toward the sculpture. They seemed proud that it existed. Bernardino De Rubeis, the ex-mayor who kept a baseball bat in his office during the 2011 *flussi*, had this to say about the sculpture: "Noi lampedusani abbiamo sempre cercato di fare la nostra parte e continueremo così, è impossibile vivere in questa isola e dimenticare cosa accade da una parte del mondo che è così vicina alla nostra." (We Lampedusans have always tried to do our part and we will continue to do so, it is impossible to live on this island and forget what happens in a part of the world that is so close to ours.)[154]

Yet the Gate of Lampedusa is slowly eroding, abraded by an unending assault of wind and sea. The sculpture is deliberately rough and unfinished so as to evoke the ongoing tragedy of the Mediterranean passage, yet even so, it has broken down further since its inauguration. Its once bright blue accent colors have faded to beige. Its tiles have begun an uneven desquamation. Iron brackets have rusted and seeped into the ceramic like bloodstains. And just beyond the bluff the sea roils under a placid guise, threatening to swallow everything and anyone into its depths. One day, too, the sea will swallow this sculpture as it has the untold numbers of people that have attempted to cross its expanse. It will be forgotten, or at best, a trace that haunts stories and photographs. It is a piece of art that, like the people it seeks to memorialize, shares with them existence in a state of temporary permanence.

Essay 2

The Camp

> The camp is merely the place in which the most
> absolute *conditio inhumana* that has ever existed on
> earth was realized: this is what counts in the last
> analysis, for the victims as for those who come after.
>
> —Giorgio Agamben

> In Italy, life is not free. This is not a prison, this is
> a camp.
> A camp is quite different from a prison.
>
> —A., twenty-four, from Nigeria

> Hunger, disease, and broken hearts took a heavy toll
> of the imprisoned population.
> Bedouin die in a cage.
>
> —E. E. Evans-Pritchard

The outskirts of Rome have the feel of an urban wasteland. Empty streets decussate the landscape. Skeletal apartment blocks stand half-finished. Abandoned parking lots languish in various states of overgrowth and decay. In the summer, the area feels even more apocalyptic than usual because of the heat. It radiates from the asphalt and pools around the body as if from a circle of Dante's inferno. No one walks these streets. In the midst of all this, the Centro di Identificazione e Espulsione (Center for Identification and Expulsion, or CIE) at Ponte Galeria hides in plain sight (figure 7). Its concrete walls and metal fences seem little out of place. This is Italy's largest migrant detention center and often the last stop for "illegal immigrants" before they are forced out of the country.

It was here that I met a young Nigerian woman named A. during my second field visit, in March 2013.[1] She stood in the middle of the room, nude. She was still wet from the shower, her body glistening in the dappled light of the windows that used newspapers for makeshift curtains. She was proud of her figure and rubbed lotion vigorously into her arms, legs, and breasts, seemingly unashamed of her nudity as she stood before me, a stranger from the outside. As her hands moved rhythmically, she talked to me. Rather, A. did

FIGURE 7.   The Ponte Galeria migrant detention center near Rome. Photograph by the author, 2012.

not just talk. It would be more accurate to say that with every sentence she issued a proclamation. She proclaimed that being detained in Bologna was better than being here in Rome. She proclaimed what she missed about Africa. She proclaimed that her breasts were beautiful. She proclaimed that she had a boyfriend on the outside who would take care of her if only she were set free. Her most vehement proclamations were reserved for the center itself. "In Italy, life is not free," she said. "This is not a prison, this is a camp. A camp is very different from a prison."

Just as A. sensed implicitly, many scholars have noted that the migrant detention centers of the twenty-first century are the grim heirs to the concentration camps of the twentieth.[2] The camp is not just a space, according to Giorgio Agamben, but the instantiation of the biopolitics that define modernity.[3] The camp is a spatial practice. It makes real the state of exception that has now become the rule. It materializes the logic of sovereignty. It exists between the temporary and the permanent. And to go one step further, the camp normalizes exception (and its corollary, emergency) in such a way that it inverts sociality to "promote un-bonding as a form of relation."[4] It is the *via negativa* of disconnection, disengagement, uncommitment, and disorder that defines the camp, and according to Agamben, that which gives order to our contemporary space and time. "Illegal immigrants" experience this unbonding today in sites like Ponte Galeria. In Italy, they have nicknamed these centers *lager*.

This essay fleshes out a genealogy of camps in modern Italy, focusing attention on the present-day migrant detention center at Ponte Galeria and its historical predecessor, the Italian-built concentration camps in eastern Libya (1929–34), or what I identify as the alpha and the omega of the camp in the modern Italian context. It tracks the ways in which mobility and state power operate at both and explores the *via negativa* lived by the people within them, many of whom already exist precariously at the edges of life. It reveals both the detention center and the concentration camp to be spaces where, paradoxically, statelessness and state power operate in full force. The migrant detention center at Ponte Galeria can also be seen as giving a permanent spatial arrangement to the contemporary logic of illegality industry. Here, people are conscripted into the medical circuits and the legal grammars of the Italian state and abstracted into the category of "illegal immigrant," coming to live it ex post facto.[5] It marks an end point of the chiasmatic movement from actuality to abstraction and fluidity to rigidity that began on the island. Put another way, if Lampedusa is an event horizon, then Ponte Galeria is its singularity.

The state of exception, the perceived threat of a mobility crisis, and the containment of a mobile populace within the neatly ordered yet oppressive space of Ponte Galeria are all haunting reminders of Italy's colonial past not so long ago. In Italian colonial Libya, the Bedouin rather than "illegal immigrants" occupied the role of dangerous, mobile Other. Their resistance to Italian occupation and purported *grande nomadismo* (great nomadism) gave rise to the most brutal of colonial policies and military actions: in 1929, almost one hundred thousand Bedouin were forcibly displaced from their homelands and sequestered in concentration camps along the bleak Cyrenaican coast. Another aim of this essay, then, is to give a history of the Libyan camps, which, with rare exceptions, have been all but excised from the scholarship on modern European imperialisms.[6] I include a general outline of their classificatory logics, their spatial layouts, and the practices of everyday life within them. This is by no means a complete picture, but it is a gesture toward the recuperation of a history that has been disavowed for too long.

Moreover, I situate Agamben's foundational theories of the camp within the Italian cultural context in which he was writing, that is, among the pronounced disavowal of Italy's colonial experience. Agamben ties the emergence of the camp—and Auschwitz, specifically—to the ultimate figure of exception under Roman law, the *homo sacer* (sacred or accursed man).[7] The Libyan camps provide a different angle on Agamben's formulation—they are always-already imbricated within empire's Mobius strip in that they were modeled, in part, on the Roman *castrum* (the camp of the Roman Legion). They not only spatialized a state of exception vis-à-vis the figure of the *homo sacer* but also recouped a moving threshold of empire—the *castrum*—in space.

The camps in colonial Libya and Ponte Galeria were both spatial responses to "threats" of unsanctioned mobilities—the former belonging to the age of European colonial imperialism, the latter tied to the forces of neoliberal empire today. In theory, the camps expressed sentiments of mastery over separate populations across different geographies and temporalities. In practice, they attempted to exercise mastery over all movements. Mobility was brought into play as a relation of force. It became something to be allocated, reappropriated, deflected, excluded, denied, deferred, disavowed, and so on within its respective polities. In Italian colonial Libya, mobility even became a juridical weapon in the form of *tribunali volanti* (flying courts). This essay weaves together the ways in which mobility consolidates and dissolves the ongoing "processes of decimation, displacement and reclamation" that constitute imperial formations.[8] It maps, with intentional ebbs and flows, the entangled trajectories of camps in modern Italy so as to reflect the uneven grounds of empire's power as well as the disparities between those who move by choice and those who are moved by force.

Italian Guantánamo

March is the cruelest month at Ponte Galeria. The raw chill of winter gives way to days that hint at warmth. Rain alternates with brilliant sunshine. Blooming grasses and cloudless skies soften the center's gunmetal fences with the promise of spring's renewal. Yet the grass and the sky are just out of reach. They are cruel reminders of a vibrant, polychrome life beyond the walls. Ponte Galeria is the largest of ten CIEs currently operating in Italy. It has 360 beds, half for men and half for women, but it is rarely at capacity.[9] All people detained here are called *ospiti* (guests), often much to their chagrin. As one man at the Trapani CIE put it in the 2014 documentary film *Limbo*: "Ti chiamano ospiti. Questa cosa si dà troppo fastidio. Almeno mi chiami 'detenuto' e non mi chiami 'ospite' se tu mi prendi solo in giro, capito?" (They call you "guests." This really bothers me. At least call me a "prisoner" and don't call me a "guest" unless you want to make fun of me, understand?) The Ponte Galeria complex once functioned as a police training facility but was repurposed in 1998 under the provision of the Turco-Napolitano law, which established temporary detention centers (CPT) for "illegal" or "irregular" immigrants in Italy without permits of stay.[10] This law expanded the 1990 Martelli law, which aimed to regularize and curb the ever-increasing migrant flows into Italy. While the Martelli law appeared to open up opportunities for migrants to work, study, and receive medical care, on the ground the state's treatment of migrants was often exceedingly harsh.[11] The laws surrounding immigration in Italy tightened further in 2008 with the passage of the so-called Security Package, the legislation that expanded the juridical framework that criminalized immigration, which, among other things, made it a crime to give aid to "irregular" migrants.

Since Italy transitioned in the mid-1970s from being a sending country of emigrants to being a receiving country for immigrants, much scholarship has documented the transformation along with the laws and politics that have accompanied it.[12] What is unique about the Italian case, according to David Forgacs, is the remarkable unity of the hardline response toward immigration across the political spectrum, particularly under Berlusconi's tenure as prime minister in the 2000s.[13] Numerous scholars have also focused attention on Italy's migrant detention centers and expanded on the ways in which they fit the logic of the camp outlined by Agamben. Examples include the work of Rutvica Andrijasevic, for whom Italy's detention centers are camps that act as "modes of temporal regulation of transit migration" among the "de-territorialization of European borders."[14] For Charlie Hailey, "Italy's system of camps combines the temporary nature of processing with the permanence of detention," and he adds that while they are classified separately into three categories, they often function interchangeably.[15] For Marco Rovelli, the camps are the physical and symbolic termini of Italy's migration politics. They materialize "una condizione di assoluta sospensione" (a condition of absolute suspension) whereby one is deprived of time, space, and life.[16] My goal here is not to repeat what has already been said but rather to enrich this body of scholarship with historical depth.

Indeed, it is logical to think of a migrant detention center like Ponte Galeria as a camp. It gives a permanent, spatial arrangement to the logic of sovereignty, that is, a state of exception that has now become the rule.[17] From Guantánamo to Sangatte, the idea of the migrant detention center as "camp" has been well established in the academic literature, especially in contemporary Europe.[18] And today, according to Bülent Diken and Carsten Bagge Laustsen, the subject of exception par excellence is the refugee, who, by default, is almost always a detainee in the camp. They write that the refugee inhabits a zone of indistinction between political states, civil rights, and social responsibilities. Contemporary discourses of migration exclude refugees from the domains of ethical responsibility and expose them to the violence of both state and civil society without legal consequences.[19] The refugee is an outsider inside and an insider outside—a new *homo sacer*—who embodies the paradox of sovereignty.[20] "In the detention center the human and the inhuman enter into a biopolitical zone of indistinction, and the detainees can be subjected to all sorts of physical and symbolic violence without legal consequences," explain Diken and Laustsen. "Banned and excluded from society, the detainee is forced to survive in an open-ended period of incarceration, sealed off by barbed wire and surveillance cameras."[21] Put another way, the detention center is a nonplace inhabited by juridical nonsubjects. It disavows the humanity of those contained within its walls.[22]

At Ponte Galeria, the detainees intrinsically sense this disavowal. For instance, the Nigerian women I talked to during my field visit in 2013 expressed their feelings of being treated as nonsubjects in comparison to animals. They said to me, "We are human beings not animals" and "Here we are treated like animals." Theirs is an innate recognition of a collapse between human and inhuman, or what might be described in theoretical terms as a threshold of desubjectivization. It is not unusual in detention centers like this. Patrick Barkham documented the same phenomenon at the notorious Woomera Immigration Reception and Processing Center in Australia, with one detainee noting, "They are dealing with us as animals, not as human beings."[23] Even Primo Levi in his well-known account of Auschwitz (from which Agamben drew inspiration for his theory of the camp) noted that prisoners "lived for months and years at an animal level" only to have that belief reinforced by the SS guards from whom "these are not *Menschen*, human beings, but animals; it's clear as the light of day."[24] Detainees thus exist at the limit between human and animal. Not only are they banned and excluded from society, but upon entering the CIE, they pass into a space that denudes them of their humanity. The center as such evacuates the space of people and replaces them with nonsubjects who are judged to be less than human. In this sense, the CIE becomes a *volkloser Raum* (people-less space), or a space that crystallizes the Italian state's biopolitical impulses. This evacuative process, writes Agamben, names the driving force of the camp understood as biopolitical machine.[25]

The camp that is the Ponte Galeria CIE, according to A.'s proclamation, exists precisely because of her unsanctioned mobilities. It is the space that has arisen out of her existence as both the object and the subject of sex trafficking and "illegal immigration." It exists to contain her and others who move against the grain of state power. At Ponte Galeria, their bodies are probed by state-sanctioned medical doctors, their minds assessed by staff psychologists, their movements controlled by police and *carabinieri*, and their legal status as subjects debated by public defenders, consular officials, and court magistrates. Whereas a prisoner's status under the law is relatively clear, everything about the *ospite* is ambiguous at Ponte Galeria. She exists between state power and statelessness. Personhood is continually redefined by parallel legal and medical grammars. She feels caught up in a biopolitical machine, caught between human and inhuman.[26] This is what A. meant when she proclaimed, "This is not a prison, this is a camp."

While other *ospiti* may not be as articulate as A., I saw them express this breakdown in other ways. For example, one man, I., had just arrived at the center. Wearing a white windbreaker and a pair of laceless shoes, he stood next to me at the threshold of the staff psychologist's office. He stared straight ahead, eyes locked level on an empty bookshelf. His smooth, unweathered skin spoke of youth, and I guessed that he was little more than twenty years old. As he underwent the long process of registration, I. hardly said a word. He was frozen. His gaze was fixed and unfocused. His stillness was haunting, like a man on a precipice about to be thrust into an unknown and precarious limbo that was not of his own making.

The Inside of Outside

The *ospiti* at Ponte Galeria spend their days being shunted back and forth among lawyers, judges, doctors, and social workers like unwanted objects as they submit to the named purpose of the center: identification and expulsion. The process begins upon arrival. Their descent into this bureaucratic leviathan is accompanied, too, by their increasing fixture into the category of "illegal immigrant." The *ospiti* have also been called many other names, including refugees, economic migrants, asylum seekers, stateless people, *sans-papiers*, displaced persons, *clandestini*, evacuees, and disaster victims. Each categorization carries its own history, and every instance of naming can be considered a political act.[27] The *ospiti* constitute what Michel Agier has called an "indistinct set of undesirables."[28] Yet the unspoken exigency that underlies every proceeding at Ponte Galeria is that all those detained are here because of their unsanctioned mobilities. They have been caught up in what Achille Mbembe has described as the "new moment of global mobility," wherein "a patchwork of overlapping and incomplete rights to rule emerges, inextricably superimposed and tangled, in which different de facto juridical instances are geographically interwoven and plural allegiances, asymmetrical suzerainties, and enclaves abound."[29] Neither the Italian state nor the European Union has authorized their movements, and as a consequence, they are marked as "clandestine" or "irregular" or "illegal" to justify their detention in the center's spatial and legal oblivion.

It became apparent from my observations that the *ospiti* at Ponte Galeria were all living in a tenuous present. Uncertain futures united them. They were subjects who existed at the limits of nation, law, space, and self in this black

hole of a place, a Dantean limbo. This limbo arose from the paradox of temporary permanence spatialized by the center. Indeed, the CIE's former name,
Centro di Permanenza Temporanea (Center of Temporary Permanence), was
itself an oxymoron; it belied a condition of stability and duration (permanence)
that was immediately negated by the precariousness of the temporary, and vice
versa. In such a way, the two terms canceled each other out and created a
vacuum. Or, as Marco Rovelli put it in *Lager italiani* (Italian lagers):[30]

> La designazione linguistica, dunque, indica già pienamente e compiuta-
> mente il senso proprio di ciò che viene a essere designato: una con-
> dizione di assoluta sospensione. Una sospensione di senso. Il centro in
> cui vige questa assoluta sospensione di senso si pone dunque come
> (non) luogo di deprivazione, di svuotamento. Uno svuotamento tanto
> da un punto di vista esistenziale (le storie ne raccontano ad abundan-
> tiam) quanto da un punto di vista giuridico.

> The linguistic designation, therefore, already fully and completely
> indicates the proper sense of what is to be designated: a condition of
> absolute suspension. A suspension of sense. The center in which this
> absolute suspension of sense is enforced therefore is set as (non)place of
> deprivation, of evacuation. An emptying as much from an existential
> point of view (the stories recount that *ad abundantiam*) as from a legal point
> of view.

If a singular truth exists here, it is that all of the *ospiti* at Ponte Galeria have
been on traumatic journeys. For instance, I was told that the female detainees
from Nigeria tend to come from its second-largest city, Kano, near the border
with Niger in the north. According to one social worker, these women were
approached by traffickers and promised a better life in Italy for $80,000 a piece,
a price that could be further discounted to $45,000 if she chose to make the
more treacherous journey to Italy over desert and sea instead of by air.[31] Im-
poverished and uneducated, many did not know they were being recruited into
the sex trade, and only upon arrival in Europe did they learn they must work
off their debt. Long before arriving at the center, these women—almost all of
them in their early twenties—had worked for months, even years, as prosti-
tutes, exchanging the bondage of poverty in Nigeria for that of sexual slavery
in Italy.[32]

Trauma and mobility are thus intimate bedfellows of the camp. Every
ospite has suffered them, usually as the result of attempting to escape the one
(trauma) through the other (mobility). Whereas the fast-and-loose potentials
of a life on the move mark the rising class of global elites, the obverse side is

that such mobilities of the rich north come at the expense of many others, usually in the global south, who remain immobilized—or even expulsed (what Saskia Sassen has called a "savage sorting")—by ever-growing social and financial inequalities.[33] The *ospiti* at Ponte Galeria tend to be people who, for one reason or another, refused their place in the globalized order. They aspired to work in Europe. They wanted to be free of poverty, sickness, and violence. They dreamed of having a better life.

Many of these *ospiti* believed in the emancipatory potentials of mobility, and they acted on those hopes. Yet instead of ameliorating life, what resulted for many of them was a total collapse of life. Entrapment in sexual slavery. Intense racial discrimination. Social exclusion. Crippling poverty. They became part of the unwanted mobile class who move furtively along lines of state power. To borrow the words of Zygmunt Bauman, "Mobility climbs to the rank of the uppermost among coveted values—and the freedom to move, perpetually a scarce and unequally distributed commodity, fast becomes the main stratifying factor of our late modern and postmodern time."[34] The glimpse into everyday life at Ponte Galeria afforded by my field visits—a glimpse into the spaces and subjects who dwell and work there—reveals its inhabitants' attempts to make the best of an intractable situation wrought by differential mobilities, reactionary immigration policies, and unstable political administrations. When I asked if the system of identification and expulsion actually worked at Ponte Galeria, the inspector in charge took a deep breath before dodging the question: "It's a system," he replied. Detainees, then, were not the only ones who felt powerless in the face of state power; so, too, did the people seemingly in charge.

Such power is dispersed among different authorities in the center, which act to complement one another. Soldiers from the Italian Army guard the front gate; police officers from the Questura di Roma (municipal police headquarters of Rome) run the intake process and accompany detainees to hearings and appointments within the center; *carabinieri* (national police) patrol the male sector; and the Ministry of the Interior oversees general operations, finances, and requests for access. These are the agencies tasked with carrying out the process of identification and expulsion. At the time of my field visit in March 2013, day-to-day operations were subcontracted to a social cooperative called Auxilium.[35] The organization held a three-year renewable-term contract making it responsible for providing food, health services (including psychological counseling), facilities maintenance, linguistic and cultural intervention, and transportation to local hospitals and clinics, and for ensuring the general well-being of the *ospiti*. In exchange, it received approximately $4.6 million per year, which works out to an average expense of $52 a day per *ospite*.[36] In 2011, the estimated management costs for social services provided to all Italian CIEs was roughly $24 million, which means that the Ponte Galeria CIE received roughly 20 percent of the annual budget allocated by the Ministry of the Interior.[37] During my visit, approximately ninety Auxilium employees were on-site for the 123 *ospiti*, an almost one-to-one ratio. I was told that staff members were on duty twenty-four hours a day. The Auxilium employees appeared to have the closest contact with detainees, and those whom I met were a highly empathetic lot. Many of them had worked there for years and had themselves come from multicultural backgrounds.

In spite of their efforts, a 2012 report by the Italian nonprofit Medici per i Diritti Umani (Doctors for Human Rights, or MEDU), which has monitored the conditions at Ponte Galeria since 2005, announced that the CIE was concomitantly "a structure which does not fully respect human dignity," as well as "a new kind of total institution, a place generating violence and exclusion," and also a "facility *genetically* unable to safeguard the dignity and fundamental rights."[38] The report noted that this system of administrative detention not only disregarded human rights but also was ineffective and costly. The center's role in countering "irregular" migration was statistically insignificant. In 2009, for example, those detained in all CIEs across Italy that year accounted for less than 2 percent of the estimated 560,000 "illegal immigrants" residing in Italy.[39] Less than half of those detained were actually deported. Many of those who were released often ended up back at the center two, three, or sometimes even four times, said the inspector in charge, who has worked at Ponte Galeria since it opened in 1998. Riots, strikes, illness, and boredom always loomed large. Days were measured in a monotonous rhythm of showers, meals, haircuts, and meetings with lawyers, guards, medics, judges, social workers, and the occasional journalist or professor. For all, waiting seemed to be the main activity: waiting to be escorted to meetings with doctors and counselors, waiting for the cafeteria to open, waiting to finally be released.

Spaces of Limbo

Ponte Galeria is surprisingly easy to access because vectors of mobility surround it: a highway, a railroad, even an airport. Each day thousands of passengers, en route to either Fiumicino airport or Rome's central train station, pass by the center. Most are totally unaware of its existence. The hypermobility of these travelers is a stark contrast to the coerced immobility of those detained within the center. Their ability to move is authorized by the Italian state vis-à-vis passports and border controls, whereas those in the center suffer the consequences for exercising the "wrong" type of mobility.

FIGURE 8.   Interior view of the women's sector at Ponte Galeria. Photograph by the author, 2013.

Inside, the male and female sectors are almost mirror images of one an-other and flank opposite sides of a central administrative building. Each has a separate cafeteria, bunkhouses, and open concrete yards (figure 8). I made note of subtle differences like the clear plexiglass panels mounted atop the fences in the men's sector to deter escapes and that the men appeared to be more heavily guarded than the women. A two-way mirror allowed *carabinieri* to monitor anyone entering and exiting the men's sector. This was absent for the women. Otherwise, the barred windows and ascetic bunkhouses all looked ex-actly the same. It looked and felt like a prison. Men and women remain seg-regated at Ponte Galeria but were free to move about their respective sectors throughout the day. They were locked into the bunkhouses at night, not un-like the *coatti* on Lampedusa more than a century ago. Even so, one social worker told me that *ospiti* did not circulate much because ethnic groups usu-ally kept to themselves in self-imposed seclusion. Each dormitory block housed four to six women who shared an open shower and Turkish toilet. Makeshift murals decorated the walls. At the entrance of one room, someone had drawn a large gray cat with glowing green eyes. Another mural showed a bird in a colorful basket of flowers.

I found the bunkhouse room to be warm and stuffy. A new electric heater pumped hot air throughout. Newspaper pages, brittle and yellowing with age, were pasted on the windows to keep out the nighttime floodlights. I talked with several Nigerian women who occupied the room. We talked over the white noise of TV soap operas and B movies dubbed into Italian. No one was watching them. Each *ospite* had her own bed, outfitted in the center's ubiquitous green tissue paper–like sheets that had been creatively transformed elsewhere around the center into clotheslines, shoelaces, washcloths, even a hammock. Dressers held hygienic products as well as stockpiles of packaged chips, brioches, and juice boxes purchased from the center's *magazzino* (storehouse) with weekly allowances. The women told me about their transfer from the detention center in Bologna. They complained about the food—prepackaged, microwaveable meals provided by an outside catering company—as well as the beds, toilets, laundry, and life in general. One woman apparently lost her voice from yelling the night before. She claimed to have had a medical emergency while locked in the bunkhouse and tried to signal the guards to no avail. The social worker was skeptical, saying that someone was always on duty, and if that person did not hear the calls, the woman could have also tried banging something on the bars. "What do we have to bang?" asked one of the other *ospite* defiantly, looking around to the chips, brioches, and juice boxes. "We have nothing."

The physical immobility experienced by the *ospiti* in the center was offset by the communicative mobility made possible by cell phones. Many detainees carried mobile phones (but without video or camera functions) that are used to call relatives, friends, and lawyers on the outside. The phones are integral to the delicate navigation of the complex bureaucracy involved in identification and expulsion. They are crucial for strategizing one's release. In a space that seems so far apart from the digitally augmented urbanism that characterizes much of contemporary Europe, the cell phone emerges as a poignant means of emancipation at Ponte Galeria. It is an instrument of communicative mobility that helps one break free from physical immobilization.[40]

It was not immobility but rather boredom that seemed to demoralize everyone I spoke with at Ponte Galeria. Mealtimes and visits to the *magazzino* broke up the day's lassitude. Many lingered at the cafeteria after lunch or made small talk with Auxilium employees at the *magazzino*. Some *ospiti* spoke of being deprived intellectually because they were not allowed to have paper or books (or anything flammable, for that matter), so reading and writing were out of the question. Auxilium did run a makeshift hair salon for the female *ospiti*, which was an important social space for the women here, a space of femininity par excellence. There were two sinks for washing hair, a set of three mirrors and plastic chairs, and a pink dresser. There was also a shower in one corner of the salon, where women could shave their legs under supervision. Razors were attentively distributed and re-collected. Here, women carefully crafted their hair and their bodies to the standards of beauty dictated by the impeccably coiffed blond woman with porcelain skin staring out from a poster overlooking the salon. Her platinum hair had been ironed straight and her violet eyes accentuated with mascara. The women at Ponte Galeria looked nothing like her. They had dark skin, crow's feet, overprocessed hair, and innumerable scars, both visible and unseen. As sex workers, many of them once offered up their beauty—and their bodies—in exchange for pay. Some forewent condoms to pocket extra cash. Their young lives centered on having sex for money. As a result, many of these women had contracted diseases, and Auxilium social workers had to explain not only the bureaucracy of political limbo but also the biological facts of medical diagnoses. At Ponte Galeria, bodies were framed in medical jargon and personhood in legal codes. Both *ospiti* and Auxilium employees constantly brokered between these two registers, which cemented the former into the category of "illegal immigrant."

Legal Grammars

The law is ever present at Ponte Galeria, and its main purpose is to sort out the consequences for all those who move in ways that are not sanctioned by state power. Much of the difficulty in navigating this legal labyrinth stems from the fact that it is not just one law but many interacting with (and counteracting) one another: the laws of the Italian state, the laws of other nation-states, and those of the European Union and the United Nations. The CIE's central mission—to identify and expel—hinges precisely on the indeterminacy of the *ospiti* before the law.[41] Its primary task is to identify a migrant's provenance and, if necessary, to expel that person from Italian territory. Yet, this is much harder to accomplish than it seems. *Ospiti* often give false names and countries of origin, usually on the advice of others, but many of them have little idea of the very tenuousness of their legal status. The immense bureaucratic machinery at work often puzzles their pro bono lawyers. Simply put, *ospiti* are effectively stateless during the long process of identification. They are caught up in a legal limbo in which the Italian state does not want them and no other state intends to claim them. However intractable that this legal quandary might seem, all cases do eventually get resolved, often with Italian state power triumphant.

Some *ospiti* are actually deported. They are put on planes at nearby Fiumi-cino airport and taken back to their purported countries of origin. Others are physically dropped off at a border and forbidden to reenter Italy for a period of five to ten years. Still others are released from the center with a decree of expulsion and a finite amount of time to leave the country by their own means. Very few successfully claim political asylum (less than 1 percent) and are issued the relevant documentation to legally stay in Italy.[42] In such ways, a migrant's stay at Ponte Galeria, much like her ambiguous status before the law, can best be described as one of temporary permanence. The *ospite* is stuck there as long as lawyers, judges, and diplomats negotiate the compli-cated network of legal sovereignties in order to determine her fate.

An *ospite's* journey into the morass of identification and expulsion begins when she arrives at the center. Few detainees have passports or identification cards, and none of them have valid permits of stay, even if some had such permits issued in the past. For instance, G.J., a thirty-two-year-old Nigerian woman, had lived in Italy for ten years. She was here legally for many of those years, working as a janitor in a hospital near Lake Como while saving money to go to design school for fashion. In 2009, her permit of stay was not renewed, and in the fall of 2012, police picked her up while she was visiting a friend in Rome. G.J. had been in Ponte Galeria for six months at the time of my field visit in 2013. Like almost all of her counterparts, G.J. did not want to leave Italy. She told me that she wanted to do all that she could to stay.

Upon arrival at the center, *ospiti* can be legally detained for forty-eight hours while they are processed and registered. During that time, a judge must de-termine two issues: (1) whether the *ospite* is a citizen who falls under the pur-view of EU directives, and (2) whether to issue a *convalida di trattenimento* (approval of detention). Hearings are held on-site. The future of each *ospite* is decided under the fluorescent lights of a cramped room filled with cheap blue chairs, faux wood paneling, overworked interpreters, and fresh-faced lawyers. The latter are allowed to visit their clients every afternoon, although not all necessarily do so. Once the *convalida* is issued—and it almost always is—the *ospite* begins an initial thirty-day period of stay. *Questura* officials work hard to identify the citizenship of each *ospite* within these first thirty days; however, it often takes much longer due to the lack of cooperation from consular officials.

Identification begins with a nationwide record check across prisons and de-tention centers in Italy and continues with consular representatives coming to the CIE to assess whether a person is Tunisian, Moroccan, Nigerian, and so on. Several Auxilium employees told me that it is not uncommon for these officials to postpone or dodge these duties entirely, leaving the CIE staff little recourse but to extend the period of an *ospite's* detention while lobbying consulates for increased cooperation. Some countries lack the adequate databases and records to make positive identifications, whereas some *ospiti* are completely off the grid, having never had records to begin with. Consulates and embassies can be very capricious too. They are sometimes very responsive, and at other times they stonewall the process. One Auxilium social worker told me that many countries do not want these migrants back, especially those who have served prison sentences in Italy. It is also the case that detainees give false countries of origin and a consular official "makes" their aliases, causing the identification process to begin anew.[43]

There is one way out of the CIE that allows for an *ospite* to exercise some semblance of agency: by asking the Italian state to legitimize their mobility by shifting one's political status from *ospite* to refugee. Being named a *rifugiato* or *profugo* (refugee)—that is, having one's mobility rendered "valid" by the state—wrests a migrant out of the center's limbo and not only accords one the rights and recognition of an Italian citizen but also forecloses the possibility of refoulement.[44] Yet such requests for political asylum are usually made as last-ditch efforts to remain in Italy and they almost always fail, said the inspector in charge. In 2011, only twenty-three requests for refugee status and/ or political asylum were approved, or 1 percent of all the *ospiti* detained in the center that year.[45] The process usually begins with lawyers, who, overwhelmed by complicated legalities, decide to apply for asylum at the last minute on behalf of their clients. The bureaucratic process is complex and drawn out, often involving hearings with local representatives of the UN Refugee Agency (UNHCR), just to buy more time for *ospiti* in Italy.

A typical day for the *questura* staff involves intake and registration, judicial hearings, consular visits, repatriations, medical accompaniments, staff meetings, and phone calls to the Ministry of the Interior, among other activities. Movement is constant. It is hard not to become blunted by the process, but the inspector in charge remains empathetic after sixteen years on the job. He is especially sensitive to the plight of migrants who arrived after the Arab Spring in 2011. Every CIE and CARA in Italy was thrown into chaos, he said, trying to accommodate the massive flows of boat migrants arriving from North Africa via Lampedusa. It was no surprise to him that so many of these people, who had fled what they thought to be dangerous revolutions in their home countries, had tried to escape from the CIE in the latter part of 2011. He implied revolt against coerced immobilization was to be expected: it was equal parts a fight and a gasp for a better life.

Medical Circuits

The days at Ponte Galeria are often saturated with medical anxieties. I spoke with one woman who complained of cold feet and blisters from her plastic flip-flops, and another who worried that a bleeding cyst meant ovarian cancer. Still others had turned inward, gazes blank, lying silently prone in bed for hours. Auxilium employed a staff of doctors, nurses, and mental health specialists to provide basic medical care to all the *ospiti* at Ponte Galeria. I saw two rooms in the central administration building dedicated to health care—one was full of patient records and medications, and the other was an office labeled *psicologia sociale* (social psychology). I learned that all detainees were given a basic medical checkup upon intake. Many had been examined before, either in prison or in other detention centers, but medical records are rarely transferred; thus, this initial check-up serves as a baseline. The process of identification and expulsion involves a full body workup. One's fixture into the category of "illegal immigrant" therefore mandates a corporeal assessment by the Italian state. At a minimum, forced medical exams violate modesty. At the other extreme, forced medical exams render the migrant's body an object to be documented, evaluated, and ultimately legislated by the Italian state. This is biopower in its most transparent form.[46]

Owing to their relatively brief stays at the CIE (usually a few weeks or months), most detainees receive only minimal treatment for chronic pathologies like hypertension, diabetes, and heart disease. The medical staff often become frustrated that medications are taken only in fits and starts, and chronic conditions are likely to be left untreated when *ospiti* are released. Auxilium employees also told me that it is not uncommon for detainees to fake their medical conditions. Similar to giving a false name and country of origin, they said some *ospiti* adopt a manipulative attitude to gain special treatment in order to get their "fix" of a particular drug or in the hopes of a temporary escape to a specialist or hospital on the outside. Such feigned medical conditions have long been commonplace in camps and prisons. The administrators in charge of the penal colonies on Lampedusa, Ustica, and Ponza frequently complained of *coatti* who faked illnesses. The remarks made by Auxilium staff in 2013 echoed those made by Giuseppe Damiani, the penal colony director of Lampedusa in 1905:[47]

Ve ne sono altri capaci di simulare e simulano tanto bene da trarre in inganno il medico. Ciò fanno per raggiungere il fine poco recondito di ottenere un trattamento migliore o qualche provvedimento di favore . . . Molti altri coatti simularono la pazzia, al fine di ottenere la libertà condizionale, sapendo che il governo di fronte a casi vari di malattie mentali suole concedere il proscioglimento, e quando è ingenerato il sospetto, tale provvedimento non venne, rinsavirono!

There are other [coatti] capable of simulation and they simulate [illness] so well as to trick the doctor. They do this to achieve the not-so-hidden goal of obtaining better treatment or some measure of favor. . . . Many other coatti simulated insanity in order to obtain parole, knowing that the government, faced with various cases of mental illness, was in the habit of granting acquittal, and when [the faking of mental illness] engendered suspicion, such that the acquittal did not happen, they [coatti] came to their senses!

Mental health is precarious in Ponte Galeria. On average, 50 percent of the ospiti are on antianxiety medications at any given time.[48] According to one of the staff psychologists, who has worked at the center for more than nine years, depression is the most common issue among detainees. To mitigate depression and anxiety, he said that it was important to involve the detainees in activities, which was an ironic proposition since I learned from other Auxilium staff members that almost all activities had been reduced or eliminated altogether. The staff psychologist also said that ospiti had access to talk therapy; however, he noted that few of them had any idea what that might entail. Instead, drugs were the easier therapeutic path—as they are in many countries, not just at Ponte Galeria—with a form of Valium (Rivotril) the antianxiety drug most frequently prescribed. In such a way, the detainee's body at Ponte Galeria is not only surveilled with medical examinations but also disciplined (and controlled) with pharmaceutics, giving rise to a form of iatrogenic violence linked explicitly to the business of "illegal immigration." Unsurprisingly, the medical circuits of examination and prescription at Ponte Galeria yoke people into the category of "illegal immigrant" by coercing the body into docility.[49] Thus medical grammars work in concert with legal categories to construct the "illegal immigrant" judicially and biologically—again, Foucauldian biopower at its finest—and to fix the detainee into a position that is always subjugated to state power.

Some migrants, particularly men who come directly from prison, arrive at Ponte Galeria already addicted to psychotropic drugs like Rivotril as well as street substances like heroin or crystal meth. Many have served prison terms for dealing drugs. While the CIE attempts to treat drug-addicted patients, it "does not have appropriate specialized competencies to manage a high number of patients in such a complex and problematic context."[50] The staff psychologist noted that a number of ospiti had antisocial tendencies and that it was a constant challenge not to aggravate them. He added that on rare occasions, detainees with grave psychological disturbances arrived at the center and that the staff worked quickly to identify them and send them on to different institutions. The staff psychologist also said that incidents of self-harm and attempted suicides have waned since 2010. Of the former, self-inflicted razor blade wounds are the most typical. Sometimes these are staged, with *ospiti* using the silver lining of cigarette packages to feign the ingestion of blades.[51] Of attempted suicides, both the psychologist and an Auxilium social worker remembered only one successful suicide in their nine years at the center. According to the MEDU report, this was the case of Nabruka Mimouni, a Tunisian woman who had lived in Italy for twenty years. She hung herself in the center on the night of May 6, 2009, the day before she was to be repatriated to Tunisia.[52]

Almost three years later, a thirty-year-old Egyptian man named Abdou Said committed suicide just days after being released from Ponte Galeria. He had been detained there for almost eight months, having arrived on Lampedusa in July 2011 and then sent onward to Rome. Said's harrowing slide toward suicide began in September of that same year, when he attempted to escape from the CIE with a group of detainees. It was one of at least four attempts at mass escape throughout the month, mostly by men who had arrived at the height of the *flussi* (flows) during the Arab Spring. Abdou Said attempted to escape with the others but was almost immediately recaptured by police. According to Angiolo Marroni, the ombudsman for prisoners' rights in Lazio, Said appeared to have been beaten and returned to the center.[53] Various accounts suggested that Said was so traumatized after this episode that he progressively lost self-control and had to be treated with psychotropic drugs for several months. His lawyer, Serena Lauri, noted a distinct change in Abdou Said's personality after the escape, which she attributed to a head injury he suffered during the breakout. According to her, when Said first entered Ponte Galeria he was almost arrogant, but after the escape "aveva lo sguardo fisso e l'espressione da persona indifesa" (he had the fixed gaze and the expression of a helpless person).[54] At the end of February 2012, Abdou Said was released from Ponte Galeria with a decree of expulsion. He had seven days to leave the country. Said went to stay with a friend in Rome, but apparently became increasingly despondent as the deadline to leave Italy approached. On March 9, 2012, he wounded himself with a razor blade and then jumped out a window to his death.

News of Said's suicide quickly reached his companions at Ponte Galeria, including his brother, who was still inside. Some 120 *ospiti*, mostly from the

Maghreb, went on a hunger strike to denounce the circumstances of Said's death. Those interminably sad circumstances were plainly linked to Italy's hardline immigration policies, which mandated Said's forced detention in the CIE. Without a state, a home, his brother, a pill to numb the pain, or even the hope of staying in Italy, Abdou Said ended his life. As to exactly why, there are no definitive answers but only speculations: delirium brought on by a traumatic brain injury, a drug-induced mood disorder, withdrawal from medication, the shame of deportation and return, the overwhelming grip of depression and anxiety. Whatever his reasons for suicide, it is a fact that Abdou Said was banned and expulsed toward the end of his life. These were the hard blows of juridical violence.

In theoretical terms, Said embodied what Agamben has called *nuda vita* (bare life). Bare life is produced through abandonment (the "ban" is central to this idea), and specifically, one's abandonment by divine and profane law.[55] Abdou Said was literally banned by the law and expulsed from the sphere of sovereignty. He was caught in limbo and seemingly had nowhere to go.[56] He lived at the inside of outside in Ponte Galeria. He was banned by the law but continued to live within its purview. He tried to escape but failed. The migrant detention center proved to be the gray zone where Abdou Said submitted to the operations of inclusive exclusion (that is, identification and expulsion) that Agamben defined as the very logic of sovereignty itself.[57] This logic of exception, as many scholars in addition to Agamben have noted, is spatialized in the form of the camp. It is the site where *homo sacer* and sovereign power continue to meet. For Abdou Said, Ponte Galeria was this camp.

Auschwitz, of course, was the ne plus ultra of the camp. It was "the most absolute biopolitical space ever to have been realized, in which power confronts nothing but pure life, without any mediation."[58] It was a biopolitical machine that produced only death. It was the form that spatialized a state of exception. It inaugurated, per Agamben, a new biopolitical *nomos* of the earth. The Greek word *nomos* is often translated as "law"; however, Agamben, following the work of Carl Schmitt, invests it with a distinctly spatial quality. Schmitt asserted that the *nomos* was a fundamental process of apportioning space. He argued that the *nomos* was originally a "fence-word" used to signify divisions, boundaries, limits, and enclosures in the spatial sense. It bracketed space, and in this process, sublimated bracketing into exception.[59] Per Schmitt, the *nomos* as law was thus inextricable from both space and exception. In his words, "The idea of designating a sphere outside the law and open to the use of force has a long history."[60]

But what of the camps that preceded Auschwitz, especially those that were built during the years immediately before its opening and that also bore the designation of "concentration camp"? An overwhelming number of these forerunners emerged in the context of American and European colonial imperialism during the early twentieth century. Examples included the *campos de concentración* built by the Spanish during the Cuban War of Independence in the late 1890s; the *reconcentrados* operated by the U.S. military in the Philippines (1901–2); the British-built system of camps in South Africa established in the Boer War (1900–1902); and the German-run extermination camp at Shark Island, Namibia, integral to the Herero genocide, the first of the twentieth century (1904–7).[61]

One of the most frequently voiced criticisms of Agamben's philosophy is its seeming "disregard for the specific histories and concrete social circumstances of present states of exception, of relations of abandonment in colonial frameworks, and of colonial and imperial relations."[62] He remains curiously silent on colonial camps. David Atkinson made the case that Agamben's silence was linked to the broader phenomenon of colonial amnesia present in Italy.[63] To Atkinson, Agamben was a product of his Italian academic environment, not only in its lack of debate about Italian colonialism but also in its failure to acknowledge and condemn colonialism's most brutal atrocities. If not ignored completely, the colonial experience in the Italian cultural imagination was characterized by misinformation, and at its most pernicious, the myth of Italian colonizers as *brava gente* (good people). It was treated as something of a "lesser" colonialism when in fact, according to Nicola Labanca, it was unusually brutal even by the standards of European colonialism.[64] Given this context, Atkinson writes, "in particular, it is surprising that [Agamben's] focus on camps, and Auschwitz as the archetypal space of exception, did not prompt some thinking on colonial ambitions, violence, and terror. For the Holocaust and Nazi expansionism can be seen as a systematic and particularly devastating form of colonialism. . . . The camps were not the aberrations it is easier to imagine, but were part of a wider imperial-colonial project."[65] In twenty-first-century Italy, migrant detention centers like Ponte Galeria are the heirs to these earlier camps in that they spatialize the state of exception in brick and mortar. The *via negativa* that delimits them as camps depends, too, as much on the legitimization of mobility as it does on medical circuits and legal grammars. It is precisely to this task of exploring the ways in which mobility shaped the camps in Italian colonial Libya and the amnesia that surrounds them that we now turn our attention.

On Camps and Nomads

All colonial enterprises rely on and generate far-reaching mobilizations of people, goods, weapons, and ideas, and Italy's occupation of Libya between 1911 and 1943 was no exception. There was constant movement between the peninsula and its *quarta sponda* (fourth shore) as well as back and forth between Italy's other colonies in the Dodecanese and eastern Africa. Large numbers of Italians also lived in the neighboring countries of Tunisia and Egypt and traveled frequently throughout the region.[66] However, the freedom of movement in Italian colonial Libya for certain populations, like troops and settlers, came at the expense of many others, like Bedouin. It actually depended on the vast immobilization of people who were believed to threaten the Italian colonial regime with their mobility. This threat was even given a name: *il grande nomadismo* (the great nomadism).

Symbolically, the "nomad" became the quintessential figure whose movements were considered dangerous in Italian colonial Libya, and for whom concentration camps were built to contain. Ruth Ben-Ghiat explains: "As a metaphor for mobility, the nomad conjured all that Fascism feared: uncontrolled movement, ephemerality, and the absence of national or territorial loyalties."[67] Yet all colonial regimes were predicated on the hierarchical application of power, which nomads jeopardized because they "require and produce nonunitary, multiple, and complex politics."[68] According to Rosi Braidotti, whose work on nomadic critical theory has opened up radical directions for rethinking mobility and subjectivity, one of the key ethical challenges for scholarship today is to offer an "accounting both spatially and temporally or historically for dramatically different forms of mobility."[69] For Braidotti, the nomad exists as an affirmative and nonunitary subject—she holds the ability to realize a mode of political belonging that is nonhierarchical and uncoupled from state power. Other scholars are less optimistic and have pointed out that the nomad is the actual subject of the *nomos* and carries within its meaning the apportionment and exclusion from space.[70] For Anne Dufourmantelle, exception was the original condition of politics and the nomad its first subject.[71] Thus, the nomad's subjective power might be seen as being on par with that of the sovereign or the *homo sacer*. Yet Gilles Deleuze and Félix Guattari, themselves well-known theorists of the nomad, concede that this power was curtailed in that "the defeat of the nomads was such, so complete, that history is one with the triumph of States. We have witnessed, as a result, a generalized critique dismissing nomads as incapable of any innovation, whether technological or metallurgical, political or metaphysical."[72] The sedentary—and the state—came to rule. And for all of the nomadic subject's possibilities of endless becoming, horizontal belonging, and harmonic difference, the nomad in theory was not necessarily the same as the nomad who actually existed in history. David Atkinson put it succinctly: "When modern theory reproduces the casual metaphor of the desert nomad as an example of a de-territorialized subject, it too runs the risk of eliding some of the very brutal histories of sedentarization that have marked North Africa."[73]

The actually existing nomads in Italian colonial Libya—the Bedouin—were forcibly denied the ability to move by the state. They were sequestered in concentration camps and the diversity of tribal and cultural differences between them effaced. All were labeled "nomads." This forced immobilization could also be described as part of an effort by the Italian colonial regime to unitize the nomad-as-subject. It was state power pushing back against the existence of what Braidotti shows to be a multilayered subject. The state opposes unruly, complex subjects who refuse neat situation within its authorized matrices of identity and citizenship. Braidotti writes, "In another paradoxical twist, the de-territorializations induced by the hypermobility of capitalism and the forms of migration and human mobility they entail, instead of challenging the hegemony of nation-states, strengthen their hold not only over territory and social space but also over identity and cultural memory."[74] In other words, the state fiercely resists (and strikes back against) nomadic subjects as conceived by Braidotti, Deleuze and Guattari, Holland, and others. What was interesting about the Italian state and its colonial regime in Libya was that the containment of the nomad-as-subject occurred through the very enunciation of nomadism itself. The Fascist regime in particular advanced the idea of a nomadic subject that was always-already unitized—a monolithic nomad that could be labeled as Bedouin or rebel or enemy, or by any other exclusionary name. The nomad was therefore rendered static and could be ranked vertically and contained spatially within lines created by the Italian state. Contrary to Braidotti's nomadic subject, this name-and-rank nomad was refused the affirmative potentials at the heart of nomadic critical theory.[75] Instead, the state-interpellated nomad was contained, or better yet, immobilized in space. In Italian colonial Libya, concentration camps were the result. In contemporary Italy, the consequences are migrant detention centers like Ponte Galeria. Put simply, to name and contain the nomad is to defuse the threat that unauthorized mobilities pose to the Italian state.

Il grande nomadismo

The most striking historical example of the Italian state's naming and containing of nomadism in the twentieth century was that of the Bedouin in Italian colonial Libya. Just a few years after Italian troops landed in Tripoli in 1911, colonial administrators identified nomadic tribes as threats to the politics of collaboration attempted at that time.[76] The archival record shows that subsequent military action in Libya was designed to suppress the nomadism of indigenous tribes, no matter if it was real or imagined. A 1916 government report on Tripolitania noted that nomads dominated the region's social order: "I nomadi predomino e l'organizzazione della loro società è rimasta intatta." (The nomads predominate and the organization of their society has remained intact.) That same report claimed that "uncolonizable" territories were the ones largely inhabited by nomads who were allegedly prone to violence.[77] Soon, the assumption of nomadic belligerence came to structure policymaking throughout colonial Libya.

Italian administrators adopted a number of strategies, ranging from bribery to brute force, to bring the "nomads" under their control. The violence was so harsh that many troops deserted, particularly the Libyan soldiers who had either enlisted or been conscripted into the Italian Army. Some joined the rebels, while others who did not want to fight against their compatriots simply left. So many Libyan battalions deserted that the governor of Cyrenaica and Tripolitania, Giovanni Ameglio, sent five thousand Libyan soldiers to Sicily in August 1915.[78] He worried that these soldiers would desert and their weapons would fall into rebel hands. They stayed in Sicily for almost a year in what Angelo Del Boca described as "campi di concentramento" (concentration camps) near the towns of Floridia and Canicattini Bagni. Because Italy had entered World War I earlier that year, the idea was for this Libyan legion to join the fight at the Austrian front; however, this plan never came to pass. The soldiers were transferred back to Libya in June 1916, but this time to Cyrenaica to offer relief to the Eritrean *askari* fighting there (*askari* was the term for indigenous troops serving in the Italian Army).[79] Apparently this forced internment on Sicily did little to stem the desertion by Libyan troops, because one year later an upset Ameglio was still writing to the Ministry of the Colonies about the desertion of indigenous soldiers and the loss of weapons that went with them.[80]

The tides of violence toward nomads shifted toward genocide in the mid-1920s, specifically with the appointment of Pietro Badoglio as marshal of Italy in 1926 and Rodolfo Graziani as vice governor of Cyrenaica that same year. A classified memo penned by Badoglio in 1925, then military chief to Mussolini, explained that the threat of nomadism could be traced back to ancient Rome. He drew parallels between the ways in which nomads once threatened to destabilize Rome's hold on Libya and the present situation in the colony. Chillingly, Badoglio argued that the only way to successfully colonize

Libya involved the total domination of nomads.[81] Not only were nomads a dilemma for the Romans, wrote Emilio De Bono, the governor of Tripolitania in 1927, but they had long troubled the Ottoman Empire. He named the problem *il grande nomadismo* (the great nomadism).[82] For De Bono, nomadism was a dangerous condition supported by historical experience.[83] Other government officials agreed, and some went so far as to single out particular tribes, such as the Magharba of the Sirtica desert, as particularly threatening. One 1927 memo by De Bono called for the "completa liquidazione del problema Mogarba" (complete liquidation of the Magharba problem), that is, the extermination of the Magharba tribe.[84] Without mincing words, De Bono called for a holocaust, pure and simple. Unfortunately, he would have the chance to put these words into action when he was named minister of the colonies in 1929 and sanctioned the construction of concentration camps in eastern Libya.[85]

Rodolfo Graziani was tasked with implementing De Bono's vision of genocide on the ground. He was the man who would "pacify" Cyrenaica and resolve its so-called nomad problem. Graziani's views of nomadism and nomads in general were famously documented in his 1932 tome, *Cirenaica Pacificata* (Cyrenaica pacified), written about his military tenure in Libya. According to him, the nomad was "anarchico, amante della più assoluta libertà ed indipendenza, intollerante di ogni freno, testardo, ignorante, eroe invincibile e bluffista" (anarchist, lover of absolute freedom and independence, intolerant of any obstruction, hard-headed, ignorant, [an] invincible and beguiling hero).[86] He described their long-standing refusal of government authority: "Refrattari ad ogni vincolo di disciplina, abituati a spaziare in territori spesso immensi e desertici, forti della loro mobilità e facilità di spostamento, pervasi dal fascino della indipendenza, sempre pronti alla guerra ed alla razzia, i nomadi hanno sempre reagito ad ogni freno di governo." (Wayward from every constraint of discipline, accustomed to moving freely in often immense and desert territories, powerful in their mobility and facility of movement, permeated by the allure of independence, always ready for war and for plunder, the nomads have always reacted to every government constraint.)[87] For Graziani, nomads were enemies of the state. The anthropologist E. E. Evans-Pritchard confirmed this sentiment in his classic 1949 ethnography about the Sanusi of Cyrenaica: "The Italians detested the Bedouin. . . . In the whole Italian literature on Cyrenaica I have not read a sentence of understanding of Romany values. Because they lived in tents without most of the goods the peasant, and even more the townsmen, regard as signs of civilization the Italians spoke of them as barbarians, little better than beasts, and treated them accordingly."[88]

What the Italian colonial regime did not anticipate was the sheer staying power of the Sanusi-led resistance in Cyrenaica. The Sanusi fraternity, established as an Islamic Order in 1843 by al-Sayyid Muhammad bin 'Ali as-Senussi, quickly gained favor in the region with its message of austerity in both faith and morals so as to reinstate the purity of early Islam. The Bedouin were particularly receptive to Sanusi asceticism because it not only complemented their already spartan lifestyle but also stood in opposition to the mysticism and ecstatic practices of Sufism that were growing in influence at the time.[89] From their base in Cyrenaica, the Sanusi extended their influence across the Sahara, the Sudan, and the Egyptian coastline over the next eighty years. Crucial to this expansion was the construction of lodges called *zawiyas* in populated areas, key oases, and transit points across the Sahara. The lodges served as important centers of education and religious training as well as administration, banking, commerce, and charity. They would later serve as an indispensable network of refuge and resupply for rebels fighting against occupation. At the moment of Italian invasion in 1911, the Sanusi Order had such a hold on Cyrenaica that it "constituted a semblance of coordinated governance and political authority in the Saharan interior—at least, as viewed in European terms."[90] To borrow Evans-Pritchard's words, theirs was a "loose Theocratic empire."[91]

The Sanusi had much to lose politically and economically with the Italian occupation and, in fact, had already suffered grave losses at the hands of European colonizers. In the early 1900s, French troops had destroyed *zawiyas* throughout the eastern Sahel (for example, Chad, Darfur, Libya, Sudan) in their bid for the Sudan and terrorized resistance fighters in Sanusi strongholds such as the desert oasis of Kufra.[92] According to Ali Ahmida, these losses inspired the Sanusi Order to anticipate and combat any future European intrusions into their space.[93] Italian colonial administrators assumed there would be resistance despite the era of negotiated collaboration after World War I. The Sanusi broadly took up the leadership of the rebellion in Cyrenaica, a cause to which many Bedouin rallied to support. Hostilities were brought to a brief détente in 1917 with the Acroma Treaty, which the Italians violated in 1923 after the Fascist regime rose to power and quickly returned to violence.

For the nine years thereafter, the Sanusi and the Bedouin waged a guerrilla war against the Italians centered on the Jabal Akhdar (Green Mountain) plateau east of Benghazi. The numbers were against them: only two thousand untrained and poorly armed men to the more than twenty thousand Italian troops.[94] Their preferred strategy of resistance: mobility. The Sanusi and the Bedouin gathered into small bands that aimed to "strike suddenly, strike hard, get out quick," and according to Evans-Pritchard, "the smallness of the Sanusi

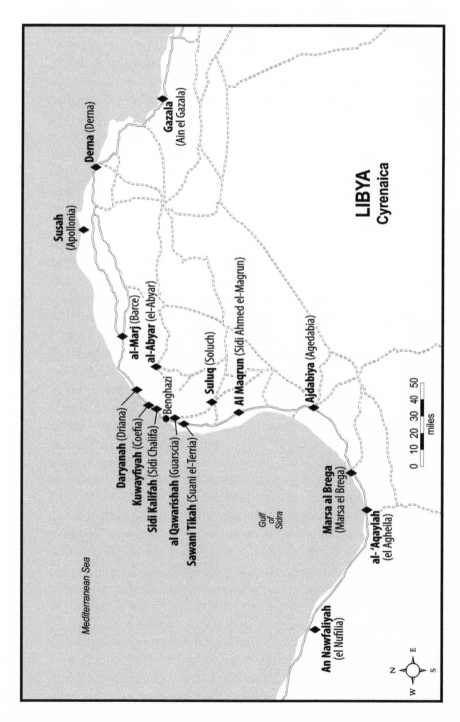

MAP 2. The Italian colonial regime built and operated sixteen concentration camps in eastern Libya from 1929 to 1933.

units and their mobility confused the slow and unwieldy Italian columns. . . . The Italians found that the blows they aimed at the enemy often struck the air."[95] Raids would often come at night, and the guerrilla bands would steal horses and destroy Italian supplies. The resistance also found its figurehead in 'Umar al-Mukhtar, a fifty-three-year-old teacher who took up arms in 1911 and led the fight against occupation for twenty years. The final years of his life were spent living on the edges of illness, starvation, and battle in the Jabal Akhdar, leading what came to be known as the *bande mobili* (mobile bands) against Italian troops. In 1931, he was captured and hanged by the Italians at age seventy-three.[96]

To counter the "dangerous" mobility of the Sanusi and the Bedouin, Italian colonial officials, led by Graziani, invoked its converse: immobilization. They forcibly marched and resettled most of Cyrenaica's Bedouin population into concentration camps between 1929 and 1933. They shut down *zawiyas* and confiscated Sanusi estates and properties. They cut off supplies and reinforcements to the *bande mobili*. They cemented up or guarded the few wells in the region. They closed the frontier and ordered the construction of a 168-mile-long barbed-wire fence along the Libya-Egypt border in 1931 to stave flows of rebel contraband.[97] Sedentarization and the stoppage of movements of people, goods, weapons, and ideas proved the orders of the day.

The System of Libyan Camps

Several hundred miles east of Tripoli on the bone-dry plains south of Benghazi, the Italian colonial administration ordered the construction of sixteen concentration camps between 1929 and 1933 (map 2). Historians estimate some one hundred thousand people, or two-thirds of Cyrenaica's mostly Bedouin population, were imprisoned here, and in the span of just four years, untold numbers of them died.[98] At least forty thousand people died in the camps proper, with the Libyan historian Yusuf Salim al-Barghathi placing the death toll even higher, between fifty thousand and seventy thousand.[99] At Soluq, the largest of the camps, some five thousand people alone died in its first year of operation.[100] Many died from disease and starvation. Others died on the forced marches across the desert, pushed against their will into the sedentary life of the camp. Still others were executed by Italian troops, usually shot or hanged, both in and outside the camps. The archival record reveals executions to be business as usual, just sterile procedures to be carried out "ad uso locale" (by local means). Altogether it was a protracted genocide that, again, remains little known outside Libya today.

The sixteen camps built within Cyrenaica were as follows: Soluq, al-Abyar, Marsa al-Brega, Sidi Ahmed el-Magrun, Ain Gazala, Driana, Sidi Chalifa, Suani al-Terria, Ajdabiya, Apollonia, Derna, Barce, al-Nufilia, Coefia, Guarscia, and el-Agheila.[101] Almost all were located within a 125-mile radius of the region's capital, Benghazi. The biggest camps—Soluq, al-Abyar, Marsa al-Brega, Sidi Ahmed el-Magrun, Ajdabiya—each contained more than ten thousand prisoners, with Soluq, the largest, at roughly twenty thousand prisoners. Each camp was built and operated at the extraordinary cost of millions of dollars each year.[102] According to Gustavo Ottolenghi, once detainees entered these camps, only half of them made it out alive. He estimated that 40 percent of all those detained at Sidi Ahmed el-Magrun perished there, as did 48 percent of the prisoners at Marsa el-Brega.[103] And while these concentration camps were not death factories in the way that Auschwitz was, life in the camps was indeed deathly living.

In a rare series of photographs housed in the Archivio Centrale dello Stato (Central State Archives) in Rome, a group of tattered men, women, and children wait for food in the chalky sands of Marsa el-Brega. The sky is cloudless and the sun high enough to erase all shadows. Several people hold their hands to their faces, either shielding themselves from the sun or gripping their heads in despair, or both.[104] Another photo reveals a claustrophobic panorama of tightly packed tents, low slung and battered, stretching far into the horizon. Still another shows a small group of men in new burnooses, faces weathered and weary, unwillingly posed for a photograph. Some are huddled so tightly they leave nothing but eyes exposed as if to turn fully inward away from the horrors of the camp.[105]

Unlike Auschwitz, where genocide took form in brick and mortar, the Libyan camps were meant to be temporary spaces. They were meant to exist for only two years at most, but instead stood for almost five.[106] A certain transparency permeated the camps' barbed-wire perimeters and woolen tents, lending a sense of easy violation to everything. Prisoners were not kept behind concrete walls but instead could stare freely unto the desert just beyond their reach. The camps expressed the Italian state's absolute control over a subjugated populace in space, but they did so with temporary, quasi-porous structures (tents and barbed wire) rather than the architectural forms of dominance typically associated with Italian colonial rule in Libya. Absent were both the monumental buildings and Italianization of autochthonous forms, which were common spatial demonstrations of Italian state power in the colonies.[107]

The temporary permanence of the camps reinforced the state's authority in different and arguably more enduring ways. It was not unlike the paradoxical foundation of contemporary refugee camps described by Michel Agier:

"Each new arrival discovers here the problem of an indefinable temporality (an endless emergency), and an exceptional situation that has become regularized and everyday."[108] The illusion of transience unmoored the Libyan camps from time and space. Here prisoners and guards lived in a tenuous caesura, unsure of quotidian survival and much less of their personal futures. The camps did not just embody the paradox of temporary permanence; they operated within a spatial and temporal parenthesis. Positioned between paradox and parenthesis, a space was opened—the concentration camp born of empire—where Italian state power was applied unevenly, and physical and psychic horrors went on unchecked.

Yet the Libyan camps were not without colonial precedent. The carceral island of Nokra, profiled in essay one, was established in 1887 off the coast of Eritrea. It was the first of these spaces, and it was linked to Italy's entwined national and colonial projects. Nokra housed fifteen hundred detainees at its maximum, many of them tribal leaders who resisted Italian occupation in eastern Africa. It operated continuously from 1887 to 1941.[109] Historians describe the conditions at Nokra as inhumane—prisoners suffered not only the oppressive heat of this barren and shadeless islet but also the hard labor and sadistic punishments meted out, often capriciously, by the guards.[110] The cruelty of daily life on Nokra, however, was by no means exceptional. In Italian colonial Libya, if anything, it was amplified across the sixteen concentration camps over several years. Much like the diversity of people contained within them, each Libyan camp was distinctive. El-Agheila was known for its violence. Ajdabiya was symbolic for its location next to a stronghold of Sanusi resistance. Soluq was the largest, complete with schools, gardens, and livestock. Every camp housed different tribes—for example, the Magharba and Ghefar tribes were detained at Ajdabiya, whereas the Zueia, Mariam, Abeidat, and Marabtin tribes were imprisoned at Marsa el-Brega.

The Libyan camps were divided into three classifications: (1) *campo di concentramento* (concentration camp), (2) *campo di rieducazione* (reeducation camp), and (3) *campo di punizione* (punishment camp). These categories recall Hannah Arendt's division of camps into Hades, Purgatory, and Hell, which "have one thing in common: the human masses sealed off in them are treated as if they no longer existed, as if what happened to them were no longer of any interest to anybody, as if they were already dead and some evil spirit gone mad were amusing himself by stopping them for a while between life and death before admitting them to eternal peace."[111] All Libyan camps were broadly referred to as *campi di detenzione* (detention camps). The first was the most common denomination, with the majority of the camps in Cyrenaica known as "concentration camps."

FIGURE 9.   Interior view of an unspecified Italian-built concentration camp in Cyrenaica, 1931.
Photograph from the author's collection.

In archival memos and telegraphs, colonial officials referred to the *concentramento* (concentration) of indigenous people as a necessary step in the surveillance of the territory, and by this logic, its control and "pacification."[112] On
the other hand, Evans-Pritchard painted a heartrending picture of anguish in
the camps: "In this bleak country were herded in the smallest camps possible
80,000 men, women, and children, and 600,000 beasts, in the summer of 1930.
Hunger, disease, and broken hearts took a heavy toll of the imprisoned population. Bedouin die in a cage."[113] According to Ali Ahmida, a scholar whose
research has helped bear witness to the Libyan camps, daily existence was continual misery (figure 9).[114] Prisoners took care of the ill and the dead, loaded
and unloaded goods, and provided forced labor in gardens and public works
projects, among other things. Starvation was ever present too, as almost all of
the tribes' livestock had perished either en route or in the camps themselves.[115]
One prisoner, Ali Muhammed Sa'ad al-'Ibidi, counted 150 hunger-related
deaths of children and elderly in one brief period. Another, Muhammad Muf-
tah 'Uthman, estimated the tribe of 'Abdalla lost more than five hundred people
to starvation alone.[116] With such starvation, humiliation, desperation, and
heartbreak, the Bedouin did not just die in a cage but lived each day in an absolute *conditio inhumana*.

The four "reeducation" camps were annexed to the larger concentration
camps at Soluq, Sidi Ahmed el-Magrun, Ajdabiya, and Marsa el-Brega. The aim
of these camps was to educate indigenous youth ages six to fourteen in the

FIGURE 10.   Aerial view of an unnamed concentration camp and the assembly gathered for an execution by hanging, circa 1931. Photograph reproduced by permission from Archivio Centrale dello Stato, Graziani Photo Archive, Rome.

ways of the Fascist regime. These children enjoyed better living conditions than most and were outfitted in new uniforms, given solid meals, and kept busy with Italian classes, physical exercise, and assemblies and marches.[117] One photograph published in the magazine *L'Italia Coloniale* shows the young prisoners at Sidi Ahmed el-Magrun spelling out "W L'Italia" (Long live Italy) with their tiny bodies.[118] At a military school in Marsa el-Brega, six hundred young boys trained to become part of the Libyan army regiments that would later invade Ethiopia in 1935.

Last, there were punishment camps, the worst of the lot. There was only one in Libya, el-Agheila, but both Nokra (Eritrea) and Dhanaane (Somalia) were officially designated as such. El-Agheila was the largest by far, with more than thirty thousand detainees passing through its gates between 1930 and 1932. Only half of them survived.[119] It was a punishment camp reserved for rebels and so-called enemies of the state (figure 10). The first thing new prisoners would have seen upon arrival was the public execution stage located at the center of the camp. These gallows were used for collective hangings. The stone wall nearby was used for executions by firing squad. According to Gustavo

Ottolenghi, there were eight tents for torture and interrogation located behind the stage, and four pits at each corner of the camp where prisoners would be lowered into isolation.[120] As if that were not enough, the prison guards designated a brothel tent where they would assault and rape young women seized against their will.

Each camp was not without its own distinct social life and systems of power. Makeshift shops were opened and gardens were planted, their proprietors either self-appointed or chosen by colonial officials from among the prisoners. Male detainees either "volunteered" or were forced into hard labor building roads and other infrastructure. Giorgio Rochat noted that at the Sidi Ahmed el-Magrun camp, for instance, "the local government office [tried] to get shopkeepers to take the initiative in constructing buildings for their own shops, so that a number of such places [would have] taken on the guise of a small center."[121] The camp at Soluq had twenty hectares of gardens, along with a hospital, school, and post office. A veterinary surgeon was on staff as were two doctors for more than thirty thousand people. From the empty desert on which the Libyan camps were built, there emerged what Michel Agier has called "camp-towns."[122] Camps created opportunities for encounter, where organic life could take root and invent new forms of sociality and power (which traditionally have the town as their locus, hence "camp-town"). Yet this was not to say that the Libyan camps were at all progressive or emancipatory. On the contrary, to borrow the words of Giorgio Rochat:[123]

> The picture that emerges from [Graziani's] report is truly depressing: tens of thousands of people huddled up against one another (as is evident from the photographs that Graziani published in his book), practically without the means of subsistence, compelled to await a meager salary for desultory road works, with a few shops as the only meeting place, an almost non-existent health service, and that at the very time when the traditional semi-nomad way of life and diet rich in meat and milk gave way forcibly to life at sea-level in overcrowded camps, with a different diet (inevitably so, once livestock had disappeared) which was not only quite inadequate but which also produced an explosion of the region's traditional diseases.

All of these Libyan camps—concentration camps, reeducation camps, and punishment camps—were ostensibly the brainchild of Pietro Badoglio, who had become governor of Libya in 1929 and had created the camps with the knowledge that they would decimate the local population. In correspondence to Graziani, Badoglio wrote sinisterly: "Bisogna anzitutto creare un distacco territoriale largo e ben preciso tra formazioni ribelli e popolazione sottomessa. Non mi nascondo la portata e la gravità di questo provvedimento, che vorrà dire la rovina della popolazione sottomessa." (We must first create a broad and well-defined territorial separation between rebel forces and subdued population. I do not deny the extent and severity of this measure, which will mean the ruin of the subjugated population.)[124] Other Italian colonizers, such as General Emilio Canevari, believed these camps to be beneficent institutions. Many like him completely disavowed the miserable existence of the people in the camps so as to reinforce the myth of Italians as *brava gente*. In his memoir of the war, Canevari wrote: "Noi non abbiamo creato 'campi di concentramento' in Cirenaica, ma solo delle 'riserve' in campi splendidamente sistemate e forniti di tutto il necessario, dalle tende di lana di camello nuove agli impianti igienici, ai servizi idrici, ecc." (We did not create "concentration camps" in Cyrenaica, but only some "reserves" in camps splendidly arranged and equipped with all the necessities, from tents of new camel wool, to hygienic installations, to water services, et cetera.)[125] Likewise, colonial propaganda painted an idyllic picture of the camps. For example, an April 1931 news report in the colonial magazine *L'Oltremare* declared the camp at Soluq to be a type of locus amoenus that boasted "l'ordine e una disciplina perfetta" (order and perfect discipline) where "regna ovunque l'igiene e la pulizia" (hygiene and cleanliness reign everywhere). His Excellency Amedeo Duca delle Puglie also visited the camps in 1931 and remarked to Graziani how lucky the detainees were for "questa nuova loro vita di onesto lavoro, di tranquilità e di pace" (this new life of honest work, tranquility, and peace) in the camps.[126]

Of course, these remarks entirely contradicted the experiences of the Bedouin actually imprisoned there. Their experiences of the camps refuted the propagandistic ideas of the camps as "splendidly outfitted reserves" and paradises of "order and perfect discipline." A remarkable series of oral histories compiled by the Libyan Studies Center in Tripoli has laid bare the brutal conditions of life in the Italian camps. One particularly moving account was that of the poet Rajab Hamad Buwaish al-Minifi, who survived the camp at el-Agheila:[127]

I have no illness except this endless aging,
Loss of sense and dignity,
And the loss of good people, who were my treasure. . . .

I have no illness except the loss of young men,
Masters of tribes,
Picked out like date fruit in daylight,

Who stood firm-chested against scoundrels,
The blossoms of our households,
Whose honor will shine despite what the ill-tongued say? . . .

I have no illness except . . .
Being imprisoned by scoundrels,
And the lack of a cohort to complain to when wronged,

The lack of those who rule with fairness,
Evenness nonexistent,
Evil leaning hard on good, dominant.

The Roman Castrum

The Libyan camps were spaces that emerged from a state of emergency—
Graziani literally declared a *stato di pericolo pubblico* (state of public danger)
for Cyrenaica in May 1930—as well as the state's weaponization of mobility.[128]
If the concentration camp was the space that actualized the state of exception (the *nomos* of the modern), the Libyan camps also suggest a complemen-
tary genealogy. These camps were modeled after a militarized space of ancient
Rome (the *castrum*) in parallel with their implicit subjective limit (the *homo
sacer*) rooted in ancient Roman law. Again, according to Agamben, the latter
embodied the originary politicization of bare life as it was brought into the
realm of the sovereignty. The *homo sacer* marked the threshold from politics
to biopolitics. Indeed, the decision on the value (or nonvalue) of life as such—
the power to make live and let die—is the biopolitical structure of modernity as
Michel Foucault argued well.[129] It was this power that Auschwitz expressed in
its purest and most horrific form.

Likewise, the Libyan camps materialized this biopolitics, but there was
more. The temporary permanence of their structures and the porosity of tents
and barbed wire had their origin in a space of militarized mobility: the
castrum.[130] Whereas the *homo sacer* was the limit figure of Roman law, the *castrum* was a traveling threshold of the Roman Empire in space. It was a short-
term military encampment used by the Roman Legion while on the march.[131]
An apportioned space par excellence, the *castrum* had a standardized grid of
streets, gates, and tent formations, which allowed for highly efficient construction and disassembly. Wherever the Legion went, so too did the sovereign power of Rome.[132] The *castrum* thus mobilized the space of empire.

Roman *castra* were "nothing more than rectangular enclosures bounded by
a rampart and ditch. . . . All these structures were based on the same concep-

tual plan; a rectangular outline with straight sides and rounded corners; the gates placed in the sides and not at the corners," according to the archaeologist Alan Richardson.[133] Camp design followed a very specific formula that could be altered per the changing needs of the Legion: the *castrum* was a square camp, bordered by a *vallum* (rampart) and ditch, an intervening perimeter space or *intervallum*, and a tented area. So good were the Romans at constructing these camps, Richardson calculated that an army of 4,200 men, each with a specific task, could erect or disassemble a *castrum* in less than two hours.[134]

Three well-known classical sources describe the form and function of the Roman *castrum*: (1) book 6 of Polybius's *Histories* (circa first and second centuries BCE), (2) book 3 of Josephus's *The Jewish War* (circa first century), and (3) Pseudo-Hyginus's lesser known *De munitionibus castrorum* (circa third century). According to Polybius, the whole camp formed a square, and "the way in which the streets are laid out and its general arrangement give it the appearance of a town. . . . After forming the camp the tribunes meet and administer an oath, man by man, to all in the camp, whether freemen or slaves. Each man swears to steal nothing from the camp and even if he finds anything to bring it to the tribunes."[135] Yet even with fealty sworn—like the declarations of *sottomissione* (submission) sworn by Bedouin at the Libyan camps—the *castrum's* rectilinear spaces ensured that men could be surveilled at all times. Josephus described the *castrum* as follows: "The camp is intersected by streets symmetrically laid out; in the middle are the tents of the officers, and precisely in the center the headquarters of the commander-in-chief resembling a small temple. Thus, as it were, an improvised city springs up, with its market-place, its artisan quarter, its seats of judgment, where captains and colonels adjudicate upon any differences which may arise."[136] The *castrum* therefore resembled something like Michel Agier's modern "camp-town." Surveillance, discipline, and punishment were also integral to the spaces of the *castrum* as was the monitoring and control of mobile troops. Both the *praetorium* (commander's tent) and the *quaestorium* (chief financial officer's tent) were flanked by the tents of the military tribunes who would hear any disputes or accusations brought against Legion members.[137] Together, this created a centralized space of authority within the *castrum*.

The Italian-built camps in Libya were laid out in almost exactly the same way. Bordered by a 1,300-yard-long perimeter, the square camps contained within them smaller squares that housed fifteen to twenty linear rows of tents. From the air, they gave the impression of a neat, controlled, rectilinear order, complete with *vallum*, *intervallum*, and tented area.[138] There were also spaces allocated for daily assemblies, food and clothing distribution, and exercise displays as well as punitive isolation and public executions. Again, there were gardens outside some camps too, usually tended by female detainees, and healthier men were often forced to work in road construction or building public works nearby. The Libyan camps, then, gave the impression of being a spatial order that housed a subjugated populace engaged in a productive colonialism.

Discipline at both *castrum* and camp was not taken lightly, and the two thousand years separating them did little to alter modes of punishment. Polybius described the death penalty issued to any soldier who was found to have violated the rules of the *castrum*. It was called the *fustuarium* (fustigation). He writes: "A court-martial composed of all the tribunes at once meets to try him, and if he is found guilty he is punished by the *fustuarium*. This is inflicted as follows: the tribune takes a cudgel and just touches the condemned man with it, after which all in the camp beat or stone him, in most cases dispatching him in the camp itself."[139] Severe flogging that resulted in death was also a common practice in the Libyan camps. Salim al-Shilwi, a prisoner at el-Agheila, recalled a man being whipped one hundred times for failing to salute a passing officer.[140] When the man refused to say "Long live the king of Italy," he was flogged seven hundred more times.[141] The poet al-Minifi lamented, "Whips lash us before our women's eyes, rendering us, useless, degraded."[142] Even worse, Salem Omram Abu Shabur, another prisoner at el-Agheila, described the forced participation in such atrocities: "Si vedevano tante torture ed impiccagioni. Tutti dovevano assistere alle esecuzioni, senza parlare, senza commentare, quasi senza piangere." (You saw so much torture and so many hangings. All were forced to witness the executions, without speaking, without comment, almost without tears.)[143]

The residues of the *castrum* haunted the camp not only among fustigations but also in the practices of everyday life. Again, Polybius described the modes of governance through terror at the *castrum*. For example, if a few soldiers broke ranks, the entire Roman Legion would be punished collectively. However, the penalty would not be the same for all: one-tenth of the legion, whether guilty or not, would randomly be put to death by *fustuarium*, often by the hands of their own cohort. The rest of the legionaries would be forced to eat barley—the food of slaves and animals—a humiliating display for a proud soldier of the Roman Empire. Of the collective punishment, Polybius writes: "As therefore the danger and dread of drawing the fatal lot affects all equally, as it is uncertain on whom it will fall; and as the public disgrace of receiving barley rations falls on all alike, this practice is best calculated both to inspire fear and to correct the mischief."[144]

Likewise, prisoners in the Libyan camps were forced to exist on a weekly ration of poor-quality barley augmented with grass, mice, insects, and whatever else could be foraged within the barbed wire, including grain pilfered from animal dung.[145] Occasionally they received a small portion of rice. Almost all prisoners in the camps were forced to turn on their compatriots and, often, to participate in their torture and execution in one way or another. Survivors tell tale after tale of being complicit witnesses, numbed to the horrors of deathly living in the camps. Zeida Attia Chet recalled: "Ad el Agheila ho assistito alla fucilazione di tre persone. Erano solo sospettate di collaborare con i nostri partigiani. Non c'erano prove e forse le prove non si sono mai cercate. Bastava solo il sospetto." (At el-Agheila, I witnessed the shooting of three people. They were only suspected of collaboration with our partisans. There were no trials, and perhaps the trials were never attempted. Only suspicion was needed.)[146] Reth Belgassem, too, witnessed the death of friends without being able to say a word, much less intervene in the proceedings: "Ammazzavano o fucilando o impiccando. Mi ricordo di uno dei miei amici e di altri tre. Furono impiccati davanti ai miei occhi . . . Ci costringevano a guardare mentre morivano i nostri fratelli." (They [Italians] killed by firing squad or by hanging. I remember one of my friends and another three. They were hanged in front of my eyes. . . . They forced us to watch while our brothers died.)[147] Executed bodies were often left hanging for days, after which the very prisoners who were forced to witness those deaths had to remove the corpses and bury them in mass graves in the hard desert soil beyond the barbed wire.[148]

At the *castrum*, mobility was always-already militarized for this was a temporary space built for the peripatetic soldiers of the Roman Legion. The Libyan concentration camps were temporary spaces built for different itinerant subjects—Bedouin nomads—thought to be militarized against the state. In design, both *castrum* and camp shared a common structure and purpose, and in such ways, they instantiated a spatial genealogy defined by mobile subjects (soldiers, nomads) and predicated on the state's instrumentalization and control of mobility. Both were threshold spaces of empire. These were also striated, surveilled, disciplinary spaces—antitheses to smooth, flexible, nomadic spaces. They were spaces of paradox too, that is, of temporary permanence—spaces that displayed the state's control over all mobilities.

Yet in Italian colonial Libya, the camp was just one expression of this control. The state appropriated and exercised other forms of mobility to advance its own ends, which set the conditions not only for the Libyan camps but also for their re-territorialization within Italy in the late 1930s and early 1940s—specifically, in *lager* built in the metropole like Risiera di San Sabba in Trieste or nearby in Croatia like Rab ("Arbe" in Italian). These were camps where biopolitics was carried to its absolute limit and the *conditio inhumana* came to be seized up within a horrifying Final Solution.

Mobility as Colonizing Force

The cruel life of the Libyan camps—these spaces where "evil leaned hard on good, dominant"—was predicated on the Italian state's naming and containing of *grande nomadismo* (great nomadism). Graziani blatantly stated that the control of mobility was paramount to defeating the rebellion: "I nomadi dovranno invece essere stabiliti nei territori del limite predesertico . . . I loro movimenti, le loro soste, i loro accampamenti dovranno essere rigidamente controllati da ufficiali di Governo e dalle truppe." (The nomads must instead be settled within the territories of the desert's edge. . . . Their movements, their rest stops, their encampments must be rigidly controlled by government officials and troops.)[149] To that end, Italian colonizers appropriated mobility—the strategy of choice of the resistance—and transformed it into a tactical weapon of the Italian state. For instance, Graziani ordered the formation of smaller, mobile bands of troops to pursue rebel leader 'Umar al-Mukhtar and his compatriots across the mountainous plateau east of Benghazi.[150] Air surveillance directed these soldiers from above, while radio and telegram relays coordinated the pursuit from below. By instrumentalizing physical and communicative mobilities, the state turned what was perceived to be the rebels' advantage—mobility—into the very strategy that crushed them in this long and bloody guerrilla war.

The power of mobility, too, was expressed by performances of imperialist hypermobility like Graziani's famous *raid automobilistico* (road trip) from Benghazi to Tripoli in June 1931 to celebrate the unity of Libya. It was a trip organized at the apex of the camps, which held close to one hundred thousand prisoners at the time. Graziani's thirty-eight-vehicle caravan traversed the 630 miles between Benghazi and Tripoli in one week so as to "orgogliosamente annunciare al mondo intero che i nemici interni sono debellati" (proudly announce to the entire world that the internal enemies have been eradicated), or more accurately, imprisoned in concentration camps.[151] To make the point, the caravan set up its comparatively luxurious accommodations next to camps like el-Agheila, giving rise to the rather perverse juxtaposition between the rows of the caravan's tents and those contained within the barbed-wire perimeters nearby. It is not unlike tourists in places like Lampedusa or Lesvos today who remain oblivious to migrant bodies that have washed ashore. The *raid automobilistico* symbolically made clear that the hypermobility of Italian colonizers depended on the forced immobility of Cyrenaica's nomads. It also announced the power of mobility as a colonizing force.

Dislocation and Dispossession

The spaces of the Libyan camps never would have been possible without the deportation of innumerable Bedouin from the earliest days of Italian occupation. These deportations began almost from the moment of invasion with the transfer of almost three thousand Libyan men to carceral islands off Italy's coast in 1911, as detailed in essay one. The forced dislocation and internment on Italy's prison islands presaged the forced dislocation and internment of Bedouin in concentration camps less than twenty years later. Nicola Labanca writes, "While deporting notables did not constitute an innovation for Italian colonialism in either its liberal or fascist articulations, deporting an entire population in order to stop anticolonial resistance . . . was without precedent."[152] Labanca referred to the most infamous of these dislocations in the latter part of 1930 when Italian officers and *askari* soldiers forcibly marched some eighty thousand people more than 600 miles across the Sahel and the Jabal Akhdar into the concentration camps.

It is important to note that a vast program of coerced dispossession preceded the hellish marches of 1930 and the enduring trauma of displacement (figure 11). Beginning in 1922, the Italian Parliament passed a series of laws that allowed for the confiscation of all land and goods belonging to the Sanusi *zawiyas*.[153] It began with the expropriation of arable lands in Tripolitania and Cyrenaica, which were transformed into farms for future Italian settlers. Often these lands were taken under the auspices of eminent domain or the owners were "convinced" to sell their land at far below market value.[154] Italian administrators reasoned that if unmoored from personal property and physical demesne, the predominantly nomadic and seminomadic population of Cyrenaica would have fewer resources with which to support the rebellion. The vast operation of dispossession continued with the closure of all *zawiyas* save the one at al-Jahbub ("Giarabub" in Italian), which was considered to be a holy site. With this closure, one report implied, Italian administrators could successfully disrupt not just the ethical-social organization of the Sanusi but also their hold on the political government of the region.[155]

While it remains difficult to find traces of the actual people imprisoned in the camps (if there were name registers, they have long since disappeared), the Italian archival record is awash with documents pertaining to this vast exercise of colonial dispossession.[156] Inventory upon inventory listed the exact number of hectares, buildings, gardens, furnishings, crops, property lines, and value of each *zawiya* as well as its proprietors and tribal affiliations. The entries in these registers of *beni confiscati* (confiscated goods) went into such detail so as to include, for example, the following: the contents of expropriated

FIGURE 11.   Italian troops raid tents and dispossess local inhabitants of their belongings during the military campaign to unite Tripolitania and Cyrenaica, June–March 1928. Photograph reproduced by permission from Archivio Centrale dello Stato, Graziani Photo Archive, Rome.

property, such as "giardino trenta palme, tre fichi, due melograni, pozzo e vasca" (garden with thirty palms, three figs, two pomegranates, well and basin); the names of the proprietor and his heirs; the numbered decree of expropriation; the monetary value of the property; and the colonial office that took possession of the land (usually the Ufficio Agrario, or Office of Agriculture). Despite the lack of name registers, one might surmise that the many landowners listed on these inventories were among those mustered into concentration camps. Dislocation closely followed dispossession.

As the camps gathered shape on the Sirtica flats in the early months of 1930, colonial officials became increasingly preoccupied with the resistance that seemed to be gaining strength in the mountains of the Jabal Akhdar. Rebels moved on horseback and struck Italian army encampments with unpredictable and brutal efficiency. Archival records show that administrative ire was increasingly directed toward 'Umar al-Mukhtar. Military operations refocused on his capture. Badoglio, then governor of Libya, even noted rather sadistically that he hoped al-Mukhtar would get a "nice surprise" from the Italian

Air Force in the form of bombs and mustard gas.[157] In July 1930, Badoglio sent an unsettling telegram to Emilio De Bono, minister of the colonies at the time, that outlined the clearing of the Jabal Akhdar and the sequestering of the local populace into concentration camps. Soldiers were ordered to shoot anyone who resisted. No one would be spared. He wrote:[158]

> Continua con massimo ordine movimento per concentramento sottomessi . . . nessun indigeno dovrà più trovarsi su altopiano, e chiunque sarà incontrato sarà passato per le armi come ribelle. È diffuso in tutta popolazione senso vero sgomento e disorientamento, perchè ormai comprendono che ribelli così isolati non potranno durarla.
>
> The movement to concentrate the subjugated [populace] continues on a maximum scale. . . . No local shall be found on the [Jabal Akhdar] plateau any longer, and anyone encountered will be shot like a rebel. A sense of true bewilderment and disorientation is diffuse in the whole population, because now they understand that rebels so isolated cannot endure.

The chosen strategy of forced dislocation and internment was meant to isolate rebels from their supply networks. In the winter of 1930, the two thousand members of the Abeidat and Marmarici tribes suffered the most brutal dislocation. Under the watchful rifles of Eritrean *askari* battalions, they were marched 600 miles across the Marmarica desert. According to Ottolenghi, 60 percent of the people died en route as did 50 percent of their livestock.[159] Those who could not keep up were either shot or simply left to die. Those who made it were imprisoned at the concentration camp of Ain el Gazala near Tobruq.

Contrary to the horrific experiences on the ground, the Italian press painted this mass dislocation as beneficial—a grand movement that would serve to quell the rebellion. An article in the December 1930 issue of *L'Oltremare* states that eighty thousand people voluntarily left the Jabal Akhdar plateau for the greener, better-watered pastures of the concentration camps built by the Italian government.[160] Of course, the Bedouin actually interned there had a completely different memory of the camps and the march. Some prisoners, such as Senussi Said, were actually made to march across the desert more than once. Imprisoned at the camp of el-Agheila, Said told of how he and other prisoners had to accompany Italian resupply caravans to Kufra, an oasis some 500 miles to the south, which today is a main transit point for human trafficking across the Sahara. He was forced to make this journey twice:[161]

Molti di noi internati fummo costretti ad accompagnare le carovane di cammelli che trasportavano i rifornimenti per i militari italiani nella zona dell'oasi di Cufra. E anche allora ci trattavano male. Io fui costretto due volte a fare il viaggio. Avanti e indietro. Ci facevano compiere il tragitto con due o trecento cammelli carichi e quando si rientrava sfiniti e affaticati dovevamo riprendere nuovamente la pista. Senza pausa. Molti a forza di queste fatiche crollavano e morivano. Molti sono morti di sete. Qualcuno veniva abbandonato lungo la pista, altri che non riuscivano più a stare in piede venivano finiti con un colpo di fucile.

Many of us detainees were forced to accompany the camel caravans that transported supplies to the Italian soldiers near the oasis of Kufra. And even then they treated us badly. I was forced to make the trip twice. Back and forth. They made us do the trip with two or three hundred camels, and when you caught up, exhausted and fatigued, we had to restart on the trail again. Without pause. Many collapsed and died from the strain of these efforts. Many died of thirst. Some were abandoned along the trail, others who could no longer stand were finished with a gunshot.

Even though the spaces of the concentration camp immobilized the majority of Cyrenaica's Bedouin, experiences like that of Senussi Said also demonstrate how such forced imprisonment was intensified through forced mobilization. What mattered here was the appearance of state control over both. Immobilization became a weapon of the Italian state and "nomads" its moving targets.

In addition to the forced movements of people, the Italian state was also intent on controlling the movement of things—namely, contraband from across the Egyptian border. To staunch these movements, Graziani ordered the construction of a 168-mile-long barbed-wire fence stretching along the traditional caravan route from Bardiyah ("Porto Badia" in Italian) on the coast to the remote desert oasis of Al Jaghbub ("Giarabub"), the holy site and Sanusi stronghold. Construction began in April 1931 and was completed in September of that same year.[162] The fence was more than six feet high and thirty feet wide. It was patrolled constantly and laced with land mines at points deemed most likely to be breached. The intention behind the fence was to further isolate rebels from networks of financial and logistical support, and the jumbled layers of barbed wire proved impossible to pass.[163] It was a strategy of isolation meant to complement the separation already created by the forced displacement and resettlement of the population into concentration camps. Taken in concert, both the fence and the camp can be considered a weapon-ized architecture created by the Italian state to control the mobility of people and things.

Flying Courts

The forced dislocations were kept in check by flight, that is, by fighter planes and aerial bombardments. While Eritrean *askari* and Italian officers attended to the Bedouin on the ground, military aviation shepherded them from above, driving "nomads" relentlessly toward the *conditio inhumana* of the camps. A different apparatus of flight—*tribunali volanti*, or "flying courts"—also sent Bedouin to the camps, and often to their death. This was so-called justice on the move.

Beginning in April 1930, the colonial administration spearheaded by Graziani set up a mobile military court that flew from point to point to put on trial whoever was suspected of participating in *atti ostili* (hostile acts) against the Italian government.[164] Simply possessing arms was considered a capital offense. Because all of Libya was under a state of emergency, Graziani argued that a mobilized system of justice was necessary: "Il tribunale venne così mobilitato e tutti i mezzi furono a disposizione perché potesse giungere con la massima rapidità ovunque necessità di servizio lo richiedesse . . . in tal modo l'azione giudiziaria procede rapida e snella." (The court had been so mobilized and all the means put at its disposition so that it could arrive, with the maximum speed, wherever its services were required. . . . In that way judiciary action proceeds quickly and smoothly.)[165] As early as 1913, the Italian colonial administration had set up various *tribunali militari speciali* (special military tribunals) to prosecute rebels across Tripolitania and Cyrenaica. Archival documents reveal that the earliest "trials" usually resulted in deportation to carceral islands like Ponza and Ustica.[166] In the 1920s, however, punishments escalated from deportation to execution. Most defendants were convicted of treason and sentenced to death. Occasionally a sentence would be commuted to life imprisonment. Those convicted were often ordinary men, either hanged or shot on site, without any chance of appeal.

What was unique about the flying courts was the speed and scale of their juridical intervention. The *tribunali volanti* would crisscross Cyrenaica by air and often would follow army regiments so as to be on-site during battles to prosecute rebels when needed.[167] The flying court was so expedient that "non appena giunge la segnalazione di un arresto in flagranza di reato, il tribunale parte e la Giudizia scende dal cielo" (just as the notification of an arrest in flagrante delicto barely arrives, the court departs and justice descends from the sky). It was a sight so common, Graziani added, "e questo è diventato così normale che quando un aeroplano giunge nel luogo ove è stato commesso un reato si sente mormorare negli accampamenti la parola «tribunale»" (and this became so normal that when an airplane arrives at a place where a crime has been committed one hears the word "tribunal" murmured throughout the encampments).[168] The court adjudicated roughly forty-three cases each month, almost all of them resulting in guilty verdicts.[169] Per Graziani, the flying courts heard 520 cases involving 809 people between April 1930 and March 1931, with approximately 250 of them ending with capital punishment.[170] According to Evans-Pritchard, these flying courts reduced rebel units by two-thirds.[171]

Under the flying courts, executions also became increasingly spectacular. For example, on July 24, 1930, four young men—Kamisc bu Abd-er-Raman, Bilesc bu Mahmud, Mohammed bu Hag Hammad, and Muftà bu Abdulla—allegedly fired their rifles at the Italian plane bombing their camel herd near Tobruq. They were arrested, convicted of "rebellion," and sentenced to death by the flying court less than one week later. At dawn on the 31st, these four men were marched out to a public plaza in Tobruq and put to death in front of a large crowd of their compatriots. All that is left of their lives—and the injustice of their deaths—is but two telegrams and a sterile, one-page report buried in an archive in Rome.[172]

The spectacle incited by Graziani and the *tribunali volanti* culminated in the capture and execution of resistance leader 'Umar al-Mukhtar in September 1931. With most of Cyrenaica's population interned in the camps and his supply lines cut off by the barbed-wire fence, al-Mukhtar regrouped with guerrilla fighters in the mountains east of Benghazi in the summer of 1931. They raided Italian conveys sporadically, taking food and a few weapons, and for the most part existed on the verge of famine and exhaustion.[173] On the evening of September 10, 1931, Italian troops moved into an area near the remote town of Slonta. There had been reports of al-Mukhtar in the area. A reconnaissance plane caught sight of a rebel group the next morning and an Italian battalion began pursuit. Spotted, rebels fled in all directions and the troops opened fire. One of the bullets killed a horse that fell and pinned its rider beneath. That rider was the seventy-three-year-old al-Mukhtar, who, after decades of resisting Italian forces, had finally been captured.[174]

In Rome, Graziani received the news of al-Mukhtar's arrest just as he was about to board a train for the famed 1931 International Colonial Exhibition in Paris.[175] He immediately caught a flight to Tripoli instead and arrived in Benghazi two days later at the same time as al-Mukhtar. The following day Graziani interrogated al-Mukhtar personally, and what emerged of this interaction was a portrait of a noble al-Mukhtar standing in silent relief against a hyperbolic

Graziani. Al-Mukhtar's brief trial by flying court was merely a staged performance of judicial proceedings. He was found guilty and sentenced to death. Upon hearing his conviction, al-Mukhtar reportedly answered: "We come from God and to God we return."[176] At 9 a.m. on September 16, 1931—just five days after he was captured—'Umar al-Mukhtar was driven across the desert to Soluq and hanged at the concentration camp in front of twenty thousand onlookers, most of them his compatriots. These included local leaders from surrounding towns as well as detainees brought in from other concentration camps nearby. His body was taken from the site and interred in a Benghazi cemetery. "The resistance died with Sidi 'Umar al-Mukhtar," wrote Evans-Pritchard years later. "The remaining fights were twitches of an already lifeless body."[177]

Graziani, not yet content with this "victory," printed flyers announcing al-Mukhtar's death and distributed them across Cyrenaica by air, dropping them from airplanes in a paper rain of propaganda.[178] These flyers declared al-Mukhtar to be the cause of Cyrenaica's ruin and his death as having been divinely ordained. They proclaimed that the magnanimous Italian state would pardon any remaining rebels who surrendered immediately, but that the state would relentlessly pursue those who did not. The message was at once all carrot and all stick. One can imagine the williwaw of flyers dropping like a curtain from the gray September sky. They would come to rest in the camps on the battered tents and the hunger-sunken faces, all exhausted souls dying in a cage: bare life on the bare plains of Cyrenaica.

Afterlives of the Libyan Camps

Despite the intentions of both Graziani and Badoglio to keep the camps open indefinitely, by the spring of 1933 all sixteen of them had been emptied. Some were repurposed as military supply bases, while others were simply abandoned to the desert. The reasons for their closure were pragmatic.[179] First, it was impossible to sustain the camps over the long term because of the chronic lack of food and water as well as ever-deteriorating sanitary and hygienic conditions. The typhus epidemic that swept through Soluq in March 1933, for example, was so severe that it forced Graziani to order its closure. Second, there was a growing need for cheap manpower to build the roads, villages, and farms for incoming Italian settlers (examined in the next essay of this book). Almost all the survivors of the camps were relocated to sites across the Jabal Akhdar, although the most fertile regions were reserved for Italian farmers. Yet these closures did not signal the end of the camp in the modern Italian context but rather the beginning of a long assault against mobile "undesirables" who threatened state power. The techniques of immobilization and punishment that began with the Libyan camps were expanded and intensified in other camps shortly thereafter, among them Dhanaane (Somalia), Jadu (Tripolitania), and Rab (Croatia) outside the peninsula, or Nazi camps like Fossoli (Modena) and Risiera di San Sabba (Trieste) within Italy. The Fascist regime established upward of one hundred camps designated as "concentration camps," most of them in Italy and the colonies, with the rest in the Balkans.[180] While the focus of this essay is on the alpha and omega of the camp in modern Italy, I touch briefly on a few of these successor camps—each of which warrants an extended critical study in its own right.

Dhanaane (Somalia)

The immediate descendant of the Libyan camps was the notoriously brutal *campo di punizione* (punishment camp) established at Dhanaane (Somalia) in 1935. It was Graziani's idea after he had been put in charge of military campaigns in eastern Africa because of his "success" in Libya. Dhanaane was a small camp, just over half a square mile designed to hold four hundred prisoners, yet it quickly expanded to imprison anyone who, in the words of Graziani, was deemed to be "elementi nocivi e potenzialmente pericolosi per il governo coloniale" (harmful and potentially dangerous elements to the colonial government).[181] It was an inhospitable place located in the dusty flatlands south of Mogadishu. It was also a symbolic place as the site where five Italian officers and a small company of *askari* defeated a superior Somali force in 1907.[182] Shabby tents provided little protection against extremes, both natural and human. At its apex in 1938, more than two thousand detainees suffered here at the same time. Of the more than 6,500 prisoners who passed through Dhanaane's gates, 3,175 of them died at a rate of four to five people per day.[183]

The horrors of Dhanaane, as at all camps, were many. Michael Tessema, an Ethiopian imprisoned here from 1937 to 1941, told not just of torture, hunger, and illness but of impossible cruelty in the face of human suffering. He told of men and women being "flogged with a whip" and "dipped headfirst into a tin filled with human excrement" and even "hanged on the wall for seven days without their feet touching the ground," resulting in amputation. There was also a woman who had a one-year-old baby who died in the camp, he said. The prisoners gathered to bury the child, but the Italian brigadier in charge forbade it. Instead, he forced a spade on the woman, who was still holding her baby's corpse, and marched her beyond the barbed-wire perimeter. And there on the hardened earth, he whipped her as she struggled to dig her own child's grave.

British troops liberated Dhanaane in 1941, and in one of history's many ironic twists, the camp was repurposed as a POW camp used for Italian soldiers. According to Gustavo Ottolenghi, 1,200 Italians and 2,000 *askari* and *zaptié* (indigenous soldiers of the Italian military) were imprisoned at Dhanaane.[184] Most were sent onward to internment camps in British India, but 300 Italians remained in the camp until it closed in 1945.[185]

Jadu (Tripolitania)

Back in Libya, racial segregation and anti-Semitism intensified during the late 1930s as Fascist Italy grew closer to Nazi Germany. In 1938, the Italian Parliament passed a series of *Leggi Razziali* (Racial Laws) aimed primarily at Jews. These laws effectively stripped Jewish people of all civil rights, confiscated their property, and opened the way for deportation to Nazi concentration camps in what was one of the most odious episodes of modern Italian history.[186] When the Racial Laws were passed, they only slightly affected the Jews of Libya, many of whom were descended from families that had lived there for centuries. At the time, the Jewish population across Libya numbered roughly 30,000, with 22,500 living in Tripolitania. Some held French citizenship or were *Tunisien Protégé Français* (Tunisian under French protection), others were British citizens, and still others were Jews that held Libyan citizenship.[187] According to Renzo De Felice, the laissez-faire attitude toward the enforcement of Racial Laws in Libya had as much to do with the important economic role that Jews played in the colony as it did with the political influence and personal interest of Italo Balbo, then governor of Libya (1933–40).[188] The rising tide of anti-Semitism disturbed the charismatic Balbo, who expended much political capital maneuvering around the Racial Laws and blocking their implementation. Unfortunately, Balbo died suddenly when his airplane was shot down over Tobruq in June 1940. The treatment of Libya's Jewish population worsened dramatically thereafter.

The enforcement of segregation and dispossession grew increasingly stringent, especially after Italy entered World War II, and in 1942, the Fascist regime inaugurated a campaign of *sfollamento*, or "clearing out" all the Jews from Libya.[189] Many people fled into the hinterlands to avoid forced deportation. Those who held British citizenship were shipped to camps in Europe: first to transit camps like Fossoli in Italy, and then onto the Nazi *lager* of Bergen-Belsen and Dachau in the spring of 1944. The Jews who were French subjects were deported to detention camps in Tunisia and Algeria. Those who held Libyan citizenship were interned at newly built concentration camps across Tripoli-tania, the largest of which was known as Jadu ("Giado" in Italian), located some 110 miles southwest of Tripoli.[190]

It was at Jadu that the Shoah arrived on Libyan shores. There were 2,584 Jews imprisoned here. Many of them were from Cyrenaica and had been loaded against their will onto camions for the five-day journey across the Sirtica desert. Survivors of Jadu described the days as being filled with illness, cru-elty, and exhaustion. According to Mushi (Moshe) Meghidish, who was im-prisoned at Jadu for a year, prisoners were given the Sisyphean task of moving heavy rocks from one end of the camp to the other, for no other purpose than tiring them out.[191] The barbed-wire fences and barren desert mountains made escape all but impossible. Almost everyone suffered from typhus and other ill-nesses that were only made worse by starvation, fatigue, and humiliation at the hands of Italian and German soldiers. In its fourteen months of operation, 562 people died at Jadu (one-fifth of those who entered), mostly from typhus.[192] British Allies liberated the camp in January 1943 and immediately took mea-sures to control the spread of disease. Prisoners were bathed, fed, and given medical care, and eventually returned to their homes in Cyrenaica. Neverthe-less, the camp at Jadu represented, to borrow the words of Eric Salerno, noth-ing less than "il perfezionamento dei campi di Soluch ed El Agheila" (the perfection of the camps of Soluq and El Agheila).[193] Thus the specter of the concentration camps that desecrated the stark beauty of the Cyrenaican plains one decade earlier returned to haunt again in extremis as Jadu, a camp born of anti-Semitism and the evil of Nazi genocide that was cresting and winnow-ing its way across Europe.

Rab (Croatia)

In that same year, 1942, the Fascist regime executed a horrific program of eth-nic cleansing in the Italian-occupied regions of Yugoslavia, primarily against the Slovene people.[194] As was the case in colonial Libya, forced deportations to camps were the favored strategy of control. There is extensive scholarship on these camps of the early 1940s to which I defer for a more detailed analy-sis, including accounts of the one built on Rab ("Arbe" in Italian), an island off the Dalmatian coast.[195] What is today a picturesque Croatian isle known for its beaches and forests, the camp at Rab was a space of absolute terror and surveillance. According to one survivor, Franc Potočnik, machine guns and barbed wire covered every angle of the camp. High-powered electric lights illuminated everything at night, not unlike the floodlights of Ponte Galeria today. Potočnik adds: "Da tali posizioni era possibile, in ogni momento, tenere i campi sotto un assoluto controllo." (From every position it was possible, in every moment, to keep the camps under absolute control.)[196]

Mario Roatta, Mussolini's then head of secret service, issued his infamous "Circolare 3C" in March 1942, a memo that elaborated a scorched-earth policy of occupation and sanctioned a genocide in the region. Roatta summarily ordered executions and demolished entire villages during the twenty-nine-month Italian occupation of the Ljubljana province (1941–43). At its apex, the camp at Rab held some 10,000 detainees, of whom 2,200 were Jewish. Surprisingly, Jews received better treatment in Rab than Slovenes, who were subjected to an official policy of *repressione* (repression). Jews fell into the category of *protezione* (protection), which warranted slightly better treatment and housing in separate barracks (instead of tents) that protected them from winter conditions.[197]

Central to Roatta's plan was what he called *la bonifica etnica* (ethnic reclamation). His aim was to eliminate all local inhabitants through execution or deportation and to replace them with Italian settlers.[198] Roatta's use of the term *bonifica* was a perverse appropriation of the language used to describe the agricultural reclamation in the colonial context. The *bonifica integrale* of Cyrenaica or the Agro Pontino centered on the creation of public works that advanced agricultural and industrial productivity. Pumps that drained marshes, tractors that plowed fields, and railways that moved goods and people were all part of the effort. Of course, the *bonifica integrale* also came at a huge human cost. The consequences of Roatta's *bonifica etnica* in Yugoslavia were lesser veiled but equally as horrific as those in Soluq, Jadu, or Dhanaane. In other words, the goal of settling an ethnically cleansed Balkan state while advancing Italy's imperialist ambitions culminated in the camp at Rab. For one violent moment, Rab existed as the cynosure between the concentration camp and the extermination camp. It was the apotheosis of Italy's twin colonial projects of demographic settlement and indigenous internment combined with the horrors of the Shoah and the savagery of a world war.

New Bedouin in a Cage

What, then, is the inheritance of the camp? Is not the camp built on Rab in 1942, with its barbed wire and open-air tents and *razzie* (raids) perpetrated against Slovenes and Jews, a residue of Soluq from ten years earlier, with its barbed wire and open-air tents and *razzie* perpetrated against Bedouin? And is not Soluq already a residue of the ancient Roman *castrum*? And is not the migrant detention center at Ponte Galeria a residue of the *castrum*, Rab, and Soluq all, with its barbed wire and open-air prison yards and *razzie* perpetrated

FIGURE 12. An *ospite* (guest) walks through the cage, the Ponte Galeria CIE, near Rome. Photograph by the author, 2013.

against "illegal immigrants"? All are manifestations of the same imperial formation expressed by the form of the camp along empire's Mobius strip.

The *ospiti* at Ponte Galeria are the new Bedouin in a cage (figure 12). Their unsanctioned mobilities are, in fact, what led to their very immobilization in today's camp. They crossed borders without passports. They lived without papers. They existed in the shadows of the law. Once detained at Ponte Galeria, many *ospiti* rebel against the limbo of temporary permanence. Revolts are frequent and tend to turn violent. Just one month before my field visit in March 2013, there was a particularly intense rebellion that began with an assault on a *carabiniere* and ended with an inferno of burning mattresses.[199] At other times, *ospiti* turn the rebellion inward onto themselves—for example, going on hunger strikes to protest their lives in this place known as "Italian Guantánamo." Sometimes dissent has been taken to harrowing extremes, as in December 2013, when a group of nine men sewed their mouths shut.[200] It was equal parts hunger strike and symbolic action—to forcibly silence themselves was a way to be heard. The *ospiti* claimed they were taking a stand against the eighteen-month maximum period of detention, which was far longer than the standard sixty days prescribed by the EU. Their actions recalled an infamous episode in Amara Lakhous's 2006 best-selling novel, *Scontro di civiltà per un ascensore a Piazza Vittorio* (Clash of civilizations over an elevator in Piazza Vittorio), arguably one of the most famous works of Italophone literature to date, in which one character, Parviz, an Iranian immigrant, sewed his mouth shut after authorities refused to grant him a permit of stay. Over the course of 2014, there were three successive occurrences of *bocche cucite* (sewn mouths) at Ponte Galeria, and the extreme protests eventually garnered the attention of Italian lawmakers. To a certain degree, the *bocche cucite* succeeded in their goal: in November 2014, the Italian Parliament passed a law that lowered the maximum stay of detention from eighteen months to sixty days. At least two of the men, however, had already been expulsed from Italy.

Successes like this are rare. More often, protests against immobilization in the center are answered by expanding the very structures of immobility. The primary result of both violent and nonviolent protests at Ponte Galeria was the creation of more severe architectures and practices of detention, including the erection of anti-escape panels atop the fences, the renovation of entryways for increased security, the installation of electronic locks and additional security cameras, and, of course, the infamous ban on shoes in 2010 (detainees can wear only flip-flops or shoes without laces). The logic behind the shoe ban—which went into effect after a series of riots and successful escapes—was that *ospiti*, even if they did escape, could not get very far with bare feet. Thus, the shoe ban, the plexiglass panels, the computerized locks, and so forth all aim to fix *ospiti* further into the limbo of the CIE. Immobilization was the punitive countermeasure to their unsanctioned mobilities.

What happens, then, when *ospiti* are released from Ponte Galeria? What happens when their lives on the inside of outside move beyond the walls of the center and back into the world at large? And more broadly, what kind of life comes after the experience of the camp? For many of the Bedouin who survived the concentration camps in Italian colonial Libya, life, now irreparably scarred by colonial violence, touched down in the built form of the village. The fates of those who passed through Ponte Galeria are lesser known as many *ospiti* choose to go underground and remain in Italy in open violation of the expulsion decrees issued to them upon release. Some live in fear of discovery and deportation. Others choose to speak out. They are the survivors of Ponte Galeria.

One man who chooses words over silence is Abd El Karim Islam. Karim was arrested near his home in Milan and taken 350 miles south to Ponte Galeria. He has lived in Italy since 1995 and speaks Italian fluently with a hint of a Milanese accent. In the 2014 film *Limbo*, Karim explains that he legally resided in the country for many years until the death of his father. That event prompted him to go "off the rails." He had to enter rehab, after which his permit of stay was not renewed. The bureaucratic machine of Ponte Galeria began its work of cementing Karim into the category of "illegal immigrant" and ordered his deportation to Egypt. He replied in consternation: "Sono più italiano che egiziano. Non c'ho una casa. Non c'ho niente. Dove vado? Non lo capisco." (I'm more Italian than Egyptian. I don't have a house there [in Egypt]. I don't have anything there. Where do I go? I don't understand.) According to Karim, the authorities tried to trick him into going to the airport but he "went crazy" and they relented. He was eventually released and returned to Milan. An avid devotee of Italian hip-hop, Karim wrote a song in 2014 about his experience in Ponte Galeria called "Tutto tace" (All is quiet).[201] Its driving beats and convulsive lyrics prove stirring counterpoints to the silence embodied by the *bocche cucite*. Karim's song also taps into what have long been the traditional concerns of Italian hip-hop: marginalization, identity, inequality, and the feeling of living on the inside of outside.[202] Whereas this was once the musical territory of southern Italians speaking back against the discrimination and prejudice levied against them in their own country, it is now the purview of people like Karim who refuse the category of "illegal immigrant" and use music to speak back against the power of the Italian state. Abd El Karim Islam refused to die in a cage, and it is only appropriate that I leave the last words to him:[203]

Da tempo	For a long time now
la maggior parte degli sfidi	most of the cops
continua appuntarmi dito	continue to point fingers at me
A trattarmi da clandestino	treating me like a *clandestino*
Dopo avermi tolto il permesso	after taking away
di soggiorno	my residence permit
Un brutto giorno	an ugly day
Hanno spaccato in due il mio	it split my world in half
mondo	
cambiando le date del mio	changing the date of my arrival
ingresso in Italia	in Italy
girando le carte in tavola	turning the tables on me
Uso le rime	I use rhymes
per raccontarvi una disavventura	to tell you of the misfortune
che mi hanno fatto vivere	that they made me live
Come possibile	how is it possible
Come un intero Stato	how can an entire State
si sia sbagliato	be so mistaken
sulle mie informazioni base	about my basic information

sulla mia vera identità
È un ventennio che vivo in questa
    nazione
Loro dichiarano che sono entrato
    nel 2007 col gommone

Vivo nel silenzio
quando mille paure dentro
e non va bene niente
anche se non mi lamento

Credo che in questo buio desto
    ci salverà solo il talento

Non è un film che vedi la
    sera al cinema
Questo è il film che parla della
    mia vita vera
In una delle peggiori galere
La mia battaglia a Ponte Galeria
Essere libero come un gabbiano
Quando in ferri alla mano
Ostaggio dello Stato
Che mi costringono
a dare l'addio a casa mia a Milano
A volare verso la città
    del Vaticano
Tanto bello che mai pensavo
Di trovarci un posto così disumano
Come il CIE
Un muro di inganni e bugie
Che brutto quando ripenso
al primo giorno dentro
In gabbia insieme d'altre migliaia
    di razze
Perse e disperse
Come me accecate dalla rabbia
Persone oneste
rinchiusi con le peggiori teste

about my true identity
it's been twenty years that I've
    lived in this nation
they declare that I arrived in
    2007 on a raft

I live in silence
with a thousand fears inside
and none of this is right
even if I don't complain

I believe that in this waking dark
    only talent will save us

It's not a film you see one
    evening at the cinema
this is a film that speaks of my
    real life
in one of the worst jails
my battle at Ponte Galeria
to be free like a seagull
when you're in handcuffs
hostage of the state
that makes me
say goodbye to my home in Milan
to fly toward the city of the
    Vatican
So beautiful that I never thought
to find there a place so inhuman
like the CIE
a wall of deceit and lies
How ugly it is when I think back
to the first day inside
in the cage together with a
    thousand other races
lost and scattered
like me blinded by rage
honest people
locked up with the worst
    [shit]heads

E meno male
che "la legge per tutti uguale"

Solo ora mi accorgo
che è un enorme cazzata scritta
    in tribunale

Vivo nel silenzio
quando mille paure dentro
e non va bene niente
anche se non mi lamento

Credo che in questo buio desto
    ci salverà solo il talento

Carabinieri
finanzieri con i cani
militari armati
Noi sempre sotto sorvegliati

Sembrava di stare in Siria o
    Baghdad
E mai me lo scordo
quel giorno all'aeroporto
Con inganno hanno tentato
di farmi prendere un volo
    senza ritorno
A cui ho riferito lo scontro
Giurando che sarei partito
    solo morto
Non sono pronto
a lasciare tutto di colpo

Tornare al paese d'origine
Non esiste
Sarete come sradicare una quercia
    dalle radici
Mia donna, famiglia, amici
Non ci sono rimedi
quando gli sbirri fanno i prepotenti

and thank goodness
that everyone is "equal before
    the law"

only now I realize
that it's an enormous load of
    shit written in court

I live in silence
with a million fears inside
and none of this is right
even if I don't complain

I believe that in this waking
    dark only talent will save us

Carabinieri
finance police with dogs
armed soldiers
we, always kept under
    surveillance

it felt like being in Syria or
    Baghdad
and I will never forget
that day at the airport
they tried to trick me
to make me take a flight without
    return
against which I chose to fight
swearing that I would only leave
    dead
I'm not ready
to leave everything in one fell
    swoop

to return to the country of origin
that doesn't exist
it would be like uprooting an
    oak at the base
my woman, family, friends
there are no remedies
when the coppers are bullies

E sono i primi hanno
  rispetto alla legge
Chi sistemerà questo sistema?
Io non credo alle cazzate della Lega
Ognuno pensa si se ne frega
Mentre scrivo 'ste pagine
La mente rifletta al cuore brutte
  immagini
Verità crude nascoste dietro
  quelle mura
Io contro tutti e non ho paura
Come ho fatto ad arrivare a tanto?
Ho bisogno di un ultimo slancio
Questo non può essere la mia fine
Fammi uscire!

and they are first with respect to the
  law
Who will fix this system?
I don't believe in the Lega's bullshit
no one gives a damn
while I write these pages
the mind reflects terrible
  images to the heart
Raw truths hidden behind those
  walls
Me against all and I'm not afraid
How did I arrive at this?
I need one last burst
this cannot be the end of me
Let me out!

The Village

I would rather live in a camp, any other camp.
I don't feel like I belong to this village, I feel out of place.

—B., sixteen, Bosnian Roma resident of La Barbuta

In Cyrenaica, in addition to the first villages of Fiorita and Alba, others will appear this year. The Muslims are happy about this most genial initiative, which acts to fix seminomadic people to the land.

—Touring Club Italiano

When I arrived at the village the first day I could not believe my eyes: a concentration camp.

—Antonio Zappador, Istrian exile at Villaggio San Marco, Fossoli

There is a faint but ever-present chemical tang to the air near the *villaggio* (village) known as La Barbuta. Even in winter the off-gasses are palpable, rising like heat from the sea of rubbish that surrounds the village perimeter. Traces of jet fuel rain down at a steady clip as the village sits directly under the glide path of Rome's Ciampino airport, almost at the edge of its runway. The sounds of decelerating engines and braking wheels surround everything with a familiar, mechanical white noise. La Barbuta is one of seven *villaggi attrezzati* (equipped villages) constructed around the Roman periphery during the past two decades to house thousands of displaced Roma (pejoratively known as "gypsies"). It is akin to a high-security trailer park. Its residents live in a patchwork grid of almost two hundred small, nondescript, white laminate houses known as "containers." Entire families live in a single room. A high metal fence posted with security cameras encircles the village. Residents live under strict rules and constant surveillance just like the *ospiti* (guests) at the nearby Ponte Galeria CIE. Entries and exits are closely monitored. There is no public transportation. Guests must be approved and registered with social services. In other

FIGURE 13.   A sea of trash surrounds the *villaggio attrezzato* (equipped village) called La Barbuta on the southeastern periphery of Rome. Photograph by the author, 2013.

words, La Barbuta segregates and sedentarizes everyone contained within its fences.

The first thing one notices about La Barbuta is the trash (figure 13). On my initial visit to the village in March 2013, the piles of rubbish were so high that, from a distance, I could barely see the red rooftops of its containers. Innumerable garbage bags, discarded mattresses, old toilets, construction debris, and every other imaginable dross littered the road leading into the village. My initial shock at the quantity of trash quickly abated as the situation veered into the realm of the absurd as I stood watching a dump truck empty the lone two trash receptacles on-site. Here was an example of the Italian state's futile provision of services to the residents of La Barbuta, a gesture made to uphold the appearance of care for those refused by society and forced to live among the refuse of the village. At first glance, the sea of trash surrounding La Barbuta might seem to reinforce the stereotypes about the Roma as being "dirty" and "uncivilized." It would be easy to mistake the rubbish as the recrement of those who live in the village, as if to imply that somehow the Roma were comfortable living in such filth. Unfortunately, many people do. The Roma have become conflated with refuse especially in the outspoken political arguments for isolating them in *villaggi* in the name of public safety and hygiene. Within the well-patrolled limits of the village, so the arguments go, the Roma can be contained and controlled.

One of the residents, R., told me that the people who lived at La Barbuta were not the ones dumping the trash. Rather, it was a whole spectrum of other people who came from Rome and the surrounding areas to offload their trash illegally, often at night. She said they dumped unspeakable things—"non puoi immaginare le cose che buttano qua" (you can't imagine the things they dump here)—and then paused to let me imagine what terrifying chattel might be found among the waste. Another resident, T., told me that each year the piles of trash get bigger and that La Barbuta now has a huge rat problem because of them. Sometimes people set fire to the trash in an attempt to curb its growth; however, this releases a toxic stew of the household chemicals illegally disposed there. At other times the chemicals seep into the village after a heavy rain. The children of both R. and T. have chronic respiratory problems as a result. R. said the chemical stench becomes so toxic in the summer that it often overpowers her. T. added, "Andiamo via se possiamo, ma non abbiamo lavoro. Come ce la facciamo?" (We would leave if we could, but we don't have work. How can we do it?)

I was surprised to find how starkly the village and the camp ran up against each other at La Barbuta. Next to the state-financed container park built in 2012, I discovered that a *campo nomadi* (nomad camp) had existed on the site for more than two decades. This camp abutted the chain-link fence that encircled the village. It was a ramshackle assemblage of makeshift trailers, tin garages, tarps, and portable toilets. Hoses that carried water and propane crisscrossed the walkways. Residents invited me into the camp to see their homes, and one man, F., said that he wanted people to know how unfairly and unjustly they were being treated by the Italian state. Embittered, he said to me: "Noi siamo italiani e vedi come il governo ci tratta." (We are Italians and look at how the government treats us.) The residents of the nomad camp were all Italian citizens belonging to the Sinti ethnic minority, a smaller subset of the larger community of European Roma. Everyone I spoke with at the camp lamented that they could not live in the village next door because it was reserved for non-Italian Roma. I was told it was a great injustice that the government handed out houses to foreign-born Roma, but they, as Italian citizens, got nothing. Instead, they were forced to live without electricity, running water, and indoor plumbing in the camp. "Non vogliamo castelli" (We don't want castles), said another resident, B., who had lived in the camp for eighteen years, "solo la fogna-tura, l'elettricità e niente spazzatura" (just sewer, electricity, and no garbage). With the construction of the village, everyone agreed that "tutte le cose sono peggiori" (all things have gotten worse).

The Sinti who live in the camp do not interact with the Roma who live in the village. They call the village residents *stranieri* (foreigners) and smart at their access to volunteers and legal aid. There is hardly any contact between them. Yet in the eyes of many European and Italian policymakers, the Roma and the Sinti are often grouped together along with the other categorizations of Roma, like the Camminanti in Sicily or the Kale in Spain. They are considered Europe's internal Others, and in Italy, they are framed predominantly in terms of nomadism and transnationalism.[1]

In the past decades, the prevailing stereotype about the Roma circulating among Italian policymakers has been that of a monolithic population on the move with little regard for national borders. They are considered to be nomads and criminals, and therefore dangerous. Certain politicians, especially those of right-wing parties like the Northern League, have wittingly conflated Roma and Sinti with criminality to such a degree that it has "helped to create and perpetuate an environment of intolerance" that has catalyzed a rising tide of racist and xenophobic violence.[2] The reality is that the majority of Roma, Sinti, Kale, and so on are sedentary. On the one hand, the illusion of Romani homogeneity allows for sustained discrimination, segregation, and violence against all Roma subgroups across Europe; and on the other, it enables organizations such as the European Roma Rights Center to lobby on their collective behalf to the EU and the UN.

This essay explores the spatial aftereffect of the camp, or the form that I have identified as the village. It is the space where many of those who have passed through the island and the camp end up. The example of La Barbuta also reveals a complex and heretofore unacknowledged enmeshment between camp and village. It shows us that the well-theorized camp is not just a space of exception, or a place for bare life, or a biopolitical paradigm of modernity, but a space that must also be seen in the context of what comes *next* to it, spatially and temporally: the village. While both the camp and the village spatialize the *via negativa* in that they "promote un-bonding as a form of relation," I argue that the village is the place in the context of modern Italy where the state harnesses inscriptions of race, ethnicity, and nationality and superimposes them on disconnection, disengagement, uncommitment, and disorder.[3]

Whereas the camp performs a collapse of distinctions per Agamben (inside-outside, life-death, human-animal, et cetera), so too does the village, and at the same time it also performs the opposite: it thickens and reinforces distinctions so that the Italian state can stamp its mark on its subjects, and that mark is either the recognition or the refusal of citizenship. Put another way, the village is a space of exception that breaks down distinctions and moves its residents toward "bare life" while simultaneously amplifying divisions that reify their difference in the face of the state. Seemingly fixed ethno-racial and ethno-national categories (Bosnian Roma, Istrian Italian, et cetera) help the Italian state not only disavow the complexity of actually existing subjectivities but also sanction discrimination and violence obliquely. In the case of La Barbuta—and as we will see in the agricultural and Muslim villages built in Italian colonial Libya and the villages constructed for *profughi nazionali* (national refugees) in the 1940s and 1950s—the form of village both heightens and obfuscates differences of ethnicity and nationality. Such differences are linked to the perceived threat of unsanctioned mobilities that are cast as an overarching danger to the Italian state.

Keeping this entanglement between camp and village in mind, this essay focuses attention on the form of the village. I draw the term "village" from the spaces themselves, including the contemporary *villaggio attrezzato* at La Barbuta along with the other examples, like the *villaggio agricolo* (agricultural village) in 1930s Italian colonial Libya and the Villaggio Santa Caterina near Turin that housed Italian *profughi nazionali* (national refugees) from the 1950s to the present. Even beyond geography, the village is close kin to the camp both historically and geographically. It stems from the Latin *villa* (country house; farm), which in turn comes from the term *vicus* (pl. *vici*, meaning "village," "neighborhood," "quarter," "hamlet," "country seat"). *Vicus* is related to the Sanskrit *vēcas* (house), the Greek *oikos* (house), the Old High German *wīch* (village), and the English suffix *-wich* or *-wick* (village) as in Greenwich or New Brunswick.[4] Scholars have noted how *vici* initially arose as temporary settlements adjacent to military encampments in ancient Rome. *Vici* developed haphazardly throughout the Roman Empire, most notably in Britain. Economic growth was their primary aim: goods and crops were traded there while troops were kept supplied and entertained. A few *vici* assumed the administrative status of towns and took on the challenges of fortification and planning, but most retained their organic quality of being ad hoc developments around military garrisons.[5] Put another way, *castrum* (camp) and *vicus* (village) aligned in Rome's imperial past just as the camp and the village do at La Barbuta on Rome's periphery today. And if the island of Lampedusa is a figurative event horizon and the camp at Ponte Galeria a singularity, then the village at La Barbuta represents a new dimension of Italy's empire.

Yet Italy was not the only state to deploy the village in imperial endeavors. For example, the British colonial government in Kenya famously implemented "forced villagization" to sequester and suppress the Kikuyu tribe in light of the Mau Mau uprising (1952–64). Similar to the way in which the Italian colonial regime forcibly interned Bedouin in concentration camps, so too did the British with Kikuyu "insurgents" in the mid-1950s. According to Caroline Elkins, there existed a series of 804 barbed-wire villages proximate to the detention camps.[6] Kikuyu women and children were imprisoned in the former, Kikuyu men in the latter. On the whole, "the British had actually detained some 1.5 million people, or nearly the entire Kikuyu population."[7] In British-ruled Kenya, as in Italian colonial Libya, the village and the camp were spaces where people were forcibly immobilized in the name of empire.

In the Italian case, however, there was a very practical difference between the form of the camp and that of the village. The village was intended to be permanent. Italian-built *villaggi* in Libya were made of stone and concrete. They were replete with modern amenities. These villages were ready for both Italians and Libyans alike to occupy for decades. Even more interesting is the fact that Italy's Libyan *villaggi* brought together two strands of Italy's colonizing project, that is, internal and external settler colonialism. The Italians chosen to populate the *villaggi agricoli* (agricultural villages) in Libya were resettled from the poorest regions of Italy. It was a demographic strategy born of the country's internal colonizing efforts, such as bringing poor northern Italian farmers to settle the Pontine Marshes south of Rome.[8] The Italian state also selected Libyans to occupy the *villaggi musulmani* (Muslim villages). Thus, the Italians and Libyans who inhabited the *villaggi* were all colonial subjects, albeit to different degrees, and bound to the ambit of the Italian colonial regime.

What interests me about the village is the ways in which this particular space throws into relief discourses of race, ethnicity, and nationality that turn on questions of citizenship. All four—race, ethnicity, nationality, citizenship—prove the filaments of this essay. Clearly, history has shown the notion of citizenship to be anything but a static category. One need only think of the contradictory and ever-changing codes of citizenship, for instance, applied to both *Pied-Noirs* and *indigènes* in French colonial Algeria.[9] Or, the differential statuses of Italian citizenship granted, for instance, to *meticci* (métis) in Eritrea (the children of "mixed" unions between Italian fathers and Eritrean mothers) and the "special Italian citizenship" offered to select Arabs in Libya examined later in this essay.[10] Citizenship is best understood as "an on-going process, a social complex and a cultural performance" that encapsulates "contradictory struggles over the definition of social membership, over categories and practices of inclusion and exclusion, and over different forms of participation in public life."[11] Who can be declared a citizen and who cannot, and why? What does citizenship mean in Italy and Europe today? What historical precedents exist for the changing terms of citizenship, particularly in Italian colonial Libya? And what role does mobility play in all of these debates?

Whereas the camp, following Agamben's line of thinking, appears to be a space beyond or antecedent to these discourses insofar as it collapses all distinctions (though surely this is not the case), time and again the village proves the form where contentious debates about citizenship—and implicitly race, ethnicity, and nationality—touch down in space. The village turns out to be the exemplary space in the context of modern Italy where the violence wrought by the accordance or refusal of citizenship in Italy's empire comes to be lived and embodied. This essay's task, then, is to theorize the village and the Italian state's co-opting of race and ethnicity to either stamp or deny its mark—citizenship—on its subjects.

The State of Nomad Emergency

In 2012, four years after the declaration of a "nomad emergency" allowed for the destruction of so-called *campi nomadi* (nomad camps) around the Roman periphery, approximately 580 Roma were forcibly resettled into the *villaggio attrezzato* (equipped village) known as La Barbuta. One hundred arrived that July. They were Macedonian Roma forced out of their camp on Via del Baiardo in the Tor di Quinto neighborhood some eighteen miles away. The majority of La Barbuta's residents arrived two months later in September of that same year. Most were Bosnian Roma from the well-established camp at Tor de' Cenci, twelve miles to the east. One forty-year-old Romani man from Montenegro described his impotence in the face of the *sgombero* (eviction): "L'ha deciso il Comune di spostarci, noi non eravamo d'accordo, abbiamo detto migliaia di volte che non volevamo venire qui. Ma avevano deciso così." (The Municipality [of Rome] decided to move us, we were not in agreement, we said thousands of times that we didn't want to come here. But they decided just like that.)[12] Even more insidiously, two employees of the city of Rome confirmed that basic services to the Tor de' Cenci camp were cut off the year before eviction and that the camp was razed for entirely political reasons, that is, to show the effectiveness of the city's so-called nomad plan.[13]

For politicians like Gianni Alemanno and Sveva Belviso, the mayor and vice mayor of Rome, respectively, at the time, the village was a solution to the "hygienic-sanitary problem" created by the "abusive" settlements of the seemingly ungovernable Roma, many of whom were EU citizens and thus legal residents in Italy.[14] Belviso saw the construction of La Barbuta as bringing to fruition Alemanno's controversial *piano nomadi* (nomad plan) drafted in 2009. The plan was part of a larger effort by then prime minister Silvio Berlusconi's government to expulse and repatriate "undesirable" EU citizens back to their countries of origin.[15] To do so, the Italian government enacted an unprecedented act of legislation: a nomad emergency decree, which declared a state of emergency over all nomadic communities in the regions of Lazio, Campania, and Lombardy. On the unruliness of the Roma and the perceived threat of their mobility, Kate Hepworth aptly sums up: "In Europe, gypsy communities—whether self-defined as Roma, Sinti, Manu's, Kale or otherwise—have historically been understood in terms of their '(real, probable or imagined) nomadism.' Defined via their mobility even when sedentary, the Roma as 'nomads' were positioned in opposition to 'settled' society; their presumed mobility was considered a proof of their rejection of the rules of sedentary society."[16] Such a decree was not unlike the state of emergency declared against the Bedouin in Italian colonial Libya some eighty years earlier. The resonances are haunting. The state of emergency allowed Alemanno to implement his nomad plan to the fullest extent—first, through the destruction of nomad camps, razed by government bulldozers; and second, with the construction of villages like La Barbuta where Roma were forcibly resettled and their collective "threat" to public safety held in check by physical and psychological isolation.

The story of La Barbuta, however, begins not in 2008 with the nomad emergency decree but rather in 1995 with the forced relocation of Italian Sinti from their settlement near Cinecittà, the famous film studio in southeastern Rome. Many of the Sinti that I spoke with remembered Cinecittà with nostalgia and remain traumatized by the move. "Siamo come i cani, ci spostano come vogliono" (We are like dogs, they move us as they want), said one Italian Sinti woman of the relocation in an interview with the Roma advocacy group Associazione 21 Luglio.[17] The decision to concentrate Roma and Sinti into settlements—then known as *campi sosta* (temporary camps)—began in earnest under Mayor Francesco Rutelli. The reasons given then were the same ones as given now: the Roma and Sinti presented a risk to hygiene and safety. Daniele Todesco notes that 80 percent of the expulsion orders issued between 1962 and 1986 across thirty-nine Italian municipalities used public health and security as justifications for coerced dislocation.[18] In November 1995, Rutelli's administration ordered the *sgombero* (eviction) of five Roma and Sinti settlements to La Barbuta. Many of the Roma had fled from ex-Yugoslavia, which in the mid-1990s was still embroiled in a brutal civil war that led to the slaughter of thousands of Bosnians.

Rutelli's order came at the time when many Italians were also struggling to come to terms with the demographic and psychic effects of four years of mass arrivals from ex-Yugoslavia, particularly Albania. The images of a drowning and desperate human sea of refugees arriving on rusting tanker ships were seared into the collective Italian consciousness not only by extensive news coverage but also in Oliviero Toscani's use of the images in his infamous Benetton advertising campaign as well as in their circulation via Gianni Amelio's acclaimed 1994 film, *Lamerica*. Arrivals were described in terms of inundation and emergency as an *esodo* (exodus) or *fuga* (escape), and also as part of a broader discourse of invasion, contamination, and contagion.[19] This anxious climate often metamorphosed into violence against Roma and Sinti, who have long been the targets of fear and assault in Italy and Europe. It was in this climate that Rutelli's plan of *trasferimento insediamenti spontanei nomadi* (transfer of spontaneous nomad settlements) was set into motion in Rome.

The resettlements of 1995 were not without protest; however, they did not trigger the sort of extreme violence that accompanied the 2008 nomad emergency declaration and the subsequent clearing of nomad camps. This time the violence was rooted in political and psychic fears surrounding the influx of hundreds of thousands of Romanians who had moved to Italy in search of economic opportunities after Romania acceded to the EU in 2007.[20] Italian politicians scrambled to find a way to deport these masses of people who had the legal right to work and live in Italy.

The tipping point toward emergency came in November 2007 with the savage murder of a forty-seven-year-old housewife named Giovanna Reggiani on the outskirts of Rome by a Romanian immigrant, Nicolai Romulus Mailat.[21] The homicide proved the flashpoint for a nationwide outcry against immigration. Anger and fear were directed toward Romanian Roma (to which Mailat was connected), resulting in a spate of violent attacks. While many Romanians living in Italy are not Roma, this distinction was often lost in public discourse. Călin Popescu Tăriceanu, Romania's prime minister at the time, flew to Italy to defuse the tension but to no avail. Instead, then prime minister Romano Prodi quickly issued an emergency decree that allowed local authorities to expel migrants they considered to be dangerous. This decree laid the groundwork for the later declaration of nomad emergency in May 2008 and aided in the reelection of Silvio Berlusconi as prime minister that same month.

Violence exploded in the days before and after the decree. Whispers of a Romani teenager attempting to kidnap a baby set off a pogrom at the Ponticelli nomad camp on the eastern periphery of Naples. A mob attacked the settlement's Romani inhabitants, sending them fleeing for their lives while burning everything else to the ground.[22] Sadly, this antiziganist pogrom was not the first in Naples nor its last: one need only think about the burning of Romani housing near the suburb of Scampia in 1999 or the stoning of the nomad camp at Poggioreale in 2014.[23] Violence against Roma and Sinti continues to be a daily part of life in much of Italy today.

In the months leading up to the nomad emergency decree in 2008, previously unrelated formations of ethnicity (Roma, Sinti), nationality (Romanians), nomadism, immigration, and violent crime became conflated into a singular danger. The declaration expanded the power of local authorities to expel whomever they saw fit and also to collect biometric data, conduct raids, and dismantle nomad camps at their own discretion. By July 2009, the danger seemed to be so clear and present that the Italian Parliament approved a so-called security package that made it a crime, inter alia, to be an undocumented migrant in Italy. Thus, in less than two decades, from the early 1990s to the present, Italy's most marginalized populations—Roma, Sinti, and foreign migrants—were reframed as problems of national security. Now that actually existing people were recategorized as threats to the general public, questions of social inclusion and integration were no longer considered priorities. Put another way, the actually existing people who also happened to be identified as migrants or Roma or Sinti were wrested away from the realm of humanity and fixed into the realm of national security.

The construction of the village at La Barbuta in 2012 was the culmination in space of years of fear, paranoia, and violence directed toward Italy's most visible and traditionally hated group of Others. The political and legislative measures exercised since 2008 in particular have led to the conflation of foreign migrants with Roma and Sinti, thereby expanding the pool of human targets for racism and xenophobia. Such targets are feared in large part because their mobilities are not sanctioned by the Italian state. As Claudia Aradau writes, "Those who do not conform to the limits and conditions set by the state become dangerous, disorderly excesses that disturb the good functioning of society. As they pose a risk to the good functioning of society itself, their neutralization or elimination can only be a logical corollary."[24] The village at La Barbuta is the space that neutralizes Italy's Roma and Sinti and eliminates the possibility of their participation in state and society. How the village neutralizes and eliminates is particularly insidious in that it shrouds its true aim of national security under the rubric of care, community, and sociality. It is ironic that La Barbuta is also known as a *villaggio di solidarietà* (village of solidarity).

The Village in the Country of Camps

Italy has been called *il paese dei campi* (the country of camps), and for many Roma and Sinti, government-built villages like La Barbuta are the latest iterations of a decades-long campaign of physical segregation and social exclusion. Italy is the only country in the EU that has actively sustained a policy of isolating Roma and Sinti into ghetto-like camps for the better part of three decades.[25] Peripheral nomad camps, however, are not "natural" spaces for Roma and Sinti, many of whom live in apartments and houses. Rather, the naturalization of camps as Romani spaces is the product of a politics that has created the so-called *problema zingari* (gypsy problem). According to Nando Sigona, the wording of "gypsy problem" belies the ambiguity and ambivalence at the heart of Italian policy toward the Romani minority: does solving the "gypsy problem" mean addressing the problems faced by Roma and Sinti, or does it mean resolving the problem that the Roma and Sinti pose to the Italian state?[26] Given the precariousness and exclusion intrinsic to living in villages like La Barbuta, the latter seems the more accurate proposition.

The passage of Roma and Sinti from camp to village was short and deeply traumatic as the interviews with La Barbuta inhabitants conducted by Associazione 21 Luglio reveal. Almost all of them wished to return to the camps they once called home. As one Romani man from Romania put it: "Mi manca tanto Tor de' Cenci, tornerei lì anche senza un container, mi basterebbe una casetta anche distrutta da rimettere a posto. I miei figli sono nati lì, cresciuti lì, hanno la residenza, il medico, la scuola, i compagni, gli amici. Siamo qua perché siamo qua, ma il cuore è lì." (I miss Tor de' Cenci a lot, I would go back there even without a container, just a small wreck of a house for me to fix up would suffice. My children were born there, grew up there, they have residence [there], the doctor, school, companions, friends. We are here because we are here, but the heart is there.)[27] Because these camps were razed to the ground during the "nomad emergency," the residents of La Barbuta, like refugees, can never go home. In this context, the village is not the destination for the latest arrivals from Lampedusa but rather a space of sequestration for people who have lived in Italy for decades, sometimes their entire lives. The label of "village" is a euphemism that changes little functionally with respect to the camp. Like the nomad camps sanctioned by the Italian government, the village is a space of legalized racism that segregates and alienates, and sustains the "condition of exceptionality through which the Roma are managed."[28]

Whether in the form of camps or villages, Romani settlements have received much attention from the Italian mass media, nonprofit organizations, supranational agencies, and academics from across disciplines.[29] Yet many Romani inhabitants in Italy, possibly even the majority, live in permanent housing. Approximately 140,000–160,000 Roma and Sinti are living in Italy; however, these are generally accepted estimates given the paucity of official statistics.[30] All groups of Roma together represent less than 1 percent of Italy's total population.[31] More than half are Italian citizens who descend from Romani communities that were established in Italy during the late Middle Ages. Before this, the

Roma are thought to have migrated from northwest India via the Middle East, arriving in Greece and the Balkans as early as the eleventh century.

Geneticists, too, have undertaken exhaustive studies to trace the origins of the Romani people by mapping the European Romani genome. They concur the Roma originated from a single population in northwestern India 1,500 years ago and date their arrival in the Balkans to 900 years ago.[32] To note, the parallels between the "colonial science" carried out in Italian East Africa in the early twentieth century (for example, measuring skull sizes) and the genome mapping of Romani people in the present day are striking insofar as both serve to biologize difference. The latter reduces difference to a scientific building block—the gene—and frames the Romani people as resolutely different in biological terms from the rest of Europe. Such "scientific" studies deserve increased ethical scrutiny for the ways in which they further alienate Europe's internal Others by reifying their difference in the seemingly incontrovertible terms of modern genetics and scientific objectivity.

There are three indigenous Romani groups in Italy: the Roma, Sinti, and Camminanti. Of the three, the Camminanti are the smallest and the least in public view. Little is known about their origins; however, the community is historically based in Sicily and travels throughout Italy for part of the year. The second group, the Sinti, arrived in the north-central Italy overland from the Balkans around the fifteenth century. Of all the Romani populations in Italy, a small portion of Sinti remains semi-itinerant owing to their work, often with traveling carnivals. One Sinti resident of La Barbuta, B., told me that he used to work with the *giostra* (carousel), but the isolation of the village now made it impossible for him to do this job. The third indigenous Romani group, the Roma, are believed to have crossed the Adriatic Sea from the Balkans and settled in the southern part of the country sometime during the fifteenth century. The minority Albanian communities known as Arbëreshë are also believed to have arrived in southern Italy in the same century. The Arbëreshë left Albania as the Ottoman Empire invaded the Balkans, with Suleiman the Magnificent capturing Belgrade in 1521. It is possible that the Roma, too, could have fled westward to escape persecution. Italy, however, was far from a safe haven. According to Shannon Woodcock, the first recorded expulsion of Roma happened in Milan in 1493—it, too, on the grounds of nomadism. She adds: "The stereotype of nomadism is a powerful discursive frame that persists at the core of contemporary anti-Romani prejudice. This stereotype is linked to a discourse that imagines the entire people as criminal, irreverent towards religion, harbouring sinister magical powers and primitive, as evidenced in promiscuity, dancing, and baby-snatching. This cluster of stereotypes has simultaneously enabled those who project them to remain settled, God-fearing and civilized, and be recognized within local administrative structures."[33]

Similar to the aforementioned genome-mapping project, the stereotypes of European Romani were united under the rubric of criminal science by the criminal anthropologist Cesare Lombroso in the late nineteenth century. His codification of gypsy criminality in *L'uomo delinquente* (The delinquent man, 1876) linked the cultural stereotypes about gypsies to the biological constitution of the Roma as a race. He writes: "Non così dirsi degli zingari che sono l'immagine viva di una razza intera di delinquente e ne producono tutte le passioni ed i vizi." (Not so to say of the gypsies who are the living image of an entire delinquent race, and they bear all the passions and vices.)[34] Lombroso goes on to describe the purportedly inhuman behaviors of gypsies, who, he claims, as a race, disregard the rules of propriety and civilization, no less the greatest taboo of all, cannibalism: "Amanti dell'orgia, del rumore, nei mercati ne fanno grandi schiamazzi; feroce, assassinano senza rimorso, a scopo di lucro; si sospettarono, anni sono, di cannibalismo." (Lovers of the orgy, of uproar, in the markets they make loud rackets; fierce, they assassinate without remorse for profit; they have been suspected of cannibalism for years.)[35] This line of race-thinking, as Hannah Arendt famously argued, not only set the foundation for Western eugenics but also established racism as the main ideological weapon of imperialistic politics, becoming the very instrument through which the new body politic of the nation-state was realized.[36]

It comes as no surprise, then, that Romani people in Italy were the targets of Fascist Racial Laws in 1938. Both Italian and foreign-born Roma bore the brunt of increased violence against them. In September 1940, the Directorate General of Public Security issued an order to expel the latter from the country and to intern Italian Roma in concentration camps. The justifications for doing so were the Roma's "natural" criminality, "essi commettono talvolta delitti gravi per natura" (they sometimes commit grave crimes by nature), and their capacity to carry out antinational activities, "vi siano elementi capaci di esplicare attività antinazionale" (there are elements capable of carrying out anti-national activity).[37]

In a move hauntingly similar to the *sgomberi* (evictions) of the twenty-first century, many Roma were forced into concentration camps by 1944, including one on the Tremiti Islands where Libyan deportees had been held for decades. Elsewhere in Europe and the Soviet Union, Romani people were not only persecuted but also exterminated with cold brutality. Estimates of the death toll range from ninety-six thousand to half a million, with the likely figure in excess of two hundred thousand in what is known as Porrajmos (the Devouring), the term for "holocaust" in the Romani language.[38] Some twenty-three thousand Roma were deported to Auschwitz-Birkenau and held in a special compound known as the *Zigeunerfamilienlager* (gypsy family camp) that was headed by the infamous doctor Josef Mengele, known for his sadistic medical experiments.

The Nazi regime was not the only one determined to destroy the Roma as a group; the Ustaše—a Fascist, terrorist movement in Croatia from 1929 to 1945—also had the same aim. The Ustaše wished to create a racially pure Croatia in the name of which they systematically murdered hundreds of thousands of Serbs, Jews, and Roma. Many of the foreign-born Roma living in Fascist Italy were actually refugees fleeing this ethnic cleansing. Deportation back to Yugoslavia meant certain death at the hands of the Ustaše. Historians have only begun to analyze the patterns of Romani persecution in Nazi-dominated Europe, and after decades of neglect, to account for the ways in which the memory of the Porrajmos still scars the European Romani community. Similar to the Bedouin of Italian colonial Libya, theirs was a genocide marginalized in part because its victims were quite literally moving targets.

Daily Life in the Village, or 22.5 Square Meters

The history of the Roma in Europe is one of perpetual exclusion and violence. Many scholars, activists, and filmmakers have brought this history to light and continue to expose the unsettling conditions of the nomad camps and the container villages in which many Roma in Italy still live today.[39] Of the eight thousand Roma and Sinti who live in or near Rome, for example, more than 60 percent live in settlements built and paid for by the municipal government (map 3).[40]

There are fine gradations in terminology for such settlements not unlike the system of Italy's migrant detention centers. *Villaggio attrezzato* (equipped village) is the most common term to describe the current container parks; it evolved from the so-called *campo attrezzato* (equipped camp) of the mid-1990s. Another term is *villaggio di solidarietà* (solidarity village), which came into use around 2013 after the center-left government came into power. Beginning in 2009, the Roman municipal government also funded the creation of *centri di raccolta Rom* (Roma collection centers). Like the sea of rubbish surrounding La Barbuta, the very name of these places links Roma with refuse, for the phrase *centri di raccolta* (collection centers) in vernacular Italian is typically associated with waste management. The name implies that Roma are to be collected, and disposed of, like trash. The intention behind these centers was to rehouse Romani families whose homes had been razed during the so-called nomad emergency in 2008. In practice, however, the centers function to further segregate

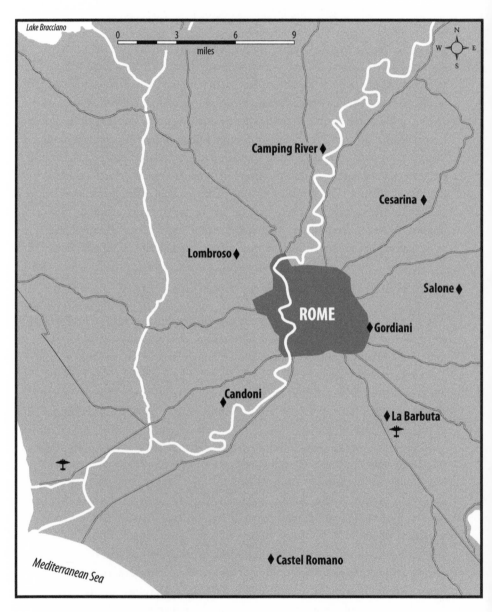

MAP 3. The government-funded *villaggi attrezzati* (equipped villages) built for Roma on the outskirts of Rome in 2016.

the Roma by ethnicity and isolate them from the rest of society, according to a report by Associazione 21 Luglio.[41] Whether village or collection center, government-built settlements for Roma share a single objective: to create a space where a distinct set of "undesirables" who threaten the Italian state with their unsanctioned mobilities can be contained and governed by law.

Residents often compare life in the village to prison. One resident of La Barbuta, twenty-eight-year-old V., spoke of the isolation of the village as incarceration: "Qui stiamo male, siamo nel nulla, è come essere a Rebibbia." (Here we are not well, we are in the nothing, it is like being at [the prison] Rebibbia.) Another occupant, twenty-year-old D., once worked at a restaurant in the city center, but the lack of public transportation prevented him from getting there and he lost his job. Like V., he described La Barbuta as a prison: "Ho sprecato due anni della mia vita, avevo un lavoro in un ristorante a Ponte Milvio, ma qui che faccio? Senza macchina non posso arrivare fin laggiù. Ti sembra normale? È come essere in prigione." (I wasted two years of my life, I had a job in a restaurant by Ponte Milvio, but here what do I do? Without [a] car I can't get there. Does that seem normal to you? It's like being in prison.)[42] Unable to work, D. often withdrew into a different, isolated world: the virtual reality of video games. Miriana, a resident of the village at Via Salone, described the mass of people living on top of one another: "Siamo tutti attaccati alla fine. Per me fa schifo, dico la verità, fa schifo perché . . . è come che fosse in un carcere." (We are all stuck [together] in the end. For me, it's disgusting, I tell the truth, it's disgusting because . . . it's like it would be in prison.)[43] In prison, at least in theory, basic needs are met and certain rights guarded. Prisoners have an identity and a sentence to serve. In the village, however, time takes on an attenuated quality as it does in the CIE of Ponte Galeria. Miriana was supposed to stay at Via Salone for only four months, after which she was promised a house. She has been waiting for three years: "Alla fine sono tre anni che stiamo qui. Ci hanno spostato qui a Salone, in mezzo al nulla." (In the end, it's been three years that we've been here. They moved us here to Salone, in the middle of nothing.) She lives with her husband and their six children in a container that measures 22.5 square meters, or 242 square feet. She does not know when, or if, they will be able to leave.

Life among the containers is bleak. As Miriana noted above, it is life in the middle of nowhere (*mezzo al nulla*), or more to the point as V. implied, it is existence in the face of oblivion (*siamo nel nulla*). At Via Salone, where Miriana lives, loud music blares, and for a while it mutes the din of crying children and bickering voices. Everybody is in everyone's business, she says. The 2013 documentary film by Stefano Liberti and Enrico Parenti, *Container 158*, records the struggle of living there. Children are bused to school more than an hour away; however, the kids report that the bus is always late and they get blamed for their tardiness. Between the reprimands and the insurmountable logistics, among other factors, many lapse into truancy.

Adults are in a similar situation when it comes to work. Employment is precarious and most often under the table. Remi, for instance, fixes cars and scooters for friends and acquaintances who pay what they can. Giuseppe once drove a van around Rome picking up scrap metal to sell to junkyards, but this ended once authorities determined he did not have the proper license. He felt the only choice left to him was to steal: "Non c'ho più il ferro. Devo avere l'autorizzazione, devo avere il formulario, devo avere la licenza . . . deve in banca trenta, quarantamila euro . . . che fo, andà a ruba? Che faccio? Devo mantenere i figli. Vado a rubà . . . eh? Ci levano il lavoro. Ci levano tutto." (I don't have the scrap metal any more. I need authorization. I need the [right] form. I need the license. I need thirty, forty thousand euros in the bank. . . . What do I do? Go to steal? What do I do? I have to support my children. I go to steal . . . eh? They take away work. They take away everything.)[44] From this perspective, life in the village seems to force one into a life of criminality. Even those like Giuseppe, who seemingly does not want to steal, feel as if they have no other choice. In the village, crossing the line from legal to illegal once again transforms illegality into a lived-in, existential category. The look of resignation on Giuseppe's face said it all: according to him, to survive as a Roma living in Italy, one must disregard the law and accept this as moral fact.

"When You Have Papers, You Have Everything"

Documenti (papers) are seen as the deus ex machina that can lift a person out of the village and, implicitly, out of a life of social exclusion, poverty, and violence. As Sasha, fifteen, another resident of Via Salone, said: "Quando c'hai documenti, c'hai tutto." (When you have papers, you have everything.) Having papers allows one to get a driver's license, buy a car, rent an apartment, and find steady work—that is, they allow access to the fundamental rights accorded to any Italian citizen. With papers, one becomes regolare (legal). Sasha continued: "Se io ero italiano, c'avevo la carta d'identità, c'avevo tutto, c'avevo. No, non sono italiano, sono zingaro . . . Se non c'hai documenti, c'hai niente." (If I were Italian, I would have an identity card, I'd have everything, I'd have. No, I'm not Italian, I'm gyspy. . . . If you don't have papers, you have nothing.) Many Romani children are born and raised in Italy, but like the second-generation children of immigrants, they have no rights to Italian citizenship, which is accorded on the basis of kinship (jus sanguinis), not birthplace (jus soli). Guido Tintori points out the irony—and the injustice—inherent in the example of third-generation Brazilians with Italian great-grandfathers gaining citizenship without so much as speaking the language or stepping foot on Italian soil, whereas second-generation children of Chinese immigrants who are born and raised in Italy have little or no recourse to citizenship. Tintori writes: "It is worth noting that long-term, non-EU, foreign residents in Italy do not enjoy any kind of political rights, not even at the local level, unless they naturalize."[45] Yet naturalization is a difficult process, one with opaque requirements that seem to change with every new government that comes into power.

Often, these changes result in Kafkaesque predicaments such as that of Brenda Salkanovic, nineteen, another resident of the village at Via Salone. In a scene from *Container 158*, Brenda speaks with a social worker about her residency status in a trailer that doubles as a bureaucratic armamentarium. Surrounded by file folders and a computer screen, Brenda learns that, despite being born and raised in Rome, she will have to declare statelessness in order to obtain a *permesso di soggiorno* (permit of stay):

SOCIAL WORKER: "Tu sei Brenda Salkanovic, vero?"
BRENDA: "Sì."
SW: "E c'hai passaporto?"
B: "No."
SW: "Non hai passaporto."
B: "No. Nessun documento."
SW: "Da dove provieni te? Visto che sei nata a Roma, poi i tuoi genitori da dove vengono?"
B: "Da Montenegro."
SW: "Montenegro. Da Nikšić?"
B: "Sì, Nikšić."
SW: "OK, Nikšić. Né papà né mamma hanno un passaporto?"
B: "Mio padre ha un passaporto ma è scaduto. L'hanno cancellato da Montenegro."
SW: "Allora, per avere cittadinanza italiana, tu devi avere una residenza ininterrotta in Italia da quando sei nata . . ."
B: "Sì, ce l'ho."
SW: ". . . fino a quando hai compiuto diciotto anni."
B: "Ce l'ho."
SW: "Tutti e due genitori, quando sei nata te, dovevano essere legalmente presenti sul territorio nazionale. Tutti e due genitori devono avere sempre avuto permessi di soggiorno per diciotto anni. E cittadinanza si chiede dal diciottesimo fino al diciannovesimo anno di vita. Non dopo. Unico modo di avere un permesso di soggiorno

adesso visto che hai diciannove anni, e non sei iscritta un paese d'origine, poi chiedi l'apolidia, e poi si chiede il permesso di soggiorno per attesa apolidia."

SOCIAL WORKER: "You're Brenda Salkanovic, right?"

BRENDA: "Yes."

SW: "And do you have a passport?"

B: "No."

SW: "You don't have a passport."

B: "No. No papers."

SW: "Where do you originate from? Since you were born in Rome, then your parents, where do they come from?"

B: "From Montenegro."

SW: "Montenegro. From Nikšić?"

B: "Yes, Nikšić."

SW: "OK, Nikšić. Neither your dad nor your mom have a passport?"

B: "My father has a passport but it expired. They cancelled it from Montenegro."

SW: "Then, to have Italian citizenship, you must have continuous residence in Italy from the time you were born . . ."

B: "Yes, I've got it."

SW: ". . . until you turned eighteen years old."

B: "I have it."

SW: "Both parents, when you were born, must have been legally present in the national territory. Both parents must have always had permits of stay for eighteen years. And one requests citizenship from eighteen to nineteen years old. Not after. The only way to obtain a permit of stay now, since you are nineteen, and you're not registered in a country of origin, then, is to request statelessness, and then, to request the permit of stay for pending statelessness."

At first, Brenda is eager and repeatedly declares that she has had continuous residency in Italy for eighteen years. Yet as the social worker explains the increasingly impossible prerequisites for citizenship—her parents' continual legal residence in Italy, the limited time frame in which to request citizenship (between eighteen and nineteen years of age), the need for her to declare statelessness—Brenda's hope deflates in a matter of seconds. She rolls her eyes and her face appears to harden with disappointment and frustration. Remi, the aforementioned auto mechanic, put it best: when you become an adult in Italy, you simply disappear. Brenda adds that when she was younger she never thought about papers, but now she thinks about them all the time, often with resignation: "Poi quando ho compiuto diciotto anni, ci penso troppo questi documenti, queste cose qua, perché vorrei avere un lavoro, no? Ma, forse potrò, forse no. Non lo so. Senza i documenti non posso fare niente." (Then when I turned eighteen, I think about these documents too much, these things here, because I would like to get a job, right? But, maybe I can, maybe not. I don't know. Without documents, I can't do anything.) Again, like Sasha, she reiterates that without papers, she has nothing.

Brenda's experience represents not only frustration with bureaucracy—which Italians, too, know all too well—but also a brand of oblique violence contained within the exercise of paperwork. The Italian state denies citizenship through the creation of bureaucratic obstacles, and this refusal of citizenship, rather than recognition, is the very stamp that the state puts on its subjects in the village. The *ospiti* in the CIE at Ponte Galeria play a different game of citizenship. They have already been recognized or are in the process of being identified as citizens who belong to a state. For those in the *villaggi*, regardless of where one was born or where one lives, that possibility is almost foreclosed from the outset. It is a different passage along the *via negativa* wherein the absence of the state—statelessness—becomes an instrument of state power. Brenda's declaration of pending statelessness is, in effect, an action of the Italian state projected onto a subject, one who is the subject of and subject to the state, which in turn recognizes her through its refusal.

While the Italian state uses the law of *jus sanguinis* to justify ethnic discrimination (in both the recognition and refusal of citizenship) and deploys statelessness to shore up state power, its creation of the *villaggio* also amplifies ethno-national divisions in space. Mariana explains these divisions while drawing the spatial layout of the village at Via Salone. She sketches a grid and explains: "Qua stanno bosniaci, ci stanno su una ventina di container. Bosniaci. Poi rumeni. Rumeni. Poi ci stanno di nuovo bosniaci, poi dopo i bosniaci arrivano i montenegrini, in mezzo a questi montenegrini ci stanno anche serbi. Non è che siamo pochi, siamo abbastanza adesso." (Here there are Bosnians, they stay in roughly twenty containers. Bosnians. Then Romanians. Romanians. Then, there are Bosnians again, and after the Bosnians there arrive the Montenegrins, and in the middle of these Montenegrins, there are also Serbians. It's not like we are few, we are quite a lot now.) In the space of the village, ethno-national divisions are clear-cut, and the proximity of the containers intensifies their boundaries. F. confirmed there was a similar situation at La Barbuta, telling me that in addition to the distinctions within the village there was an even greater division between the Italian-born Roma and Sinti, like himself, and all the other foreign-born Roma. In precisely this way, the village is a striated space both within and without, a space where difference is amplified and overseen by the state. It is a space that Loïc Wacquant would call "advanced marginality," the "regime of sociospatial relegation and exclusionary closure that has crystallized in the post-Fordist city as a result of the uneven development of the capitalist economies and the recoiling of welfare states."[46]

Similar to the matrices of race and class that shape the American hyperghetto or the French *banlieue*, the *villaggio* is given form by institutional logics of segregation and aggregation that are distinctly Italian. In one way, the *villaggi* are linked to the modern development of the *periferia romana* (Roman periphery), and in particular, the aestheticization of this periphery in post–World War II Italian literature and cinema. In particular, works like Pier Paolo Pasolini's *Ragazzi di vita* (The Ragazzi, 1955) and *Una vita violenta* (A violent life, 1959), and his film *Accattone* (1961) introduced audiences to the bleak landscapes and violent existence inhabited by Rome's lumpenproletariat. Scenes of Italy's urban marginality were broadcast around the world. Even in death, the famous image of Pasolini's lifeless, brutalized body deserted on a beach near Ostia underscored the unbidden barbarism of the Roman periphery. Thus, the images of poverty and violence linked to present-day *campi nomadi* and *villaggi attrezzati* have as their aesthetic precursors the Roman underclass of a not-so-distant past.

Additionally, both the nomad camp and the equipped village are connected to the historical logics of segregation, concentration, and citizenship rooted in Italy's colonial project in Libya. The following section traces the interwoven passages of Bedouin and colonists from the concentration camps on the Cyrenaican plains to the *villaggi agricoli* (agricultural villages) and *villaggi musulmani* (Muslim villages) built along the Jabal Akhdar (Green Mountains) in the 1930s and 1940s, and whose differential mobilities, like those of Roma and Sinti today, complicated the notions of race, ethnicity, and citizenship in the face of the Italian state.

The Village as Colonial Destiny

The Jabal Akhdar, or Green Mountain, region of Cyrenaica has been touted as one of Libya's most beautiful and also its most fertile (figure 14). The Greek historian Herodotus famously wrote of Cyrene's "three amazing seasons" and compared Libya's crops to the abundant harvests of Babylonia.[47] Even today, the plateau erupts into virid splendor after the rains. Junipers and pines line earthen terraces that are reminiscent of faraway New Mexican mesas. The ruins of Cyrene, too, stand on a hillside in view of the sea. Headless statues and empty tombs seem to testify, after so many centuries, to "the powerful but

FIGURE 14.   Ruins of an Italian-built *podere* (homestead) in the Jabal Akhdar region of Cyrenaica, Libya, 2005. Photograph reproduced by permission from Sean Anderson.

unrecorded race that once dwelt in that annihilated place," to quote the poet Horace Smith on Ozymandias.[48] Likewise, the region has a well-earned reputation for political unrest. Herodotus described the violent, almost sadistic conflicts that took place among Greeks, Persians, and Barkaians near the town of Barce (also Barqa) in the fifth century BCE. Forces clashed in underground tunnels around the besieged city, and among the many atrocities committed, men were impaled and women's breasts cut off and hung along the walls.[49] In 2017, the city remained a hotbed of sectarian violence. It saw intense fighting during the Libyan Civil War and emerged as a stronghold for Islamic State militants. Thus, violence and agricultural fecundity have long been hallmarks of the Jabal Akhdar. This was little different under Italian rule.

When Italian troops landed in Tripoli, roughly 198,000 people inhabited Cyrenaica, according to the last Ottoman census conducted in 1911.[50] Most belonged to seminomadic tribes that made their homes in the Jabal Akhdar, subsisting on livestock herded seasonally throughout the plateau. Federico Cresti notes that Cyrenaica was among the most "Arabized" regions outside Saudi Arabia after the Muslim conquests of the seventh century.[51] The spread of Islam through the Maghreb institutionalized discrimination against ethnic and religious minorities, like Berbers and Christians, and often forced their assimilation. In the eleventh century in particular, Cyrenaica was overrun with Arabs from the east. More than one million men, women, and children made their way across the region, which the fourteenth-century historian Ibn Khaldun famously described as a swarm of locusts destroying everything in its path. This influx solidified the Arabization of North Africa. The sixteenth century marked the beginning of Ottoman rule in Libya, and for the next two hundred years, more or less, the Sublime Porte assumed a laissez-faire approach to governance. The pashas installed in Tripoli and Benghazi were left to their own devices to collect tributes and manage allegiances; some, such as Ahmed Bey Qaramanli in Tripoli, established dynasties of their own.[52] In Cyrenaica, the religious political order of the Sanusi set up a state-like system of government that superseded Ottoman authority in practice. Yet all this changed when European powers began to stake claims on African territory, first through explorations and then through formal entreaties. The so-called Scramble for Africa culminated with the Berlin Conference of 1884–85, which effectively partitioned the continent into European colonies.

In Cyrenaica, explorers such as Agostino Cervelli (1811–12), Paolo Della Cella (1817), Gerhard Rohlfs (1868–69), Giuseppe Haimann (1881), and Pietro Mamoli (1881) extensively documented the natural environment, and many called for Italy to take over the administration of the region from the Ottoman Empire. In July 1884, for example, the Milan-based La Società d'Esplorazione Commerciale in Africa (Society for Commercial Exploration in Africa) petitioned the Italian Ministry of Foreign Affairs to push the Sublime Porte for territorial concessions in Cyrenaica under the auspices of agricultural colonization.[53] The president of the society, Manfredo Camperio, declared his intentions to found *colonie agricole* (agricultural colonies) in Cyrenaica, and argued there was precedent for the Ottomans to concede land because they had done so for the German government in Syria and Palestine after a similar request. Less than a decade later, the journalist Guglielmo De Toth suggested in an 1895 letter to the Ministry of Foreign Affairs that it was no longer necessary to ask for concessions as the Ottoman Empire was about to fall and that Italians should profit from its ruination: "L'Impero Ottomano sta per fallire. Lo sfascio è imminente . . . E non sarebbe il caso di utilizzare coteste rovine, tentandone l'acquisto almeno in parte?" (The Ottoman Empire is about to fall. The collapse is imminent. . . . And wouldn't it be the case to exploit these ruins, to attempt the acquisition thereof at least in part?)[54] In 1909, the Jewish Territorial Organization, led by John Walter Gregory, made a trip to Cyrenaica to assess the possibility of founding a Jewish state there. Gregory ultimately decided that it lacked sufficient natural resources to support a large Jewish population but said that Italy should colonize it instead.[55] It was against this backdrop that Italian troops invaded Tripoli in September 1911.

Valorization of a "Land Ruined by Nomads"

The first years of Italian occupation in Cyrenaica were characterized by a politics of conciliation and cooperation. Historians such as Angelo Del Boca, Federico Cresti, Dirk Vandewalle, and Nicola Labanca have covered these events in detail; therefore I will limit my description to the broadest of strokes in order to focus attention on the villages built for the arrival of the colonists known as the Ventimila in 1938. To summarize, the Sanusi order initially allied with Ottoman forces to resist Italian colonization; however, this changed with the Acroma Pact, signed between the head of the Sanusi, Sayyid Idris, and the Italian colonial administration in April 1917. This pact established a tenuous ceasefire while ceding control of almost all of Cyrenaica to the Sanusi, save for a small coastal strip that went to the Italians. Further statutes issued after World War I, like the 1919 Legge Fondamentale (Fundamental Law), established a special category of Italian citizenship for certain Libyans and aimed to solidify Italy's control over Cyrenaica and Tripolitania vis-à-vis a politics of cooperation.[56]

In the following years, Italian offices and organizations dedicated to agricultural colonization took root throughout Libya. In 1921, the Ufficio per i Servizi Agrari della Cirenaica (Office of Agrarian Services of Cyrenaica) was established under the direction of Armando Maugini, who would later become head of the powerful Istituto Agronomico per l'Oltremare (Overseas Agricultural Institute). The latter oversaw agricultural development throughout the Italian colonies and played a critical role in planning the settlements for the Ventimila. Maugini famously called Cyrenaica "un paese rovinato dai nomadi" (a land ruined by nomads) but worked tirelessly to transform the region into an agricultural arcadia.[57] He, like so many others, was intent on the *valorizzazione* (valorization) of Libya.

Similar to the tropes of the civilizing mission or the colonized subject as child, the rhetoric of valorization infused the entire Italian colonial project, not only in Libya but also in eastern Africa. These were lands that needed Italian intervention in order to show the world their "value" as well as that of Italy as a colonizing power. The term itself, *valorizzazione*, is ambiguous and polysemous. It connotes a simultaneous process of exploitation, valuation, and valorization. It can be qualified by many adjectives too: for example, moral, commercial, economic, political, agricultural, and touristic valorization were all arguments made for Italy's colonial practices in Libya. Indeed, "agricultural" was the most common qualifier of the noun (viz. *valorizzazione agricola*) as it related to Cyrenaica. Policymakers shrouded violent acts such as the unwarranted disposal of Bedouin property and the mass internment in concentration

camps under the rhetoric of agricultural valorization, as if economic ends justified such savage means.

The plans to bring *valorizzazione* to fruition in Cyrenaica centered on agriculture, and at first, through the "cooperation" between Italians and Arabs
such as that fostered by the joint Società Agricola Italo-Araba (Italo-Arab Agricultural Society) in 1921. According to Federico Cresti, certain policymakers in Rome championed the idea of an agricultural consortium between
Italians and Libyans—the so-called Consorzio Nazionale di Emigrazione e
Lavoro (National Consortium of Emigration and Labor)—that was to be composed of two-thirds Italians and one-third Libyans.[58] However, there is little
to suggest this organization ever developed beyond the initial planning phases,
especially as the character of colonial operations shifted when the Fascist regime came to power in 1922. In the place of an agricultural consortium based
on joint Italian-Libyan participation, what developed instead were *colonie
penali agricole* (agricultural penal colonies) where Libyans were criminalized, imprisoned, and forced into hard labor in the service of agricultural
valorization.

Agricultural Penal Colonies

The *colonie penali agricole* built in the early 1920s served as the structural and
functional precursors of the *villaggi agricoli* (agricultural villages) and *villaggi musulmani* (Muslim villages) built in the mid to late 1930s. It is a space where the
island, the camp, and the village all metaphorically meet. In Tripolitania, the agricultural penal colony of Sghedeida, about eight miles southeast of Tripoli,
held 400 prisoners. The 1929 Touring Club Italiano guidebook claimed it looked
a bit like the Roman countryside with undulating terrain and eucalyptus trees.[59]
There were three agricultural penal colonies in Cyrenaica: Coefia (Kuwayfiyah),
about eight miles to the northeast of Benghazi, which housed 150 detainees;
Berca (Al-Berka), located in Benghazi proper, had roughly 100 along with 4 Italian administrators and 15 *agenti indigeni* (indigenous agents) who presumably
enforced day-to-day operations; and Castellaccio, three miles from Benghazi
with 100 prisoners, 4 Italian administrators, and 8 indigenous guards.[60] Contemporaneous articles in the Fascist magazine *L'Italia Coloniale* revealed three of the
four agricultural penal colonies were founded between 1921 and 1923 (Castellaccio was built in 1928), more than seven years before the system of concentration
camps in Cyrenaica. As in the camps, detainees were exclusively *indigeni* (natives), although there were some debates about transferring Italian *coatti* (prisoners) from Italy's carceral islands to serve out the remainder of their sentences in
the Libyan fields.[61] This plan, however, never came to pass.

As on Ustica, Ponza, and Lampedusa, detainees in these agricultural penal colonies were housed in *cameroni* (large rooms) that were locked at night. For example, most of Sghedeida's 400 prisoners were held twenty-five to a room, whereas those singled out for solitary confinement were detained in one of fifty-six isolation cells.[62] Most were transfers from the overcrowded civil prison, Castello di Tripoli. They both slept and cooked in the *cameroni* and were guarded by two battalions of Eritrean *askari* (soldiers) who camped in *tukuls* (huts) outside the central building. The detainees husbanded animals and manned 125 hectares of crops, among them almonds, mulberry, citrus, olives, and Australian acacia. In a quintessential example of colonial stereotyping, Edoardo Maggiolini waxed enthusiastically about the necessity of hard labor for "lazy Arabs" in a 1928 article about Sghedeida:[63]

L'arabo trova nel carcere non una punizione che lo avii a redenzione ma una lusinga al suo abito di infingardaggine contemplativa onde fu nato che si risolveva in premio quello che doveva essergli castigo. Occorreva un incitamento, un obbligo di lavoro che lo togliesse alla sua pigra sonnolenza atavica.

The Arab finds in prison not a punishment that directs him toward redemption, but rather an enticement to his habit of contemplative idleness; so that it turned out what should have been a punishment ended up a reward. An incentive was needed, an obligation of work that would take away his lazy, atavistic indolence.

According to Maggiolini, agricultural labor provided both the material and moral incentive, that is, *valore* in both senses of value and valor. Prisoners would have the chance to earn a small stipend, but more importantly, in his opinion, their work would offset the costs of detention while fostering social renewal and moral improvement among the prisoners. Crops could eventually be sold and laborers rented out to private enterprises for a fee. Maggiolini added that Sghedeida was to be a model for prisoner work-release programs in the metropole, obviously unaware that such programs had existed informally throughout Italy's carceral archipelago since the turn of the century. What was unique about the agricultural penal colonies in Libya was the way in which they were linked to the message of *valorizzazione agricola* (agricultural valorization) that was used to justify Italy's colonial presence there.

Both Sghedeida in Tripolitania and Berca in Cyrenaica were proximate to formal schools and offices of colonial agriculture. Of the former, the famed Regia Scuola di Agricoltura (Royal School of Agriculture), inaugurated in February 1914, was just a few miles away. This school provided the administrative support for agricultural endeavors in the colony, including experimental projects. The vast orchards and grapevines of the latter, Berca, abutted the Regia Ufficio per i Servizi Agrari della Cirenaica (Royal Office of the Agricultural Services of Cyrenaica), an entomology museum, and a new park, the seventeen-hectare Bosco del Littorio (Forest of the Lictor). Both Berca and Coefia in Cyrenaica expanded under the direction of prison warden Francesco Stagno. According to a 1926 article in *L'Italia Coloniale*, Stagno and his indigenous prisoners transformed a wasteland into "un podere fertilissimo che può competere con i più ubertosi terreni metropolitani" (a fertile homestead that can compete re with the most uberous plots in the metropole).[64] Attilio Teruzzi, governor of Cyrenaica from 1926 to 1928, took a special interest in both agricultural penal colonies, declaring them institutions indispensable to colonial development. He noted that Libyan prisoners were to prepare the plots for colonists before their arrival so that the Italians "non si troveranno così a dare fatica e denaro in un lavoro improbo" (will not find themselves as such expending energy and money on grueling work).[65]

Several photographs housed in the archive of the Istituto Agronomico per l'Oltremare in Florence provide a record of the grueling work that took place in these agricultural penal colonies.[66] One photograph (presumably of Coefia or Berca) shows about a dozen men dressed in white uniforms hunched over, at work in a grove of saplings. Some are digging with shovels, others with their bare hands. Still others have what appear to be canvas seed bags slung across their shoulders like the plantation slaves of an earlier era in the American South. They were putting down roots for what Tito Cicinelli described in 1932 as a "vera oasi lussureggiante in mezzo ad una plaga desertica" (truly lush oasis in the middle of a desert playa).[67] Another photograph shows three dozen men scattered about a dirt-filled yard drawn low into various poses ranging from crouch to cower. They are weaving on giant floor looms. The camera caught many in midstroke; one can almost hear the rat-a-tat of their shuttles at work. The man standing at the center of the frame projects authority over the scene. His crossed arms and wide stance hint at military training, but perhaps more accurately they recall the stilted postures of Mussolini himself. He oversees the proceedings. No one looks at him.

Teruzzi called for the construction of additional agricultural penal colonies for they would advance not only the economy of Italian colonial Libya but also its civilizing mission. Again, he deploys the "moral and material" dyad common to Italian colonial rhetoric:[68]

D'altre parte il Governo avrà, con il lavoro salutare dei detenuti indigeni, anticipato materialmente quei sussidi e quegli aiuti che normalmente dà per la colonizzazione. Da un'opera altamente educatrice e civilizzatrice sarà quindi ricavato un utile pratico per la economia della Cirenaica.

On the other hand, the Government, with the salutary work of indigenous prisoners, will have anticipated materially those subsidies and those aids that are normally given for colonization. From a highly edifying and civilizing endeavor, then, a practical utility for Cyrenaica's economy will be extracted.

By 1940, however, few, if any, additional agricultural penal colonies were operating in Libya. Sghedeida and Berca still existed, but Coefia had been privatized by that time. Interestingly, the Touring Club Italiano guidebook published that same year classified Sghedeida not as an agricultural penal colony but rather as a "centro rurale" (rural center) that was the "opera dei carcerati musulmani del vicino penitenziario" (work of Muslim prisoners of the nearby penitentiary).[69] The rural center was another name given to the agricultural village, and this shift in nomenclature also represented a transfer in function. The segregation, incarceration, and forced labor of natives were no longer the domain of the penal colony (or the camp, for that matter), but instead they became that of the village.

Zawiyas

The rise of *villaggi* (villages) in both Libya and metropolitan Italy was part of the Fascist regime's twin projects of *bonifica* (land reclamation) and *colonizzazione demografica* (demographic colonization). Villages were constructed in the name of reclamation and populated in the name of demographic colonization. As Mia Fuller notes, "The government intended the settlements to be 'ethnic Italian islands,' and with very few exceptions, writers represented them as such. In practice, however, Italians in the settlements were anything but isolated."[70] Sometimes these villages were referred to as *città nuove* (new towns) or *centri rurali* (rural centers); however, this nomenclature lacks the categorizing power of the village. In Italian colonial Libya, there was a sharp distinction between *villaggi agricoli* (agricultural villages) and *villaggi musulmani* (Muslim villages, also referred to as indigenous villages). Libyan workers housed in the latter built the former for the incoming masses of Italian colonists in 1938 known as the Ventimila. Perversely, many of those laborers were Bedouin survivors of the concentration camps who had been forcibly relocated and resettled once again by the Italian state away from their traditional homelands.

The *zawiya* (also *zaouie*; in Italian, *zavia*) can be seen as the symbolic ante-cedent to the *villaggio agricolo*. When the Sanusi order took hold in the mid-nineteenth century, life in Cyrenaica became organized around this space. Although defined as an Islamic school or monastery, the *zawiya* was always much more than that. It served as an educational center, social hub, and node for economic, religious, political, and cultural networks. It was, in effect, the center of rural life. The founder of the Sanusi order, Sayyid Mohammed, the Grand Sanusi, established Cyrenaica's first *zawiya* in Al Bayda near the ruins of Cyrene in 1843.[71] He entreated his followers to spread the Sanusi doctrine and founded new *zawiyas* throughout the region. In his history of Libya, John Wright describes how the system of *zawiyas* offered hospitality in exchange for proselytization: "The *zawiyas*, which were colleges, monasteries, and mar-kets, were often built on tribal boundaries and at watering places on the trade and pilgrim routes, and travellers who halted there to take advantage of the three days' free hospitality offered, were subjected to Sanusi doctrine."[72] By the 1880s, *zawiyas* numbered thirty-eight in Cyrenaica, eighteen in Tripolitania, and seventeen in nearby Egypt. Among the most influential was the *zawiya* built at Ajdabiya, which was the very same site where Italians erected one of the most brutal concentration camps in the early 1930s.

Given their important role in Cyrenaican society, it was no surprise that Ital-ian colonizers targeted *zawiyas* for destruction, particularly after the appoint-ment of Rodolfo Graziani as vice governor of Cyrenaica in 1926. As part of his campaign to "pacify" Cyrenaica, Graziani declared the region in a *stato di pericolo pubblico* (state of public danger) in May 1930, which allowed him carte blanche to forcibly dispossess, dislocate, and decimate anyone at will. Italian archival records show the systematic targeting and dismantling of Cyrenaican *zawiyas*, as detailed in essay two.[73] These efforts advanced at a steady crescendo in the late 1920s and culminated in a royal decree issued on December 22, 1930, which called for the confiscation of all property belonging to *zawiyas* in Cyre-naica.[74] As soon as all remaining *zawiyas* were shut down in 1931, the Italian regime in short order promoted the village as the fulcrum of rural life in the colony.

In 1926, the Banco di Roma bolstered its "economic penetration" of Cyre-naica by financing the construction of the region's first planned agricultural settlement at al-Qawarisha (Guarscia, or "Guarscià" in Italian), located about six miles south of Benghazi. Plans show this agricultural village spanned thirty-five hectares and included ten houses, farmland, several wells, a small church, a school, and police headquarters. It was built in conjunction with the Unione Coloniale Italo-Araba (Italo-Arab Colonial Union), a short-lived business co-

operative founded in 1922. The village's design was one of extreme simplic-
ity, and its buildings were constructed with very poor materials (for example,
seaweed insulation).[75] By 1937, only fourteen Italian families were left in this
village.

The Banco di Roma had been active in Libya since the turn of the century.
In fact, this selfsame bank had brick-and-mortar outposts throughout the Italian colonies. Its architecture was often exulted in postcards and newspaper ads.
The Italian government had charged this Vatican-supported bank with increasing Italy's economic holdings in Libya, especially in light of French advances
in the Tibesti Mountains to the south. The bank opened a branch in Tripoli in
1907, followed by others in Benghazi, Derna, Homs, Misurata, and Zliten
shortly thereafter. It offered loans and made investments in industry and infrastructure, much to the chagrin of the Ottoman pasha then in power. Some
of the bank's more unusual investments included an ice factory and an outfit
for the preparation of ostrich feathers.[76]

The Banco di Roma director, Enrico Bresciani, was a strong proponent of
Italy's demographic colonization of Libya. Like many Italian politicians at the
time, he believed immigration to the colonies was an effective strategy of
"peaceful penetration." His vision was one of rural utopia with gainfully employed natives laboring for Italian colonists: "È la migliore e più efficace forma
di penetrazione pacifica . . . Vorrei insomma creare qualche modesta fattoria
con contadini italiani, assoldando gli indigeni per la lavorazione della terra."
(It is the best and most efficient form of peaceful penetration. . . . In sum, I
would like to create some modest farmsteads with Italian peasants, hiring the
indigenous to work the land.)[77] The problem with Bresciani's plan was that
the best lands were not for sale. The solution, according to Attilio Teruzzi,
Cyrenaica's governor from 1926 to 1928, was expropriation.

Bureaucratic agencies were created to accomplish this task. They were
among the many new entities created by the Fascist regime, which would
come to be infamous for its bureaucratic redundancies. Federico Cresti
notes that a type of *cassa di colonizzazione* (colonization bank) that would
serve as an intermediary for property transactions between indigenous
landowners and future colonists in Cyrenaica had been in the works for
years but never came to fruition.[78] Instead, two organizations were founded
in 1932 to serve the explicit purpose of developing land in Cyrenaica and
settling Italian farmers there: the Istituto Nazionale Fascista per la Previ-
denza Sociale (Fascist National Welfare Institute) and the Ente per la Colonizzazione della Cirenaica (Agency for the Colonization of Cyrenaica,
which later became the Ente per la Colonizzazione della Libia). While the

agricultural and demographic valorization of the region through the creation of planned agricultural settlements was the primary objective of these agencies, they also identified transportation infrastructure as critical to their initiatives, that is, vectors of mobility.

Roadwork

Road construction began in earnest across the Jabal Akhdar in the early 1930s. Terrain that had once been the provenance of nomadic tribes soon came to be decussated by concrete and bitumen. Bridges, culverts, and guardrails became as common of features of the landscape as were junipers and broom. In practice, these new roads were the vectors along which Italian colonizers controlled the movement of people and goods. Metaphorically, they were the mark of the Italian state incised onto the territory, much like the accordance or refusal of citizenship would be its stamp on the populace. Roads symbolized conquest, domination, possession, and power over others, as was the case in many other European colonies in Africa. Roads made manifest the nexus of empire and mobility.

Nowhere was the link between roads and Italian colonial domination made clearer than in Angelo Piccioli's massive 1933 tome, *La nuova Italia d'Oltremare* (The new overseas Italy). He writes of the moral significance of Italian-built roads in Libya:[79]

> Questo grande sviluppo di vie di communicazione ha anche un grande significato morale: le strade costituiscono, dopo la conquista, la più durevole presa di possesso. Anche l'indigeno—sopratutto l'indigeno—comprende che l'opera stradale è opera di dominio durevole: che essa è la vera presa di possesso della colonia: si crea soltanto sui suoli che si intende dominare per sempre.
>
> This great development of communication channels also has great moral significance: the roads constitute, after the conquest, the most durable hold of possession. Even the native—above all the native—understands that roadwork is the endeavor of enduring dominion, that it is the true taking of possession of the colony. [Roads] are only created on the land that they are meant to dominate forever.

The native—"above all the native"—understood the meaning of enduring dominion all too well. They were the ones who toiled in the dust and heat to build these roads, and were paid almost nothing for their labor. Sometimes they were conscripted into the travail. Forced labor was a fact of life in the system of Italian-built concentration camps from 1929 to 1933. Male prisoners from the camps were commonly dragooned into roadwork, cutting, grading, and paving the coastal highway between Sirte and Benghazi.

Piccioli describes the 150 miles of new roads built along a trajectory from Sidi Ahmed El Magrum to Ajdabya, Marsa Brega, and El Agheila—exactly the line of concentration camps extending southwest from Benghazi. These new roads, in his words, "non solo saranno civile strumento di valorizzazione della colonia ma dovranno cooperare rapidamente allo stroncamento della ribellione" (not only will be a civilizing instrument of valorization of the colony, but also shall quickly contribute to the overthrow of the rebellion).[80] Ironically, the prisoners forced to build these roads were put into camps for fear of their alleged participation in that very rebellion.

Roadwork made for a wretched life. Conditions were brutal. A photo of road construction in the Jabal Akhdar circa 1930–34, housed in the Archivio Centrale dello Stato, captures the drudgery: a group of twenty men, most of them dark-skinned and wearing turbans, haul rocks in wheelbarrows to build a road that stretches out toward an empty horizon (figure 15).[81] The sky is

FIGURE 15.   Roadwork near Sidi Abdalla on the *strada nord gebelica* (north Jabal road) circa 1930–34. Photograph reproduced by permission from the Archivio Centrale dello Stato, Graziani Photo Archive, Rome.

cloudless, the sun relentless. In the foreground a shovel lays temporarily abandoned, perhaps belonging to the man who is hunched and squatted nearby,
who seems to carve away uselessly at the road with a chisel. To his right, two
men walk toward the camera with wheelbarrows filled with rocks. To his left,
two more walk away looking to deposit their payloads farther down the road.
Still others are chiseling, leveling, and shoveling like machines.

Three figures make eye contact with the camera. The two men to the left
of the frame appear to be Italian laborers both by the caps they are wearing
and the fact that they are working on what appears to be a concrete guardrail.
They are spared from hauling rocks. The other Italian in the photo is partially
hidden from view; however, his suit and trilby mark him as the authority on
scene. The third man making eye contact is a very dark-skinned man almost
at dead center of the frame. He is holding a shovel in his left hand. His body
is perpendicular from the camera but he has turned his head to glance at the
lens. In both countenance and pose he seems to ask of the cameraman, "Why
are you taking my photo?"

One can imagine the fatigue and despair of these laborers returning to the
inhumane conditions of the camp after a long day of roadwork. Some of their
accounts have been documented in an oral history project organized by the
Libyan Studies Center in Tripoli. However, since the fall of Qaddafi's regime
in 2011 and ensuing civil war in Libya, access to these records has become difficult. Nonetheless, a few voices have emerged to provide testimony, including
that of Rajab Hamad Buhwaish al-Minifi, a poet and survivor of the concentration camp El Agheila. His epic poem "Dar al-Agaila" (Under such conditions) describes the forced labor that was part of his internment:[82]

> I have nothing except the dangers of the roadwork
> My bare existence
> Returning home without a morsel to move down a gullet.
>
> Whips lash us before our women's eyes,
> Rendering us useless, degraded,
> Not even a matchstick among us to light a wick . . .
>
> I have no illness except about the saying of "Beat them,
> No pardon,"
> And "With the sword extract their labor," . . .
>
> What a wretched life,
> And when they're done with the men, they turn on the women.

Al-Minifi's poem directly contradicts the myth of Italians as good colonizers epitomized by the trope of Italians as *brava gente* (good people). With the sword, Italians extracted labor. Between 1929 and 1932, an estimated 575 miles of new roads were built in Cyrenaica, most with carceral labor, at a cost of what would be approximately $52 million today when adjusted for inflation.[83] E. E. Evans-Pritchard noted in his seminal 1949 study of Cyrenaica, "It was intended that they [Bedouin] should constitute a cheap reserve of labor for general unskilled work and for seasonal labor on the farms of Italian colonists."[84]

Even after the dissolution of the camps, Bedouin survivors continued to toil on Italian roads. An estimated 20–25 percent of the survivors from the camps, all able-bodied men, labored in roadwork, particularly on the construction of the new coastal highway known as the *litoranea libica*.[85] Stretching 1,100 miles from the Tunisian to the Egyptian border and built in just two years (1935–37), this highway was celebrated as a symbol of Italy's colonial successes in Libya. It was completed just in time for Mussolini's visit in 1937. A triumphal arch—the Arch of the Philaeni—was erected at its halfway point on the border of Tripolitania and Cyrenaica. A tourist guidebook to Italian colonial Libya declared the arch, "segno definitivo e immutabile, vincitore dello spazio e del tempo" (definitive and immutable sign, victor of space and time), an enduring monument to Italian empire.[86]

The fervor of roadwork not only symbolized Italian domination over Libya but also gave the appearance of colonial productivity. According to Martin Moore, the *Daily Telegraph* correspondent who accompanied the Ventimila colonists to Cyrenaica in 1938: "The Italians say that there is no unemployment in Libya, and when one observes the feverish road-making and building activity one can well believe that statement. The laboring Arab is better off today than he has ever been, and the same is probably true—or soon will be true—of the agricultural and pastoral Arab."[87] What Moore was referring to was the resettlement of "the agricultural and pastoral Arab" from concentration camps into Muslim villages, that is, the movement from a purgatorial space of temporary permanence (the camp) to another (the village) where the state harnesses inscriptions of race, ethnicity, and nationality to put its stamp on its subjects.

The Ventimila, Muslim Villages, and Fuorusciti

A news brief buried in the August 1933 issue of the *Rivista delle Colonie Italiane* offers a glimpse into what awaited Bedouin survivors in life after the camp.[88] It suggests that the Italian colonial government might return them to their homelands but not to their nomadic lifestyles. The news brief details how survivors would be relocated tribe by tribe to various agricultural centers of the colony where they would be put to work raising crops and tending livestock. The first tribe moved was the Obeidat, beginning in early June 1932. Over the course of four weeks, nine thousand survivors from the Marsa El Brega camp were ferried by boat to coastal regions near Derna and Tobruq. Several thousand livestock followed by land. The news brief concludes:

> Così, il primo e più importante spostamento di popolazioni cirenaiche in campi di produzione agricola è un fatto compiuto, ed il Governo in breve disporrà per il ritorno ai paesi di origine degli altri gruppi ancora concentrati, ridonando a ciascuno di essi la vita agricola che gli eventi politici avevano momentaneamente imposto di sospendere.

> Thus, the first and most important movement of Cyrenaican populations to fields of agricultural production is an accomplished fact, and the government will shortly arrange the return of the other groups still concentrated [in camps] to their homelands, restoring to each of them the agricultural life that political events had to suspend momentarily.

Between 1932 and 1933, Bedouin survivors of the camps were forcibly relocated throughout Cyrenaica.[89] For members of the Obeidat tribe, the memory of violent dislocation must have still been fresh, for only two years earlier they were forcibly marched 600 miles across the Marmarica desert with 60 percent of the tribe dying en route. Gustavo Ottolenghi describes the long-term psychic fallout of this forced relocation among Bedouin survivors. With their livestock decimated and arable lands expropriated by Italians, survivors had little choice but to work for Italians in construction, roadwork, mining, and fishing. Ottolenghi notes this subjugation resulted in grave psychic disorders that caused a few to commit suicide, while it produced in the majority conditions of apathy, abulia, and intolerance that profoundly affected their socioeconomic development for decades.[90] This is the long echo of trauma wrought by imperial formations.

Although the dislocations from the camps paralleled the routes to the camps, Graziani insisted survivors would not return to their "vita libera e nomade" (free and nomadic life). In an April 1934 memo to Governor Italo Balbo, Graziani fatuously reasoned that dislocation creates the opposite effect: "All'opposto, l'attuale dislocazione, pur dando ampio respiro alle necessità di pascolo e di semina, risponde ai più rigorosi criteri di controllo e di vigilanza politica delle popolazioni." (On the contrary, the current dislocation, while giving ample breath to the needs of grazing and sowing, meets the most rigorous criteria for political control and vigilance of the populations.)[91] These dislocations hardly fulfilled the needs of pasture or husbandry. In fact, they resulted in quite the opposite. What they did prove, however, was how the Italian state engaged mobility once again as an inimical technique of control and subjugation.

The dissolution of camps led to another forced dislocation of Bedouin, this time to villages in inhospitable regions. This time, too, Bedouin were moved under the auspices of agricultural productivity instead of the threat of nomadism. (There is evidence that, at least for a brief time, several concentration camps were repurposed for a different set of mobile subjects; the camps were transformed into rest stops for Italian tourists and business travelers.)[92] The coercive resettlement of Bedouin was part of Governor Italo Balbo's alleged recalibration of indigenous policy from Graziani's heavy-handed violence to one of paternal benevolence. The anthropologist E. E. Evans-Pritchard saw through this scheme:[93]

> In any case, the Italians intended to take the best arable land of the country for themselves. . . . They planted by mass emigration colonies of metropolitans on extensive stretches of the best tribal lands, excluding the Bedouin from the whole tableland, both for pasturing and for sowing, section by section as it was taken over for exploitation. Under Balbo's scheme of development, which aimed at destroying the Bedouin way of life, they were to be settled as far as possible in village communities in these areas, where they would live and cultivate under the same rigid State control to which Italian nationals were subjected. The whole of northern Cyrenaica was thus expropriated for State purposes, the more fertile areas for metropolitan colonists, and the less fertile for the urbanized and semi-urbanized Arabs or such Bedouin as could be induced to submit to State direction and forsake their traditions.

By 1938, the movement toward agricultural life, which was part and parcel of Italian fascism's well-documented advancement of ruralism, culminated spatially in the *villaggi* (villages) of the Jabal Akhdar. In Italy, the archetype of Fascist ruralism and the model for planned rural settlements were the farmsteads of the Agro Pontino (Pontine Marshes). The Romans called these marshes Pomptinae Paludes. Malaria flourished here among the silt and swamp. These marshes were long thought to be uninhabitable after centuries of failed attempts to drain this alluvial plain. It was only with Mussolini's ambitious program of land reclamation, the *bonifica integrale*, that the marshes were transformed into fecund agricultural fields and modern new towns. Tens of thousands of peasants were relocated from northern Italy to work this land south of Rome. They were given a *podere* (homestead), a plow, and several hectares. They were charged with growing wheat and other crops in this former marsh, or in the parlance of the times, helping the soil meet its fertile destiny. The resettlement of northern Italians to the Agro Pontino was one of the most extensive programs of internal colonization ever undertaken in twentieth-century Europe, and one that remains little known outside of Italy.[94]

The Agro Pontino became shorthand for Fascist rural planning in the metropole. In Libya, the synonym for planned rural settlement was the Ventimila. Literally meaning "twenty thousand," the Ventimila signified the mass transfer of Italian colonists to Libya in 1938. As in the Agro Pontino, these colonists were peasants who were relocated to villages throughout the Jabal Akhdar plateau and charged with growing crops and raising livestock. Again, *Daily Telegraph* reporter Martin Moore accompanied the Ventimila, noting: "The Libyan enterprise appears in its true perspective when considered simply as an extension of *bonifica*. From reclamation of the Pontine Marshes to reclamation of Libyan sands is a natural step. Both are tremendous and costly achievements; between them they may provide a livelihood for hundreds of thousands of the poorest peasantry."[95]

Moore was on the caravan of seventeen ships that left the Sicilian city of Siracusa with great fanfare in October 1938. It was bound for Tripoli, carrying the Ventimila to their new lives on the *quarta sponda* (fourth shore). The colonists numbered close to sixteen thousand (in spite of the Ventimila moniker), the majority of whom were assigned to homesteads in Cyrenaica. Agricultural *villaggi* had been built in Tripolitania as well; however, Balbo staked his plan to colonize Libya demographically on the fertile tablelands of the east. His ultimate aim was to bring three hundred thousand Italians to Libya over the next ten years.[96]

The press widely covered the arrival of the Ventimila. Photos of steamer ships with cheering crowds made the front pages in Italy. So, too, did images of smiling families laden with suitcases and personal belongings being loaded onto military lorries labeled by village and bound for Cyrenaica. These photographs became some of the most famous images of Italy's colonial project in Libya.

Everything had been prepared for the colonists before their arrival. Their *poderi* (homesteads) had been built and outfitted. Their fields already tilled and planted. Roads connected homesteads to rural centers complete with schools, churches, wells, stores, and a *casa del fascio* (Fascist headquarters). Almost all of this had been accomplished with indigenous labor, paid well below any living wage. To give an idea of the Ventimila's exorbitant cost, the Italian state invested millions of *lire* in demographic colonization between 1938 and 1939

FIGURE 16.   An unnamed agricultural village cuts a striking figure against the Jabal Akhdar plateau, Cyrenaica, Libya, 1938. Photograph reproduced by permission from Istituto Luce, Rome.

alone, which would equate to approximately $90 million in 2018.[97] Despite Italian colonists' contracts to pay off the debt of ownership, the enterprise never turned a profit.

Set against the arid steppe of the Jabal Akhdar plateau, the *villaggi* cut a striking figure (figure 16). All of the structures were whitewashed and gleaming. Italo Balbo had intended for these villages to be islands of Italian ethnicity; however, as Mia Fuller notes, in practice the villages were anything but isolated insofar as local Arabs were always part of the everyday lives of settlers.[98] Another *Daily Telegraph* correspondent, G. L. Steer, also accompanied the Ventimila to Cyrenaica and described the villages that had been prepared for them:[99]

At each new address they found a village centre, with a handsome modern church of dazzling white and slim, simple lines; Fascist headquarters with a young official in boots to tell them what to do, which they were only too pleased to know; a school and a post office, and a shop where one got something for nothing and which was called a cooperative; all in the same functional block, softened only by Roman colonnades and whitewashed without spot. If they had enjoyed a knowledge of aesthetic, they would have said that this centre was beautiful. From it they were conducted to little white boxes of uniform design which sprinkled the plain at equidistance round the central block, shown their uniform four rooms and the beds in fertile rows, and walked round the uniform acreage, spread with the first shoots of uniform crops, of their little estates.

Uniform, Roman, slim, simple lines: Steer precisely summarizes the aesthetic of Fascist architecture. His description also reveals a condescending attitude toward the peasant colonists. To Steer, as well as to many Italian colonists already settled in Libya, the Ventimila were uneducated and themselves in need of a civilizing mission. Paola Hoffman, an Italian born in 1927 in Benghazi, where her father practiced medicine, and raised in Cyrenaica until 1941, describes in her memoir seeing the Ventimila colonists for the first time: "Arrivarono i «Ventimila» e ci apparvero tanti poveri Cristi da incoraggiare, da imboccare, da aiutare con tutto ciò che ci capitasse tra le mani . . . Un po' selvaggi lo erano, ma nel senso buono, affettuoso, patetico." (The Ventimila arrived and they appeared to us like so many poor Christs to encourage, feed, and help with everything that came into our hands. . . . They were a little savage, but in the good sense, affectionate, pathetic.)[100] Hoffman also notes that one doctor believed the new colonists were so uncivilized that they had to be instructed in how to use the bathrooms at their new homesteads.

The Ventimila were both the subjects and the objects of Italy's civilizing mission in Libya. On the one hand, they were to carry out the Italian state's project of demographic colonization, while on the other, they were perceived as needing to be tamed and acculturated. Everyday life was complicated for the Ventimila. They faced the challenges, inter alia, of nonarable land, confusing land ownership contracts, diffident locals, and geographic isolation. Scholars have delved deeply into each of these challenges and have together produced a body of academic literature that incisively documents and problematizes the formation, operation, and "long decolonization" of colonists' agricultural villages in Libya.[101] What has received less attention has been the *villaggi musulmani* (Muslim villages) built for the indigenous population, including the Bedouin survivors of the camps.

In Tripolitania, there were twelve agricultural villages built for Italian colonists and two Muslim villages. In Cyrenaica, where the efforts of the Ventimila were focused, there were eleven agricultural villages and six Muslim villages (map 4).[102] The colonists' villages bore the names of famous historical figures as if manifesting a book of illustrious men: Crispi, D'Annunzio,

Luigi di Savoia, Oberdan, and so on. The names of the Muslim villages pur-portedly corresponded to traditional place-names or "la poesia del mondo musulmano" (the poetry of the Muslim world), according to a 1939 article in the *Rivista delle Colonie*.[103] They were hopeful and optimistic names: Alba (dawn), Deliziosa (delightful), Fiorita (blossom), Nuova (new), Risorta (re-surge), Verde (green), Vittoriosa (victorious).

The foreign press repeatedly described these Muslim villages as little more than showcase efforts, or "window dressing," again in the words of Steer. He rejoined, "That may be so; but at least they represent an improvement on the methods of a predecessor [Graziani] who prepared to put the entire native pop-ulation of Cyrenaica into concentration camps."[104] Both the camp and the village, although different spaces, had the same goal: to sedentarize the local population.

By design, each Muslim village followed the same architectural formula: central plaza, mosque, minaret, director's office (*mudiriyya*), school, coffee-house, covered market (*suq*), and a smattering of private residences. Fuller notes that these new settlements paradoxically "reduced Islamic settlement to its essential signifiers" and became "artificial renderings of the very social con-figurations Italians had uprooted."[105] They were, in her words, reductionist stage-sets not unlike the Hotel Uaddan in Tripoli or the Libyan Pavilion at the Mostra Triennale d'Oltremare, Italy's largest colonial exhibition held at Naples in 1940.[106]

By appearance, the Muslim villages looked similar to the *villaggi* built for Italian settlers, save for the towering minaret that subordinated all else around it. The minaret signified that these places were without doubt Muslim and therefore non-Italian spaces. The *poderi* (homesteads) were also much smaller than those in the villages built for colonists, about five hectares each compared with twenty.[107] As with the roads that led to these villages, they were built by the very people whose territory had been expropriated by the Italian state. Moore described the scene in 1940: "Hundreds of Arabs under Italian super-vision were hewing stone, mixing cement, making roads, and rolling boulders from the areas destined for cultivation. This was part of Balbo's compensa-tion for having turned the Arabs off the uplands between Benghazi and Derna to make way for the incoming Italian settlers."[108] Not only were these Bed-ouin dispossessed and forcibly dislocated in the name of Italian colonization, but they were also "rewarded" with hard labor.

A photograph of indigenous farmers attempting to till a field of rocks on a *podere* near Fiorita can only be described as a fool's errand.[109] To the left of the frame, a man stands behind his emaciated cow, its ribs and sunken hips fitted with a makeshift plow. Two other men work sparse rows of withered

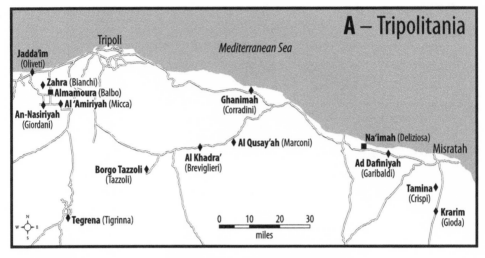

A – Tripolitania

Tripoli

Mediterranean Sea

Jadda'îm (Oliveti)

Zahra (Bianchi)
Almamoura (Balbo)
Al 'Amiriyah (Micca)

An-Nasiriyah (Giordani)

Ghanimah (Corradini)

Al Qusay'ah (Marconi)

Na'imah (Deliziosa)

Misratah

Al Khadra' (Breviglieri)

Borgo Tazzoli (Tazzoli)

Ad Dafiniyah (Garibaldi)

Tamina (Crispi)

Tegrena (Tigrinna)

Krarim (Gioda)

0   10   20   30
miles

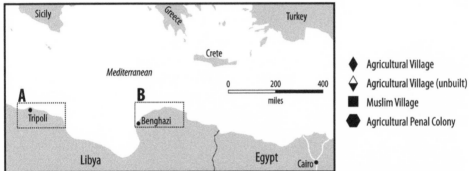

Sicily

Greece

Turkey

Crete

Mediterranean

A

B

Tripoli

Benghazi

0   200   400
miles

Libya

Egypt

Cairo

◆ Agricultural Village
◇ Agricultural Village (unbuilt)
■ Muslim Village
⬢ Agricultural Penal Colony

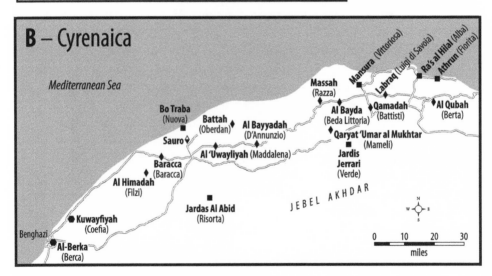

B – Cyrenaica

Mediterranean Sea

Mansura (Vittoriosa)
Labraq (Luigi di Savoia)
Ra's al Hilal (Alba)
Athrun (Fiorita)

Massah (Razza)

Bo Traba (Nuova)

Battah (Oberdan)

Al Bayyadah (D'Annunzio)

Sauro

Al Bayda (Beda Littoria)

Qamadah (Battisti)

Al Qubah (Berta)

Qaryat 'Umar al Mukhtar (Mameli)

Al 'Uwayliyah (Maddalena)

Baracca (Baracca)

Jardis Jerrari (Verde)

Al Himadah (Filzi)

JEBEL AKHDAR

Jardas Al Abid (Risorta)

Kuwayfiyah (Coefia)

Benghazi

Al-Berka (Berca)

0   10   20   30
miles

MAP 4. The *villaggi agricoli* (agricultural villages) and *village musulmani* (Muslim villages) built in Tripolitania and Cyrenaica in the 1930s.

crops already desiccated by the heat. A group of women and children stands in front of a new, windowless, quadrate house, bearing witness to this lost cause.

The political goal of building the Muslim villages was the "complete assimilation of elements of Arab population into an Italianized sedentary community," according to Douglas Johnson. He specifies the goal, "civilizing and Italianizing the Bedouin."[110] Nomads would be transformed into farmers. They would become productive members of Italian society. To the point, an English-language photo book published by the Istituto Agricolo Coloniale juxtaposes two photos—one of tatterdemalion Bedouin tents and the other of orderly plazas and colonnades in new Muslim villages—with a caption that reads: "The transformation of nomad life in sedentary [sic] in the new Moslem villages of 'Alba' and 'Fiorita.'"[111] A 1939 article in the *Rivista delle Colonie* explains the rationale behind this transformation, which is that sedentarization leads directly to civilization: "La creazione di centri di coltivazione terriera era infatti derivata dal concetto di fissare al suolo quelle popolazioni nomadi e di contribuire così decisivamente all'evoluzione della loro civiltà verso forme superiori." (The creation of land cultivation centers was in fact derived from the concept of fixing those nomadic populations to the soil and thus contributing decisively to the evolution of their civilization toward superior forms.)[112]

The Muslim villages were to be used not only to contain and civilize the Bedouin survivors vacated from the concentration camps but also to centralize and concentrate the influx of *fuorusciti* (refugees, sing. *fuoruscito*) who had fled the ongoing violence in Libya, and who, by 1934, had begun to return in droves. More than twenty thousand had fled into neighboring Egypt. Others escaped westward, with more than seven thousand refugees crossing over to Tunisia and Algeria. Three thousand *fuorusciti* were in the Tunisian city of Sfax alone. Still others fled farther afield, some as far away as Sudan and Damascus.[113]

Archival records show that Italian colonial officials were deeply concerned with *rimpatrio* (repatriation) of this new class of mobile subjects. Categorically, *fuorusciti* met the modern definition of refugee—that is, someone forced to flee his or her country because of war, violence, or persecution. Yet the name *fuorusciti* does not translate directly as such. It stems from the verb *fuoriuscire*, which is a compound word (*fuori* [outside] + *uscire* [to exit]). It roughly translates as "to spill out, to pour out." Being a *fuoruscito* has a diluvial quality to it, and indeed Italian colonial officials were fearful of being overwhelmed by the flood of these returning refugees.

They sought to control the *fuorusciti* by limiting the places to which they could return and by refusing to restitute their goods and property. Angelo Del Boca tells the story of a *fuoruscito* named Mohammed Fgheni who had fled from Cyrenaica to Tunisia. Decrepit and blind with old age, Fgheni applied to return to Libya in May 1934. Then Italian minister of the colonies Emilio De Bono responded to Fgheni's request himself:[114]

> Se egli [Fgheni] desidera venire a passare gli ultimi anni della sua vita in Tripolitania, mantengo la promessa fatta dal mio predecessore . . . ma non consentirò assolutamente che egli ritorni sul Gebel, dove ebbe a spiegare la sua opera deleteria. Egli potrebbe solo fissarsi nella località che fin d'ora stabilisco, e cioè Homs, ove gli farei passare un assegno mensile di lire 400 necessario per vivere. Maggiori concessioni di queste non sono disposto a fargli.
>
> If he [Fgheni] wishes to spend the last years of his life in Tripolitania, I will maintain the promise made by my predecessor [Luigi Feder-zoni] . . . but I absolutely will not consent to his return to the Jabal [Akhdar] where he had deployed his deleterious work. He could only settle in a location that I am now setting up, namely Homs, in which I would pass along to him a monthly check of 400 *lire* [that is] necessary to live. More concessions than these I am not willing to make to him.

Although their reentry took place over a number of years, Italian colonial officials insisted that *fuorusciti*, like nomads, needed to be immobilized and controlled. Rarely were they called *profughi* (refugees) or *deportati* (deportees), for these terms implied criminal activity, that is, active rebellion against Italian rule. Instead, *fuorusciti* proved a threat by their sheer number to the colonial order in Cyrenaica. They outnumbered the Ventimila settlers by almost two to one. What is more, the *fuorusciti* represented a new category of mobile subjects who simultaneously embodied refugee and repatriate. Theirs was a hapless congregation caught up in the tides of war. The *fuorusciti* would also become the historical antecedent for Italians returning from the colonies just ten years later, many of whom were repatriated into refugee camps throughout the Italian peninsula in the late 1940s and 1950s. Although there were attempts to regulate the movements of both populations, it is worth noting that the Italian state treated the *rimpatriati* (repatriates) far better than the *fuorusciti*.

The Italian state controlled the *fuorusciti* by giving them nothing or, as in the case of Mohammed Fgheni, by confining their return to spaces like the *villaggi musulmani*. The press corps, for the most part, framed the reception of these villages positively. Moore writes: "In other respects the Arab farmer is on exactly the same footing as the Italian colonists who have displaced him. . . . Rising fully equipped out of nothingness, they [the villages] are also calculated to impress the Arabs with the benevolent power of Italy."[115] Interestingly, Moore uses the same adjective—"equipped"—to describe the Muslim villages as that which is used to describe the *villaggi attrezzati* (equipped villages) like La Barbuta built to contain the Roma seventy years later.

In another example, G. Z. Ornato, writing for the Touring Club Italiano in 1939, notes the "happy" reception of the villages: "In Cirenaica, oltre ai primi villaggi di el Atrum e di Ras Hilal, altre ne sorgeranno quest'anno . . . I Musulmani sono felici di questa iniziativa genialissima, che vale a fissare alla terra gente seminomade, la quale viveva essenzialmente della pastorizia." (In Cyrenaica, in addition to the first villages of El Atrum [Fiorita] and Ras Hilal [Alba], others will appear this year. . . . The Muslims are happy about this most genial initiative, which acts to fix to the land seminomadic people who essentially live by pastoralism.)[116] For Francesco Barone, writing for the *Rivista delle Colonie* in 1938, the Muslim villages represented a continuation of "la leale collaborazione di opera fra metropolitani e musulmani che è da anni felicemente in atto" (the loyal collaboration of work between metropolitans and Muslims that for years has been happily in place).[117] The press gave the impression that Muslim villages were happy, genial, loyal, collaborative, and benevolent spaces.

The archival record, however, tells a different story. A 1942 memorandum on the "colonizzazione musulmana" (Muslim colonization) housed in the archive of the Istituto Agronomico Oltremare in Florence reveals that the Libyans who accepted *poderi* from the Italian state made little effort to cultivate them.[118] Evans-Pritchard notes, "The Italians experienced difficulty in finding Arab colonists for even these thirty-two holdings [at Fiorita and Alba], for the Bedouin showed no inclination to work as serfs the lands they had worked as freemen."[119] Most of the fields lay fallow. Wells did not produce enough water for irrigation. Families subsisted on handouts from the Italian state. The memo lamented that Italy would never see a return on its investment. And as if to add salt to the wound, the text smarts at the ingratitude of the inhabitants of the *villaggi musulmani*. The memo not only expresses disbelief at the manifestations of the inhabitants' discontent but also dismisses their claims as absurd and exaggerated:[120]

In via di massima i coloni, anziché di dimostrare della riconoscenza per quanto è stato fatto e si fa continuamente per la loro, danno delle continue manifestazioni di malcontento ed accampano invece delle pretese, il più delle volte esagerate ed assurde.

By and large the [Muslim] settlers, instead of showing gratitude for what has been done for and continues to be done for them, they give rise to continuous manifestations of discontent, and instead, they advance pretenses that are most often exaggerated and absurd.

The consternation expressed by the memo is seemingly without gall or guile. The text is conspicuously amnesic. It forgets (or disavows) that the land the Italian state "gifted" as *poderi* and *villaggi* was actually expropriated from these inhabitants in the first place. It also forgets (or disavows) the broader efforts to control Bedouin mobility that underpinned this cycle of expropriation and restitution: coerced deportations and dislocations, concentration camps, forced labor, flying courts, mass dispossession, and states of nomad emergency, all of which culminated in the genocide of tens of thousands of Bedouin. With the "gift" of *villaggi musulmani*, Evans-Pritchard writes, "the Bedouin believed that [Balbo] intended to destroy them by guile as surely as Graziani had destroyed them with machine gun and bomb."[121] The memo further lends credence to the villages as "window dressing," for it notes that many *poderi* were built but remained unoccupied. The villages of Deliziosa and Nuova, for instance, each had fifty *poderi* under construction, but all were suspended because of World War II.[122]

After the war, Douglas Johnson described Bedouin tents as still being pitched beside Italian-built *poderi* well into the late 1960s but noted: "Increasingly this relic [of] survival of the nomadic era is being abandoned and total occupation of the *Ente* farmhouses . . . is proceeding at an accelerated pace."[123] Today, if they still exist, most *villaggi musulmani* stand in ruins. Some were repurposed as warehouses for grain and livestock.[124] At Alba, for instance, the colonnades of the central plaza have been covered and partitioned into storage areas. The neighboring *villaggio* of Fiorita is empty. Its structures have yellowed with dust and age like parchment. In the countryside nearby, storm clouds gather above an abandoned *podere* (figure 14). It stands alone among the spring greenery of the Jabal Akhdar. Erumpent weeds have overtaken its interior; its outside is weathered and crumbling. The land, once expropriated by Italians, is taking back the building. No longer is this farmhouse the symbol of Italian colonial conquest in Libya but rather its tombstone.

Special Italian Citizenship, or Minor Citizens

The *villaggi musulmani* spatialized ethno-religious segregation in Italian colonial Libya much in the same way as the *villaggi attrezzati* segregate people on the periphery of Rome today. These were villages built to house non-Italians in which Arab, Muslim, Bedouin, and Libyan all reduced to one monolithic "Other" who could be contained and controlled in space. And like the residents of today's *villaggi attrezzati*, those in the *villaggi musulmani* were bound up in predicaments of citizenship. Whereas the Muslim village actualized difference in space, the Italian state intensified difference vis-à-vis a special form of citizenship for its inhabitants.

It was called the *cittadinanza italiana speciale* (special Italian citizenship) and was inaugurated by royal decree on January 9, 1939. This form of citizenship also went by other names and previous iterations: *cittadinanza italiana libica* (Italian-Libyan citizenship) as well as *piccola cittadinanza* (little citizenship), better translated as "minor citizenship." Its subjects were called *cittadini italiani libici speciali* (special Italian-Libyan citizens).

As an instrument of state power, special Italian citizenship was a particularly brilliant weapon. On the one hand, it gave the Italian state the appearance of benevolence. By seeming to offer the rights and privileges of citizenship to select subjects in Libya, the state reinforced the optics of Italians as good colonizers. On the other hand, the Italian state did so with the tacit understanding that few people, if any, would apply for said citizenship. In practice, special Italian citizenship served to isolate Libyans juridically just as the *villaggi* segregated them spatially.

Before 1939, élites in Libya had the opportunity to apply for full Italian citizenship under a law passed twenty years earlier.[125] Most were employees of the colonial administration whose employment depended on their presumptive application to become citizens. Yet to become an Italian citizen, one must have been willing to give up one's *statuto personale* (personal status) under Islamic or "customary" law.[126] Traditionally, the *statuto personale* governed transactions related to marriage, property, and most importantly, inheritance. Anyone wanting to apply for Italian citizenship would have to accept Italian civil code as governance in these domains. Assimilation was mandatory. According to Evans-Pritchard, "Employees of the administration could not feel that any advantages they might derive from [Italian citizenship] could compensate for loss of status before the religious courts in matters of personal law, a loss considered shameful even by whole-hearted collaborators."[127]

The 1919 law was unusual in the panoply of rights it accorded to those who gave up their *statuto personale* in exchange for Italian citizenship. First, it abolished the condition of *sudditanza coloniale* (colonial subjecthood). New citizens were demarcated by their geography, not their ethnicity or religion. The law created *cittadini italiani della Tripolitania* (Italian citizens of Tripolitania) and *cittadini italiani della Cirenaica* (Italian citizens of Cyrenaica). Second, it created two parliaments, one in Tripolitania and one in Cyrenaica, responsible for legislating local matters. Third, the law gave these new Italian citizens the right to vote. In other words, the 1919 law established a semblance of legal equality between citizens of the metropole and those of the colony, even though this parity was rarely carried out in practice.

After the Fascist regime rose to power, things began to change. A 1927 law reversed many of the 1919 provisions. It abolished the two parliaments, rescinded the right to vote, and reclassified citizenship on the basis of ethnonationalism as opposed to geography. The 1927 law created *cittadinanza italiana libica* (Italian-Libyan citizenship). Under this law, *cittadini italiani libici* (Italian-Libyan citizens) were *diminuto jure*, that is, of diminished juridical status. Their civil rights were not only subordinate to those of metropolitan citizens but also applicable only in colonial Libya. If Italian-Libyan citizens were to travel to Italy, their citizenship would mean nothing. They would be treated as colonial subjects. Furthermore, having given up the *statuto personale* the Italian-Libyan citizen would have no recourse to customary law to settle disputes nor have the full rights of an Italian citizen under the Italian civil code. Metaphorically, one was stuck between a juridical rock and a hard place. With one legislative stroke, writes Evans-Pritchard, "Arabs ceased to be *cittadini italiani* and became *cittadini italiani libici*. . . . In general, the Arabs were no longer equal with the Italians before the law."[128]

Gradated forms of citizenship began to emerge in the colonies under the Fascist regime. Certain populations were privileged over others, and this division always broke along racial lines. More rights were accorded to those in Libya and the Aegean Islands whose *mediterraneità* (Mediterraneanness) was believed to link metropole and colony both racially and culturally. Italian-Libyan citizenship was held up as the gold standard of colonial citizenship, with *cittadinanza italiana egea* (Italian-Aegean citizenship) a close second.[129] In Eritrea, Somalia, and Ethiopia, citizenship was never an option. The state of *sudditanza coloniale* (colonial subjecthood) was never abolished nor was a singular "Italian-African citizenship" imagined after the three colonies were united into Africa Orientale Italiana (Italian East Africa) in 1936.[130] Italian state power once again exercised its oblique violence through the categorical refusal of citizenship.

Instead, a series of *leggi razziali* (Racial Laws) intensified segregation in this newly united Italian East Africa. In 1937, the regime enforced antimiscegenation laws, which forbade interracial marriage, sexual relations, and the paternal acknowledgment of interracial children.[131] In July 1938, Mussolini issued his famous Manifesto of Race, which was followed by the passage of Fascist Racial Laws four months later that stripped Jews of their civil rights and targeted them for exile and then extermination. In the colonies the application of Racial Laws varied by context and degree. Giulia Barrera notes, "Italians were in agreement with their government over the subordination of the colonized, but they disagreed with the forms that such subordination should assume. Many Italians violated the race laws; but mixing with Africans did not necessarily mean being on friendly terms with them."[132]

Italian East Africa bore the brunt of the Fascist Racial Laws, whereas colonial Libya sought to assimilate its colonized subjects vis-à-vis Muslim villages and minor citizenship. After all, Libya was Mediterranean. It was Italy's *quarta sponda* (fourth shore), and as of January 1939, it officially became an administrative region of Italy. Four coastal provinces—Tripoli, Misurata, Benghazi, and Derna—were annexed into the Italian nation-state. Only residents of these provinces were eligible for special Italian citizenship. Those living in Fezzan, the large region bordering the Sahara, or those in southern Cyrenaica, had neither a path to minor citizenship nor basic civil protections.

What made the 1939 iteration of colonial citizenship different from those of 1919 and 1927 was the preservation of the *statuto personale* (personal status) in matters of governance. Those with *cittadinanza italiana speciale* (special Italian citizenship) had recourse to both Italian civil code and Islamic customary law to settle conflicts and broker agreements. Yet this citizenship was still considered subordinate to that of metropolitan Italians. A 1938 article in *Rivista delle Colonie* made this explicit:[133]

> I Libici non sono infatti considerati sudditi, ma cittadini minoris iuris; essi hanno la garanzia della libertà individuale ed è stata riconosciuta loro la inviolabilità del domicilio e della proprietà, come pure il diritto a concorrere a determinate cariche civili e militari nella Colonia e l'esercizio professionale in Colonia ove ne abbiano i titoli necessari.
>
> The Libyans, in fact, are not considered subjects, but minor citizens [*minoris iuris*]; they have the guarantee of individual freedom and the inviolability of their domicile and property has been recognized, as well as the right to compete for certain civil and military positions in the colony and for professional work for which they have the necessary qualifications.

In other words, special Italian citizenship was minor citizenship, that is, something less than before the law (*minoris iuris*). Those who held it existed in a limbo, halfway between subject and citizen. Access to it was uneven and discriminatory. Under it, civil rights were conditional and their enforcement erratic. As the stamp the Italian state put on its subjects, special Italian citizenship was a noncommittal gesture. It was just as much "window dressing" of a body politic as Muslim villages were stage sets of Islamic space. Together, the *villaggio musulmano* and *cittadinanza italiana speciale* worked to segregate colonized subjects spatially and isolate them juridically. Put simply, space and law were harnessed into the service of Italian empire.

In 2017, the Italian Senate took up debate on special forms of citizenship for migrants. Whereas Italian citizenship had traditionally been granted on the basis of kinship (*jus sanguinis*, literally "right of blood") rather than birthplace (*jus solis*, literally "right of the soil"), legislative reforms would create two intermediary forms of citizenship for those under eighteen years old: *jus solis temperato* and *jus culturae*.[134] The first is citizenship by right of soil (*jus solis*) tempered (*temperato*) by certain conditions—one must be born in Italy to foreign parents, at least one of these parents must have been legally resident in the EU for a minimum of five years, and a declaration of citizenship must be made before turning eighteen. Such conditions are almost impossible to fulfill, as demonstrated earlier by the case of Brenda Salkanovic in the documentary *Container 158*. The second is citizenship by right of culture (*jus culturae*). This path to citizenship is reserved for foreign-born children who arrived in Italy before the age of twelve, attended at least five years of primary or secondary school, and completed at least one educational stage (for example, elementary school). Both *jus culturae* and *jus solis temperato* require the support of an applicant's parents, who are required to make a declaration to the state on the applicant's behalf.

All of these conditions, combined with the morass of debates and deal making that often grinds the legislative process to a halt, can quickly turn the dream of Italian citizenship into a lost cause. Once again the Italian state exercises its power through the recognition or refusal of citizenship, and once again it creates the conditions under which people become caught in limbo, suspended between citizen and subject. This was the case with *cittadini italiani speciali* (special Italian citizens) in colonial Libya. It is the case with many migrants in Italy today. It was also the case with Italians returning from the colonies and expropriated territories after World War II, who found themselves lost in a land that was at once familiar and strange, national refugees in a country that was supposed to be their home.

Villages for National Refugees

In the years after World War II, millions of people were on the move. Borderlines were redrawn, territories shifted, and the long, fitful process of decolonization had begun among European colonial possessions in Africa and Asia. Colonists returned home in droves. An estimated five to seven million people returned from the colonies, although to say "return" would be a misnomer since for many of them it was their first time stepping foot on the Continent. Andrea Smith calls these returnees "Europe's invisible migrants," a little-studied demographic that, en masse, calls into question the very definitions of citizenship and nationality at precisely the moment nation-states were trying to position themselves in the postwar geopolitical order.[135]

In Italy, they were called *profughi nazionali* (national refugees). More than seventy thousand Italian colonists returned from Libya in the decade after World War II, many of them the selfsame migrants who arrived in Cyrenaica with the Ventimila. Some fifty-seven thousand colonists left Eritrea in those same years, the majority of whom repatriated to Italy. The biggest influx of refugees came not from the Italian colonies but rather from the Istrian peninsula in present-day Croatia and Slovenia. Up to two hundred thousand ethnic Italians fled the ascendant Tito regime in a modern-day exodus from the region known as the Julian March.[136]

Whether returning colonist or Istrian exile, all found themselves immured together in a series of 109 *campi profughi* (refugee camps) scattered throughout Italy in the late 1940s and 1950s. In some camps, the *profughi nazionali* (national refugees) were housed, sometimes for years, with Jewish survivors of concentration camps who were en route to Israel.[137] Sometimes these camps were called *centri di raccolta profughi* (refugee collection centers). They were the direct historical precedents of today's *centri di raccolta Rom* (Roma collection centers). For all colonists, exiles, and survivors, time spent in the *campi profughi* added to the trauma of ongoing displacement.

M. was a young girl when her family fled Istria for Italy. One of five children, M. told me she spent nine years—her entire adolescence—moving from refugee camp to refugee camp. She began her journey in a camp near Udine but was soon moved far south to one of the largest camps at Altamura, some thirty miles southwest of Bari. The camp was originally built to house prisoners of war, which it did so for a short time before it was transformed into a refugee camp.

Profughi nazionali (national refugees) stayed in the camps for years. Children were born and raised in the *capannoni* (warehouses). Weddings were celebrated. Funerals marked. Celebrities came out of the camps too, including famed race car driver Mario Andretti, who was originally from Motovun (Istria) and spent seven years in a camp near Lucca before immigrating to the United States, and Italian national basketball coach Romeo Sacchetti, who was born at Altamura and lived there for two years. Renowned chef Lidia Bastianich was born in the coastal city of Pula (Istria) and fled with her family to Italy, where they lived for two years in a refugee camp housed in the former Nazi extermination camp of Risiera San Sabba near Trieste.

Alongside Istrian exiles, another little-known demographic moving through the refugee camps at the time were the thirteen thousand Italian children who had been evacuated from Libya.[138] Aged four to fourteen, many were the children of Ventimila settlers. With Libya thought to become a main battleground for World War II, the children were told to pack for vacation and were sent to the metropole in June 1940. For many it would be their first time in Italy. Little did they know their odyssey would last for years. Maria Giorlandino, for example, left at age six and returned at twelve. Elda Gava left as a girl and returned at nineteen, her mother noting in dialect, "Che bela tosa che l'è tornada" (What beautiful lady has returned). These children were sent to summer camps (*colonie estive*) either in the mountains or at the seashore. Angelo Del Boca notes there was not a single family in Tripolitania or Cyrenaica that did not have at least one child evacuated to the *colonie estive* in 1940.[139] By summer's end, war made their return to Libya untenable and the Fascist regime transformed the summer camps into schools designed to mold the children into *piccoli fascisti* (little Fascists).

When the regime fell in 1943, however, all organization disintegrated and the Italian children of Libya were abandoned. Some found refuge with relatives. Others passed through convents and monasteries. Still others ended up in the *campi profughi* (refugee camps). Some children eventually made it back to Libya, where they found both families and homes irrevocably changed. Parents had died. Siblings refused to accept them. Mothers did not recognize their children. Jole Mezzavilla Ferrara described her return to Libya: "Partiti bambini siamo tornati grandicelli insomma e ricordo che la mamma è svenuta." (We left as children, we came back quite a bit older, you know, and I remember my mom fainted.) She continued: "Quella notte abbiamo dormito non più dico io nelle stazioni, per terra, o nei campi profughi. Ci rendemmo conto che eravamo a casa finalmente." (That night, I say, we no longer slept in stations, on the floor, or in refugee camps. We realized that we were finally home.)[140]

Back at the Altamura camp near Bari, M. told me that her family of *esuli* (exiles) from Istria eventually left for another camp at Marina di Carrara (Tuscany), where they stayed for several years before finally arriving at what she called the *casermette* (shacks) of Borgo San Paolo on the outskirts of Turin. Archival photos show these *casermette* to be no more than shantytowns, composed of muddy streets and dilapidated shacks, not unlike the *campi nomadi* (nomad camps) today. M. lived there until her family was assigned an apartment in Villaggio Santa Caterina in 1955, a public housing complex in Turin required to allocate 15 percent of its inventory to national refugee families (figure 17). She, along with dozens of other Istrian Italians, still lives there today.

Compared with Italy's contemporary migration crisis, the Italian state did much in the 1950s and 1960s to support the resettlement and integration of both Istrian refugees and returning colonists. The 1952 Scelba Law, for instance,

FIGURE 17. The Villaggio Santa Caterina outside Turin was built for *profughi nazionali* (national refugees) from Istria in the early 1950s. Photograph by the author, 2016.

established a variety of protections for them, including monthly subsidies and quotas for public housing and employment. The law obligated businesses contracted with the state to hire *profughi nazionali* as 5 percent of their workforce. Another law passed in 1958 increased this quota to 10 percent for businesses employing more than fifty people and guaranteed that employment for a minimum of two years. Refugees received other protections in the form of public housing allocations, vocational training, and university scholarships.[141] Political will made much happen, many thanks in part to the Opera per l'Assistenza ai Profughi Giuliani e Dalmati (Organization for Aid to Julian and Dalmatian Refugees).

After their time in the *campi profughi*, the Italian state helped resettle many Istrian refugees into "villages" like Villaggio Santa Caterina in Turin. Sometimes these were neighborhoods within a larger metropolitan area such as the Villaggio Giulio-Dalmati in Rome. This particular village originally housed workers who built the Esposizione Universale Roma in 1942; however, six years later it was repurposed to accommodate thousands of Istrian *profughi*. Other examples include the Villaggio Dalmazia in Novara and the Villaggio Giuliani e Dalmati in Busto Arsizio that opened in the mid-1950s, which were apartment complexes similar to the Villaggio Santa Caterina in Turin. All were built with the specific purpose of moving Istrian refugees out of temporary camps and into permanent housing.

Sometimes the village was born directly from a camp, as in the case of the Villaggio San Marco at Fossoli near Modena. This village arose from rehabilitated barracks of the Fossoli concentration camp. Fossoli gained notoriety during World War II as a *Polizei Durchgangslager*, a transit camp for Italian Jews, the antechamber to Nazi *lager* in Germany and Poland. Yet its fortunes shifted quickly after the war. After brief stints as an Allied-run prison camp, displaced persons camp, and Catholic orphanage, Fossoli transformed into a village for Istrian refugees in 1954 and remained as such until 1970. One refugee, Antonio Zappador, recounted his disbelief upon arrival there:[142]

> Quando arrivai al villaggio il primo giorno non potevo credere ai miei occhi: un campo di concentramento . . . Ma non riuscivo a capacitarmi dallo stupore e mi dico che mi hanno tirato un brutto scherzo . . . Il villaggio si chiamava San Marco ma fuori, per la gente del posto noi eravamo "i triestein dal camp."

> When I arrived at the village on the first day I couldn't believe my eyes: a concentration camp. I couldn't understand my astonishment, and I told myself that they'd pulled a nasty joke on me. The village was called San Marco but outside, among the locals, we were the "Triestines of the camp."

In another case, Fertilia, the village for Istrian refugees, was previously a *villaggio agricolo* (agricultural village) created for Italy's internal colonization project. Fertilia was one of the Fascist new towns in Sardinia, founded in 1936 and built concurrently with those in the Agro Pontino in Lazio as well as those for the Ventimila in Libya.[143] All construction on Fertilia stopped with the outbreak of World War II and the *villaggio* was left unfinished. In 1947 it was turned over to a group of Istrian refugees to finish the construction and make it their home. These *profughi* and their descendants have lived there ever since.

I paid a visit to the community of Istrian refugees at Villaggio Santa Caterina in March 2016 and, specifically, the local clubhouse that serves as the headquarters of the Istrian Italian community of Piedmont.[144] It was clear to me that the memory of being a national refugee was very much alive at the club. One of M.'s friends, E., insisted they were a group of *profughi* (refugees) not *rimpatriati* (repatriates). She told me the *rimpatriati* (repatriates) were those who came back from Africa and the Aegean—in other words, returning colonists. "Non siamo stati colonizzati. Non siamo stati mai una colonia," she said of Istrian Italians. (We were never colonized. We were never a colony.)

From the vantage point of the Italian state and the international political order, both returning colonists and Istrian refugees were considered Italian. However, internally, both groups articulated feelings of being doubly exiled.[145] Neither could return home as both Istria and the colonies had been ceded to other states. Nor were they at home in Italy, where they often met with discrimination and resentment. Pamela Ballinger notes that Istrian refugees often spoke of being "stranieri a casa nostra" (foreigners in our own home).[146] Likewise, returning colonists from Libya felt "dimenticati" (forgotten) by the state, the public, and historians in postwar Italy. They constituted a forsaken demographic caught in the tumultuous space between imperialism and nationalism.[147]

Similar to the rhetoric linked to Europe's current migration crisis as well as contemporary immigration in the United States, refugees and colonists were thought to be taking away jobs from "native-born" Italians. One Istrian refugee, Bruno, remembers being taunted with the refrain: "Tornate a casa vostra, ci portate via il lavoro. Perché non tornate a casa vostra, siete tutti fascisti." (Go back to your home, you're taking away jobs from us. Why don't you go home, you're all fascists.)[148] On the contrary, the refugees who left Istria were hardly Fascists. Many were fleeing from the *foibe* massacres (1943–47), in which Yugoslav partisans targeted and murdered ethnic Italians. The refugees had endured the loss of everything to come to Italy.[149] Their trauma ran as deep and cavernous as the karst where the massacres took place. For example, E. told me her mother had already lost three children, including two in the *foibe*, before arriving in Italy. According to E., she was a woman haunted by that loss for the rest of her life.

In the *campi profughi* of the 1940s and 1950s, and the brick-and-mortar villages that arose from them, inhabitants drew clear lines of distinction between *profughi* (refugees) and *rimpatriati* (repatriates). E. described for me a "mixed marriage" between a *profugo* and a *rimpatriato* in a camp near Turin. She said the *rimpatriato* was Greek, but in further conversation it became clear that said Greek was a returning Italian colonist from Rhodes. E.'s husband told me about another "mixed marriage" in the camp between a *profuga* and a *meridionale* (southern Italian). The southerner had been a *carabiniere* (police officer) stationed in Turin when he met and fell in love with an Istrian refugee. They have been married for more than fifty years and living in Villaggio Santa Caterina, and still this man is known throughout the clubhouse as *il meridionale* (the southerner). In the ghettoized spaces of the camp and the village, the self-policing of exilic categories (for example, *profugo, rimpatriato, meridionale*) is well practiced among inhabitants, as if those already forced outside Italian society by coerced mobilities seek not only to maintain but also to reinforce their specific expressions of marginalization and the boundaries that bind them.

When I asked E.'s husband, F., about his memories of returning colonists, he told me a story about a particular dinner with *rimpatriati* from Eritrea. He traveled to the *campo profughi* (refugee camp) in the city of Tortona, also in Piedmont, which housed a large community of 1,500 Istrian exiles and returning colonists. The "camp" existed in a large palazzo named Caserma Giuseppe Passalacqua, which today serves as Tortona's city hall. This was a *centro di raccolta profughi* (refugee collection center) and archival records show that culinary division was one of the ways that inhabitants self-policed their exilic boundaries. There were three kitchens at the camp: one for Istrian exiles, one for "Greeks," and a third for everyone else.[150] F. described a raucous dinner with the "Eritreans" at Tortona. He said they had dressed up in traditional African costumes and made a traditional African meal, couscous. "And they were black, as black as your wool coat," he said to me. When I asked him to expand on this statement, he said the "Eritreans" were children of mixed unions and that their skin color was black.

More than sixty years later, memories of race and Otherness still occupied a place in F.'s experience of the *campo profughi*. Exilic boundaries became entangled with racial ones, and inhabitants not only preserved but also practiced fully the racial segregation that Italian colonial architects and planners had hoped to accomplish in cities like Addis Ababa. The Istrian *profughi* that I spoke with in Turin simultaneously Otherized *rimpatriati* while sharing a sense of solidarity with them. They all lived at Italy's margins, either invisible to postwar Italian society or, at its worst, as objects of its discrimination.

Citizenship, too, was in play. The Istrian refugees that I met at Villaggio Santa Caterina all spoke of "opting" (*optare*) for Italian citizenship. The language of option stems directly from the 1947 Paris Peace Treaty, which laid out the terms for Italy's reparations after World War II, including the formal surrender of colonial territories. The treaty stipulated that Italian citizens domiciled in a territory transferred by Italy to another state (for example, Yugoslavia) would have the option to become citizens of that state, or they could opt to retain Italian citizenship provided they relocate to Italy within one year of the treaty coming into force.[151] E. described to me the urgency with which her family left Istria after "opting" for Italian citizenship for fear of further oppression under Tito. She had to pare down her life's possessions to only ten pounds, the limit of what she could bring to Italy. Unlike the gradations of *cittadinanza italiana speciale* (special Italian citizenship) in colonial Libya, the Italian state gave Istrian refugees the option for full citizenship under purview of the Paris Peace Treaty.

Yet some Istrian refugees arrived clandestinely in Italy and refused to opt until decades later. One woman I spoke with in Villaggio Santa Caterina remained *apolide* (stateless) as she moved for years among the refugee camps. Still others, by way of bureaucratic errors and database omissions, remained without a *codice fiscale* (social security number). For example, Maria Luisa, an Istrian *profuga* born in Fiume in 1941 and living in Rome, discovered her *codice fiscale* was incomplete in 2014 when she went to a local hospital and could not be served because there was no record of her being Italian. Another *profuga*, Maria Grazia, could not report a crime because she too was without a *codice fiscale*.[152] Put another way, the Italian state once again harnessed inscriptions of race, ethnicity, and nationality to put its stamp on its subjects—be they Istrian *profughi*, "special Italian citizens" in colonial Libya, or Roma living in *villaggi attrezzati*—and it does so via the recognition or refusal of citizenship.

It might be said that all refugees bear an indelible scar on the spirit. At the ex–concentration camp of Fossoli, Istrian exiles softened their scar tissue by creating their own refuge at Villaggio San Marco. One refugee, Antonio Zappador, said the village was a place where "niente e nessuno è riuscito a distruggere la nostra autentica italianità istriana" (nothing and no one succeeded in destroying our authentic Istrian Italianness).[153] Life went on here for seventeen years. Some people moved away and made their lives elsewhere, and by the late 1960s, just a few Istrian refugee families remained. On March 7, 1970, they were moved to a public housing complex in nearby Carpi, and the Villaggio San Marco was closed for good.

The End of the Village?

In July 2017, a fiery inferno destroyed part of the *villaggio attrezzato* of La Barbuta outside Rome (figure 18). The blaze started around noon and quickly blackened the sky with a column of smoke that stopped traffic on roads and in the air above. It gathered and billowed like a thunderhead. The fire started in the trash heaps that lined the village periphery—that is, in the same place where one of the residents, R., had told me years before, "Non puoi immaginare le cose che buttano qua" (You can't imagine the things they dump here). What made the fire so toxic was the burning of the hazardous waste (for example, electrical appliances, household chemicals). From Google Earth, one can see the twisted and charred remains of more than a dozen of the white laminate houses known as "containers." They look incinerated as if by napalm. While the cause of this particular fire was not specified, both local politicians and the media were quick to assign blame to the Roma who lived at La Barbuta.

Figure 18. Smoke rises from the *villaggio attrezzato* (equipped village) of La Barbuta, 2017. Photograph by Alessandro Serranò and reproduced by permission from Agenzia Fotografica Giornalistica (AGF), Rome.

Stereotypes were mobilized to sway political and public opinion against the Roma and in favor of closing La Barbuta. The Roma were once again painted as "uncivilized" and "criminal," an untoward collective intent on living outside the law. For instance, local right-leaning politician Adriano Palozzi called the fire "l'ennesimo episodio di illegalità" (the umpteenth episode of illegality). Of other fires at La Barbuta, he said previously, "È più che evidente che all'interno dell'insediamento attrezzato, a fronte di persone che scelgono di vivere civilmente, ce ne siano altre che non conoscono o fanno finta di non conoscere le regole di convivenza collettiva." (It is more than evident that within the equipped village, in the face of people who choose to live civilly, there are others who do not know or pretend not to know the rules of collective coexistence.)[154] The regional president of Lazio, Nicola Zingharetti, was even blunter: "Oggi brucia ancora La Barbuta, superato ogni limite. Non è un caso, spesso è criminalità." (Today La Barbuta burns again, exceeding every limit. It is not coincidence; often it is crime.)[155] At the national level, the July 2017 fire prompted parliamentary representative Fabio Rampelli to file an inquiry with the Ministry of the Interior asking: "Perché sia a oggi possibile che all'interno del campo possano entrare ingenti quantità di materiale rubato o venduto per essere 'stoccato' illegalmente nel campo e quindi bruciato."

(Why is it possible today that around the camp there can be enormous quantities of stolen or contraband goods "stored" illegally in the camp and then burned.)[156] These are but a few examples of the ways in which Roma stereotypes were deployed in the wake of the fires at La Barbuta.

By framing the matter as one of public safety—as happened in 2008 with the declaration of *emergenza nomade* (nomad emergency), and even earlier, in 1930 with the *stato di pericolo pubblico* (state of public danger) declared against the Bedouin of colonial Libya—the discourse of security opens up the possibility for the Italian state to declare an emergency again and thereby justify the use of force against Roma and Sinti. Residents of nearby towns intensified their protests against the toxic fires and petitioned for the closure of La Barbuta. Their cries have not fallen on deaf ears. While debates about closing the *villaggi attrezzati* have circulated since 2015, the July fire prompted the municipal establishment to give a definitive timeline: La Barbuta will close by 2020.

Exactly how the Roman government would close this village of 4,500 residents prompted concerns from Michela Micheli, interim director of the newly formed Ufficio Speciale Rom, Sinti e Camminanti (Special Office of Roma, Sinti, and Camminanti). "A La Barbuta ha avuto avvio la prima sperimentazione di Roma Capitale per la chiusura del campo," she said. "Si sta cercando di portare a termine . . . [di] attuare un progetto di accompagnamento guidato, assistito, alla fuoriuscita delle persone dal campo." (At La Barbuta, Roma Capitale has launched its first experiment in the closure of the camp. It is trying to carry out . . . to actualize a project of guided accompaniment assisting the egress of the people from the camp.)[157] Micheli uses the term *fuoriuscita* to describe the removal of Roma from La Barbuta, the very same term employed by Italian colonial officials in the mid-1930s to describe the influx of Bedouin refugees, *fuorusciti*, returning to Libya. The term's liquid connotation, "to spill out, to pour out," captured the anxiety of Italian colonial officials of being inundated by refugees. In much the same way, Micheli is a municipal official worried about the many soon-to-be-created Romani *fuorusciti* of the *villaggio attrezzato*. The implication: from the fire will come a flood.

The closure of La Barbuta in 2020 is just not soon enough for some residents and political officials. Presciently, in October 2017, members of the ruling political party in Rome, Movimento Cinque Stelle (M5S), began to push for the Italian Army to quell the "emergency" at La Barbuta. M5S activists have gone on record as saying:[158]

Siamo di fronte a un'emergenza talmente grave e complessa . . .
I roghi tossici sono veri e propri reati penali e come tale vanno trattati . . .

Ed in quanto reati la competenza non può essere imputata alla Giunta Capitolina ma alle autorità competenti: il Prefetto e le forze dell'ordine.

We are faced with a very serious and complex emergency. . . . The toxic fires are true and proper criminal offenses and should be treated as such . . . and with regard to crime, expertise cannot be ascribed to the municipal government but rather to competent authorities: the Prefect and the law enforcement.

The M5S are building a case for state intervention at La Barbuta. They are hitting all the pertinent discursive notes—public safety, criminality, emergency—that have led to state violence in the past. It is the same rhetorical constellation that preceded the razing of *campi nomadi* (nomad camps) in 2009 and the creation of concentration camps in colonial Libya in 1929. If the village of La Barbuta is closed by force, then what new space of exclusion will take its place? What additional challenges will this newly unmoored group of "undesirables" face as a consequence of their coerced displacement? In other words, for those who have passed through the island, the camp, and the village, where to next in empire's Mobius strip?

This precarious life of ongoing displacement and discrimination prompted one Romani woman, Laura Halilovic, to take refuge in the art form that best displaces and re-creates reality: film. At nineteen, Halilovic made a documentary, *Io, la mia famiglia rom, e Woody Allen* (Me, my Roma family, and Woody Allen, 2009), the only Roma-directed feature to emerge from Italy in the past decade.[159] Elsewhere in Europe, Roma-directed films have gained traction and visibility; however, in Italy the *campi nomadi* have remained largely the provenance of Italian directors. For example, the acclaimed film *A Ciambra* (2017), directed by Jonas Carpignano, trains its lens on a Romani protagonist, Pio, and his life in a Romani community in Calabria. Reviews of the film celebrate its neorealist ethos yet note its polished finish thanks in part to executive producer Martin Scorsese.

Laura Halilovic's film has none of *A Ciambra*'s slick production value, but it gives an unfiltered glimpse into the life of Laura's Romani family and the long-term repercussions of their resettlement from nomad camp into public housing. Her film opens with a meditation on citizenship and its inadequacy in representing her identity. She narrates the initial voiceover:

Io sono nata in Italia. Ho la carta d'identità italiana. Però il mio passaporto è della Bosnia. E ogni anno devo dare le impronte digitali per rinnovare il mio permesso di soggiorno. Ma la mia identità è ancora un'altra: io sono rom.

I was born in Italy. I have an Italian identity card. But my passport is from Bosnia. And every year I have to get fingerprinted to renew my permit of stay. But my identity is still yet another: I am Roma.

By opening with a declaration of her identity, Halilovic sets the intention of the film: this is a film that speaks as Roma. Indeed, much of it is shot in the Romani language and dubbed into Italian. It is set in northern Italy, the hazy flatlands and gray skies of Lombardy serving as counterpoints to the colorful clothing and gold jewelry of the Romani women.

The Halilovic family moved into public housing around 1999, and the film zeroes in on this trauma of sedentarization as that which continues to define them. Halilovic sets up a dichotomy between their vibrant life in the camp and their quasi-anhedonic life in the apartment by juxtaposing home videos of birthday parties and snowball fights in the former against interior shots of empty rooms and neatly arranged furniture in the latter. She waxes nostalgic for life in the camp:

Mi ricordo che la mia baracca era piena di gente. Mi piaceva la confusione. Tutti che parlavano ad alta voce. Adesso dopo dieci anni che viviamo in questo appartamento penso sempre meno al campo. A volte mi manca ancora quella vita e tanti momenti felici che mi sono rimasti impressi nel cuore.

I remember my shanty was full of people. I liked the confusion. Everyone talked at high volume. Now after ten years that we've lived in this apartment I think less about the camp. Sometimes I still miss that life and the many happy moments that remain impressed on my heart.

For Laura's father, the *campo nomadi* was a space of security and freedom. "Ecco com'era nel campo . . . più libero, più tranquillo. Ero più sicuro quando dovevo lasciare la famiglia per andare a lavorare." (That's how it was in the camp . . . more free, more tranquil. I felt safer when I left the family to go to work.) The film romanticizes life in the *campo nomadi* not just in voiceovers and interviews but also in scenes showing Laura's extended family who still live in a camp nearby. Her grandmother tells stories. A cousin reads coffee grounds. Children play together outside. Life there seems rich, happy.

Halilovic also comments on the *villaggi attrezzati* (equipped villages) where the municipal government has relocated many Roma. In one scene the camera follows a young Romani girl walking briskly among the uniform containers of one village. "Quando vedo queste casette tutte uguali, chiuse dentro un recinto di ferro, mi vengo in mente campi di concentramento," says

Halilovic in a voiceover. (When I see these houses all the same, locked within an iron fence, concentration camps come to mind.) The follow shot of the young girl hastening through the *villaggio* serves a dual purpose: it forces viewers to identify with her and it also symbolizes the pursuit and persecution of Roma. To confirm this symbolism, Halilovic in the next shot cuts to archival footage of Roma in a concentration camp, their striped uniforms clearly visible.

The camp, the village, and the Halilovic apartment are the spaces of Romani life in this film. The *campo nomadi* serves as the bastion of Romani culture, and of all the spaces, it is the one under greatest threat. Tension builds throughout the documentary as Laura's extended family battles an order of *sgombero* (eviction). They have twenty-four hours to vacate the camp or face being physically removed by force. The agony and frustration are palpable. Laura's uncles had purchased the land, but that did not seem to matter. They enlisted a lawyer's help to appeal the eviction, but again, there appeared to be little hope of victory given the discrimination against Roma. In the lawyer's words, "Purtroppo è inutile negarlo. Voi siete dei zingari. Non siete certamente ben considerati né dal comune né tantomento dalla popolazione d'intorno." (Unfortunately it is useless to deny it [the eviction]. You are gypsies. You are certainly not well regarded by the municipal government or by the inhabitants around here.) In short, *sgombero* was imminent, and Laura's uncle begrudgingly concludes that the best course of action would be to accept this injustice and move on to another place.

Laura's grandmother, however, is not so easily accepting of the impending *sgombero*. Distraught, disheveled, and smoking heavily, she opines: "Ora ci mandano via ma io non so dove andare. Non so veramente dove andare. Vado davanti al comune, dal sindaco. Mi metto lì con la tenda e resto lì." (Now they send us away and I don't know where to go. I really don't know where to go. I'll go to city hall, to the mayor. I'll pitch my tent and remain there.) Then her distress transforms into defiance. Her wizened face, its lines the etchwork of decades, hardens with anger. She seems to reach a breaking point, as perhaps did the inhabitants of La Barbuta who, tired of their containment in the *villaggio attrezzato*, allegedly set fire to it, or the *ospiti* (guests) of Ponte Galeria who burned mattresses in protest of their detention. Laura's grandmother professes in broken Italian: "Lo sai cosa faccio, un chilo o due di benzina e fatto bruciare tutto. Andare tutto bene per me." (You know what I'll do, a kilo or two of gasoline, and I'll burn it all. That'll be all good for me.)

To burn everything would leave nothing left for anyone to take. It would close out the possibility for injustice, inequality, discrimination, and persecution—a singularity of nothing. Yet the impulse to destroy brings with it the potential to start anew. Fire evokes purification and rebirth, for in death there is life. What, like a phoenix, might then arise from these metaphorical ashes? Laura's grandmother rejoins, "non si muore come si vuole" (you do not die as you wish). While rare is the choice in dying, the real privilege is having the choice to live as one chooses. This is impossible for anyone cemented into the substrata of imperial formations and the disorientation of empire's Mobius strip. For those who are caught up in these endless loops of power, the time feels ripe for conflagration, for everyone deserves the chance and the choice of living a full life.

Coda

If I hadn't gone to that kind of place I wouldn't have realized the beauty that exists in that enormous bleakness.

—Chiura Obata

It feels ten degrees colder at Manzanar than anywhere else in the Owens River valley. Set between California's Sierra Nevada to the west and the Inyo Mountains to the east, the valley is both desolate and dramatic. Few trees grow here. The wind and granite cut sharply, especially in winter. The mountains rise up like snow-covered fangs, impenetrable to all but the most experienced climbers.

Manzanar functioned as a concentration camp from 1942 to 1945 where ten thousand Japanese Americans and Japanese immigrants were unjustly imprisoned on the basis of their race (figure 19). It was part of a greater system of concentration camps (inaccurately called "war relocation centers") built on American soil that interned 120,000 Japanese throughout the West. More than half of these people were U.S. citizens. Some historians have described the forced detention of the country's own citizens as one of the darkest episodes in American history.[1]

The Manzanar War Relocation Center was originally called the "Owens Valley Reception Center," an appellation strikingly similar to the *centri di accoglienza* (welcome centers) for contemporary migrants in Italy described in this book's previous essays. Other similarities exist between Manzanar and Italy's islands, camps, and villages. For instance, its geographical isolation brought to mind Lampedusa, but instead of the Mediterranean Sea, the mountains surrounded the camp to form an impassable limit. Its scale and rectilinear layout

FIGURE 19.   Remains of the Manzanar concentration camp, Owens River valley, California, 2017.
Photograph reproduced by permission from Paul Myers.

reminded me of aerial photos I saw in Italian archives of the Soluq concentration camp in colonial Libya. The testimonies of the *Nisei* (second-generation Japanese Americans) interned in the cramped conditions of Manzanar's tar-paper barracks recalled for me the same laments of Roma living in overcrowded trailers in villages like La Barbuta.[2]

The point here is that sites like Manzanar, Lampedusa, Soluq, and La Barbuta are all bound up in empire's Mobius strip. They represent the historical echoes and the contemporary exercise of imperial formations that hinge on the exertion of power over others—a power that rests on the control of mobility. Empire rises and falls by the struggle of those who move by choice and those who are moved by force.

The story that I have written of Italy's islands, camps, and villages—and the people among them who are moved or immobilized coercively—unfolds and entangles with mobility regimes operating across myriad times and places. Sometimes these stories rest so close to home that we no longer see them as consequences of empire. Nor do we attend carefully enough to the links between contemporary crises of migration and detention and the historical ones that preceded them.

In the years I spent writing this manuscript in the United States, I sought out sites where imperial formations manifested close to home: in part for inspiration, and in part as confirmation that empire indeed depends on the control of mobility. One could easily write the story of empire's Mobius strip in the United States at places like Manzanar, where *Nisei* who were deemed a threat to the state were contained and isolated in the early 1940s.

Or, the California missions where Spanish settlers in the late eighteenth century forcibly marshaled indigenous peoples onto ranches and estates, leading to what the historian Kevin Starr has called nothing less than "wholesale anthropological devastation."[3]

Or, military outposts like Fort Sill, Oklahoma, where wide-ranging Plains Indian tribes such as the Comanche were captured and imprisoned during the 1860s and 1870s in the bloody conflict for the American frontier.

Or, the ruins of Chinatown in San Jose, California, that burned to the ground by arson in 1887, a flashpoint for anti-immigration biases that led to the Chinese Exclusion Act being made permanent.

Or, carceral islands like Alcatraz or Guantánamo, both sites of imprisonment for those deemed to be extreme threats to the state.

Or, the system of migrant detention centers across the United States, the largest in the world, in which any noncitizen is made vulnerable to internment and deportation.

The examples are seemingly endless. Whether Japanese Americans, California indigenous peoples, Plains Indians, Chinese immigrants, Bedouin, Roma, Sinti, migrants, refugees, asylum seekers, exiles, nomads, *coatti* (prisoners), *confinati* (confined), *deportati* (deportees), *fuorusciti* (refugees), *profughi nazionali* (national refugees), and many others—all have been forced to move or have been immobilized against their will. They are shunted into and among spaces of exclusion like the island, the camp, and the village.

The control of mobility is the fulcrum of empire. The power over movement equates to power over people. It creates mobility-generated inequality, a condition that resonates deeply across geographies and generations and that has intensified in our contemporary moment. Unsanctioned mobilities have once again been cast as a "threat" in this second decade of the twenty-first century. Xenophobia and racism not only have been operating at their most brazen and unapologetic in decades but also have fomented the relentless violence and cruelty that characterize the exercise of imperial power. In the United States and elsewhere, the trauma linked to migration and detention does not discriminate. It scars men and women alike: families separated at borders, deportees returned "home" to violence and persecution, and countless others ensnared in the illegality industry.

What is more, enormous profits are being made off those who are most vulnerable. The illegality industry is worth billions, if not trillions, worldwide.

Ruben Andersson notes that migrants are often used as crude bargaining chips to increase funding for military budgets and humanitarian aid.[4] For example, one nonprofit organization in the United States was awarded a government contract for $458 million in 2018 to run shelters for migrant children separated from their families in Texas, one of which was in a converted Wal-Mart. Over the past decade, this nonprofit, Southwest Key Inc., has received $1.5 billion in funding from the U.S. government for its "unaccompanied alien children program."[5] Thus border zones are not just territorial boundaries but also margins of profit and loss. Migrant lives no longer just hang in the balance but are calculated on balance sheets. Earnings will only grow as the illegality industry continues to expand apace. According to the UN Refugee Agency, more than sixty-eight million people were forcibly displaced in 2018 as a result of conflict or persecution, the highest level ever on record. The divide between those who move by choice and those who move by force grows wider and starker. Empire expands its reach while tightening its grip.

And yet there may still be hope. Some, like the artist Chiura Obata, have found beauty in the bleakness. A Japanese immigrant and art professor at the University of California, Berkeley, Obata gained renown in the 1920s and 1930s for his woodblock prints and landscape paintings of California's high country. His views of Yosemite still rival those of his contemporary, photographer Ansel Adams.

In 1942, however, Obata was among the 120,000 Japanese forcibly "relocated" to concentration camps like Manzanar. He ended up in Utah at the Topaz War Relocation Center with 9,000 other internees, the majority of whom hailed from the San Francisco Bay Area. While interned, Obata mobilized his fellow artists to establish an art school in the camp, for he believed art could lend strength and hope to those detained.

"Sincere creative endeavoring, especially in these stressing times, I strongly believe will aid in developing a sense of calmness and appreciation which is so desirable and following it come sound judgment and a spirit of cooperation," wrote Obata. "In such manner I feel that the general morale of the people will be uplifted."[6]

Some of Obata's illustrations of Topaz bore witness to the quotidian brutalities of daily life there, such as internees complying with bureaucratic regulations or another being shot along the barbed wire while walking his dog. Others of Obata's paintings were more poetic, evoking the paradox between the natural beauty of the high desert and the constructed confines of the camp.

One of these works is the painting *View of Topaz* (figure 20), a watercolor on silk commissioned by the Japanese American Citizens League for First Lady Eleanor Roosevelt. The painting gives prominence to the emptiness of sky and

FIGURE 20. *View of Topaz, Japanese Relocation Camp* (1942), a painting by Chiura Obata, shows the concentration camp in Utah where the artist was interned from 1942 to 1943. Image provided by the Franklin D. Roosevelt Library and Museum and reproduced by permission from Kimi Kodani Hill.

earth. Moonlight renders the negative space serene, bathing the landscape in a silvery haze. The eye is drawn to nature's sacred trinity of moon, mountains, and desert that occupies the background and the foreground of the painting.

At the middle ground the haze clears to reveal a fence, guard tower, and barracks painted heavy in black, an unnatural weight to an otherwise ephemeral scene. The camp haunts and partitions the landscape. It stands isolated and alienated in nature just as the people imprisoned within it were isolated and alienated in their own country.

Yet fences eventually fade into the desert, as does the one in this painting. Barracks become small and insignificant in the face of the age-old mountains. Obata's painting reminds us that the darkness of places such as the camp is only temporary. It will dissolve under the greater forces of nature—today Topaz lies in ruins—and over time hope will emerge from the bleakness and the blight once again.

Acknowledgments

Every academic book depends on the enduring support and goodwill of many people and institutions. Mine is no exception. Every word, every sentence, every idea in it connects back to conversations I have had, or lectures I have heard, or experiences that I have lived with others. This manuscript is infinitely better for it.

The majority of writing took place during my fellowship year at the Stanford Humanities Center (SHC), where I had the good fortune to be named the 2014–15 Marta Sutton Weeks Fellow. The time spent with my colleagues there proved invaluable to shaping the book in its present form. I am grateful to all the fellows in my year, especially Attiya Ahmad, Marquis Berry, Joseph Boone, J. P. Daughton, Fred Donner, Erika Doss, Bruno Perreau, Joan Ramon Resina, and Barb Voss. I also owe many thanks to the supportive SHC staff, including Director Caroline Winterer, as well as Robert Barrick, Roland Hsu, and Patricia Terrazas.

Thanks to a Charles A. Ryskamp Fellowship from the American Council of Learned Societies I was able to extend my stay at Stanford for the 2015–16 academic year. I am grateful to everyone in the Department of French and Italian for welcoming me as a visiting scholar, in particular Dan Edelstein, Robert Harrison, David Lummus, Christine Onorato, and Laura Wittman. In the greater Stanford community, I am thankful for the support of John Evans, Jenny Martinez, Sarah Ogilvie, Sarah Sussman, and Beth Van Schaack.

I was fortunate to have been chosen as the Lauro De Bosis Lecturer in the History of Italian Civilization at Harvard University in the fall of 2012, where I spent six months conducting research in the university's inestimable libraries. I am ever grateful to my colleagues in the Department of Romance Languages and Literatures, including Francesco Erspamer, Annalisa Sacchi, Pierluigi Sacco, and Jeffrey Schnapp. I thank Kathy Coviello and Mike Holmes for making everything happen administratively. The library staff was indispensable to my research, and I owe thanks to Joanne Bloom, Joseph Garver, András J. Riedlmayer, Jonathan Rosenwasser, and Vanessa Venti for their help. Also at Harvard, a huge thank-you to Michael Herzfeld and Nea Herzfeld for always delightful conversations and delicious meals. To my circle of friends in Boston, you made my stay wicked awesome. Thank you, Case Lance Brown and Aparna Keshaviah, Peter Cahn and Donald Hess, Anne Carney and John Ochsendorf, Rachel Jacoff, and Karina Xavier and José-Luis Galache.

I also owe thanks to the Oscar Broneer Traveling Fellowship at the American School for Classical Studies at Athens (ASCSA) for enabling me to spend the spring of 2013 in Greece. My time in Athens reminded me how citizenship and democracy are still being contested even at the very site where they were born, as did my fruitful conversations with ASCSA colleagues Nick Blackwell, Sean Corner, Tarek Elemam, Sara Frank, Margie Miles, Jana Mokrisova, and Director Jim Wright.

I am very thankful to have in my corner the wisdom, wit, and support of Emily Andrew, editor extraordinaire at Cornell University Press. I am grateful to everyone at the press for making the publication process truly enjoyable from start to finish. I owe thanks to the three anonymous peer reviewers, the Editorial Board, and the Faculty Board for believing in this project and offering valuable feedback that unequivocally made this a better book. Thank you to Mike Bechthold for creating the beautiful maps that illustrate every essay. Likewise, many thanks to Susan Storch for creating an index that is a work of art.

I am very grateful to my friends and colleagues who accompanied me during my fieldwork throughout Italy. A special thank-you to *New York Times* correspondent Elisabetta Povoledo for her gracious hospitality in Rome and for her strength during our visit to the migrant detention center at Ponte Galeria. I am grateful to Gabriele Proglio, who made the trip to Villaggio Santa Caterina with me in Turin. I am also thankful for my colleagues Suzanne Stewart-Steinberg and Ruth Lo from my alma mater, Brown University, who came with me to La Barbuta and spent hours debriefing about the experience. Also in Rome, I owe thanks to Catherine Brice, Rachel Donadio, Monica Larner, Gaia Pianigiani, and Ruth Raymond as well as the staff of the American Academy in Rome, my home away from home in the Eternal City.

In Italy, I have a long list of people to thank. Without them my fieldwork and archival research would have been impossible. They include the staff and *ospiti* at the CIE Ponte Galeria who spoke with me about their experiences; the residents of La Barbuta who invited me into their homes; the indefatigable staff at the Archivio Storico Diplomatico, which houses the papers of the Ministero dell'Africa Italiana (ASMAI); the staff of the Archivio Centrale dello Stato (ACS); the archivists at the Istituto Agronomico per l'Oltremare (IAO), Antonella Bigazzi, Laura Bonaiuti, and Patrizio Paoli; Matteo Zannoni and Cristiano Migliorelli (Istituto Luce); Fabrizio Nava (Ministero degli Affari Esteri); Antonio Taranto (Archivio Storico di Lampedusa); Daniele Monaci and Manuela

Monaci (Farchikalà, Lampedusa); Vito Ailara (Centro Storia e Documentazione Isola di Ustica); Luigi Usai and Bruna Usai (Formia); Carlo Marone (Ponza); Iole Lianza (Mostra Triennale d'Oltremare, Naples); Giulia Moretti (ZaLab); Giulia Bianchini (Fossoli); Dirk Moses and Valerie McGuire (European University Institute).

In the United States and Canada, I am very grateful for the support and feedback of colleagues who read earlier drafts of these essays, attended my conference presentations, and invited me to present my research at their institutions. Many thanks to Ali Ahmida, Jenny Chio, Jonathan Combs-Schilling, Bob Davidson, Alain-Philippe Durand, Rebecca Falkoff, Claudio Fogu, David Forgacs, Nelson Graburn, Kimi Kodani Hill, Lucienne Kroha, Amara Lakhous, Dean MacCannell, Juliet Flower MacCannell, Ara Merjian, Àine O'Healy, Dana Renga, Luca Somigli, Barbara Spackman, Rhiannon Welch, and Simona Wright. Thank you to Sean Anderson for the beautiful photos of Italian ruins in Cyrenaica.

I also owe thanks to my fellow 2017–18 Nantucket Project scholars for their cheerleading and support throughout the final steps of the publication process, especially Kate Brosnan, Allister Chang, Pulkit Datta, Lindsay Morris, Genevieve Lang, Daniela Papi, Ana Reyes, Laura Rittenhouse, and Raegan Sealy.

To my colleagues at my former institution, the University of Oklahoma, thank you: Lucas Bessire, Kristin Dowell, Pamela Genova, Jason Houston, Misha Klein, Nancy LaGreca, Bob Lemon, Monica Seger, Monica Sharp, Maurizio Vito, and Logan Whalen. My research was supported in part by grants from the Office of Vice President of Research, the College of Arts and Sciences, the College of International Studies, and the OU Board of Regents.

To my colleagues at the Acus Foundation, a hearty thank-you: especially Joseph Helms and Pamela Helms, as well as Lynne Gumina, Janice Sager, Sarah Weiss, and the cadre of dashing preceptors.

To Mia Fuller and Ruth Ben-Ghiat, my colleagues in intellect and friends in heart, a very special thank-you. This book also honors the memory of Scott Spradlin, my kindred spirit who left too soon.

I feel very fortunate to have wonderful friends and family members who have been there for me throughout all of life's ebbs and flows: my dog Brownie, Aileen Feng, the entire Hom family, Jay Hopler and Kimberly Johnson, the staff of Kepler's Books, Jennifer Madden and Jeff Reed, the Myers clan, Allison Rayne and Jason Manley, Kelli and Nic Rogl, Jim and Jan Sylvester, Jodi Sylvester, and Nikki Sylvester. To Lee and Julie Moncton, my family of the heart, you were there for me when all things fell apart, and I am forever grateful. Last but not least, Paul Myers, thank you for teaching me to see in new ways, and most importantly, thank you for love.

Notes

Introduction

1. Stoler 2008, 192.

2. Stoler and McGranahan 2007, 8.

3. The original name of this avenue was the Via dell'Impero, or the "Road of the Empire." It was changed to its present name, Via dei Fori Imperiali (Road of the Imperial Forums), after the fall of the Fascist regime in 1943.

4. All translations from Italian are mine unless otherwise noted.

5. Herzfeld 2009, 264–75.

6. Stoler and McGranahan 2007, 33–35.

7. The academic literature on empire is vast and replete with deep scholarly lineages. Historians including Ruth Ben-Ghiat, Jane Burbank, Frederick Cooper, and Victoria De Grazia have consistently pioneered new ways in which we study empire, as have anthropologists such as Mia Fuller and Ann Laura Stoler. World-systems theorists such as Giovanni Arrighi, Michael Hardt, Antonio Negri, and Immanuel Wallerstein have also transformed our thinking on the imperial, particularly in relation to capital. Likewise, the field of postcolonial studies established by scholars such as Homi Bhabha, Edward Said, and Gayatri Spivak has taken to task the cultural norms and values generated by empire, figuratively embodying the Italian tradition of *la critica militante* (militant criticism) with their work. Representative examples include Arrighi 2010; Ben-Ghiat 2015; Bhabha 2005; Burbank and Cooper 2010; Chatterjee 2012; De Grazia 2006; Fuller 2007; Hardt and Negri 2000; Said 1978, 1993; Spivak 1988; Stoler 2008, 2016; Wallerstein 2011.

8. UNHCR (UN Refugee Agency). Figures at a Glance. August 2018. http://www.unhcr.org/en-us/figures-at-a-glance.html (accessed August 8, 2018).

9. Agier 2011, 53, 71.

10. On the dream of migrating to Italy while in Dadaab, see Rawlence 2016, 278–83. On the growing Dadaab diaspora, see *Dadaab Stories: 500,000 Refugees. Countless Stories*, created by K. Ryan Jones and Rafiq Copeland, FilmAid International, www.dadaabstories.org (accessed August 4, 2018).

11. Rovelli 2006, 189. Emphasis in the original.

12. Stoler and McGranahan 2007, 8–9. See also Stoler 2016, 4–10.

13. Referring to a decentralized and de-territorialized globalized sovereignty, Hardt and Negri (2000, xiv) also note: "Empire has no boundaries, Empire's rule has no limits."

14. Bauman 1988, 2.

15. Urry 2007, 46–54.

16. Elliott and Urry 2010, 8.

17. Agier 2011, 23.

18. Fernando and Giordano 2016. See also De Genova 2017b, 9–17.

19. Mbembe 2003, 31.

20. Representative examples of scholarship on the crisis of migration and detention in the Mediterranean include Albahari 2015; Andersson 2014, 2017; Cabot 2014; De Genova 2017a; Feldman 2012; Giordano 2014; and Lucht 2012.

21. Andersson 2014, 15–16, 107–8.

22. Giordano 2014, 115–20.

23. Arendt 1976, 296–97.

24. From 1876 to 1976, an estimated twenty-six million Italians emigrated from Italy to destinations abroad. See Choate 2008, 1.

25. Ben-Ghiat and Hom 2016, 4–9. See also Fiore 2017.

26. On Italian diasporas, see Baldassar and Gabaccia 2010; Gabaccia 2000; Harney 1998, 2016; Ruberto and Sciorra 2017.

27. Ben-Ghiat and Hom 2016, 4.

28. Ben-Ghiat 2015, 23. See also Behdad 1994; Rosaldo 1989; Spackman 2017.

29. Fuller 2007, 29. See also Jonas 2011.

30. Bhabha 2005, 121–31.

31. Fuller 2007, 49. See also Hom 2012.

32. Braudel 1995.

33. Braudel 1995, 171–73.

34. Representative examples of scholarship on Italian colonial history include Ben-Ghiat 2015; Cresti 2011; Del Boca 2005, 2010a, 2010b; Di Giulio and Cresti 2016; Iacopini 2015; Labanca 2002; Marchi 2010; Ottolenghi 1997; Pergher 2018; Rochat 1973, 1991; Ryan 2018; Salerno 2005; and Segrè 1974. On Italian postcolonial studies, see Andall and Duncan 2005, 2010; Ben-Ghiat and Fuller 2005; Palumbo 2003; Ponzanesi and Merolla 2005; Romeo and Lombardi-Diop 2012; and Spadaro 2013.

35. Ballinger 2016b.

36. Parati 2005.

37. Del Boca 2005; Locatelli 2016.

The Island

1. Lampedusa's migrant detention center is currently classified as a Centro di Primo Soccorso e Accoglienza (Center of First Aid and Welcome) by the Italian Ministry of the Interior.

2. Much has been written about the spectacle of the border on Lampedusa and elsewhere. As representative examples of scholarship, see Albahari 2015; Andersson 2014; Cabot 2014; Cuttitta 2012; De Genova 2002, 2013; O'Healy 2016; Proglio and Odasso 2018. On the politics of humanitarian interventions, see Fassin and Pandolfi 2010.

3. In 2013, TripAdvisor ranked Lampedusa's Isola dei Conigli (translated in English as "Rabbit Island") as the best beach in the world.

4. Stoler and McGranahan 2007, 8.

5. On insular regimes of inclusion and exclusion in the Mediterranean, see Baldacchino 2010, 2014; Bernadie-Tahir and Schmoll 2014; Loyd and Mountz 2014; Staniscia 2011; Triandafyllidou 2014.

6. On the transit networks and multidirectional movements of the Mediterranean, see Abulafia 2011; Braudel 1995; Chambers 2008; Clancy-Smith 2011; Fogu and Re 2010; Horden and Purcell 2000; Matvejevic 1998. Sadly, human cargo has long been a part of these networks, not just in the Mediterranean but also worldwide. On islands like Lampedusa, where the exclusionary dynamics of contemporary migration take form in space, one need not look very far for other examples, such as Christmas Island and Nauru, which house detention facilities for Australia (Pugliese 2010), or the Canary Islands, where West African migrants to Spain are stopped and held (Andersson 2014, 70–73). They are a far cry from the likes of Ellis Island or Angel Island in the past and perhaps closer in spirit to Solzhenitsyn's gulag archipelago.

7. Perera 2009, 4. The *Journal of Island Studies* also offers an interdisciplinary scholarly forum that tracks the ways in which islands, meeting points of land and sea, are interconnected sociopolitical spaces.

8. See Baldacchino 2014, 58–60, as well as the discussion of islands in Braudel 1995, 148–67.

9. Said 1993, 320. To be clear, Edward Said referred specifically to the contradictory relations between culture and empire.

10. On this, see Andrijasevic 2010, 150–52; Cuttitta 2012, 51–54; Pugliese 2011. See also Agamben 1998, 1999, and essay two of this book.

11. Andersson 2014, 67–68, 95–97. See also Andersson 2017.

12. The Lampedusa airport was built for €16.7 million in 2012. All historical currency conversions were calculated using the website *Historical Currency Converter*, edited by Rodney Edvinsson, Stockholm University, http://www.historicalstatistics .org/Currencyconverter.html (accessed August 5, 2018).

13. Sgroi 2007. See also Gatti 2007, 289.

14. Founded in 2008, the Archivio di Memorie Migranti is an extraordinary repository of migrant testimonies, both written and oral. In 2012 the organization began work on the Lampedusa project, which will help "transform the image of Lampedusa, through activities of communication and advocacy, from a place of emergency and foreign invasion to a symbolic place in which the memory of discrimination can help bring to light new forms of human relationships and the recognition of mutual rights between people of different origins." *Archivio memorie migranti*, Circolo Gianni Bosio: Casa della Memoria e della Storia, http://www.archiviomemoriemigranti .net/ (accessed September 13, 2018).

15. Since the mid-2000s, a vast body of scholarly literature and first-person narratives of migration has been published in Italy. Some authors, such as Pap Khouma and Amara Lakhous, have written best sellers that are widely known throughout the country. Others are more obscure, published by small regional presses with limited distribution. Yet autobiographies and journalistic accounts about migrant life in Italy seem to be a cottage industry, and many texts foreground the journey to the country—and the passage through Lampedusa—as a key element of their narratives. Examples of such texts include De Pasquale and Arena 2011; Del Grande 2008, 2010; Lanza 2014; Liberti 2008; Maragnani and Aikpitanyi 2007, among many others.

Scholarly works on migration narratives are also numerous; for representative examples, see Benelli 2013; Burns 2013; Parati 2005; Ponzanesi and Merolla 2005; Triulzi and McKenzie, 2013.

16. Gatti cites €150 per person as the price of passage in the mid-2000s. Gatti 2007, 195; see also Gatti 2005 and the documentary film *A sud di Lampedusa* (2008).

17. Hamood 2006, 45–47. See also Bensaâd 2001, 2002, 2007; Lucht 2011, 2012, 160–76.

18. As cited in Hamood 2006, 46.

19. Human Rights Watch 2009, 71.

20. Gatti notes the illegality industry generated €1.5 million each month in Dirkou. Gatti 2007, 196.

21. Human Rights Watch (2009, 75) notes that the accounts of Kufra "should be read as a snapshot of a continuous, traumatic journey. The description of abuse in Kufra should not be read in isolation but as part of a continuum of hardship and abuse." On the use of poison gas in Kufra in the 1930s, see Del Boca 2010b, 189–97.

22. As cited in *Come un uomo sulla terra* 2008.

23. On the transit economy that has developed around migrants and refugees in camps and along routes, see Agier 2011, 152–55; Pliez 2002.

24. Andersson 2014, 117–18.

25. Braudel 1995, 171–73.

26. To note, Zuwarah was a key transit point in Italian colonial Libya, acting as the western terminus for the 73-mile-long railway built between Tripoli and Zuwarah in the 1920s, one of the very few constructed by the Italian colonial administration. See Touring Club Italiano 1929, 302–6. In terms of contemporary migration, most boats are crudely retrofitted to be just seaworthy enough to endure the 186-mile trip from Libya to Lampedusa, several days at sea in good weather. Many are actually stolen and ready to be abandoned on arrival. The boats vary in form and in name, which is reflected in the Italian: *barcone* (large boat or pontoon), *gommone* (inflatable raft or rubber dinghy), *peschereccio* (fishing trawler), *carretta del mare* (tramp steamer). Yet it is perhaps the name for these vessels in Arabic that best captures their true essence: they are simply known as "death boats" (*qawaarib al-mawuut*) across the Maghreb. According to the UN Refugee Agency (UNHCR), on average, one person in ten dies on the journey from Libya. On other trans-Mediterranean routes, see Andersson 2014, 78–80; Forgacs 2016; Monzini, Pastore, and Sciortino 2004, 50–51.

27. During the Arab Spring in 2011, the numbers of people making the journey across the Mediterranean increased exponentially. Their plight, too, has become increasingly familiar to the general public thanks to films such as *Harragas* (2009), by Algerian filmmaker Merzak Allouache, and *I nostri anni migliori* (2012), by Matteo Calore and Stefano Collizzolli. Migrants from North Africa are called *Haraagha* in Arabic, from the verb "to burn," which stems from the common practice of burning one's documents prior to being detained.

28. According to Hamood, the price of the Mediterranean crossing has fluctuated between €800–€1,200 since the early 2000s. Hamood 2006, 50; Monzini, Pastore, and Sciortino 2004, 50.

29. On the *respingimenti* (pushbacks), see Albahari 2015, 41; Andersson 2017, 76; Forgacs 2016; Locchi 2014. Flows of migrants have increased along the central

Mediterranean route into Europe since the mid-2000s after Spain funneled millions of euros to governments in western Africa to effectively shut down migration externally (Andersson 2014, 33–65). Frontex, the EU border management agency, outlines four main routes of "illegal immigration" into Europe: the Western Mediterranean (Morocco/Spain), Central Mediterranean (Libya/Italy), Eastern Mediterranean (Turkey/Greece), and Western Balkan (Serbia/Hungary). The majority of "illegal immigrants" in the EU are visa over-stayers, arriving on tourist visas and staying beyond their duration (Scheel 2017). Those who cannot afford the airfare cross into the EU illicitly, with the central Mediterranean route being the most popular (Frontex 2014, 7–8).

30. Forgacs 2016, 189.

31. European Court of Human Rights, *Hirsi Jamaa and Others v. Italy*, case no. 27765/09, accessed August 5, 2018, http://hudoc.echr.coe.int/sites/eng/pages /search.aspx#{%22dmdocnumber%22:[%22901565%22],%22itemid%22:[%22001 -109231%22]}. This case was brought to court by eleven Somali nationals and thirteen Eritreans who were intercepted by Italian authorities south of Lampedusa in May 2009 and returned to Tripoli. The court found in favor of the migrants and awarded them approximately $19,000 each (€15,000) in nonpecuniary damages. In the concurring opinion by Judge Pinto De Albuquerque appended to the case, he eloquently summed up the complexities of the situation: "The Hirsi case is about the international protection of refugees, on the one hand, and the compatibility of immigration and border control policies with international law, on the other hand. The ultimate question in this case is how Europe should recognize that refugees have 'the right to have rights,' to quote Hannah Arendt. . . . Refugees attempting to escape Africa do not claim a right of admission to Europe. They demand only that Europe, the cradle of human rights idealism and the birthplace of the rule of law, cease closing its doors to people in despair who have fled from arbitrariness and brutality. That is a very modest plea, vindicated by the European Convention on Human Rights. We should not close our ears to it" (*Hirsi Jamaa and Others v. Italy*, 60, 80).

32. IOM 2014, 109; UNHCR 2014, 1. Of Italy's population of 61 million, approximately 4.9 million are migrants. Of the 139,000 people rescued in 2014, half were from Syria and Eritrea, and the rest were from other countries. On migration statistics, see UN International Organization on Migration, *Migration Data Portal*, https:// www.iom.int/ (accessed August 4, 2018).

33. IOM 2014, 109–37.

34. Cuttitta 2012, 25–71.

35. For details on the legislation of immigration and citizenship in Italy, see Albahari 2015; Forgacs 2016; Tintori 2016; and essay three in this book.

36. Zaccaria 2013, 169.

37. Gatti 2007, 335.

38. Gatti 2007, 344.

39. Zaccaria 2013, 170.

40. Dal Lago, 2012.

41. On the state of exception spatialized by Lampedusa's CPT, see Andrijasevic 2010; Vassallo Paleologo 2012.

42. Claviez 2013, 8.

43. As presented in the audio documentary "Turchi: Storie di elicotteri e barche a Lampedusa" (2009). On the construction of the migrant detention center and the creation of Lampedusa as borderland, see Cuttitta 2012, 43–45, 81–84.

44. "Lampedusa, scontri tra migranti e polizia" 2009.

45. Ziniti 2011b.

46. "Berlusconi da Gheddafi" 2008.

47. Triandafyllidou 2014, 13–15.

48. According to Human Rights Watch, Italy spent €5.5 million on migrant detention in Libya circa 2003. Human Rights Watch 2006, 101.

49. Human Rights Watch 2009, 75. This report identifies a total of sixteen dedicated migration detention facilities: Misratah, Zlitan, Az-Zawiyah, Garabulli, Surman, Towisha, Zuwarah, Kufra, Ganfuda (Benghazi), Al-Qatrun, Ajdabiya, Sirte, Sabratah, Bani Walid, Jawazat, and Bin Gashir. The journalist Gabriele Del Grande, who has spent years traveling in Libya and runs the blog *Fortress Europe*, visited detention sites in the south of the country and identified at least four additional detention "camps" in the southwest of the country: three located in Shati, Ghat, and Birak, which act as holding centers for migrants arrested at the border with Algeria and Niger, and another in Sabha, which is a larger facility to which people detained in Shati, Ghat, and Birak are eventually sent (Del Grande 2009).

50. As cited in Dietrich 2005.

51. Fagan 2010, 106.

52. For details about the treatment of migrants in Libyan detention centers, see Drudi 2013; Eltahawy 2012; Zerai 2013. On Liu's visit to Libyan detention centers, see "MSF President Dr. Joanne Liu on horrific migrant detention centres in Libya," September 8, 2017. https://www.youtube.com/watch?v=Ppb_5hJCF98 (accessed August 5, 2018).

53. Pugliese 2010, 106.

54. The classical sources that mention Lampedusa (Lopadussa) include it as part of Africa rather than Sicily or Europe. See Pliny the Elder's *Natural History* (book 3, chapter 14, as well as book 5, chapter 8); Ptolemy's *Geography* (listed as both Anemussa and Lopadusa, 4, 3, 44), and Strabo's *Geography* (book 17, chapter 3, §16). On *garum* production in the Mediterranean, see Curtis 1978; Ponsich and Tarradell 1965.

55. See Bonaffini 1997; Bono 1989, 1993; Davis 2003, 2009.

56. The actual statistics on the number of slaves along the Barbary Coast vary but were certainly in the tens of thousands. For an in-depth discussion of slave counts, see Davis 2003, 3–26; also Bono 1993, 192–98; Braudel 1995, 754–55. Barbary pirates were not the first to practice slavery in the Mediterranean; it was a widespread practice in the ancient Mediterranean, especially in Rome. For a general overview, see Bradley and Cartledge 2011.

57. Bono (1993, 194–95) estimates that in the second half of the sixteenth century, there were twelve thousand Muslim slaves in Sicily alone (or 1 percent of the population) and twenty thousand more in Naples. He adds that Muslim slaves were present to greater and lesser degrees throughout Italy for much of the sixteenth century, as were Christian slaves in the Maghreb, with Algiers and Tunis the chief centers of slavery.

58. Davis 2009, 41.

59. Ciappara 2004, 178.

60. "Lampedusa Island," *Encyclopaedia Brittanica*, accessed August 5, 2018, http://www.britannica.com/EBchecked/topic/328858/Lampedusa-Island.

61. Stritmatter and Kositsky 2013, 88.

62. Stritmatter and Kositsky 2013, 93.

63. On the protracted end of the Mediterranean slave trade, see Davis 2009, 26.

64. Gregory 1996, Appendix A: Lampedusa, 283–86. See also Staines 2008, 393–410.

65. Pasley 1810, 81–82.

66. Gregory 1996, 286.

67. Staines 2008, 407–10; Zerafa 2011.

68. Zerafa 2011.

69. Sanvisente 1849, 87.

70. Sanvisente 1849, 87–88.

71. Sanvisente 1849, 46–47, 91–100.

72. Sanvisente 1849, 53.

73. Sanvisente 1849, 77.

74. Sanvisente 1849, 111–12.

75. Mancini 1978, 42–43; Maslah 2012, 84.

76. Martucci 1999, 324.

77. Representative examples of the extensive scholarship on the Italian South include Dickie 1999; Moe 2002; Petrusewicz 1998; Schneider 1998.

78. Farini was a staunch supporter of the Risorgimento, and he kept up a frequent correspondence with Cavour. After Unification, he would go on to briefly serve as Italy's fourth prime minister (December 1862–March 1863), resigning due to poor health. The famous quote that conflates the Italian South with Africa comes from Farini's letter to Cavour dated October 27, 1860, available in *La liberazione del Mezzogiorno e la formazione del Regno d'Italia: Carteggi di Camillo Cavour*, vol. 3 (Bologna: Zanichelli, 1952), 207–8. I am grateful to Sara Troyani for identifying the source of this quotation.

79. On this, see Ballinger 2002; Choate 2008; Welch 2016b; Wong 2006.

80. For an overview of the political circumstances and legislative measures leading up to the creation of *domicilio coatto*, see Garfinkel 2011.

81. Fozzi 2010, 235–85.

82. Archivio di Stato di Agrigento. Inventario 26, Busta 111 1862, Censimento 1862. As cited in Maslah 2012, 91.

83. Archivio di Stato di Agrigento. Inventario 26, Busta 111 1862, Censimento 1862. As cited in Maslah 2012, 91.

84. Archivio Vescovile di Agrigento, Lampedusa, Processetti matrimoniali, N° 167, 1860–1888. As cited in Maslah 2012, 88.

85. Maslah 2012, 96–97.

86. Fozzi 2010, appendix, table 1, 304–5.

87. Giovanni Fragapane, "Il confine e i lager di Mussolini" (unpublished manuscript, 2014). Text acquired by the author at the Lampedusa Historical Archive. Fragapane is the ex-mayor of Lampedusa and a resident expert on the island's history.

88. On brigandage and its repression in Italy, see Fozzi 2010; Martucci 1980; Molfese 1966. Article 2 of the Pica law abrogated due process and sanctioned death by firing squad of anyone believed to be a brigand: "I colpevoli del reato di brigantag-

gio, i quali armata mano oppongono resistenza alla forza pubblica, saranno puniti colla fucilazione, o co' lavori forzati a vita correndovi circostanze attenuanti." (Those guilty of the crime of brigandage, who resist the police with armed hands, will be punished by firing squad, or if there are extenuating circumstances, with hard labor for life.) Full text of the law available at "Legge per la repressione del brigantaggio," Università degli Studi Firenze, Sistema Bibliotecario di Ateneo, http://www.sba .unifi.it/CMpro-v-p-567.html (accessed August 5, 2018).

89. Damiani 1905.

90. Damiani 1905, 45. One U.S. dollar traded at approximately 5 lire in 1905. At this historical currency rate, the prison budget was calculated to be $19,500, or roughly $500,000 today when adjusted for inflation. Figures were calculated using the websites *Historical Currency Converter*, edited by Rodney Edvinsson, Stockholm University, http://www.historicalstatistics.org/Currencyconverter.html and *U.S. Inflation Calculator*, CoinNews Media Group LLC, http://www.usinflationcalculator.com/ (accessed December 9, 2018).

91. Damiani 1905, 46.

92. Damiani 1905, 37.

93. Damiani 1905, 14–18.

94. Damiani 1905, 29.

95. In 1877, Errico Malatesta famously led an insurrection against the Italian state and was forced into a life of exile, moving among the network of anarchist colleagues around the world. He was arrested in 1898 upon a brief return to Italy, convicted of seditious association, and sentenced to *domicilio coatto* on Lampedusa (on this, see Mantovani 1982, 16–17). See also Turcato 2012, 178–79.

96. According to Ailara and Caserta (2012, 39), 1,367 prisoners were taken to the Tremiti Islands, 920 to Ustica, and the rest to Favignana, Ponza, and Gaeta. See also Archivio Storico del Ministero dell'Africa Italiana (ASMAI), Libia, Pos. 112/1, fasc. 1–10. "Sudditi libici relegati in Italia," (1913–18).

97. ASMAI, Libia, Pos. 112/1, fasc. 10. Memo from Ministero dell'Interno to Ministero delle Colonie, "Spese per relegati arabi all'isola di Ponza" (September 28, 1914).

98. El-Hesnawi 1988, 108–9.

99. Campbell 2017, 226–32; Del Boca 2005, 80–82.

100. Ottolenghi 1997, 159–62.

101. "Testimony of Jacob Gabrie Leul, Extract from Affidavit 11," in *Documents on Italian War Crimes* 1949–50, 14–15.

102. As cited in Le Houerou 1994, 86.

103. "Colonia di Assab," *Rivista di discipline carcerarie* 23 (1898): 407. Although no author is given for this article, Ambra Boldetti (1977, 513) contends that it was written by Martino Beltrani-Scalia, then director general of prisons in Italy.

104. Archivio Centrale dello Stato (ACS), "Telegram from Crispi to Governor of Eritrea," September 19, 1894, *Crispi Roma* cit., fasc. 647 (I), f. 10. As cited in Boldetti 1977, 512.

105. Caputo 1899, 261–67.

106. Caputo 1899, 265. For more on the living conditions at Assab, see Mucciarelli 1899.

107. Caputo 1899, 267 (emphasis in the original).

108. While el-Hesnawi (1988) cites 594 as the number of Libyan deportees after Shara Shatt, Vito Ailara and Massimo Caserta (2012, 35) argue the figure was five times higher, or 2,975. Of the 920 prisoners off-loaded at Ustica, 5 had died en route and were thrown overboard, and 127 more died shortly thereafter from the ensuing cholera epidemic and other diseases.

Beginning in the early 2000s, scholarship concerning the Libyan deportees blossomed in Italy, particularly thanks to the interest of local archives, historians, and historical societies. The *deportati* were the subject of a series of conferences held from 2000 to 2004 throughout Italy's carceral archipelago (Tremiti Islands 2000, Favignana 2001, Ponza 2002, Ustica 2004). The proceedings from these meetings offer the most detailed analyses to date of the deportees' experience on the islands (Sulpizi and Sury, 2002, 2003; Ghezzi and Sury 2004; Sury and Malgeri 2005). Italian historians have also worked closely with their Libyan counterparts, many of them affiliated with the Libyan Studies Center, who have also published work on the deportees (on this, see al-Jefa'iri 1989; also Baldinetti 2003, 2010).

The historical links between Libya and islands such as Ustica and Ponza have also been renewed over the years through personal ties and symbolic acts. In 2004, for example, the Libyan government paid for the renovation of the Muslim cemetery on Ustica and sent an annual delegation from Libya to pay their respects. One year the delegation included the son of 'Umar al-Mukhtar, the leader of the rebellion in Cyrenaica who was executed by Italians in 1931. There was also a small monument dedicated to the Libyan deportees in the Ponza cemetery and an open-air mausoleum on San Nicola in the Tremiti Islands. In 2010, the Centro Studi e Documentazione Isola di Ustica (Ustica Study Center and Archive) organized a major exhibition about the *deportati* that traveled to universities, archives, schools, and also to the Libyan Studies Center in Tripoli.

109. On this, see Ebner 2011.

110. As cited in Ailara and Caserta 2012, 45. For more on the everyday operations related to the *deportati*, Cutrera made a full report to the inspector general of the public security, Adolfo Lutrario, on December 11, 1911. See Sury and Malgeri 2005, 136–43; Archivio Centrale dello Stato (ACS), Ministero dell'Interno, Direzione generale di pubblica sicurezza, Divisione polizia giudiziaria, 1913–15, b. 71. See also Genco 1989.

111. Valera 1912. On Mussolini's initial stance against the Italian occupation of Libya and his tenure as editor of *Avanti!*, see De Felice 1965, 103–5, 136–76; Mack Smith 1981, 14–24.

112. Ailara and Caserta 2012, 59.

113. Ailara and Caserta 2012, 60.

114. Graziosi 2002.

115. ASMAI, Libia, Pos. 112/1, fasc. 3. Ministero delle Colonie, Ufficio Politico, "Elenco nominativo degli individui arrestati durante le operazioni militari di Gasr Jeffren che trovansi relegati all'isola di Ponza" (n.d.). There is no date on the document; however, other memos related to the listed prisoners are dated September 1913.

116. ASMAI, Libia, Pos. 112/1, fasc. 5. Memo from Ministero dell'Interno to Ministero delle Colonie, "Deportazione di arabi nella colonia di Ponza" (April 18, 1913).

117. ASMAI, Libia, Pos. 112/2, fasc. 17. Romeo Nappi, "Cenni sul funzionamento amministrativo della colonia penale di Ponza con speciale riguardo alla gestione per gli arabi deportati" (February 6, 1914).

118. ASMAI, Libia, Pos. 112/2, fasc. 16. Romeo Nappi, "Esame della proposta di trasferire da Ponza a Lampedusa la colonia di deportati arabi" (February 10, 1915).

119. Of the 778 deportees in the second wave to Ustica, 730 of them hailed from the Sirtica region, the vast expanse of desert that occupies the border between Tripolitania and Cyrenaica. See ASMAI, Libia, Pos. 112/2 (1915–18), fasc. 19. "Riepilogo degli indigeni imbarcati sul Piroscafo 'Re Umberto' partito il 12 giugno 1915 per Ustica." On the increase to 1,400 *deportati*, see ASMAI, Libia, Pos. 112/2 (1915–18), fasc. 19. Riservato from Ministero della Guerra to Ministero delle Colonie (January 24, 1916).

120. ASMAI, Libia, Pos. 150/8 (1914–38), fasc. 25. Memo no. 69264 from Ministero dell'Interno to Ministero delle Colonie, "Confino nel Regno di cittadini libici" (May 13, 1923).

121. Ailara and Caserta 2012, 72–73.

122. Scalarini 1992, 71. See also Ebner (2011, 103–38) for more extensive treatment of the *confinati* throughout the broader carceral archipelago.

123. Scalarini 1992, 86–95. See also ASMAI, Libia, Pos. 150/7 (1919–34), fasc. 24. Memo from Lorenzo Leone to Ministero delle Coloniale, "Relazione sull'insegnamento italo-arabo ai confinati libici in Ustica" (July 31, 1924).

124. ASMAI, Libia, Pos. 150/7 (1919–34), fasc. 24. Memo from Ministero dell'Interno to Ministero delle Colonie, "Abdalla Belaon fu Hamed, confinato politico arabo" (January 4, 1932).

125. ASMAI, Libia, Pos. 150/7 (1919–34), fasc. 24. Memo from Graziani to Ministero delle Colonie, "Abdalla Belaon. Confinato politico" (September 5, 1932).

126. ASMAI, Libia, Pos. 150/7 (1919–34), fasc. 24. Memo from Ministero dell'Interno to Ministero delle Colonie, "Confinato politico Abdalla Belaon" (March 11, 1933).

127. ASMAI, Libia, Pos. 150/7 (1919–34), fasc. 24. Memo from Ministero delle Colonie to the Governo di Tripoli & Bengasi, "Relegati libici ad Ustica" (June 30, 1934).

128. Ballinger 2007, 722.

129. Ballinger 2007, 721–22n23. For a general overview of the migrations of decolonization in Europe, see Smith 2003.

130. Clandestine Italians who returned to Libya faced arrest and up to three months in prison; on this, see Ballinger 2016a, 33–34.

131. Ballinger 2016a, 34.

132. Locatelli 2016, 143–46.

133. Del Boca 2010b, 468–77; St. John 2008, 142. In 1978, Qaddafi established what is today known as the Libyan Studies Center but was originally called the Center for the Study of the Jihad of the Libyans against the Italian Occupation (St. John 2008, 167–68).

134. Del Boca 2010b, 469. In 1972, the Associazione Italiani Rimpatriati dalla Libia (Association of Italians Repatriated from Libya) was founded to connect and unite

those expulsed by Qaddafi. It is still active today. On this, see "Chi Siamo," Associazione Italiani Rimpatriati dalla Libia Onlus, http://www.airl.it/ (accessed August 5, 2018).

135. Erlanger 2001; Malinarich 2001.

136. Nigro 2008; Scherer and Freeman 2008.

137. As cited in Dionne 1986.

138. As cited in Mazzeo 2012.

139. Strazzeri 2011.

140. "Lampedusa, lo spot del governo per rilanciare il turismo," produced by AgenParl, 2011, accessed January 5, 2015, http://www.youtube.com/watch?v=9oRaER4mOKo.

141. On tourism and the development of the Italian nation-state, see Hom 2015.

142. Istituto Nazionale di Statistica (ISTAT), *Annuario statistico italiano* (Rome: ISTAT, 2012), 516.

143. "Lampedusa 25 agosto-1 settembre," Amnesty International Italia, http://www.amnesty.it/campi-estivi/lampedusa (accessed August 5, 2018).

144. "Silvio Berlusconi a Lampedusa," March 30, 2011, accessed August 5, 2018, http://www.youtube.com/watch?v=KlJRDdFOfP0.

145. Ziniti 2011a. See also Nicolini 2013, 91.

146. As cited in Ziniti 2011a.

147. Nicolini 2013, 80.

148. O'Healy 2016, 152.

149. Fanon 2004, 4, 6.

150. Foucault 1994, 125–65.

151. Lanza 2014, 151. See also "Carta di Lampedusa," http://www.lacartadilampedusa.org/index.html (accessed August 5, 2018).

152. As presented in the audio documentary "Turchi: Storie di elicotteri e barche a Lampedusa" (2009).

153. Bolzoni 2008.

154. Bolzoni 2008.

The Camp

1. I conducted two field visits to the Ponte Galeria CIE, in July 2012 and March 2013. For the latter visit, the Italian Ministry of the Interior granted me permission to visit the CIE along with my colleague from the *New York Times*, Elisabetta Povoledo. We spent eight hours in the center speaking with everyone who agreed to be interviewed by us, including administrators, social workers, *carabinieri*, and a number of female and male *ospiti*. Given the legal sensitivity of the proceedings at the CIE, I have chosen to identify the people we interviewed by their initials or their occupations. I am deeply grateful to all of them for their willingness to shed light on this place and its processes that so often remain in the dark. A portion of this essay was originally published as "Becoming *Ospite*: Hospitality and Mobility at the Centre of Temporary Permanence," in *Italian Mobilities*, edited by Ruth Ben-Ghiat and Stephanie Malia Hom, 88–110 (London: Routledge, 2016). It is reproduced here by permission from Taylor & Francis UK.

2. On the concentration camp and its contemporary heirs, see Agier 2011, 183–90; Bauman 2002, 113–17; Diken and Laustsen 2005, 79–91; Marchetti 2006, 125–39; Stone 2017; Waters 2010, 92–97. On Ponte Galeria specifically, see Di Cesare 2014, 71–81.

3. Agamben 1998, 15–29, 174–75. See also Agamben 2005, 1–31; Schmitt 2006, 98–99.

4. Diken and Lausten 2005, 147–48, 155–62.

5. Andersson 2014, 125–26.

6. The limited but growing scholarship on the Libyan camps includes Ahmida 2005; Atkinson 1999, 2012; al-Barghathi 1981; al-Barghathi and Suri 1985; Bu Sha'alah 1984; Del Boca 2005, 2010a, 2010b; el-Hesnawi 1988; Labanca 2002, 2005; al-Maimuni and al-'Amari 2006; Ottolenghi 1997; Rochat 1991; Salerno 2005, 2008; Santarelli et al. 1986.

7. Agamben 1998, 17–20, 166–80.

8. Stoler 2008, 193.

9. During my field visit to Ponte Galeria on March 21, 2013, there were 123 *ospiti* on site (50 women and 73 men), according to statistics provided to me by Auxilium. More than half of the women were from Nigeria; the others hailed from Bosnia, Cameroon, Chile, China, Colombia, Cuba, Honduras, Morocco, Romania, Serbia, and Tunisia. Of the men, the majority also came from Nigeria, followed by others from Afghanistan, Albania, Bangladesh, Chile, the Czech Republic, Egypt, Gambia, Georgia, Honduras, India, Moldavia, Morocco, the Philippines, Romania, Russia, Senegal, Serbia, Tanzania, and Tunisia. As of January 2018, there were four categories of migrant detention centers operating across Italy: (1) Centri di Accoglienza (Centers of Welcome); (2) Centri di Primo Soccorso e Accoglienza (Centers of First Aid and Reception); (3) Centri di Accoglienza per Richiedenti Asilo (Centers of Assistance for Asylum-Seekers, CARA); and (4) Centri di Identificazione e Espulsione (Centers of Identification and Expulsion, CIE). All were formerly known as Centri di Permanenza Temporanea (Centers of Temporary Permanence, CPT) under the 1998 Turco-Napolitano law; however, the "Security Package" legislation passed in 2009 divided them into specialized categories. For details, see "Centri per l'immigrazione," Governo Italiano, Ministero dell'Interno. http://www.interno.gov.it/it/temi/immigrazione-e-asilo/politiche-migratorie/centri-limmigrazione (accessed August 5, 2018).

10. Di Cesare 2014, 84–86; Rovelli 2006, 220.

11. One need only think of the infamous *sbarchi* (landings) of Albanian boat migrants at Brindisi and Bari in 1991. Fleeing the fallen communist regime, migrants arrived en masse on rusting tanker ships. The iconic images of this human sea have been seared into Italian cultural memory by photographs and news reports. It was (and remains) a critical cynosure in the imaginary of emergency in contemporary Italy. During the Brindisi landing in August 1991, some twenty thousand migrants were sequestered in the local soccer stadium with little food and water (much less due process of law) and deported back to Albania within weeks (see Albahari 2015, 35–44). Despite such treatment, migration to Italy has only increased with the worldwide economic downturn in 2008 and the violent conflicts spreading across sub-Saharan Africa and the Middle East.

12. For a critical overview of the history and legislation of citizenship in Italy, see Hepworth 2012; Oliveri 2012; Tintori 2016. See also essay three of this book.

13. Forgacs 2016, 175–76.

14. Andrijasevic 2010, 149.

15. Hailey 2009, 251.

16. Rovelli 2006, 189.

17. Agamben 1998, 15–29, 174–75.

18. On this, see Bigo 2007; Caloz-Tschopp 2004; Hailey 2009, 242–59; Le Cour Grandmaison, Lhuilier, and Valluy 2007; Marchetti 2006; Stone 2017, 121–22; Valluy et al. 2005.

19. Diken and Laustsen 2005, 84–86.

20. Agamben 1998, 20–29, 71–74.

21. Diken and Laustsen 2005, 84–85. On barbed wire and the creation of the concentration camp, see Netz 2004, 128–227.

22. According to Marc Augé (1995, 82), nonplaces are spaces of transience that are evacuated of organic society (for example, airports, highways, metros). He writes that nonplaces "do not integrate other places, meanings, traditions, and sacrificial, ritual moments but remain, due to a lack of characterization, non-symbolized and abstract spaces." They are zones of indistinction par excellence. On migrants as nonsubjects, see also Dal Lago 2012, 205–35.

23. Barkham 2002. One of the most rigorous lines of critique of Agamben's core concepts (for example, *homo sacer*, exception, and the camp) has questioned the ways in which Agamben utilizes the Aristotelian distinction between forms of "life"—*bios* and *zoē*—and their intersections with death (necropolitics, thanatopolitics). On this, see Mbembe 2003; Murray 2006; Norris 2005. In later work, Agamben has taken issue with the distinction between human and animal; see Agamben 2004.

24. Levi 1989, 75, 111. See also Frankl 1984, 49–50.

25. Agamben 1999, 85.

26. The state of suspension is not unique to the Ponte Galeria CIE. Rather, it is the prevailing characteristic of all detention centers, refugee camps, transit zones, and related spaces of exception. Zygmunt Bauman (2002, 114) put it thus: "Refugee camps boast a new quality: a frozen 'transience,' an on-going, lasting state of temporariness, a duration patched together of moments, none of which is lived through as an element of, and a contribution to, perpetuity." Michel Agier (2011, 71–78) describes this state of existence-on-standby as the "interminable insomnia of exile."

27. Varikas 2007, 133–43.

28. Agier 2011, 23.

29. Mbembe 2003, 31.

30. Rovelli 2006, 189.

31. In 2013, the going rate for trafficking to Italy was €60,000 for passage by air and €35,000 for passage by land, according to social workers at the Ponte Galeria CIE. All historical currency conversions were calculated using the website *Historical Currency Converter*, edited by Rodney Edvinsson, Stockholm University, http://www.historicalstatistics.org/Currencyconverter.html (accessed August 5, 2018).

32. On Nigerian women and the sex trade in Italy, see Aikpitanyi 2011; Kara 2009, 89–92; Maragnani and Aikpitanyi 2007; Okojie and Prina 2004.

33. Sassen 2014, 4; see also Hsu 2010. On global mobile elites, see Elliott and Urry 2010, 8–9, 63–64.

34. Bauman 1988, 2.

35. For twelve years, the Italian Red Cross ran day-to-day operations at Ponte Galeria; however, on the heels of violent riots at the center in 2010, Auxilium was awarded the government contract to take over management. In December 2014, Auxilium lost the contract to a French company, Gestione Penitenziari e Servizi Ausiliari (GEPSA), which specializes in the management of penal institutions and detention centers. GEPSA is a subsidiary of the UK-based Cofely holding company, which in turn is run by the Paris-based GDF Suez, one of the largest energy conglomerates in the world. In sum, a multinational corporation focused on cost savings and efficient management now operates the CIE at Ponte Galeria, and by all accounts, life in the center has taken a drastic turn for the worse. On this, see Di Benedetto Montaccini and Zandonini 2014.

36. MEDU (Medici per i Diritti Umani) 2012, 7. According to MEDU, the operating budget of Ponte Galeria was €3.6 million a year, which is a cost of €41 on average per day per detainee.

37. MEDU 2012, 7. MEDU notes the annual budget for all migrant detention centers in Italy was €18.6 million in 2012.

38. MEDU 2012, 17, 19 (emphasis in the original).

39. MEDU 2012, 16.

40. The fetishization of the mobile phone among migrants is not limited to Ponte Galeria but is rather common across Italy. In his ethnography of Ghanaian migrants in Naples, Hans Lucht (2012, 88) explains: "The mobile phone is a necessary tool for arranging work situations with employers . . . for keeping in contact with family members at home. . . . The mobile phone is also the quintessential symbol of having connections to the world, to another social and political reality. It contains the promise or potentiality of connectedness. . . . The acquisition of a 'powerful' mobile phone may be viewed as a kind of magical reversal of one's exclusion from the circulation of materials and symbolic goods or, perhaps, as one of 'the avenues of re-enchantment' that thrives in circumstances in which real participation is denied."

41. Cristiana Giordano (2014, 115–20) illustrates the extreme degrees to which legal documents interpellate hierarchies of migrant subjects in Italy, prompting many of her informants to ask: "Who does the law want me to be?" Italy's ever-changing juridical framework hems migrants into increasingly abstruse categorizations, and only the submission to being categorized legally and recognized by the state allows one access to what Hannah Arendt (1976, 296–97) has famously called "the right to have rights." In such ways, the Italian state maintains a powerful border regime that exercises a monopoly over movements and legalities in a concerted effort to keep "undesirables" out no matter what their label, migrant or otherwise.

42. MEDU 2012, 22.

43. On the suspicion of "false" refugees, see Agier 2011, 110–11.

44. The widely adopted 1951 Convention Relating to the Status of Refugees defines the rights of refugees (and in later revisions, also those of internally displaced people and stateless persons). According to Article 1 of this document, "The term 'refugee' shall apply to any person who . . . owing to well-founded fear of being per-

secuted for reasons of race, religion, nationality, membership of a particular social group or political opinion, is outside the country of his nationality and is unable or, owing to such a fear, is unwilling to avail himself of the protection of that country; or who, not having a nationality and being outside the country of his former habitual residence as a result of such events, is unable or, owing to such fear, is unwilling to return to it." See Ghandi 2012, 14.

45. MEDU 2012, 11.

46. Foucault 1990, 2003. On asylums and mental health in modern Italy, see Forgacs 2014, 197–262; on the experience of immigrants within that system, see Giordano 2014. On the corporeality of migrants, see Ticktin 2011, 207–18.

47. Damiani 1905, 33–34.

48. MEDU 2012, 11.

49. Michel Foucault (1988, 1995) is considered an authority on the body and the mind as political sites, and the institutions designed to control them. See also Giordano 2014, 78–79, 183–84; Ticktin 2011, 89–127.

50. MEDU 2012, 11.

51. MEDU 2012, 10.

52. MEDU 2012, 10. Further details about Nabruka Mimouni's life and death are given on a Facebook page established in her memory: https://www.facebook.com/SegnaliamoIlRazzismo/posts/479466645452948 (accessed February 11, 2015). In the popular press she was sometimes referred to as Mabruka Mimouni or Mimuni.

53. Brogi 2012.

54. Cosentino 2012.

55. Building on the work of Foucault and Agamben, Didier Bigo (2005, 3–4) has theorized a specific form of governmentality, which he calls the "banopticon," that arises from a logic of permanent exceptionalism linked to the detention of foreigners. It becomes spatialized in the form of the camp. He adds that the "detention of foreigners considered 'would-be criminals' in camps is, for the present time, the locus that concentrates and articulates heterogeneous lines of power diffracted into society. . . . This is rooted in the routinization of the monitoring of groups on the move through technologies of surveillance, and is further linked to a will to monitor the future. . . . The detention camp for foreigners is for the banopticon the equivalent of what the prison was for the panopticon of Foucault."

56. Abdou Said could be considered a *homo sacer* (sacred or accursed man), a man who incarnated one extreme of the state of exception (the other pole is the sovereign). For Agamben (1998, 71–74), the *homo sacer* was a man banned by the law and, owing to that ban, could be killed by anyone but not ritually sacrificed. On the one hand, the killing of the sovereign was something more than a homicide (lese-majesty), while on the other hand, the killing of the *homo sacer* was something less. Agamben (1998, 84–85) elaborates on the definition of *homo sacer*: "At the two extreme limits of the [political] order, the sovereign and *homo sacer* present two symmetrical figures that have the same structure and are correlative: the sovereign is the one with respect to whom all men are potentially *homines sacri*, and the *homo sacer* is the one with respect to whom all men act as sovereigns. . . . They [*homines sacri*] constitute instead the originary exception in which human life is included in the political order in being exposed to an unconditional capacity to be killed."

57. Agamben 1998, 27–29.

58. Agamben 1998, 170–71.

59. Schmitt 2006, 67–70, 98–99.

60. Schmitt 2006, 98.

61. Agamben (1998, 166) mentions these earlier camps only briefly in *Homo Sacer*: "What matters here is that in both cases, a state of emergency linked to a colonial war is extended to an entire civil population. The camps are thus born not out of ordinary law . . . but out of a state of exception and martial law." On the development of colonial camps, see also Atkinson 2012; Diken and Laustsen, 2005, 40–43; Hyslop 2011; Kamiński 1982, 30–69; Stone 2017, 11–33.

62. Bignall and Svirsky 2012, 6.

63. Atkinson 2012, 169–73.

64. Labanca 2005, 27.

65. Atkinson 2012, 171–72. On the damages caused by Italian colonialism, see Jerary 2005.

66. According to Mark Choate (2008, 83–86), Italians made up seven-eighths of Tunisia's resident European population by 1900, or seventy thousand of its eighty thousand residents. The distinct lack of French settlers, especially compared with neighboring Algeria, led one leading French colonial theorist to call for Tunisia to be redesignated from "settlement colony" to "colony of exploitation" as in central Africa or French Indochina, with the Italians among those meant to be exploited.

67. Ben-Ghiat 2015, xvii.

68. Braidotti 2011, 8.

69. Braidotti 2011, 10. For Braidotti, like Gilles Deleuze and Félix Guattari, the subject is nonunitary. Instead, it is a "process ontology" that is neither linear nor rational, but rather constantly in a state of becoming. Collective assemblages and relations of exteriority mediate such subjectivities—Deleuze and Guattari would call them "rhizomatic"—and the result is subjects that, according to Braidotti (2011, 21), are "stripped of [their] old genderized, racialized, normalized straightjacket and relocated into patterns of different becoming" (becoming-cyborg, becoming-woman, et cetera). As a result, such becoming-subjects can unsettle structural inequalities and help rethink difference in much more fluid, horizontal, and harmonic terms. See also Braidotti 1994; Deleuze and Guattari 1987, 233–309.

70. Schmitt 2006, 70, 78.

71. Anne Dufourmantelle (2013, 14–15) describes exception in terms of exile, which she argues was the first condition of humanity. According to her, the earliest social groups were nomadic, and they depended on the unconditional hospitality of others who were happy to grant it because they too might be in need of such refuge given their tenuous nomadic existence. On hospitality and migration in Italy, see Hom 2016, 101–5.

72. Deleuze and Guattari 1987, 394. Eugene Holland (2011, 65–98) imagines an affirmative relationship between state and subject vis-à-vis nomad citizenship. The nomad citizen is a subject who can positively cocreate herself within nonstate and noncapitalist forms of society. This citizenship arises immanently, that is, from the self-coordinating articulations of related difference and the horizontal distribution of multiple sovereignties, all to the mutual benefit of everyone involved. According to

Holland, nomad citizenship harnesses the power of the nonunitary subject—in a "power-with" not "power-over"—to actualize a mode of political belonging that is neither limited to politics nor limited to the state. The nomad's multiple allegiances foment small-scale participatory democracy and, implicitly, a fuller way of inhabiting the world.

73. Atkinson 1999, 118.

74. Braidotti 2011, 18.

75. Braidotti 2011, 236–38.

76. After a handful of resounding military defeats, including the Battle of Gasr Bu Hadi in April 1915, Italian colonial administrators shifted their focus from military coercion to more "collaborative" strategies of colonization. This shift culminated with the Acroma pact signed on April 17, 1917, between Italian administrators and the leader of the Sanusi order. The pact established a tentative cease-fire and lent to the Sanusi an ambiguous degree of sovereignty over most of Cyrenaica (Del Boca 2010a, 278–83, 339–41). On nomadism in Italian colonial Libya, see also Atkinson 1999, 2007; Ben-Ghiat 2012, 2015, 28–32.

77. Archivio Storico del Ministero dell'Africa Italiana (ASMAI), Libia, Pos. 126/1 (1913–19), fasc. 2. *Relazione sullo schema di ordinamento politico-amministrativo della Tripolitania, Governo della Tripolitania, Ufficio Politico Militare* (1916), 6, 9.

78. ASMAI, Libia, Pos. 126/1 (1913–19), fasc. 2. *Relazione sullo schema di ordinamento politico-amministrativo della Tripolitania, Governo della Tripolitania, Ufficio Politico Militare* (1916), 301. See also ASMAI, Libia, Pos. 115/3 (1911–26), fasc. 31–34. "Riservatissimo." Telegram no. 48 from Giovanni Ameglio to Ministry of the Colonies (July 26, 1915). Ameglio noted that the Libyan soldiers would sleep in their Bedouin tents near Floridia. Archival records show additional correspondence between Ameglio and the Prefect of Siracusa as well as the War Ministry about the camp administration as well as the decline in troop morale during their months in the camp. To boost their spirits, Ameglio suggested that the troops be taken on a tour of Italy so as to "offrire loro occasione di apprezzare realmente lo spettacolo di bellezza, di progresso e forza combattiva che offre oggi la nostra Patria" (offer them the occasion to truly appreciate the spectacle of beauty, progress, and combative force that our Patria offers today). ASMAI, Libia, Pos. 115/3 (1911–26), fasc. 31–34. "Riservata speciale," Memo from Ameglio to Ministero delle Colonie (September 18, 1915).

79. Del Boca 2010a, 301. On *askari* soldiers, see also Ben-Ghiat 2015, 118–66.

80. ASMAI Libia, Pos. 115/3 (1911–26), fasc. 29. "Diserzione ascari libici," Memo from Ameglio to Ministero delle Colonie (June 1, 1917).

81. ASMAI, Libia, Pos. 122/31 (1925–29), fasc. 289. "Riservatissimo personale. Situazione in Libia e condotta militare da seguire," Memo from Pietro Badoglio to Mussolini (October 23, 1925).

82. ASMAI, Libia, Pos. 122/31 (1925–29), fasc. 287. "Riservato. Notiziario informazioni," Memo from Emilio De Bono to Minister of the Colonies, Luigi Federzoni; Governor of Cyrenaica, Attilio Teruzzi; Commando Truppe (December 10, 1927), 3.

83. The popular colonial press in Italy also lent credence to De Bono's opinion; see Biagio 1932; Dei Gaslini 1933; Ricci 1922.

84. ASMAI, Libia, Pos. 150/5 1924–28, fasc. 6 bis. "Inizio operazione," Memo from Emilio De Bono to Minister of the Colonies (December 27, 1927).

85. Attilio Teruzzi, the governor of Cyrenaica from December 1926 to January 1929 (and Graziani's supervisor), established two *colonie penali agricole* (agricultural penal colonies) at Berka and Coefia for *detenuti indigeni* (indigenous criminals), which could be considered precursors to the larger system of concentration camps established in 1929. According to Teruzzi, the agricultural penal colonies were temporary measures. Prisoners would begin the cultivation of grapes, citrus, and so forth, and once the crops began producing a harvest, Italian colonists would take over. In this way, indigenous prisoners did the hardest work (Teruzzi 1931, 323–25). Archival documents also reveal a discussion in 1928 about transferring domestic *coatti* (prisoners), particularly *mafiosi*, who were serving sentences on carceral islands such as Ustica and Ponza to these agricultural penal colonies in Cyrenaica; however, this never came to pass (more on agricultural penal colonies in essay three). ASMAI, Libia, Pos. 150/38 (1919–34), fasc. 172. "Istituzione di colonie agricole militari," Memo from Corrado Zoli to Ministero dell'Interno (April 2, 1928).

86. Graziani 1932, 119.

87. Graziani 1932, 120.

88. Evans-Pritchard 1949, 196.

89. Chapin-Metz 1987. On the history and culture of the Sanusi Order, see Ahmida 2009, 73–102; Baldinetti 2010, 30–33; Evans-Pritchard 1949, 1–89; Ryan 2018; Serra 1933, 6–54; Vandewalle 2012, 18–20.

90. Atkinson 1999, 102.

91. Evans-Pritchard 1945b, 65.

92. Lobban and Dalton 2014, 35–36. On Sanusi *zawiyas*, see Evans-Pritchard 1945a, 183–87.

93. Ahmida 2009, 102.

94. Evans-Pritchard 1945b, 71.

95. Evans-Pritchard 1945b, 71, 72.

96. 'Umar al-Mukhtar's life and death have been famously celebrated in the 1981 film *Lion of the Desert*, which is a Libyan production directed by Moustapha Akkad that recounts the al-Mukhtar's years of resistance in Cyrenaica. Shot on location, it also depicts the coerced subjugation and forced march of Bedouin tribes across Cyrenaica into Italian-built concentration camps and includes historical footage of the camps themselves. The film was banned in Italy until 2009. On this, see Fuller 2017.

97. Graziani 1932, 188–89. On antinomad strategies in Italian colonial Libya, see also Atkinson 1999, 2012; Del Boca 2010b, 200–201; Evans-Pritchard 1945b, 73–74; Jongmans 1964, 225–46; Piccioli 1933, 239–41.

98. Atkinson 1999, 111; Del Boca 2005, 179; 2010b, 183; Rochat 1973, 100–102; 1986, 95–103; Vandewalle 2012, 30–32.

99. Quoted in Ahmida 2005, 44.

100. Del Boca 2010b, 183.

101. Ottolenghi 1997, 98.

102. Ottolenghi 1997, 207–9. In the fall of 1932, Soluq briefly turned into a tourist attraction when 108 Italian cruise passengers paid a visit there and saw "le scuole e gli orti che hanno suscitato la più bella impressione per il grado di progresso raggiunto"

(the schools and gardens that created the most beautiful impression of the degree of progress achieved). "Cronache coloniali" 1932.

103. Ottolenghi 1997, 173.

104. Archivio Centrale dello Stato (ACS), Fondo Rodolfo Graziani, Archivio Fotografico, N° Inventario 52/17.3, Pos. Cb 36a 2, Album 13.

105. "Come il generale Graziani pacificò la Cirenaica" 1932.

106. Ottolenghi 1997, 107.

107. Fuller 2007, 107–47; von Henneberg 1996a.

108. Agier 2011, 70.

109. Del Boca 2005, 80–82.

110. Ottolenghi 1997, 159–62.

111. Arendt 1958, part III, 445.

112. ASMAI, Libia, Pos. 150/22 (1913–33), fasc. 97. Telegram from Badoglio to De Bono (July 7, 1930), noting the successful "movimenti di concentramento di popolazione" (movements of concentration of population). Building the camps involved a two-step process: first, the clustering of "nomads" into camps near Italian military strongholds, and second, moving these camps farther into the Sirtica desert to remove them from the reach of 'Umar al-Mukhtar. Furthermore, according to *La formazione de l'impero coloniale italiano* (1938, 544): "I campi vennero circondati da reticolato, i pascoli controllati, la circolazione sottoposta a misure di vigilanza speciali." (The camps were surrounded by barbed wire, the pastures controlled, and the circulation put under special measures of surveillance.)

113. Evans-Pritchard 1949, 189.

114. Ahmida 2005, 48; 2006, 182–83; 2009, 103–40.

115. El-Hesnawi 1988, 248.

116. Ahmida 2005, 48. See also al-Barghathi 1981; al-Barghathi and Suri 1985; al-Maimuni and al-'Amari 2006.

117. Ottolenghi 1997, 157.

118. "Dislocamenti a Sidi Ahmed el Magrum" 1932.

119. Ottolenghi 1997, 164.

120. Ottolenghi 1997, 163.

121. Rochat 1986, 102.

122. Agier 2011, 132–34.

123. Rochat 1986, 102–3.

124. ACS, Carte Graziane, busta 1, fasc. 2, sottofasc. 2. Also cited in Ahmida 2005, 43; and Del Boca 2010b, 178.

125. As cited in Del Boca 2010b, 186. For an especially rosy view of the camps, see Lischi 1934, 132–38.

126. "Notiziario d'Oltremare" 1931.

127. Quotations from Rajab Hamad Buwaish al-Minifi's poem, "Dar al-Agaila" (Under such conditions), have been excerpted from Ali Ahmida, *Forgotten Voices: Power and Agency in Colonial and Postcolonial Libya*, 49–51 (New York: Routledge, 2005). They are reproduced here with permission from Taylor & Francis Group LLC Books. In addition to Ahmida's translation, the full text of the poem in Arabic with a rough translation into English is available online at "Libyana: Al-Agaila concentration

camp (a poem)," Khelwat el-MrabiT, http://www.libyana.org/history/agaila/pm
.html (accessed August 5, 2018).

128. ASMAI, Libia, Pos. 150/22 (1913–33), fasc. 97, pacco 55/10. "Cirenaica: stato
di pericolo pubblico." Graziani made the actual declaration of the *stato di pericolo pubblico* on May 16, 1930; however, most of Libya had already been under a different state
of emergency—a *stato di guerra* (state of war)—since January 1, 1928. On this, see
ASMAI, Libia, Pos. 150/22 (1913–33), fasc. 97. Telegram from Graziani to Ministero
delle Colonie (October 1, 1930).

129. Agamben 1998, 71–86, 127–37.

130. Del Boca 2010a, 183–84; Ottolenghi 1997, 102.

131. Dando-Collins 2010, 65–69; Hanel 2007, 395–416; Trousset 1974, 142–46.

132. On the exercise of state military power, the philosopher Paul Virilio (1975, 120,
174–75) evokes the *castrum* insofar as he argues that "castramentation" was the ideal
geometric expression of the calculated expansion of state power in space and time.
The Roman Empire imposed a type of linear, geometrical state power, which included, for instance, a general outline of camps and fortifications, a marking of
boundaries by lines, and an increasingly rigid segmentarity in all property. Castrametation, then, was and is the apotheosis of striated space. On this, see also Deleuze
and Guattari 1987, 211–13; Monk 1998.

133. Richardson 2004, 3.

134. Richardson 2004, 15–16.

135. Polybius 2011, 377, 381.

136. Josephus (Titus Flavius) 1927, 601.

137. Polybius 2011, 375; see also Le Bohec 1994, 132–33.

138. Ottolenghi 1997, 102–3.

139. Polybius 2011, 391.

140. Similar punishments were issued for Italian southerners who failed to salute
the flag or praise the king under the 1863 Pica law (see essay one).

141. Ahmida 2005, 48.

142. Quoted in Ahmida 2005, 49.

143. Salerno 2005, 96.

144. Polybius 2011, 395.

145. Ahmida 2005, 48.

146. Salerno 2005, 103.

147. Salerno 2005, 93.

148. Al-Maimuni and al-'Amari 2006, 103–7.

149. Graziani 1932, 123.

150. ASMAI, Libia, Pos. 134/26 (1925), fasc. 196. Ernesto Mombelli, "Riservatissimo
Personale, Governo della Cirenaica, Gabinetto, N. 02" (January 7, 1924), 2–3.

151. ASMAI, Libia, Pos. 150/28, fasc. 130. "Da Bengasi a Tripoli in automobile:
Come 38 macchine nel deserto annunciano che la Libia è unificata," *Giornale d'Oriente*
(June 28, 1931); see also Graziani 1932, 216–17.

152. Labanca 2005, 31.

153. ASMAI, Libia, Pos. 150/7 (1919–34), fasc. 16. Memo from Badoglio to De
Bono, "La confisca dei beni senussiti esistenti in Cirenaica" (August 19, 1930).

154. El-Hesnawi 1988, 221–31.

155. ASMAI, Libia, Pos. 150/7 (1919–34), fasc. 15. A. Fantoni, "La natura giuridica degli Auqaf delle zavie senussite della Cirenaica" (August 11, 1930): 3–4. See also *La formazione de l'impero coloniale italiano* 1938, 544.

156. ASMAI, Libia, Pos. 150/7 (1919–34), fasc. 17–23. Each file in this archival folder gives a detailed record by region (for example, Ajdabiya, Benghazi, Derna, Barce, Cirene) of the goods confiscated from the Sanusi *zawiya*.

157. ASMAI, Libia, Pos. 150/21 (1913–36), fasc. 90. Telegram from Badoglio to Siciliani and De Bono (January 10, 1930).

158. ASMAI, Libia, Pos. 150/21 (1913–36), fasc. 90. Telegram from Badoglio to De Bono, "Riservatissimo personale" (July 7, 1930).

159. Ottolenghi 1997, 162. After several years in the camps, Giorgio Rochat (1991, 81–83) estimated that roughly 90–95 percent of sheep, goats, and horses died as did approximately 80 percent of camels and cows. Thus, the livelihood of the Bedouin perished in or en route to the camps.

160. "La pulizia del Gebel Cirenaico" 1930, 498–99.

161. As cited in Salerno 2005, 101.

162. Piccioli 1933, 239–42.

163. Atkinson 1999, 115–16; el-Hesnawi 1988, 240; Graziani 1932, 224–25.

164. *La formazione de l'impero coloniale italiano* 1938, 546. See also Rochat 1986, 70n81. Flying courts were not limited to Libya. In fact, their scope was expanded in East Africa during the late 1930s. Whereas deportations emptied Libya of *capi notabili* (notable leaders) from 1911 onward, flying courts ruthlessly executed young Ethiopian leaders, sometimes hundreds of people at a time. See Campbell 2017, 257–61.

165. Graziani 1932, 139.

166. ASMAI, Libia, Pos. 112/1 (1913–18), fasc. 2. Memo from A. Capone to Tribunale Militare di Guerra (September 22, 1913).

167. Graziani 1932, 139.

168. Graziani 1932, 139.

169. El-Hesnawi 1988, 239; see also al-Barghathi 1981, 115.

170. Graziani 1932, 144.

171. Evans-Pritchard 1949, 188.

172. ASMAI, Libia, Pos. 150/27 (1922–34), fasc. 124. Memo from Graziani to Ministry of the Colonies, "Condanne capitali" (August 4, 1930).

173. "La fine di Omar el Muctar" 1931.

174. Vellani 1931.

175. Graziani 1932, 269. On the capture and execution of al-Mukhtar, see also Goglia 1986; Rainero 1986.

176. Graziani 1932, 270–72.

177. Evans-Pritchard 1949, 190.

178. Vellani 1931, 806.

179. Ottolenghi 1997, 168–71; Rochat 1986, 103–15.

180. *Campi di concentramento* (concentration camp) was but one type of camp established by the Fascist regime. Other designations included *località di internamento* (place of internment), *campi di transito* (transit camp), *campi di lavoro coatto* (forced labor camp), and *campi per prigionieri di guerra* (prisoner of war camp). An invaluable resource for the history of Fascist camps is the website created and managed by

Andrea Giuseppini and Roman Herzog: http://www.campifascisti.it (accessed August 5, 2018).

181. Ottolenghi 1997, 165. See also ACS, Fondo Graziani, busta 11, fasc. 8. Telegram from Graziani to Santini (April 18, 1937). Ruth Ben-Ghiat's unpublished manuscript in progress, "Prisoners of War: Italian Captives in Germany, Great Britain, and France, 1940–50," investigates the detention of Italian prisoners of war (POWs) in Europe and around the globe.

182. Pesenti 1932.

183. Statistics cited from "Testimony of Michael Tessema" and "Testimony of Blatta Bekele Hapte Michael," in *Documents on Italian War Crimes Submitted to United Nations War Crimes Commission by the Imperial Ethiopian Government*, vol. 2, *Affidavits and Published Documents* (Addis Ababa: Ministry of Justice, 1949–50), 11–13, 16–17. See also Campbell 2017, 231–34, 316–17.

184. Ottolenghi 1997, 166.

185. Ottolenghi 1997, 166. For further details, see the firsthand account by Domenico Salvatori, an Italian soldier stationed in Libya who was captured and held in the POW camp at Dehradun (India) for almost two years. Salvatori 1989, 58–123.

186. Levis Sullam 2018, 59–108.

187. Roumani 2008, 28–29.

188. De Felice 1985, 169. De Felice's study of Libyan Jewry remains the definitive work on the subject. On this, see also Goldberg 1980, 1990; Hatefutsoth 1980; Roumani 2008; Salerno 2008; Simon 1992.

189. De Felice 1985, 179–84.

190. Maurice Roumani (2008, 33) notes that roughly three thousand Jews from Tripolitania were sent to the hard-labor camp of Sidi Azaz near Homs, where they were employed to build the railroads and highways that conducted war supplies to the front. Given the persecution of Jews across Europe at the time, these laborers were treated relatively well. They were paid for their work and allowed to practice their religious beliefs, thanks in no small part to Moshe Haddad, an engineer from Tripoli who managed the Sidi Azaz camp.

191. As cited in Salerno 2008, 105. Further testimonies in Hebrew about life in the Jadu concentration camp are available on the website of the Documentation Center of North African Jewry during World War II of the Ben-Zvi Institute, Jerusalem. See http://www.ybz.org.il/?CategoryID=582 (accessed August 5, 2018).

192. Roumani 2008, 35.

193. Salerno 2008, 112.

194. The human costs of World War II in ex-Yugoslavia were enormous, with deaths numbering upward of one million people. Nazi troops deported the Jewish population to concentration and extermination camps, the Croatian Ustaše (a Fascist party) murdered Serbs and Roma en masse, the Serbian Chetnik movement perpetrated ethnic cleansing against Muslims and Croats, and Italians targeted the Slovenian population. War crimes charges have never been brought against Italian officers for their role in the Yugoslav genocide. On this, see Kersevan 2008, 61, and the 1989 BBC documentary film *Fascist Legacy*, directed by Ken Kirby.

195. Myriad concentration camps were built between 1940 and 1943 in Italy. Some of the most notorious included Gonars and Visco (Udine), Monigo and Chiesanuova

(Veneto), and Renicci (Arezzo); the scholarship on these camps is extensive. Representative examples include Di Sante 2001; Finzi 2004; Galluccio 2003; Kersevan 2008; Reale 2011.

196. As cited in Kersevan 2008, 115.

197. As cited in Kersevan 2008, 161–62.

198. Ballinger 2002, 139; Del Boca 2005, 241–45.

199. "Un nigeriano rifiuta l'espulsione" 2013. It is also important to acknowledge the many Italian nonprofits, international agencies, and individual citizens that have organized countless protests and lobbied tirelessly for the closure of Ponte Galeria since the day it opened in 1998. Their campaigns have brought sustained attention to the center's human rights violations, its violation of the Italian constitution, and its affront to democratic society. One of the most vocal organizations has been LasciateCIE Entrare (Let Us Enter CIE), also known as Mai più CIE (No more CIE), which has launched an effort to close down all migrant detention centers in Italy.

200. "Choc nel Cie di Roma" 2013. See also Di Cesare 2014, 56–59. On migrants' self-harm, see also Ticktin 2011, 201–17.

201. Abd El Karim Islam performs "Tutto tace" during the closing credits of the 2014 film *Limbo*. It is also available on YouTube: https://www.youtube.com/watch?v=DDx8jQDmjb4 (accessed August 5, 2018).

202. Pacoda 2000.

203. The lyrics of Abd El Karim Islam's song, "Tutto tace" are reproduced here with permission from ZaLab, a documentary filmmaking collective and production company based in Rome and Padova. The song appears in the closing credits of the 2014 film *Limbo* directed by Matteo Calore and Gustav Hofer, and produced and distributed by Zalab. In addition to the film, the song can be viewed online at "Tutto tace, Karim and Micaela," Omar Abd El Karim, https://www.youtube.com/watch?v=DDx8jQDmjb4 (accessed December 18, 2018).

The Village

1. Scholars have been more careful than policymakers in considering the heterogeneity of Roma populations. The academic literature is extensive, especially in political science and sociology. Representative works of scholarship on Roma in Italy include Alunni 2012; Clough Marinaro 2009, 2014; Daniele 2011; Forgacs 2014; Impagliazzo 2008; Special issue on Roma and Sinti in Contemporary Italy, *Journal of Modern Italian Studies* 2011; Piasere 2005, 2008; Sigona 2003, 2005, 2010.

2. Human Rights Watch 2011, 3.

3. Diken and Laustsen 2005, 147–48, 155–62.

4. "Vicus" as defined in Lewis and Short 1879.

5. Arthur 2004; Wacher 1995, 20–21.

6. Elkins 2005, 233–68.

7. Elkins 2005, xiv.

8. Fuller 2004.

9. Cooper 2014; Mamdani 1996; Parolin 2009, 94–114; Saada 2012.

10. On race in Italian colonial Eritrea, see Barrera 2003a.

11. Berdahl 2005, 236–37. The interdisciplinary field of citizenship studies is vast, and the debates and definitions of citizenship have been deliberated extensively in journals such as *Citizenship Studies* and in representative scholarly works such as Brubaker 1998; Isin and Turner 2002; Ong 1999; Turner and Hamilton 1994. In the Italian context, see Ballinger 2007; Tintori 2016.

12. Associazione 21 Luglio 2014, 11. On eviction in modern Rome, see Herzfeld 2009, 263–66.

13. Associazione 21 Luglio 2014, 10.

14. Gianni Alemanno is a right-wing politician who was once part of the neofascist party in Italy. Similar to Fascist officials who made arguments for "cleansing" colonial Libya in the name of public health and security, Alemanno's vice mayor, Sveva Belviso, has gone on the record as saying: "Chiederemo al Governo di rinnovare lo stato di emergenza sulla base di un'effettiva problematica igienico-sanitaria che insiste sulle realtà abusive presenti sul territorio." (We will ask the government to renew the state of emergency on the basis of an actual hygienic-sanitary problem, which insists on the abusive realities present in the territory.) On this, see "Ed ora, senza la figura del commissario straordinario, come verrà gestita l'emergenza nomadi?" 2011.

15. Sigona 2005, 2010.

16. Hepworth 2012, 434.

17. Associazione 21 Luglio 2014, 30. On the Cinecittà refugee camp, see Steimatsky 2009.

18. As cited in Piasere 2005, 164. See also Herzfeld 2009, 31.

19. Jean-Léonard Touadi, the first black deputy in Italy's lower house of Parliament, pinpoints the Albanian arrivals of 1991 as the beginning of Italy's "slow approach to racism" (Human Rights Watch 2011, 6). See also Welch 2016a.

20. "Italy Starts Deporting Romanians," *BBC News*, November 5, 2007, accessed August 5, 2018, http://news.bbc.co.uk/2/hi/europe/7078532.stm. A 2013 report by Caritas Migrantes (2013, 11) notes that Romanians constituted 21 percent of all immigrants to Italy.

21. Aradau 2012, 43–45; Woodcock 2012. For news coverage of the Reggiani killing, see Fisher 2007.

22. Human Rights Watch 2011, 47–49.

23. Forgacs 2014, 283–85; Sigona 2012, 71–72.

24. Aradau 2012, 48–49. See also Feldman 2012, 51–54.

25. European Roma Rights Center 2000; Clough Marinaro 2009, 265–66. In June 2015, the Civil Court of Rome ruled that La Barbuta and other camps and villages established for Roma were a form of segregation and discrimination based on ethnic grounds, breaching both Italian and European law. The lawsuit was brought against the Municipality of Rome by the European Roma Rights Center, Amnesty International, and the Open Society Foundations. On this, see European Roma Rights Center 2015.

26. Sigona 2012, 72.

27. As cited in Associazione 21 Luglio 2014, 24.

28. Clough Marinaro 2014, 552. See also van Baar 2015.

29. For example, the Council of Europe and the European Court of Human Rights have repeatedly condemned the Italian state's ghettoization and discrimina-

tion against Roma and Sinti. The European Roma Rights Center (ERRC) and Associazione 21 Luglio continually advocate for Romani rights. Artists, journalists, and scholars also call attention to contemporary discrimination against Roma and Sinti.

30. Forgacs 2014, 274; Sigona 2012, 75; 2010, 144.

31. Aradau 2012, 44; Forgacs 2014, 274.

32. Mendizabal et al. 2012.

33. Woodcock 2012, 53.

34. Lombroso 2011, 240.

35. Lombroso 2011, 241.

36. Arendt 1976, 38–64.

37. Ministero dell'Interno, Direzione Generale della Pubblica Sicurezza, Divisione Polizia, Sezione Terza to Prefetti Regno et Questore Roma. Telegram of circular n. 63462/10 (September 11, 1940). The memo is reprinted in its entirety as a photograph in Boursier 1999, 18.

38. Weiss-Wendt 2013, 1.

39. The nomad camps in Italy have a long categorical history linked to the government's systematic policies of *segregare* (segregation), *concentrare* (concentration), and *allontanare* (removal). All are grouped under the category of *campo nomadi* (nomad camp). However, to label as "camp" what were often settlements that existed for decades in the same place (for example, Casilino 900, once the largest encampment outside Rome, was founded in the 1960s) gives the impression of a spontaneous, ad hoc settlement that serves to reinforce the stereotype of Romani rootlessness. At various times in their history, nomad camps have been subdivided into categories, among them *campo rom* (Roma camp), *campo sosta* (temporary camp), *campo tollerato* (tolerated camp), *campo attrezzato* (equipped camp), and *campo abusivo* (abusive camp). The latter, "abusive camp," resonates illegality, and it emerged in the wake of the nomad emergency decree to describe any settlement that was not "approved" by the government. Many "abusive camps" sprung up after the destruction of Casilino 900 in 2009 and were targeted by authorities for extirpation. The verb for such demolitions is *sgomberare*, which contains within it simultaneous meanings that are impossible to capture in a single English word: "eviction," "clearing out," "removal," "move," "evacuation." In the context of nomad camps, the verb always contains an implicit element of force, and the proper noun, *sgombero* (plural, *sgomberi*), always designates coerced removal.

40. Associazione 21 Luglio 2013, 5n7. In 2013, eight *villaggi* (villages) and three *centri di raccolta Rom* (Roma collection centers) were funded by the municipal government of Rome.

41. Associazione 21 Luglio 2013, 48–49. The three *centri di raccolta Rom* in Rome are Via Salaria (2009), via Amarilli (2010), and "Best House Rom" (2012). All are located on the outskirts of the city, most often in repurposed industrial buildings. In 2013, 680 Roma lived in these collection centers.

42. Both V. and D. are cited in Facondi 2012.

43. Miriana is cited in *Container 158* 2013.

44. Giuseppe is cited in *Container 158* 2013.

45. Tintori 2016, 122.

46. Wacquant 2008, 2–3.

47. Herodotus, *The Histories*, book IV, 4.198–4.199. As cited in Herodotus 2009, 362.

48. Smith 1818.

49. Herodotus, *The Histories*, book IV, 4.200–4.205. As cited in Herodotus 2009, 362.

50. Cresti 2011, 23.

51. Cresti 2011, 23.

52. Vandewalle 2012, 16–17.

53. Archivio Storico del Ministero dell'Africa Italiana (ASMAI), Libia, Pos. 101 (1878–1906), fasc. 1. "N. 175. Risposta alla Nota 148 del Registro Turco Div. Politica," Memo from Manfredo Camperio to Ministry of Foreign Affairs (July 30, 1884). On the Society for Commercial Exploration in Africa, see Kemény 1973.

54. ASMAI, Libia, Pos. 101 (1878–1906), fasc. 5. "Tripoli Italiana," Letter from Guglielmo De Toth to Ministry of Foreign Affairs (July 2, 1895).

55. Cresti 2011, 52–57.

56. Del Boca 2010a, 339–41; Vandewalle 2012, 27–30. The contemporaneous deportations of Libyans to Italian prison islands such as Ustica and Ponza rendered the politics of cooperation attempted by the Italian colonial regime both disingenuous and ineffective.

57. For Maugini (1924, 109–10), the pastoral economy of nomadic Bedouin had left Libya in a state of abandonment, decay, and, in keeping with the best Orientalist tropes, progressive decadence: "Tutto dinota l'abbandono, la decadenza, nella quale il paese langue ed immiserisce . . . Economia esclusivamente pastorale, primitivo, senza freno, significa dunque decadenza progressivo del territorio e delle popolazioni, depopolamento, carestie periodiche, epidemie." (Everything denotes the abandonment, the decay, in which the country languishes and impoverishes. . . . [An] exclusively pastoral economy, primitive, without brakes, signifies the progressive decadence of the territory and the populations, depopulation, periodic famines, epidemics.)

58. Cresti 2011, 70.

59. Touring Club Italiano 1929, 301.

60. Cicinelli 1932, 502.

61. Cicinelli 1932, 499.

62. Maggiolini 1928; Ravizza 1926, 334.

63. Maggiolini 1928, 168.

64. "La colonia penale agricola di Bengasi" 1926, 196. See also Cresti 2011, 78; Touring Club Italiano 1929, 445, 462.

65. Teruzzi 1931, 324.

66. Istituto Agronomico per l'Oltremare. Photographic Archive. Album 5 LY 2222, *Libya (autori vari)*, circa early 1930s.

67. Cicinelli 1932, 501.

68. Teruzzi 1931, 324.

69. Touring Club Italiano 1940, 397.

70. Fuller 2007, 173. See also Von Henneberg, 1996b.

71. Wright 2010, 92. See also Evans-Pritchard 1949, 192–95. On the Sanusi relationship with Italian colonialism, see Ryan 2018.

72. Wright 2010, 93.

73. ASMAI, Libia, Pos. 150/7 (1919–34), fasc. 17–23. Each file in this archival folder gives a detailed record by region (for example, Ajdabiya, Benghazi, Derna, Barce, Cirene) of the goods confiscated (*beni confiscati*) from the Sanusi *zawiyas*.

74. ASMAI, Libia, Pos. 150/7 (1919–34), fasc. 16. Confisca beni della Senussia (R.D. 22/12/1930 N°1944) (1925–30). On the broader phenomenon of confiscation in modern Italy, see Brice 2014. The French employed a similar strategy of *zawiya* dispossession and dismantling in the Tibesti Mountains when making a bid to control Chad in 1901. After the strategic failure of *pénétration pacifique* (peaceful penetration), French battalion chief Georges-Mathieu Destenave applied a bellicose approach to gaining control of the region, which included targeting Sanusi strongholds. See Evans-Pritchard 1949, 28; Triaud 1995, 600–602.

75. Maugini 1927, 141. See also Bartolozzi 1936, 121; Cresti 2011, 60–61; Teruzzi 1931, 318.

76. Capresi 2007, 34–35. See also Gheriani 2007.

77. Letter from Bresciani to Banco di Roma headquarters (April 13, 1908). Archivio Storico Banca di Roma (ASBR), VIII. 1.4.2, busta 28, fasc. 108, anno 1908. As cited in Capresi 2007, 35. Others, like Crispi, believed colonization was the only way to stem the demographic losses occurring with immigration to the Americas and elsewhere. See Ben-Ghiat and Fuller 2005; Welch 2016b.

78. Cresti 2011, 74.

79. Piccioli 1933, 912.

80. Piccioli 1933, 958. This particular stretch of road near the concentration camps was a pet project of Graziani, who visited road crews there in early August 1930. On this visit, see "Cronache coloniali: Cirenaica Il generale Graziani visita le concessioni del Gebel" 1930. Furthermore, a June 1934 article published in the Touring Club Italiano's magazine, *Le Vie d'Italia*, confirms that the majority of roadwork in Cyrenaica was performed by indigenous labor. See Fantoli 1934, 437–48.

81. Archivio Centrale dello Stato (ACS), Fondo Graziani, Archivio Fotografico, Inventario 52/17.3, busta 1, fasc. 36. Cirenaica. "Strada nord gebelica presso Sidi Abdalla" circa 1930–34. On the retro of the photograph, accreditation is given to "Studio Fotografico Cav. V. Dinami, Bengasi." On Dinami's colonial photographic production in Cyrenaica, see Prestopino 1999. Interestingly, a photo album of road construction in Libya is missing from this same archival file. The archival index notes there should be an album of twenty-four photographs of "Come è stata costruita una strada" (How a road was constructed). This is not the first incident of colonial files gone missing in an Italian archive.

82. Quotations from Rajab Hamad Buwaish al-Minifi's poem, "Dar al-Agaila" (Under such conditions), have been excerpted from Ali Ahmida, *Forgotten Voices: Power and Agency in Colonial and Postcolonial Libya*, 49–51 (New York: Routledge, 2005). They are reproduced here with permission from Taylor & Francis Group LLC Books. In addition to Ahmida's translation, the full text of the poem in Arabic with a rough translation into English is available online at "Libyana: Al-Agaila concentration camp (a poem)," Khelwat el-MrabiT, http://www.libyana.org/history/agaila/pm.html (accessed August 5, 2018).

83. Piccioli 1933, 966. One dollar traded at approximately 19 *lire* in 1932. At this historical currency rate, the cost of Italian road construction in Cyrenaica was 55 million *lire*, or the equivalent of $2.89 million in 1932. Figures were calculated using the websites *Historical Currency Converter*, edited by Rodney Edvinsson, Stockholm University, http://www.historicalstatistics.org/Currencyconverter.html and *U.S. Inflation*

Calculator, CoinNews Media Group LLC, http://www.usinflationcalculator.com/ (accessed August 5, 2018).

84. Evans-Pritchard 1949, 225.

85. ACS, Fondo Graziani, busta 11, fasc. 14, sottofascicolo 9. Telegram from Graziani to Balbo (April 26, 1934). Giambattista Biassuti (2004, 292–93) estimates a ratio of twelve thousand indigenous laborers to one thousand Italians involved in the construction of the *litoranea libica*. He also estimates an additional twenty-three thousand indigenous laborers built the public works (homesteads, wells, roads, et cetera) in preparation for the arrival of the Ventimila in 1938. On the *litoranea libica*, see also Hom Cary 2007, 331–33, 354–60; *La strada litoranea della Libia* 1937; McLaren 2005, 35–38; Segrè 1990, 295–98.

86. De Agostini 1938, 27–28. The Italian-built coastal highway remains the main artery connecting eastern and western Libya today. In 2013, a consortium of Italian companies won a $1.29 billion contract to refurbish 250 miles of the highway. The deal was part of the 2008 Italy-Libya Friendship Pact, which, inter alia, sanctioned the refoulement of boat migrants off the Lampedusan coast detailed in essay one. See "Italian Group Wins $1.29bn Libyan Coastal Road Contract" 2013.

87. Moore 1940, 177.

88. "Cronache coloniali: Cirenaica. La riorganizzazione delle popolazioni indigene" 1933.

89. Del Boca 2010b, 216–17. See also "Cirenaica: Provvedimenti civili in zona di Agedabia dopo il ritorno delle popolazioni alle loro sedi" 1934.

90. Ottolenghi 1997, 169–72.

91. ACS, Fondo Graziani, busta 5, fascicolo 9, sottofascicolo 6. Memo from Graziani to Balbo (April 26, 1934).

92. "Cronache coloniali: Cirenaica. Posti di ristoro per i viaggiatori" 1934, 59. The repurposed camps included those with the reputations of being the most violent: Sidi Ahmed el-Magrun, al-Agheila, Marsa El Brega, Ajdabiya.

93. Evans-Pritchard 1949, 199. Evans-Pritchard served in the British Army during World War II, and in 1942 he was posted to the British Military Administration in charge of governing Cyrenaica.

94. On the development of Fascist new towns in the Agro Pontino, see Caprotti 2007; Dalzini 2005; Fuller 2004; Ghirardo 2013, 109–15; ; Stewart-Steinberg 2016. Mia Fuller's unpublished manuscript "Mussolini Threshing Still: Inertia Memoriae, Italy, and Fascist Monuments" explores the symbolic legacy of these Fascist new towns in Italy and beyond.

95. Moore 1940, 213–14.

96. *The Italian Empire: Libya* 1940, 63. See also Segrè 1974, 102–12.

97. *The Italian Empire: Libya* 1940, 65. In 1939, one dollar traded at approximately 19 *lire*, that is, a conversion of 945 million *lire* to roughly $5 million.

98. Fuller 2007, 173.

99. Steer 1939, 154.

100. Hoffman 1990, 127–28. Salvatore Bono (2006) describes Hoffman's memoir as the most effective and incisive testimony about everyday life in Italian colonial Libya.

101. Ballinger 2016b; Capresi 2007; Cresti 2011; Fowler 1973; Fuller 2007; Johnson 1973; Lembo 2011; Pergher 2018; Sherkasi 1973; Von Henneberg 1996a.

102. In Tripolitania, the agricultural villages were (in Italian, with present-day Libyan place-names transliterated from Arabic): Balbo (Almamoura), Borgo Tazzoli (Tazzoli), Breviglieri (Al Khadra'), Corradini (Ghanimah), Crispi (Tamina), Garibaldi (Ad Dafiniyah), Gioda (Krarim), Giordani (An-Nasiriyah), Marconi (Al Qusay'ah), Micca (Al'Amiriyah), Oliveti (Jadda'im), and Tigrinna (Tegrena). The Muslim villages were Bianchi (Zahra) and Deliziosa (Na'imah). In Cyrenaica, the agricultural villages were Baracca (Baracca), Battisti (Qamadah), Beda Littoria (Al Bayda), Berta (Al Qubah), D'Annunzio (Al Bayyadah), Filzi (Al Himadah), Luigi di Savoia (Labraq), Maddalena (Al 'Uwayliyah), Mameli (Qaryat 'Umar al Mukhtar), Oberdan (Battah), Razza (Massah). The Muslim villages were Alba (Ra's al Hilal), Fiorita (Athrun), Nuova (Bo Traba), Risorta (Jarda Al Abid), Verde (Jardis Jerran), Vittoriosa (Mansura). The agricultural village of Sauro was built but never occupied (Capresi 2007, 58).

103. Barone 1939, 808.

104. Steer 1939, 164. Almost immediately after their dissolution, the Italian colonial press began to "spin" the concentration camps in Libya as productive spaces. For example, an article in the March 1934 issue of *Rivista delle Colonie Italiane* claims that certain populations did not want to leave the camps because the quality of life was so much better in them: "A questo proposito è molto significativo il fatto che parecchi gruppi di popolazioni, quando ebbero libertà di fare ritorno alle loro sedi normali, chiesero di rimanere nei campi in cui erano stati concentrati . . . hanno preferito restare là, dove le condizioni di vita sono confortanti e dove, per di più, hanno sott'occhi lo spettacolo dei loro figli amorosamente educati e curati dal Governo." (In this regard it is very significant the fact that several groups of people, when they had the freedom to return to their normal homelands, asked to remain in the camps in which they were concentrated. . . . They preferred to remain there, where the conditions of life are comforting, and moreover, where they have under their eyes the spectacle of their children being lovingly educated and cared for by the government.) "Cronache coloniali: Cirenaica. Ritorno di fuoruscito" 1934.

105. Fuller 2007, 193. A newsreel produced by Istituto Luce documented the opening of the first Muslim village, La Fiorita, in Cyrenaica on May 3, 1939. See Archivio Luce, "Primo villaggio agricolo mussulmano," directed by Arnaldo Ricotti, https://patrimonio.archivioluce.com/luce-web/detail/IL5000019708/2/primo-villaggio-agricolo-mussulmano.html (accessed August 5, 2018).

106. Fuller 2007, 195. See also Anderson 2010, 10.

107. Cresti 2011, 222–23; Touring Club Italiano 1940, 387, 426.

108. Moore 1940, 187–88.

109. *Cirenaica: Some Photographic Representations of Italy's Action* 1946, 40.

110. Johnson 1973, 190.

111. *Cirenaica: Some Photographic Representations of Italy's Action* 1946, 38.

112. Neri 1939, 402.

113. ASMAI, Pos. 150/21 (1913–36), fasc. 89. "Rientro e sottomissione fuoruscito libici in Egitto (1929–36)." See also Biassuti 2004, 287; Cresti 2011, 169; Del Boca 2010b, 219–21; Moore 1940, 184. It is worth noting that the term *fuoruscito* also described ethnic Italians who left the Habsburg Empire during World War I to return to Italy as well as Italian citizens who were antifascists that fled Italy during the regime. Whether in the context of the Habsburg Empire, Italian colonial Libya, or Fascist Italy, a *fuoruscito* is

a person who leaves his or her country of origin for political reasons and resides abroad in exile.

114. Del Boca 2010b, 220.

115. Moore 1940, 189–90.

116. Ornato 1939, 47.

117. Barone 1938, 1632.

118. Istituto Agronomico Oltremare (IAO), Centro Documentazione Inedita, Fasc. 2091, Memo from Cosimo Manni, President of the Ente per la Colonizzazione della Libia to Ministry of Italian Africa, "Promemoria della colonizzazione musulmana" (January 26, 1942).

119. Evans-Pritchard 1949, 225–26.

120. IAO, "Promemoria della colonizzazione musulmana" 1942, 5.

121. Evans-Pritchard 1949, 226.

122. IAO, "Promemoria della colonizzazione musulmana" 1942, 6. Another memo housed in the IAO archive describes how difficult living conditions forced the native populations to "stray" from their assigned *poderi*. IAO, Centro Documentazione Inedita, Fasc. 2092, Memo from Blundo, Prefecture of Derna, to Vice Governor General in Tripoli, "Rapporti con i nativi rientrati nel breve period di occupazione della Libia Orientale da parte delle truppe inglesi" (June 23, 1941).

123. Johnson 1973, 206–7.

124. Anderson 2010, 10–11; Capresi 2007, 242–43.

125. Reggio Decreto June 1, 1919, and Reggio Decreto October 31, 1919. See Renucci 2005. Renucci's article was republished in 2010 at the Archive ouverte en Sciences de l'Homme et de la Société. I cite this version throughout, which is available at https://halshs.archives-ouvertes.fr/halshs-00463636v2/document (accessed August 5, 2018).

126. The 1919 law was inspired by the French law regarding colonial citizenship in Algeria that same year. See Cooper 2014, 6; Renucci 2005, 1.

127. Evans-Pritchard 1949, 215.

128. Evans-Pritchard 1949, 214.

129. Mondiani 1939, 69–70. See also Deplano 2017, 135–39; Rappas 2017.

130. Mondiani 1939, 68. On the irresolute ways in which the Italian state treated ex–colonial subjects living in Italy after World War II, see Deplano 2017, especially 139–59 on citizenship.

131. Fuller 2007, 35. See also Barrera 2003b.

132. Barrera 2003b, abstract.

133. "L'Italia per i suoi sudditi musulmani" 1938, 1186.

134. "I 'nuovi italiani' nella riforma della cittadinanza" 2017; "Il Senato rinvia la discussione sullo Ius soli" 2017. See also Fiore 2017, 185–88.

135. Smith 2003, 10–13. With the return of colonists from overseas after World War II, Smith notes that Europe became the site of immigration rather than emigration for the first time in a century.

136. The numbers on returning colonists are soft, at best. The Libyan numbers were calculated using Italian census data from 1942 and British Military Administration census data in 1962. The Eritrea numbers were calculated using Italian census data from 1939 and 1949. Maximalist figures for the Istrian-Dalmatian exodus are

close to 350,000 (as cited in Ballinger 2002, 1); however, the current scholarly consensus estimates that number to be closer to 180,000–200,000.

137. These Jewish survivors living in Italy numbered seventy thousand. On Jewish survivors in displaced person camps after World War II, see Hom 2017.

138. *Vacanze di Guerra* 2010. All testimonials regarding the thirteen thousand children evacuated from Libya in 1940 are cited from this documentary film.

139. Del Boca 2010b, 311–15. Adding to the trauma of already-splintered families, by 1941 more than half of Italian colonists in Cyrenaica had abandoned their agricultural villages and fled to Tripolitania and Tunisia. The Allied forces sacked the villages on the Jabal Akhdar plateau in early 1942.

140. As quoted in *Vacanze di Guerra* 2010.

141. Molinari 2006, 90–91.

142. As cited in Stermieri 2016. See also Molinari 2006, 101.

143. Lo 2013.

144. In 1992, residents of Villaggio Santa Caterina created the Associazione Nazionale Venezia Giulia e Dalmazia (National Association Venezia Giulia and Dalmatia). This organization actively promotes the memory of Istrian exodus and the ongoing effects of that experience. See Associazione Nazionale Venezia Giulia e Dalmazia, Centro studi Padre Flaminio Rocchi, http://www.anvgd.it/ (accessed August 5, 2018).

145. Pamela Ballinger (2002, 198) calls the Istrians "doubly exiled," whereas Andrea Smith (2003, 24) calls the population of European returning colonists "doubly diasporic."

146. Ballinger 2002, 198.

147. Iacopini 2015; Ryan 2017. Libyan-Italians have a robust online presence via the Associazione Italiani Rimpatriati dalla Libia at http://www.airl.it/ (accessed August 5, 2018). It was founded after 1970 when Qaddafi expulsed the remaining twenty thousand Italians residing in Libya.

148. Molinari 2006, 105. Ballinger (2002, 203) confirms similar discrimination among the Istrian exiles she interviewed in Trieste.

149. The *foibe* massacres were a four-year stretch of violence between 1943 and 1947 in the region that today comprises northeastern Italy, western Slovenia, and northeastern Croatia. The *foibe* refer to the naturally occurring sinkholes in the geologic karst where Yugoslav partisans buried the ethnic Italians living in Yugoslav territories that they had targeted and killed en masse. See Ballinger 2002, 129–67; Oliva 2009, 22–26.

150. "I luoghi dell'esodo in Piemonte," n.d.

151. Article 19 of the Paris Peace Treaty stipulated the "option" of citizenship. In the aftermath of "opting" for Italy or not, Ballinger (2002) documents with great sophistication the turbulent histories of exile between those who left (*andati*) and those who stayed (*rimasti*).

152. As cited in Coda 2014. See also Veneziani 2015.

153. As cited in Stermieri 2016.

154. "Ciampino, incendio al campo nomadi La Barbuta" 2017; "Incendio nel campo rom 'La Barbuta'" 2015.

155. "Brucia ancora La Barbuta" 2017.

156. Grilli 2017b.

157. "Ciampino, sopralluogo parlamentare a La Barbuta" 2017.

158. Grilli 2017a.

159. *Io, la mia famiglia rom e Woody Allen* 2009. I owe many thanks to Àine O'Healy for introducing me to Halilovic's work. Romani cinema is a burgeoning genre elsewhere in Europe, and the first Romani film festival, Ake Dikhea?, was held in October 2017 in Germany. In Italy, documentaries and films by Italian directors concerning the Roma are also emerging, including *Container 158* (2013); *Fuori Campo: storie dei rom in Italia* (2015); and *A Ciambra* (2017).

Coda

1. On Japanese internment in the United States, see Daniels 1971, 2004; Muller 2001; Starr 2015, 225–27. On the pernicious euphemism of "relocation center," see Hirabayashi 1994.

2. Muller 2001, 36–37.

3. Starr 2015, 41.

4. Andersson 2014, 66–97, 273–81.

5. Fernandez and Benner, 2018.

6. As cited in Kodani Hill 2000, 38. See also Wang 2018.

WORKS CITED

A sud di Lampedusa. 2008. Film. Directed by Andrea Segre, with Stefano Liberti and Ferruccio Pastore. Rome: ZaLab.

Abulafia, David. 2011. *The Great Sea: A Human History of the Mediterranean*. Oxford: Oxford University Press.

Agamben, Giorgio. 1998. *Homo Sacer: Sovereign Power and Bare Life*. Translated by Daniel Heller-Roazen. Stanford, CA: Stanford University Press.

———. 1999. *Remnants of Auschwitz: The Witness and the Archive*. Translated by Daniel Heller-Roazen. Stanford, CA: Stanford University Press.

———. 2004. *The Open: Man and Animal*. Translated by Kevin Attell. Stanford, CA: Stanford University Press.

———. 2005. *State of Exception*. Translated by Kevin Attell. Chicago: University of Chicago Press.

Agier, Michel. 2011. *Managing the Undesirables: Refugee Camps and Humanitarian Government*. Translated by David Fernbach. Cambridge, UK: Polity Press.

Ahmida, Ali. 2005. *Forgotten Voices: Power and Agency in Colonial and Postcolonial Libya*. London: Routledge.

———. 2006. "When the Subaltern Speak: Memory of Genocide in Colonial Libya 1929–33." *Italian Studies* 61 (2): 175–90.

———. 2009. *The Making of Modern Libya*. 2nd ed. Albany: SUNY Press.

Aikpitanyi, Isoke. 2011. *500 storie vere sulla tratta delle ragazze africane in Italia*. Rome: Ediesse.

Ailara, Vito, and Massimo Caserta. 2012. *I relegati libici dal 1911 al 1934*. Ustica, Italy: Edizioni del Centro Studi e Documentazione Isola di Ustica.

Albahari, Maurizio. 2015. *Crimes of Peace: Mediterranean Migrations at the World's Deadliest Border*. Philadelphia: University of Pennsylvania Press.

Alunni, Lorenzo. 2012. "'After All, They Are Nomads, Aren't They?' Roma Transnationalism and Health Issues." MMG Working Paper 12–20, Max Planck Institute for the Study of Religious and Ethnic Diversity.

Andall, Jacqueline, and Derek Duncan, eds. 2005. *Italian Colonialism: Legacy and Memory*. Oxford: Peter Lang.

———, eds. 2010. *National Belongings: Hybridity in Italian Colonial and Postcolonial Cultures*. Oxford: Peter Lang.

Anderson, Sean. 2010. "The Light and the Line: Florestano di Fausto and the Politics of *Mediterraneità*." *California Italian Studies* 1 (1): 1–13. http://escholarship.org/uc/item/9hm1p6m5#page-6.

Andersson, Ruben. 2014. *Illegality Inc.: Clandestine Migration and the Business of Bordering Europe*. Berkeley: University of California Press.

———. 2017. "Rescued and Caught: The Humanitarian-Security Nexus at Europe's Frontiers." In *The Borders of "Europe": Autonomy of Migration, Tactics of Bordering*, edited by Nicholas De Genova, 64–94. Durham, NC: Duke University Press. Andrijasevic, Rutvica. 2010. "From Exception to Excess: Detention and Deportation across the Mediterranean Space." In *The Deportation Regime: Sovereignty, Space, and the Freedom of Movement*, edited by Nicholas De Genova and Nathalie Peutz, 147–65. Durham, NC: Duke University Press.

Aradau, Claudia. 2012. "The Roma in Italy: Racism as Usual?" In *Roma in Europe: Migration, Education, Representation*, edited by Anca Pusca, 43–50. New York: International Debate Education Association.

Arendt, Hannah. 1958. *The Origins of Totalitarianism: Parts I–III*. 2nd ed. Cleveland: Meridian Books, World Publishing. Originally published 1951 by Schocken Books.

———. 1976. *Imperialism: Part Two of the Origins of Totalitarianism*. Rev. ed. New York: A Harvest Book, Harcourt. Originally published 1951 by Schocken Books.

Arrighi, Giovanni. 2010. *The Long Twentieth Century: Money, Power, and the Origins of Our Times*. Rev. ed. London: Verso.

Arthur, Paul. 2004. "From Vicus to Village: Italian Landscapes, AD400–1000." In *Landscapes of Change: Rural Evolutions in Late Antiquity and the Early Middle Ages*, edited by Neil Christie, 103–33. London: Routledge.

Associazione 21 Luglio. 2013. *Campi nomadi s.p.a. Segregare, concentrare e allontanare i rom: I costi a Roma nel 2013*. Rome: Associazione 21 Luglio.

———. 2014. *Terminal Barbuta. Il "villaggio della solidarietà" La Barbuta a Roma. Presente e future di un "campo" per soli rom*. Rome: Associazione 21 Luglio.

Atkinson, David. 1999. "Nomadic Strategies and Colonial Governance: Domination and Resistance in Cyrenaica, 1923–32." In *The Entanglements of Power: Geographies of Domination/Resistance*, edited by Joanne P. Sharp, Paul Routledge, Chris Philo, and Ronan Paddison, 93–121. London: Routledge.

———. 2007. "Embodied Resistance, Italian Anxieties, and the Place of the Nomad in Colonial Cyrenaica." In *In Corpore: Bodies in Post-Unification Italy*, edited by Charlotte Ross and Loredana Polezzi, 56–79. Madison, NJ: Fairleigh Dickinson Press.

———. 2012. "Encountering Bare Life in Italian Libya and Colonial Amnesia in Agamben." In *Agamben and Colonialism*, edited by Marcelo Svirsky and Simone Bignall, 155–77. Edinburgh: Edinburgh University Press.

Augé, Marc. 1995. *Non-Places: An Introduction to the Anthropology of Supermodernity*. Translated by John Howe. London: Verso.

Baldacchino, Godfrey. 2010. *Island Enclaves: Offshoring Strategies, Creative Governance and Subnational Island Jurisdictions*. Montreal: McGill-Queen's University Press.

———. 2014. "Islands and the Offshoring Possibilities and Strategies of Contemporary States: Insights on/for the Migration Phenomenon on Europe's Southern Flank." *Island Studies Journal* 9 (1): 57–68.

Baldassar, Loretta, and Donna Gabaccia, eds. 2010. *Intimacy and Italian Migration: Gender and Domestic Lives in a Mobile World*. New York: Fordham University Press.

Baldinetti, Anna, ed. 2003. *Modern and Contemporary Libya: Sources and Historiographies*. Rome: Istituto Italiano per l'Africa e l'Oriente.

——. 2010. *The Origins of the Libyan Nation: Colonial Legacy, Exile, and the Emergence of a New Nation-State*. London: Routledge.

Ballinger, Pamela. 2002. *History in Exile: Memory and Identity at the Borders of the Balkans*. Princeton, NJ: Princeton University Press.

——. 2007. "Borders of the Nation, Borders of Citizenship: Italian Repatriation and the Redefinition of National Identity after World War II." *Comparative Studies in Society and History* 49 (3): 713–41.

——. 2016a. "Beyond the Italies: Italy as a Mobile Subject?" In *Italian Mobilities*, edited by Ruth Ben-Ghiat and Stephanie Malia Hom, 20–45. London: Routledge.

——. 2016b. "Colonial Twilight: Italian Settlers and the Long Decolonization of Libya." *Journal of Contemporary History* 51 (4): 813–38.

Barghathi, Yusuf Salim al-. 1981. "The Concentration Camps and the Harm Resulting from the Italian Invasion of Libya." In *'Umar al-Mukhtar, nashatuhu wa-jihaduhu min 1862 ilá 1931: dirasat fi harakat al-jihad al-Libi: a'mal al-nadwah al-'ilmiyah allati 'aqadaha Markaz Dirasat Jihad al-Libiyin Didda al-Ghazw al-Itali* ['Umar Al-Mukhtar—his early life and his jihad from 1862 to 1931, Studies in the Libyan Jihad Movement: Proceedings of the Scientific Session Convened by the Center of the Study of the Jihad of Libyans against the Italian Invasion], edited by 'Aqil Al-Barbar et al., 113–49. Tripoli, Libya: al-Markaz.

Barghathi, Yusuf Salim al-, and Salah al-Din Hasan Suri. 1985. *Al-Mu'taqalat al-fashistiyah bi-Libiya: Dirasah tarikhiyah* [The Fascist concentration camps in Libya: An historical study]. Tripoli, Libya: Markaz Dirasat Jihad al-Libiyin Didda al-Ghazw al-Itali.

Barkham, Patrick. 2002. "No Waltzing in Woomera." *The Guardian*, May 25. Accessed August 8, 2018. http://www.theguardian.com/uk/2002/may/25/immigration.australia.

Barone, Francesco. 1938. "Terre italiane d'oltremare. Note e rassegne. Case popolari nella Libia orientale. Villaggi agricoli per musulmani a Derna." *Rivista delle Colonie* 12, no. 12 (December): 1630–32.

——. 1939. "Terre Italiane d'Oltremare. Note e rassegne. La toponomastica dei nuovi villaggi." *Rivista delle Colonie* 13, no. 6 (June): 799–810.

Barrera, Giulia. 2003a. "The Construction of Racial Hierarchies in Colonial Eritrea: The Liberal and Early Fascist Period (1897–1934)." In *A Place in the Sun: Africa in Italian Colonial Culture from Post-Unification to the Present*, edited by Patrizia Palumbo, 81–115. Berkeley: University of California Press.

——. 2003b. "Mussolini's Colonial Race Laws and State-Settler Relations in Africa Orientale Italiana (1935–41)." *Journal of Modern Italian Studies* 8 (3): 425–43.

Bartolozzi, Enrico, ed. 1936. *Nuove costruzioni rurali in Libia*. Studi e monografie, 4 bis. Rome: Istituto Nazionale di Economia Agraria.

Bauman, Zygmunt. 1988. *Globalization: The Human Consequences*. Cambridge, UK: Polity.
———. 2002. *Society under Siege*. Cambridge, UK: Polity.
Behdad, Ali. 1994. *Belated Travelers: Orientalism in the Age of Colonial Dissolution*. Durham, NC: Duke University Press.
Benelli, Elena. 2013. "Migration Discourses in Italy." *Conserveries mémorielles*. Special issue on Frontiers, Barriers, Horizons: Re-examining the History and Memories of Migration. 13. Accessed August 8, 2018. http://cm.revues.org /1419.
Ben-Ghiat, Ruth. 2012. "Italian Fascism's Empire Cinema: *Kif Tebbi*, the Conquest of Libya, and the Assault on the Nomadic." In *Postcolonial Cinema Studies*, edited by Sandra Ponzanesi and Marguerite Waller, 20–31. London: Routledge.
———. 2015. *Italian Fascism's Empire Cinema*. Bloomington: Indiana University Press.
Ben-Ghiat, Ruth, and Mia Fuller. 2005. "Introduction." In *Italian Colonialism*, edited by Ruth Ben-Ghiat and Mia Fuller, 1–12. New York: Palgrave Macmillan.
Ben-Ghiat, Ruth, and Stephanie Malia Hom. 2016. "Introduction." In *Italian Mobilities*, edited by Ruth Ben-Ghiat and Stephanie Malia Hom, 1–19. London: Routledge.
Bensaâd, Ali. 2001. "Voyage au bout de la peur avec les clandestins du Sahel." *Le Monde Diplomatique*, September, 16–17.
———. 2002. "La grande migration africaine à travers le Sahara." Special issue on "Le sahara, cette «autre Méditerranée»." *Méditerranée* 99 (3–4): 41–52.
———. 2007. "The Mediterranean Divide and Its Echo in the Sahara: New Migratory Routes and New Barriers on the Path to the Mediterranean." In *Between Europe and the Mediterranean: The Challenges and the Fears*, edited by Thierry Fabre and Paul Sant-Cassia, 51–69. New York: Palgrave Macmillan.
Berdahl, Daphne. 2005. "The Spirit of Capitalism and the Boundaries of Citizenship in Post-Wall Germany." *Comparative Studies in Society and History* 47 (2): 235–51.
"Berlusconi da Gheddafi, siglato l'accordo: «Uniti sull'immigrazione»." 2008. *Corriere della Sera*, August 30. Accessed August 8, 2018. http://www.corriere.it/esteri /08_agosto_30/berlusconi_libia_gheddafi_bengasi_478ee3f4-767e-11dd-9747 -00144f02aabc.shtml.
Bernadie-Tahir, Nathalie, and Camille Schmoll. 2014. "The Uses of Islands in the Production of the Southern European Migration Border." *Island Studies Journal* 9 (1): 3–6.
Bhabha, Homi. 2005. *The Location of Culture*. Rev. ed. London: Routledge.
Biagio, Pace. 1932. "La pacificazione della Cirenaica e il regime dei nomadi occidentali." *Riviste delle Colonie Italiane* 6, no. 5 (May): 329–42.
Biassuti, Giambattista. 2004. "La politica indigena italiana in Libia: Dall'occupazione al termine del governorato di Italo Balbo (1911–40)." PhD diss., Università degli Studi di Pavia.
Bignall, Simone, and Marcelo Svirsky. 2012. "Introduction." In *Agamben and Colonialism*, edited by Marcelo Svirsky and Simone Bignall, 1–16. Edinburgh: Edinburgh University Press.
Bigo, Didier. 2005. "Global (In)security: The Field of the Professionals of Unease Management and the Ban-opticon." *Traces: A Multilingual Series of Cultural Theory* 4: 34–87.

———. 2007. "Detention of Foreigners, States of Exception, and the Social Practices of Control of the Ban-Opticon." In *Borderscapes: Hidden Geographies and Politics at Territory's Edge*, edited by Prem Kumar Rajaram and Carl Grundy-Warr, 3–33. Minneapolis: University of Minnesota Press.

Boldetti, Ambra. 1977. "La repressione in Italia: Il caso del 1894." *Rivista di storia contemporanea* 6, no. 4 (October): 481–515.

Bolzoni, Attilio. 2008. "La porta che guarda l'Africa in ricordo di chi non è mai arrivato." *La Repubblica*, June 26. Accessed August 8, 2018. http://www.repubblica.it/2008/06/sezioni/cronaca/sbarchi-immigrati-1/porta-immigrati/porta-immigrati.html.

Bonaffini, Giuseppe. 1997. *Un mare di paura: Il Mediterraneo in età moderna*. Palermo: Sciascia.

Bono, Salvatore. 1989. *Siciliani nel Maghreb*. Mazara del Vallo, Italy: Liceo Ginnastico Gian Giacomo Adira.

———. 1993. *Corsari nel Mediterraneo: Cristiani e musulmani fra guerra, schiavitù e commercio*. Milan: Mondadori.

———. 2006. "Memorie e nostalgie degli Italiani di Libia." In *La Libia tra Mediterraneo e mondo islamico*, edited by Federico Cresti, 35–54. Milan: Dott. A. Giuffrè Editore.

Boursier, Giovanna. 1999. "Gypsies in Italy during the Fascist Dictatorship and the Second World War." In *In the Shadow of the Swastika: The Gypsies during the Second World War*, edited by Donald Kendrick, Vol. 2, 13–36. Hatfield, UK: University of Hertfordshire Press.

Bradley, Keith, and Paul Cartledge, eds. 2011. *The Cambridge World History of Slavery*. Vol. 1, *The Ancient Mediterranean World*. Cambridge: Cambridge University Press.

Braidotti, Rosi. 1994. *Nomadic Subjects: Embodiment and Sexual Difference in Contemporary Feminist Theory*. New York: Columbia University Press.

———. 2011. *Nomadic Theory: The Portable Rosi Braidotti*. New York: Columbia University Press.

Braudel, Fernand. 1995. *The Mediterranean and the Mediterranean World in the Age of Phillip II*. Translated by Siân Reynolds. Berkeley: University of California Press. Originally published 1949 by Libraire Armand Colin.

Brice, Catherine. 2014. "Confiscations et séquestres des biens des exilés politiques dans les États italiens au XIXe siècle: Questions sur une pratique et projets de recherches." *Diaspora: Circulations, migrations, histoire* 23–24: 147–63.

Brogi, Paolo. 2012. "Ex recluso si suicida per disperazione: Sciopero della fame al Cie di Ponte Galeria." *Corriere della Sera*, March 16. Accessed January 28, 2018. http://roma.corriere.it/roma/notizie/cronaca/12_marzo_16/suicida-ex-ospite-cie-pontegaleria-2003713113930.shtml.

Brubaker, Rogers. 1998. *Citizenship and Nationhood in France and Germany*. Cambridge, MA: Harvard University Press.

"Brucia ancora La Barbuta, Zingharetti 'Troppo incendi dolosi, è criminalità.'" 2017. *Corriere della Sera*, July 10. Accessed August 8, 2018. http://roma.corriere.it/notizie/cronaca/17_luglio_10/roma-incendi-barbuta-zingaretti-dolosi-criminalita-8af8f1aa-6582-11e7-a5ea-ffe2be8246f0.shtml.

Bu Sha'alah, Sa'd Muhammad. 1984. *Min dakhil al-mu'taqalat: Dirasah tarikhiyah tahliliyah* [From inside the concentration camps: An analytical historical study]. Tripoli, Libya: al-Munshaah al-'Aammah.

Burbank, Jane, and Frederick Cooper. 2010. *Empires in World History: Power and the Politics of Difference.* Princeton, NJ: Princeton University Press.

Burns, Jennifer. 2013. *Migrant Imaginaries: Figures in Italian Migration Literature.* Oxford and Bern: Peter Lang.

Cabot, Heath. 2014. *On the Doorstep of Europe: Asylum and Citizenship in Greece.* Philadelphia: University of Pennsylvania Press.

Caloz-Tschopp, Marie-Claire. 2004. *Les étrangers aux frontiers de l'Europe et le spectre des camps.* Paris: La Dispute.

Campbell, Ian. 2017. *The Addis Ababa Massacre: Italy's National Shame.* Oxford: Oxford University Press.

Capresi, Vittoria. 2007. "I centri rurali libici: L'architettura dei centri rurali di fondazione costruiti in Libia—colonia italiana—durante il fascismo (1934–40)." PhD diss., Technische Universität Wien.

Caprotti, Federico. 2007. *Mussolini's Cities: Internal Colonialism in Italy, 1930–39.* Amherst, NY: Cambria Press.

Caputo, Ferdinando. 1899. "Assab e le Colonie penitenziarie nell'Eritrea." *Rivista di discipline carcerarie* Anno 24, no. 7 (July): 261–67.

Caritas Migrantes. 2013. *XXIII Rapporto Immigrazione 2013: Tra crisi e diritti umani.* Report. Accessed August 8, 2018. http://www.caritas.it/caritasitaliana /allegati/3960/SintesiRapportoImmigrazione.pdf.

Chambers, Iain. 2008. *Mediterranean Crossings: The Politics of an Interrupted Modernity.* Durham, NC: Duke University Press.

Chapin-Metz, Helen, ed. 1987. *Libya: A Country Study.* Washington, DC: Federal Research Division.

Chatterjee, Partha. 2012. *The Black Hole of Empire: History of a Global Practice of Power.* Princeton, NJ: Princeton University Press.

Choate, Mark. 2008. *Emigrant Nation: The Making of Italy Abroad.* Cambridge, MA: Harvard University Press.

"Choc nel Cie di Roma, nove immigrati si cuciono la bocca per protesta." 2013. *Corriere della Sera*, December 22. Accessed August 8, 2018. http://roma .corriere.it/roma/notizie/cronaca/13_dicembre_21/cie-roma-quattro -immigrati-si-cuciono-bocca-protesta-c856418c-6a5f-11e3-aaba-67f946664e4c .shtml.

"Ciampino, incendio al campo nomadi La Barbuta: Denso colonna di fumo." 2017. *Corriere della Sera*, June 5. Accessed August 8, 2018. http://roma.corriere.it /notizie/cronaca/17_giugno_05/ciampino-incendio-campo-nomadi-barbuta -densa-colonna-fumo-577e1d30-4a09-11e7-80a9-c638c3a4067c.shtml.

"Ciampino, sopralluogo parlamentare a La Barbuta. Roma Capitale: 'Chiusura entro il 2020.'" 2017. *ilmamilio.it, L'informazione dei Castelli romani*, August 1, 2017. Accessed August 8, 2018. https://www.ilmamilio.it/c/comuni/868-ciampino -sopralluogo-parlamentare-a-la-barbuta-roma-capitale-chiusura-entro-il-2020.html.

Ciappara, Frans. 2004. "Christendom and Islam: A Fluid Frontier." *Mediterranean Studies* 13: 165–87.

Cicinelli, Tito. 1932. "Creazione di colonie agricole per connazionali in Cirenaica."
Rivista di diritto penitenziario: Studi teorici e pratici 3: 497–509.

"Cirenaica: Provvedimenti civili in zona di Agedabia dopo il ritorno delle popolazioni alle loro sedi." 1934. *Rivista delle Colonie* 8, no. 2 (February): 131–32.

Cirenaica: Some Photographic Representations of Italy's Action. 1946. Florence: Istituto Agricolo Italiano.

Clancy-Smith, Julia A. 2011. *Mediterraneans: North Africa and Europe in an Age of Migration, c. 1800–1900.* Berkeley: University of California Press.

Claviez, Thomas. 2013. "Introduction." In *The Conditions of Hospitality: Ethics, Politics, and Aesthetics on the Threshold of the Possible*, edited by Thomas Claviez, 1–12. New York: Fordham University Press.

Clough Marinaro, Isabella. 2009. "Between Surveillance and Exile: Biopolitics and the Roma in Italy." *Bulletin of Italian Politics* 1 (2): 265–87.

———. 2014. "Rome's 'Legal' Camps for Roma: The Construction of New Spaces." *Journal of Modern Italian Studies* 19 (5): 541–55.

Coda, Mario. 2014. "Esuli senza codice." *Azione Tradizionale* (blog). July 5. Accessed August 8, 2018. http://www.azionetradizionale.com/2014/05/07/esuli-senza -codice/.

"Come il generale Graziani pacificò la Cirenaica: Precisa documentazione contro le denigrazioni straniere." 1932. *L'Italia Coloniale* 9, no. 2 (February): 24–25.

Come un uomo sulla terra. 2008. Film. Directed by Andrea Segre and Dagmawi Yimer, with Riccardo Biadene. Rome: ZaLab.

Container 158. 2013. Film. Directed by Enrico Parenti and Stefano Liberti. Rome: ZaLab.

Cooper, Frederick. 2014. *Citizenship between Empire and Nation: Remaking France and French Africa, 1945–60.* Princeton, NJ: Princeton University Press.

Cosentino, Raffaella. 2012. "Viaggio dentro i CIE tra pestaggi, psicofarmaci, e strani suicidi." *Corriere della Sera*, April 10. Accessed January 29, 2018. http://www .corriere.it/inchieste/viaggio-dentro-cie-pestaggi-psicofarmaci-strani-suicidi /f86e60d4-82f3-11e1-b660-48593c628107.shtml.

Cresti, Federico. 2011. *Non desiderare la terra d'altri: La colonizzazione italiana in Libia.* Rome: Carocci.

"Cronache coloniali: Cirenaica. Il generale Graziani visita le concessioni del Gebel." 1930. *Rivista delle Colonie* 4, no. 9 (September): 817–18.

"Cronache coloniali: Cirenaica. La crociera in Cirenaica dei volontari di guerra." 1932. *Rivista delle Colonie Italiane* 6, no. 10 (October): 802–3.

"Cronache coloniali: Cirenaica. La riorganizzazione delle popolazioni indigene." 1933. *Rivista delle Colonie Italiane* 7, no. 8 (August): 670–71.

"Cronache coloniali: Cirenaica. Posti di ristoro per i viaggiatori." 1934. *Rivista delle Colonie Italiane* 8, no. 1 (January): 59.

"Cronache coloniali: Cirenaica. Ritorno di fuorusciti." 1934. *Rivista delle Colonie Italiane* 8, no. 3 (March): 221–22.

Curtis, Robert Irvin. 1978. "The Production and Commerce of Fish Sauce in the Western Roman Empire: A Social and Economic Study." PhD diss., University of Maryland.

Cuttitta, Paolo. 2012. *Lo spettacolo del confine: Lampedusa tra produzione e messa in scena della frontiera.* Milan: Mimesis.

Dal Lago, Alessandro. 2012. *Non-persone: L'esclusione dei migranti in una società globale*. 5th ed. Milan: Feltrinelli.

Dalzini, Alda. 2005. *La terra promessa: Breve storia della bonifica delle paludi pontine*. Latina, Italy: Museo Piana delle Orme.

Damiani, Giuseppe. 1905. *Il domicilio coatto: Colonia di Lampedusa*. Palermo: Stab. Tip. A. Giannitrapani.

Dando-Collins, Stephen. 2010. *Legions of Rome: The Definitive History of Every Imperial Roman Legion*. London: Quercus.

Daniele, Ulderico. 2011. "'Nomads' in the Eternal City: Local Policies and Roma Participation in the 'Emergency' Era." *Géocarrefour* 86 (1): 15–23.

Daniels, Roger. 1971. *Concentration Camps U.S.A.: Japanese Americans and World War II*. New York: Holt, Rinehart & Winston.

——. 2004. *Prisoners without Trial: Japanese Americans in World War II*. Rev. ed. New York: Hill and Wang.

Davis, Robert. 2003. *Christian Slaves, Muslim Masters: White Slavery in the Mediterranean, the Barbary Coast, and Italy 1500–1800*. New York: Palgrave Macmillan.

——. 2009. *Holy War and Human Bondage: Tales of Christian-Muslim Slavery in the Early-Modern Mediterranean*. Santa Barbara, CA: Praeger, ABC-Clio.

De Agostini, Giovanni. 1938. *La Libia turistica*. Milan: Ente Turistico ed Alberghiero della Libia.

De Felice, Renzo. 1965. *Mussolini il rivoluzionario, 1883–1920*. Turin: Einaudi.

——. 1985. *Jews in an Arab Land: Libya, 1835–1970*. Translated by Judith Roumani. Austin: University of Texas Press.

De Genova, Nicholas. 2002. "Migrant 'Illegality' and Deportability in Everyday Life." *Annual Review of Anthropology* 31: 419–47.

——. 2013. "Spectacles of Migrant 'Illegality': The Scene of Exclusion, the Obscene of Inclusion." *Racial and Ethnic Studies* 36, no. 7: 1–19.

——, ed. 2017a. *The Borders of "Europe": Autonomy of Migration, Tactics of Bordering*. Durham, NC: Duke University Press.

——. 2017b. "The Borders of 'Europe' and the European Question." In *The Borders of "Europe": Autonomy of Migration, Tactics of Bordering*, edited by Nicholas De Genova, 1–35. Durham, NC: Duke University Press.

De Grazia, Victoria. 2006. *Irresistible Empire: America's Advance through Twentieth-Century Europe*. Cambridge, MA: Belknap Press of Harvard University Press.

De Pasquale, Elena, and Nino Arena. 2011. *Sullo stesso barcone: Lampedusa e Linosa si raccontano*. Todi, Italy: Tau Editrice.

Dei Gaslini, Mario. 1933. "L'anima e il volto degli arabi libici." *L'Oltremare* 7, no. 7 (July): 287–90.

Del Boca, Angelo. 2005. *Italiani, brava gente?* Vicenza, Italy: Neri Pozza Editore.

——. 2010a. *Gli Italiani in Libia: Tripoli bel suol d'amore, 1860–1922*. Rev. ed. Vol. 1. Milan: Mondadori.

——. 2010b. *Gli Italiani in Libia: Dal Fascismo a Ghedaffi*. Rev. ed. Vol. 2. Milan: Mondadori.

Del Grande, Gabriele. 2008. *Mamadou va a morire: La strage dei clandestini nel Mediterraneo*. Rome: Infinito Edizioni.

———. 2009. "Frontiera Sahara: I campi di detenzione nel deserto libico." *Fortress Europe* (blog). January 2. Accessed August 8, 2018. http://fortresseurope .blogspot.com/2006/01/frontiera-sahara-i-campi-di-detenzione.html.

———. 2010. *Il Mare di Mezzo al tempo dei respingimenti*. Rome: Infinito Edizioni.

Deleuze, Gilles, and Félix Guattari. 1987. *A Thousand Plateaus: Capitalism and Schizophrenia*. Translated by Brian Massumi. Minneapolis: University of Minnesota Press.

Deplano, Valeria. 2017. *La madrepatria è una terra straniera: Libici, eritrei e Somali nell'Italia del dopoguerra (1945–60)*. Florence: Le Monnier.

Di Benedetto Montaccini, Veronica, and Giacomo Zandonini. 2014. "Ponte Galeria, 'la Guantanamo italiana,' la situazione al Cie dopo il cambio gestione." *La Repubblica*, December 22. Accessed August 8, 2018. http://www.repubblica.it /solidarieta/immigrazione/2014/12/22/news/ponte_galeria_la _guantanamo_italiana_la_situazione_al_cie_di_ponte_galeria_dopo_il _cambio_gestione-103531674/?ref=search.

Di Cesare, Donatella. 2014. *Crimini contro l'ospitalità: Vita e violenza nei centri per gli stranieri*. Genoa: Il Melangolo.

Di Giulio, Francesca, and Federico Cresti, eds. 2016. *Rovesci della fortuna: La minoranza italiana in Libia dalla seconda guerra mondiale all'espulsione 1940–70*. Arricia, Italy: Aracne.

Di Sante, Costantino, ed. 2001. *I campi di concentramento in Italia: Dall'internamento alla deportazione, 1940–45*. Milan: FrancoAngeli.

Dickie, John. 1999. *Darkest Italy: Nation and Stereotypes of the Mezzogiorno, 1860–1900*. New York: St. Martin's Press.

Dietrich, Helmut. 2005. "The Desert Front—EU Refugee Camps in North Africa?" *Statewatch* (blog), March 12. Accessed August 8, 2018. http://www.statewatch .org/news/2005/mar/12eu-refugee-camps.htm.

Diken, Bülent, and Carsten Bagge Laustsen. 2005. *The Culture of Exception: Sociology Facing the Camp*. London: Routledge.

Dionne, E. J., Jr. 1986. "Italian Isle, Site of U.S. Base, Is Fearful of Qaddafi's Anger." *New York Times*, May 27. Accessed August 8, 2018, http://www.nytimes.com /1986/05/27/world/italian-isle-site-of-us-base-is-fearful-of-qaddafi-s-anger .html.

"Dislocamenti a Sidi Ahmed el Magrum." 1932. *L'Italia Coloniale* 9, no. 3 (March): 37.

Documents on Italian War Crimes Submitted to United Nations War Crimes Commission by the Imperial Ethiopian Government. 1949–50. Vols. 1–2. Addis Ababa: Ministry of Justice.

Drudi, Emilio. 2013. "L'inferno dei profughi libici a Burshada." *Buongiorno Latina*, June 9. Accessed August 8, 2018. http://www.buongiornolatina.it/linferno -dei-profughi-libici-a-burshada.

Dufourmantelle, Anne. 2013. "Hospitality—Under Compassion and Violence." In *The Conditions of Hospitality: Ethics, Politics, and Aesthetics on the Threshold of the Possible*, edited by Thomas Claviez, 13–23. New York: Fordham University Press.

Ebner, Michael. 2011. *Ordinary Violence in Mussolini's Italy*. Cambridge: Cambridge University Press.

"Ed ora, senza la figura del commissario straordinario, come verrà gestita l'emergenza nomadi? «Il Piano del Comune va avanti»" 2011. *iltempo.it*, November 22. Accessed August 8, 2018. http://www.iltempo.it/roma-capitale/2011/11/22 /news/br-ed-ora-senza-la-figura-del-commissario-straordinario-come-verra -gestita-l-emergenza-nomadi-il-piano-del-comune-va-avanti-784562.

Elkins, Caroline. 2005. *Imperial Reckoning: The Untold Story of Britain's Gulag in Kenya.* New York: Henry Holt.

Elliott, Anthony, and John Urry. 2010. *Mobile Lives.* London: Routledge.

Eltahawy, Diana. 2012. "Migrants in Libya: 'They Don't Treat Us Like Humans.'" *Amnesty International News* (blog), September 18. Accessed August 8, 2018. www.amnesty.org/en/news/blog-migrants-libya-they-don-t-treat-us-humans -2012-09-18.

Erlanger, Steven. 2001. "Four Guilty in Fatal 1986 Berlin Disco Bombing Linked to Libya." *New York Times*, November 14. Accessed August 8, 2018. http://www .nytimes.com/2001/11/14/world/4-guilty-in-fatal-1986-berlin-disco-bombing -linked-to-libya.html.

European Roma Rights Center. 2000. *Campland: Racial Segregationo of Roma in Italy.* Country Report Series No. 9. October. Budapest: European Roma Rights Center.

——. 2015. "Municipality of Rome Condemned for La Barbuta Camp." *ERRC Newsletter*, June 10. Accessed August 8, 2018. http://www.errc.org/article /municipality-of-rome-condemned-for-la-barbuta-camp-for-the-first-time-in -europe-an-official-roma-only-settlement-ruled-discriminatory/4369.

Evans-Pritchard, E. E. 1945a. "The Distribution of Sanusi Lodges." *Africa* 15 (4): 183–87.

——. 1945b. "The Sanusi of Cyrenaica." *Africa* 15 (2): 61–79.

——. 1949. *The Sanusi of Cyrenaica.* Oxford: Clarendon Press.

Facondi, Lara. 2012. "Rom, udienza su La Barbuta: 'Viviamo come in un carcere." *Nuovopaesesera.it*, November 9. Accessed January 23, 2013. http://www .paesesera.it/Cronaca/Rom-udienza-su-La-Barbuta-Viviamo-come-in-un -carcere.

Fagan, Andrew. 2010. *The Atlas of Human Rights: Mapping Violations of Freedom around the Globe.* Berkeley: University of California Press.

Fanon, Frantz. 2004. *The Wretched of the Earth.* Translated by Richard Philcox. New York: Grove Press. Originally published 1963 by Présence Africaine.

Fantoli, Amilcare. 1934. "Le strade della Cirenaica." *Le Vie d'Italia* 40 (June): 437–48.

Fascist Legacy. 1989. Film. Directed by Ken Kirby. London: BBC Productions.

Fassin, Didier, and Mariella Pandolfi, eds. 2010. *Contemporary States of Emergency: The Politics of Military and Humanitarian Interventions.* New York: Zone Books.

Feldman, Gregory. 2012. *The Migration Apparatus: Security, Labor, and Policymaking in the European Union.* Stanford, CA: Stanford University Press.

Fernandez, Manny, and Katie Benner. 2018. "The Billion-Dollar Business of Operating Shelters for Migrant Children." *New York Times*, June 21, A15.

Fernando, Mayanthi, and Cristiana Giordano. 2016. "Refugees and the Crisis of Europe." Hot Spots. *Cultural Anthropology*, June 28. https://culanth.org /fieldsights/911-refugees-and-the-crisis-of-europe.

Finzi, Daniele. 2004. *La vita quotidiana di un campo di concentramento fascista: Ribelli sloveni nel querceto di Renicci-Anghiari (Arezzo)*. Rome: Carocci.

Fiore, Teresa. 2017. *Pre-occupied Spaces: Remapping Italy's Transnational Migrations and Colonial Legacies*. New York: Fordham University Press.

Fisher, Ian. 2007. "Romanian Premier Tries to Calm Italy after a Killing." *New York Times*, November 8. Accessed August 8, 2018. http://www.nytimes.com/2007/11/08/world/europe/08italy.html?_r=0.

Fogu, Claudio, and Lucia Re, eds. 2010. Special issue on "Italy in the Mediterranean." *California Italian Studies* 1 (1). Accessed August 8, 2018. https://escholarship.org/uc/ismrg_cisj/1/1.

Forgacs, David. 2014. *Italy's Margins: Social Exclusion and Nation Formation since 1861*. Cambridge: Cambridge University Press.

——. 2016. "Coasts, Blockades and the Free Movement of People." In *Italian Mobilities*, edited by Ruth Ben-Ghiat and Stephanie Malia Hom, 175–99. London: Routledge.

Foucault, Michel. 1988. *Madness and Civilization: A History of Insanity in the Age of Reason*. Translated by Richard Howard. 2nd ed. New York: Vintage Books.

——. 1990. *The History of Sexuality*. Vol. 1. Translated by Robert Hurley. New York: Vintage Books.

——. 1994. *The Order of Things: An Archaeology of the Human Sciences*. New York: Vintage Books. Originally published 1966 by Éditions Gallimard.

——. 1995. *Discipline and Punish: The Birth of the Prison*. Translated by Alan Sheridan. 2nd ed. New York: Vintage Books.

——. 2003. *Society Must Be Defended: Lectures at the Collège de France, 1975–76*. Edited by Mauro Bertani and Alessandro Fontana. Translated by David Macey. New York: Picador.

Fowler, Gary L. 1973. "Decolonization of Rural Libya." *Annals of the Association of American Geographers* 63, no. 4 (December): 490–506.

Fozzi, Daniela. 2010. *Tra prevenzione e repressione: Il domicilio coatto nell'Italia liberale*. Rome: Carocci.

Frankl, Viktor. 1984. *Man's Search for Meaning: An Introduction to Logotherapy*. Translated by Ilse Lasch. 3rd ed. New York: Simon & Schuster.

Frontex. 2014. *Annual Risk Analysis, 2014*. Warsaw: Frontex.

Fuller, Mia. 2004. "Tradition as a Means to the End of Tradition: Farmers' Houses in Italy's Fascist-Era 'New Towns.'" In *The End of Tradition?*, edited by Nezar AlSayyad, 171–86. London: Routledge.

——. 2007. *Moderns Abroad: Architecture, Cities, and Italian Imperialism*. London: Routledge.

——. 2017. "1931: Il leone del deserto e il suo boia." In *Storia mondiale dell'Italia*, edited by Andrea Giardina, 629–44. Rome and Bari: Laterza.

Fuocoammare. 2016. Film. Directed by Gianfranco Rosi. Rome: Stemal Entertainment, Istituto Luce/Cinecittà, Rai Cinema, Les Films d'Ici, Arte France Cinema, Kino Lorber.

Gabaccia, Donna. 2000. *Italy's Many Diasporas*. London: Routledge.

Galluccio, Fabio. 2003. *I lager in Italia: La memoria sepolta nei duecento luoghi di deportazione fascisti*. Civezzano, Italy: Nonluoghi Libere Edizioni.

Garfinkel, Paul. 2011. "Forced Residence in Liberal Italy: A Pre-history." *Journal of Modern Italian Studies* 16 (1): 37–58.

Gatti, Fabrizio. 2005. "Io, clandestino a Lampedusa." *L'Espresso*, October 7. Accessed August 8, 2018. http://espresso.repubblica.it/palazzo/2005/10/07/news/io-clandestino-a-lampedusa-1.594.

———. 2007. *Bilal: Viaggiare, lavorare, morire da clandestini*. Milan: Bur.

Genco, Mario. 1989. "L'agonia dei deportati libici nella colonia penale di Ustica." *Studi piacentini* 5 (1): 89–113.

Ghandhi, Sandy, ed. 2012. *Blackstone's International Human Rights Documents*. 8th ed. Oxford: Oxford University Press.

Gheriani, Omar. 2007. "Banco di Roma and the 'Penetrazione Pacifica' of Tripolitania." *A Gateway into History: Scattered Papers from Libyan History* (blog). April 15. Accessed August 8, 2018. http://abughilan.blogspot.com/2007/04/banco-di-roma-and-penetrazione-pacifica.html.

Ghezzi, Carla, and Salaheddin Hasan Sury, eds. 2004. *Terzo Convegno su gli esiliati libici nel periodo coloniale: 30–31 ottobre 2002, Isola di Ponza*. Rome: Istituto italiano per l'Africa e l'Oriente.

Ghirardo, Diane. 2013. *Italy: Modern Architectures in History*. London: Reaktion Books.

Giordano, Cristiana. 2014. *Migrants in Translation: Caring and Logics of Difference in Contemporary Italy*. Berkeley: University of California Press.

Goglia, Luigi. 1986. "The Capture, Trial and Death of Omar al-Mukhtar in the Italian Press." In *Omar al-Mukhtar: The Italian Reconquest of Libya*, translated by John Gilbert, 173–203. London: Darf.

Goldberg, Harvey E., ed. 1980. *The Book of Mordechai: A Study of the Jews of Libya*. Philadelphia: Institute for the Study of Human Issues.

———. 1990. *Jewish Life in Muslim Libya: Rivals & Relatives*. Chicago: University of Chicago Press.

Graziani, Rodolfo. 1932. *Cirenaica pacificata*. Milan: Mondadori.

Graziosi, Paolo. 2002. "L'organizzazione sanitaria nella colonia penale di Ustica (1911–1912)." *Lettera del Centro Studi e Documentazione Isola di Ustica* Anno 4, nos. 11–12 (July–December): 33–36.

Gregory, Desmond. 1996. *Malta, Britain, and the European Powers, 1793–1815*. London: Associated University Presses.

Grilli, Fabio. 2017a. "La Barbuta come la 'terra dei fuochi': Il M5s spinge per l'intervento dell'Esercito." *Roma Today*, October 24. Accessed August 8, 2018. http://tuscolano.romatoday.it/morena/la-barbuta-chiesta-applicazione-legge-terra-dei-fuochi.html.

———. 2017b. "Manifestazione e consiglio straordinario: I roghi de La Barbuta scaldano l'estate." *Roma Today*, July 14. Accessed August 8, 2018. http://tuscolano.romatoday.it/consiglio-straordinario-manifestazione-prefettura-roghi-la-barbuta.html.

Hailey, Charlie. 2009. *Camps: A Guide to 21st-Century Space*. Cambridge, MA: MIT Press.

Hamood, Sara. 2006. *African Transit Migration through Libya to Europe: The Human Cost*. Special Report. Cairo: American University in Cairo, Forced Migration and Refugee Studies.

Hanel, Norbert. 2007. "Military Camps, *Canabae*, and *Vici*: The Archaeological Evidence." In *A Companion to the Roman Army*, edited by Paul Erdkamp, 395–416. Oxford: Blackwell.

Hardt, Michael, and Antonio Negri. 2000. *Empire*. Cambridge, MA: Harvard University Press.

Harney, Nicholas. 1998. *Eh Paesan! Being Italian in Toronto*. Toronto: University of Toronto Press.

———. 2016. "Italian Mobilities and Circulating Diasporas in Neoliberal Times." In *Italian Mobilities*, edited by Ruth Ben-Ghiat and Stephanie Malia Hom, 46–67. London: Routledge.

Harragas. 2009. Film. Directed by Merzak Allouache. Paris: Libris Films.

Hatefutsoth, Beth. 1980. *Libya: An Extinct Jewish Community*. Tel-Aviv: Nahum Goldmann Museum of the Jewish Diaspora.

Hepworth, Kate. 2012. "Abject Citizens: Italian 'Nomad Emergencies' and the Deportability of Romanian Roma." *Citizenship Studies* 16 (3): 431–49.

Herodotus. 2009. *The Landmark Herodotus: The Histories*. Edited by Robert B. Strassler. Translated by Andrea Purvis. New York: Random House.

Herzfeld, Michael. 2009. *Evicted from Eternity: The Restructuring of Modern Rome*. Chicago: University of Chicago Press.

Hesnawi, Habib W. el-. 1988. *The Story of the Libyans' Jihad (Resistance) against Italian Colonialism, 1911–43: Illustrations, Documents, and Statistics*. Tripoli, Libya: A Libyans' Jihad Studies Centre Publication.

Hirabayashi, James. 1994. "'Concentration Camp' or 'Relocation Center': What's in a Name?" *Japanese American National Museum Quarterly* (Autumn): 5–10.

Hoffman, Paola. 1990. *La mia Libia*. Genoa: Marietti.

Holland, Eugene W. 2011. *Nomad Citizenship: Free-Market Communism and the Slow-Motion General Strike*. Minneapolis: University of Minnesota Press.

Hom, Stephanie Malia. 2012. "Empires of Tourism: Travel and Rhetoric in Italian Colonial Libya and Albania, 1911–43." *Journal of Tourism History* 4 (3): 281–300.

———. 2015. *The Beautiful Country: Tourism and the Impossible State of Destination Italy*. Toronto: University of Toronto Press.

———. 2016. "Becoming *Ospite*: Hospitality and Mobility at the Center of Temporary Permanence." In *Italian Mobilities*, edited by Ruth Ben-Ghiat and Stephanie Malia Hom, 88–110. London: Routledge.

———. 2017. "DP Camps and *Hachsharot* in Italy after the War." Digital Media Review. *Italian American Review* 7 (1): 109–12.

Hom Cary, Stephanie. 2007. "Destination Italy: Tourism, Colonialism, and the Modern Italian Nation-State, 1861–1947." PhD diss., University of California Berkeley.

Horden, Peregrine, and Nicholas Purcell. 2000. *The Corrupting Sea: A Study of Mediterranean History*. Oxford, UK: Blackwell.

Hsu, Roland, ed. 2010. *Ethnic Europe: Mobility, Identity, and Conflict in a Globalized World*. Stanford, CA: Stanford University Press.

Human Rights Watch. 2006. *Libya: Stemming the Flow: Abuses against Migrants, Asylum Seekers and Refugees*. New York: Human Rights Watch.

———. 2009. *Pushed back, Pushed around: Italy's Forced Return of Boat Migrants and Asylum Seekers, Libya's Mistreatment of Migrants and Asylum Seekers*. New York: Human Rights Watch.

———. 2011. *Everyday Intolerance: Racist and Xenophobic Violence in Italy*. New York: Human Rights Watch.

Hyslop, Jonathan. 2011. "The Invention of the Concentration Camp: Cuba, Southern Africa, and the Philippines." *South African Historical Journal* 63 (2): 251–76.

"I luoghi dell'esodo in Piemonte. Alessandria e provincia. Caserma Giuseppe Passalacqua, corso Alessandria 62, Tortona." n.d. *L'Esodo istriano-fiumano-dalmata in Piemonte*. Digital Exhibition. Istituto Piemontese per la Storia della Resistenza e della Società Contemporanea 'Giorgio Agosti.' Accessed August 8, 2018. http://intranet.istoreto.it/esodo/luogo.asp?id_luogo=11.

I nostri anni migliori. 2012. Film. Directed by Matteo Calore and Stefano Collizzolli. Rome: ZaLab.

"I 'nuovi italiani' nella riforma della cittadinanza: L'impatto dello ius soli in Italia." 2017. *La Repubblica*, June 15. Accessed August 8, 2018. http://www.repubblica.it/solidarieta/diritti-umani/2017/06/15/news/i_nuovi_italiani_nella_riforma_della_cittadinanza_l_impatto_dello_ius_soli_in_italia-168145760/.

Iacopini, Luigi Scoppola. 2015. *I 'dimenticati': Da colonizzatori a profughi, gli italiani in Libia 1943–74*. Foligno, Italy: Editoriale Umbra.

"Il Senato rinvia la discussione sullo Ius soli. Zanda: Ora la maggioranza non c'è." 2017. *Rai News*, September 12. Accessed August 8, 2018. http://www.rainews.it/dl/rainews/articoli/Il-Senato-rinvia-la-discussione-sullo-Ius-soli-Zanda-ora-la-maggioranza-manca-2b778d97-9fc0-4b1f-8e7e-d1b3c1aff57e.html.

Impagliazzo, Marco, ed. 2008. *Il caso zingari*. Milan: Leonardo International.

"Incendio nel campo rom 'La Barbuta.'" 2015. *Il Tempo*, July 21. Accessed August 8, 2018. http://www.iltempo.it/roma-capitale/2015/07/21/news/incendio-nel-campo-rom-la-barbuta-983009/.

Io, la mia famiglia rom e Woody Allen. 2009. Film. Directed by Laura Halilovic. Italy: 2 + 1 and Zenit Arte Audiovisive, in collaboration with Rai Tre, Aria Viva.

IOM (International Organization for Migration). 2014. *Fatal Journeys: Tracking Lives Lost during Migration*. Edited by Tara Brian and Frank Laczko. Geneva: International Organization for Migration.

Isin, Engin, and Bryan Turner, eds. 2002. *Handbook of Citizenship Studies*. London: Sage.

"Italian Group Wins $1.29bn Libyan Coastal Road Contract." 2013. *Global Construction Review*, August 15. Accessed August 8, 2018. http://www.globalconstructionreview.com/news/italian-group-wins-129bn-libyan-coastal-road-contr/.

The Italian Empire: Libya. 1940. New York: Italian Library of Information.

Jefa'iri, Mohamed al-. 1989. *The Libyan Deportees in the Prisons of the Italian Islands: Documents, Statistics, Names, Illustrations*. Tripoli: Libyan Studies Center.

Jerary, Muhammad T. 2005. "Damages Caused by the Italian Fascist Colonization of Libya." In *Italian Colonialism*, edited by Ruth Ben-Ghiat and Mia Fuller, 203–8. New York: Palgrave.

Johnson, Douglas L. 1973. *Jabal al-Akhdar, Cyrenaica: An Historical Geography of Settlement and Livelihood.* Research Paper No. 148. Chicago: University of Chicago, Department of Geography.

Jonas, Raymond. 2011. *The Battle of Adwa: African Victory in the Age of Empire.* Cambridge, MA: Belknap Press of Harvard University Press.

Jongmans, D. G. 1964. *Libie, land van de dorst.* Uitgevers Te Meppel, Netherlands: J. A. Boom en Zoon.

Josephus (Titus Flavius). 1927. *The Jewish War.* Bks. 1–3. Translated by H. St. J. Thackeray. Loeb Classical Library. London: William Heinemann.

Journal of Modern Italian Studies. 2011. Special issue on Roma and Sinti in Contemporary Italy. 16 (5): 583–666.

Kamiński, Andrzej J. 1982. *Konzentrationslager 1896 bis heute: Eine Analyse.* Stuttgart: Verlag W. Kohlhammer.

Kara, Siddarth. 2009. *Sex Trafficking: Inside the Business of Modern Slavery.* New York: Columbia University Press.

Kemény, Anna Milanini. 1973. *La Società d'Esplorazione Commerciale in Africa e la politica coloniale (1879–1914).* Florence, Italy: La Nuova Italia, Pubblicazioni della Facoltà di Lettere e Filosofie dell'Università degli Studi di Milano.

Kersevan, Alessandra. 2008. *Lager italiani: Pulizia etnica e campi di concentramento fascisti per civili jugoslavi 1941–43.* Rome: Nutrimenti.

Kodani Hill, Kimi, ed. 2000. *Topaz Moon: Chiura Obata's Art of the Internment.* Berkeley, CA: Heyday Books.

"La colonia penale agricola di Bengasi." 1926. *L'Italia Coloniale* 3, no. 10 (October): 196.

"La fine di Omar el Muctar." 1931. *L'Italia Coloniale* 8, no. 10 (October): 157–59.

La formazione de l'impero coloniale italiano. 1938. Vol. 1, "Le prime imprese coloniali: La rinascita coloniale." Milan: Fratelli Treves.

"La pulizia del Gebel Cirenaico." 1930. *L'Oltremare* 4, no. 12 (December): 498–99.

La strada litoranea della Libia. 1937. Verona: Officine Grafiche A. Mondadori.

Labanca, Nicola. 2002. *Oltremare: Storia dell'espansione coloniale italiana.* Bologna: Il Mulino.

——. 2005. "Italian Colonial Internment." In *Italian Colonialism*, edited by Ruth Ben-Ghiat and Mia Fuller, 27–36. New York: Palgrave Macmillan.

"Lampedusa, scontri tra migranti e polizia. Un incendio devasta il Cie: 24 feriti." 2009. *Corriere della Sera*, February 18. Accessed August 8, 2018. http://www.corriere.it/cronache/09_febbraio_18/lampedusa_incendio_cie_scontri_immigrati_forze_ordine_43a1d466-fdb2-11dd-aa50-00144f02aabc.shtml.

Lanza, Angela. 2014. *La storia di uno è la storia di tutti, con il testo della carta di Lampedusa.* Guidonia, Italy: iacobellieditore.

Le Bohec, Yann. 1994. *The Imperial Roman Army.* London: B. T. Batsford.

Le Cour Grandmaison, Olivier, Gilles Lhuilier, and Jérôme Valluy, eds. 2007. *Le retour des camps? Sangatte, Lampedusa, Guantanamo.* Paris: Éditions Autrement.

Le Houerou, Fabienne. 1994. *L'épopée des soldats de Mussolini en Abyssinie.* Paris: L'Harmattan.

Lembo, Daniele. 2011. *La Libia Italiana: Italo Balbo, l'esercito dei ventimila e la colonizzazione demografica della Libia.* Rome: IBN Editore.

Levi, Primo. 1989. *The Drowned and the Saved*. Translated by Raymond Rosenthal. New York: Vintage Books.

Levis Sullam, Simon. 2018. *The Italian Executioners: The Genocide of the Jews of Italy*. Translated by Oona Smyth with Claudia Patane. Princeton, NJ: Princeton University Press.

Lewis, Charlton T., and Charles Short. 1879. *A Latin Dictionary*. Rev. ed. Oxford: Clarendon Press.

Liberti, Stefano. 2008. *A sud di Lampedusa: Cinque anni di viaggi sulle rotte dei migranti*. Rome: Edizioni minimum fax.

Limbo. 2014. Film. Directed by Matteo Calore and Gustavo Hofer. Rome: ZaLab.

Lion of the Desert. 1981. Film. Directed by Moustapha Akkad. Tripoli: Falcon International Productions.

Lischi, Dario. 1934. *Viaggio di un cronista fascista in Cirenaica*. Pisa: Nistri-Lischi Editori.

"L'Italia per i suoi sudditi musulmani." 1938. *Rivista delle Colonie*, September, 1177–91.

Lo, Ruth. 2013. "The Architecture and Planning of Fascist New Towns in Sardinia." *SAH Newsletter*, March 14. Accessed August 8, 2018. http://www.sah.org/publications-and-research/sah-newsletter/sah-newsletter-ind/2013/03/14/the-architecture-and-planning-of-fascist-new-towns-in-sardinia.

Lobban, Richard A., Jr., and Christopher H. Dalton. 2014. *Libya: History and Revolution*. Santa Barbara, CA: Praeger, ABC-CLIO.

Locatelli, Francesca. 2016. "Migrating to the Colonies and Building the Myth of 'Italiani brava gente': The Rise, Demise, and Legacy of Settler Colonialism." In *Italian Mobilities*, edited by Ruth Ben-Ghiat and Stephanie Malia Hom, 133–51. London: Routledge.

Locchi, Maria Chiara. 2014. "The Mediterranean Sea as European Border: Trans-Mediterranean Migration, Forced Return and Violation of Rights." In *Borders, Fences, Walls: State of Insecurity?*, edited by Elisabeth Vallet, 11–26. London: Ashgate.

Lombroso, Cesare. 2011. *L'uomo delinquente studiato in rapporto all'antropologia, alla medicina legale ed alle discipline carcerarie*. Bologna: Il Mulino. Originally published 1876 by Hoepli.

Loyd, Jenna M., and Alison Mountz. 2014. "Managing Migration, Scaling Sovereignty on Islands." *Island Studies Journal* 9 (1): 23–42.

Lucht, Hans. 2011. "The Killing Seas." *New York Times*, May 18, A27.

——. 2012. *Darkness before Daybreak: African Migrants Living on the Margins in Southern Italy Today*. Berkeley: University of California Press.

Mack Smith, Denis. 1981. *Mussolini*. London: Weidenfeld and Nicolson.

Maggiolini, Edoardo Vacca. 1928. "La colonia penale di Sghedeida." *L'Italia Coloniale* 5, no. 8 (August): 168–69.

Maimuni, Ibrahim al-'Arabi al-'Amari al-, and Fathi Abu-'l-Qasim al-'Arabi al-'Amari. 2006. *Dhikrayat Mu'taqal al'Uqaila* [Memoirs of the el-Agheila concentration camp]. Tripoli: Libyan Studies Center.

Malinarich, Nathalie. 2001. "Flashback: The Berlin Disco Bombing." *BBC News*, November 13. Accessed August 8, 2018. http://news.bbc.co.uk/2/hi/europe/1653848.stm.

Mamdani, Mahmood. 1996. *Citizen and Subject: Contemporary Africa and the Legacy of Late Colonialism.* Princeton, NJ: Princeton University Press.

Mancini, Enzo. 1978. *Le isole del sole: Natura, storia, arte, turismo delle Pelagie (Lampedusa, Linosa, Lampione).* Milan: Mursia.

Mantovani, Vincenzo. 1982. "Fuga da Lampedusa." *Rivista anarchica* 12 (100): 16–17.

Maragnani, Laura, and Isoke Aikpitanyi. 2007. *Le ragazze di Benin City: La tratta delle nuove schiave dalla Nigeria ai marciapiedi d'Italia.* Milan: Melampo.

Marchetti, Chiara. 2006. *Un mondo di rifugiati: Migrazioni forzate e campi profughi.* Bologna: EMI.

Marchi, Luca. 2010. *Libia 1911–2011: Gli italiani da colonizzatori a profughi.* Udine, Italy: Storia Kappa Vu.

Martucci, Roberto. 1980. *Emergenza e tutela dell'ordine pubblico nell'Italia liberale: Regime eccezionale e leggi per la repressioen dei reati di brigantaggio, 1861–65.* Bologna: Il Mulino.

———. 1999. *L'invenzione dell'Italia unita, 1855–64.* Milan: Sansoni.

Maslah, Amina. 2012. "Migrazioni isolane nel canale di Sicilia tra 1843 e 1900." *Palaver* 1: 83–98.

Matvejević, Predrag. 1998. *Il Mediterraneo e l'Europa.* Milan: Garzanti.

Maugini, Armando. 1924. *Relazione sull'attività dell'Ufficio per i servizi agrari della Cirenaica.* Benghazi, Libya: Unione Tipografia Editore.

———. 1927. "La colonizzazione della Cirenaica." In *Per le nostre colonie*, edited by Istituto Agricolo Coloniale Italiano di Firenze. Florence: Vallecchi Editore, 131–56.

Mazzeo, Antonio. 2012. "Elogio Pd dei lager modello Lampedusa." *Peacelink: Telematica per la pace*, January 11. Accessed August 8, 2018. http://www.peacelink.it/migranti/a/35370.html.

Mbembe, Achille. 2003. "Necropolitics." Translated by Libby Meintjes. *Public Culture* 15 (1): 11–40.

McLaren, Brian. 2005. *Architecture and Tourism in Italian Colonial Libya.* Seattle: University of Washington Press.

MEDU (Medici per i Diritti Umani [Doctors for Human Rights]). 2012. *Behind Higher Fences: Report on the Identification and Deportation Centre of Ponte Galeria in Rome.* Rome: Medici per i Diritti Umani.

Mendizabal, Isabel, and Oscar Lao, Urko M. Marigorta, Andreas Wollstein, Leonor Gusmão, Vladimir Ferak, Mihai Ioana, Albena Jordanova, Radka Kaneva, Anastasia Kouvatsi, Vaidutis Kučinskas, Halyna Makukh, Andres Metspalu, Mihai G. Netea, Rosario de Pablo, Horolma Pamjav, Dragica Radojkovic, Sarah J.H. Rolleston, Jadranka Sertic, Milan Macek, Jr., David Comas, Manfred Kayser. 2012. "Reconstructing the Population History of European Romani from Genome-Wide Data." *Current Biology* 22: 2342–49.

Moe, Nelson. 2002. *The View from Vesuvius: Italian Culture and the Southern Question.* Berkeley: University of California Press.

Molfese, Franco. 1966. *Storia del brigantaggio dopo l'Unità.* Milan: Feltrinelli.

Molinari, Maria Luisa. 2006. *Villaggio San Marco, Via Remesina 32, Fossoli di Carpi: Storia di un villaggio per profughi giuliani.* Quaderni di Fossoli. Turin: EGA Editore.

Mondiani, Gennaro. 1939. "Il problema della cittadinanza ai sudditi coloniali." *Rivista delle Colonie* 8, no. 1 (January): 51–72.

Monk, Daniel Bertrand. 1998. "The Art of Castramentation." *Assemblage 36* (August): 64–83.

Monzini, Paola, Ferruccio Pastore, and Giuseppe Sciortino. 2004. *Human Smuggling to/through Italy*. Special Report on "The Human Smuggling and Trafficking in Migrants: Types, Origins and Dynamics in a Comparative Interdisciplinary Perspective." Rome: Centro Studi di Politica Internazionale.

Moore, Martin. 1940. *Fourth Shore: Italy's Mass Colonization of Libya*. London: Routledge.

Mucciarelli, Carlo. 1899. "Cenno sulle condizioni sanitarie della Colonia Coatti e degli Agenti di custodia in Assab, dal 26 giugno 1898 al 16 febbraio 1889." *Rivista di discipline carcerarie* Anno 24, no. 7 (July): 267–81.

Muller, Eric. 2001. *Free to Die for Their Country: The Story of the Japanese American Draft Resisters in World War II*. Chicago: University of Chicago Press.

Murray, Stuart J. 2006. "Thanatopolitics: On the Use of Death for Mobilizing Political Life." *Polygraph* 18: 191–215.

Neri, Italo. 1939. "Politica indigena: I centri agricoli musulmani della Libia." *Rivista delle Colonie* 13, no. 3 (March): 401–3.

Netz, Reviel. 2004. *Barbed Wire: An Ecology of Modernity*. Middletown, CT: Wesleyan University Press.

Nicolini, Giusi, with Marta Bellingreri. 2013. *Lampedusa: Conversazioni su isole, politica, migranti*. Turin: Edizioni Gruppo Abele.

Nigro, Vincenzo. 2008. "1986, quando Craxi pensò di attaccare la Libia." *La Repubblica*, October 31. Accessed August 8, 2018. http://ricerca.repubblica.it /repubblica/archivio/repubblica/2008/10/31/1986-quando-craxi-penso-di -attaccare-la.html.

Norris, Andrew, ed. 2005. *Politics, Metaphysics, and Death: Essays on Giorgio Agamben's Homo Sacer*. Durham, NC: Duke University Press.

"Notiziario d'Oltremare." 1931. *L'Oltremare* 4 (April): 151.

"Nuovi sbarchi a Lampedusa, i migranti arrivati nel 2011 sono 50mila." 2011. *Il Messaggero*, August 16. Accessed January 5, 2015. http://www.ilmessaggero.it /home_initalia/primopiano/nuovi_sbarchi_a_lampedusa_i_migranti _arrivati_nel_2011_sono_50mila/notizie/159726.shtml.

O'Healy, Àine. 2016. "Imagining Lampedusa." In *Italian Mobilities*, edited by Ruth Ben-Ghiat and Stephanie Malia Hom, 152–74. London: Routledge.

Okojie, Christiana E. E., and Franco Prina, eds. 2004. *Trafficking of Nigerian Girls to Italy = Il traffico delle ragazze nigeriane in Italia*. Turin: UN Interregional Crime and Justice Research Unit (UNICRI).

Oliva, Gianni. 2009. *Esuli. Dalle foibe ai campi profughi: la tragedia degli italiani di Istria, Fiume, e Dalmazia*. Milan: Mondadori.

Oliveri, Federico. 2012. "Migrants as Activist Citizens in Italy: Understanding the New Cycle of Struggles." *Citizenship Studies* 16 (5–6): 793–806.

Ong, Aihwa. 1999. *Flexible Citizenship: The Cultural Logics of Transnationality*. Durham, NC: Duke University Press.

Ornato, G. Z. 1939. "I Ventimila al lavoro nelle terre libiche." *Le Vie d'Italia* 45, no. 1 (January): 36–47.

Ottolenghi, Gustavo. 1997. *Gli italiani e il colonialismo: I campi di detenzione italiani in Africa*. Milan: SugarCo Edizioni.

Pacoda, Pierfrancesco. 2000. *Hip hop italiano: La CNN dei poveri*. Turin: Einaudi.

Palumbo, Patrizia, ed. 2003. *A Place in the Sun: Africa in Italian Colonial Culture from Post-Unification to the Present*. Berkeley: University of California Press.

Parati, Graziella. 2005. *Migration Italy: The Art of Talking Back in a Destination Culture*. Toronto: University of Toronto Press.

Parolin, Gianluca. 2009. *Citizenship in the Arab World: Kin, Religion and Nation-State*. Amsterdam: Amsterdam University Press.

Pasley, Sir Charles William. 1810. *Essay on the Military Policy and Institutions of the British Empire*. London: D.N. Shury for Edmund Lloyd.

Perera, Suvendrini. 2009. *Australia and the Insular Imagination: Beaches, Borders, Boats and Bodies*. London: Palgrave Macmillan.

Pergher, Roberta. 2018. *Mussolini's Nation-Empire: Sovereignty and Settlement in Italy's Borderlands, 1922–43*. Cambridge: Cambridge University Press.

Pesenti, Gustavo. 1932. *Danane: Nella Somàlia italiana, nel XXV anniversario del combattimento (9–10 febbraio 1907)*. Milan: L'Eroica.

Petrusewicz, Marta. 1998. *Come il Meridione diventa una questione: Rappresentazioni del Sud prima e dopo il Quarantotto*. Soveria Mannelli, Italy: Rubbinetto.

Piasere, Leonardo. 2005. *Popoli delle Discariche: Saggi di antropologia Zingari*. 2nd ed. Rome: CISU.

——. 2008. *I Rom d'Europa*. 3rd ed. Rome: Laterza.

Piccioli, Angelo. 1933. *La nuova Italia d'Oltremare: L'opera del fascismo nelle colonie italiane*. Milan: Mondadori.

Pliez, Olivier. 2002. "Vieux réseaux et nouvelles circulations entre les deux rives due Sahara." Special issue on "Le sahara, cette «autre Méditerranée»." *Méditerranée* 99 (3–4): 31–40.

Polybius. 2011. *The Histories*. Bks. 5–8. Translated by W. R. Paton. Revised by Frank W. Walbank and Christian Habicht. Loeb Classical Library. Cambridge, MA: Harvard University Press.

Ponsich, Michel, and Miguel Tarradell. 1965. *Garum et industries antiques de salaison dans la Méditerranée occidentale*. Paris: Presses Universitaires de France.

Ponzanesi, Sandra, and Daniela Merolla, eds. 2005. *Migrant Cartographies: New Cultural and Literary Spaces in Post-Colonial Europe*. Lanham, MD: Lexington Books.

Prestopino, Francesco. 1999. *Una città e il suo fotografo: La Bengasi coloniale (1912–41)*. Milan: La Vita Felice.

Proglio, Gabriele, and Laura Odasso, eds. 2018. *Border Lampedusa: Subjectivity, Visibility and Memory in Stories of Sea and Land*. New York: Palgrave Macmillan.

Pugliese, Joseph. 2010. "Transnational Carceral Archipelagoes: Lampedusa and Christmas Island." In *Trans-Mediterranean: Diasporas, Histories, Geopolitical Spaces*, edited by Joseph Pugliese, 105–24. Brussels: Peter Lang.

——. 2011. "Spectres of the Muselmann: Guantanamo Bay 'Theme Park' and the Torture of Omar Khadr." In *Torture: Power, Democracy and the Human Body*, edited by Shampa Biswas and Zahi Zalloua, 158–87. Seattle: University of Washington Press.

Rainero, Romain. 1986. "The Capture, Trial and Death of Omar al-Mukhtar in the Context of the Fascist Policy for the 'Reconquest' of Libya." In *Omar al-Mukhtar: The Italian Reconquest of Libya*, translated by John Gilbert, 119–203. London: Darf.

Rappas, Alexis. 2017. "Propriété et souverainetés imperiale et nationale dans la Méditerranée orientale de l'entre-deux-guerres." *Revue d'Histoire Moderne et Contemporaine* 64 (3): 64–89.

Ravizza, Adelgiso. 1926. "La conquista morale: La giustizia." In *La rinascita della Tripolitania: Memorie e studi sui quattro anni di governo del conte Giuseppe Volpi di Misurata*, 321–36. Milan: Mondadori.

Rawlence, Ben. 2016. *City of Thorns: Nine Lives in the World's Largest Refugee Camp.* New York: Picador.

Reale, Luigi. 2011. *Mussolini's Concentration Camps for Civilians: An Insight into the Nature of Fascist Racism.* London: Vallentine Mitchell.

Renucci, Florence. 2005. "La strumentalizzazione del concetto della cittadinanza in Libia negli anni Trenta." *Quaderni fiorentini per la storia del pensiero giuridico moderno* 33–34: 319–42.

Ricci, Leonardo. 1922. "Centri abitati e tribù nomadi." In *La Cirenaica: Geografia, economica, politica*, edited by Olinto Marinelli, 87–106. Milan: Antonio Villardi Editore.

Richardson, Alan. 2004. *Theoretical Aspects of Roman Camp and Fort Design.* BAR International Series 1321. Oxford, UK: British Archaeological Reports.

Rochat, Giorgio. 1973. *Il colonialismo italiano.* Turin: Loescher Editore.

——. 1986. "The Repression of Resistance in Cyrenaica (1927–31)." In *Omar al-Mukhtar: The Italian Reconquest of Libya*, translated by John Gilbert, 35–115. London: Darf.

——. 1991. *Guerre italiane in Libia e in Etiopia.* Treviso, Italy: Pagus Edizioni.

Romeo, Caterina, and Cristina Lombardi-Diop, eds. 2012. *Postcolonial Italy: Challenging National Homogeneity.* New York: Palgrave Macmillan.

Rosaldo, Renato. 1989. "Imperialist Nostalgia." Special issue on Memory and Counter-Memory. *Representations* 26 (Spring): 107–22.

Roumani, Maurice R. 2008. *The Jews of Libya: Coexistence, Persecution, Resettlement.* Brighton, UK: Sussex Academic Press.

Rovelli, Marco. 2006. *Lager italiani.* Milan: Bur Edizioni.

Ruberto, Laura, and Joseph Sciorra. 2017. *New Italian Migrations to the United States.* Vols. 1–2. Urbana: University of Illinois Press.

Ryan, Eileen. 2017. Review of *I 'dimenticati': Da colonizzatori a profughi, gli italiani in Libia 1943–74*, by Luigi Scoppola Iacopini, *Modern Italy* 22, no. 3 (August): 349–50.

——. 2018. *Religion as Resistance: Negotiating Authority in Colonial Libya.* Oxford: Oxford University Press.

Saada, Emmanuelle. 2012. *Empire's Children: Race, Filiation, and Citizenship in the French Colonies.* Translated by Arthur Goldhammer. Chicago: University of Chicago Press.

Said, Edward. 1978. *Orientalism.* New York: Vintage Books.

——. 1993. *Culture and Imperialism.* New York: Vintage.

Salerno, Eric. 2005. *Genocidio in Libia: Le atrocità nascoste dell'avventura coloniale italiana (1911–31)*. Rome: Manifestolibri.

——. 2008. *Uccideteli tutti. Libia 1943: Gli ebrei nel campo di concentramento fascista di Giado*. Milan: Il Saggiatore.

Salvatori, Domenico. 1989. *Prigioniero in India: Vita quotidiana e grande storia nel diario di un ufficiale*. Edited by Gianfranco Porta. Brescia, Italy: Grafo.

Santarelli, Enzo, Giorgio Rochat, Romain Rainero, and Luigi Goglia. 1986. *Omar al-Mukhtar: The Italian Reconquest of Libya*. Translated by John Gilbert. London: Darf.

Sanvisente, Bernardo. 1849. *L'isola di Lampedusa, eretta a colonia dal munificentissimo sovrano Ferdinando II*. Naples: Dalla Reale Tipografia Militare.

Sassen, Saskia. 2014. *Expulsions: Brutality and Complexity in the Global Economy*. Cambridge, MA: Harvard University Press.

Scalarini, Giuseppe. 1992. *Le mie isole*. Milan: FrancoAngeli.

Scheel, Stephan. 2017. "'The Secret Is to Look Good on Paper': Appropriating Mobility within and against a Machine of Illegalization." In *The Borders of "Europe": Autonomy of Migration, Tactics of Bordering*, edited by Nicholas De Genova, 37–63. Durham, NC: Duke University Press.

Scherer, Steve, and Adam Freeman. 2008. "Italy Warned Libya of Bombing, Saved Qaddafi's Life." *Bloomberg News*, October 30. Accessed January 5, 2015. http://www.bloomberg.com/apps/news?pid=newsarchive&sid=asdtPeIfTReg&refer=us.

Schmitt, Carl. 2006. *The Nomos of the Earth in the International Law of the Jus Publicum Europaeum*. Translated by G. L. Ulmen. New York: Telos Press Publishing.

Schneider, Jane, ed. 1998. *Italy's Southern Question: Orientalism in One Country*. Oxford: Berg.

Segrè, Claudio. 1974. *Fourth Shore: The Italian Colonization of Libya*. Chicago: University of Chicago Press.

——. 1990. *Italo Balbo: A Fascist Life*. Berkeley: University of California Press.

Serra, Fabrizio. 1933. *Italia e Senussia (Vent'anni di azione coloniale in Cirenaica)*. Milan: Fratelli Treves.

Sgroi, Ornella. 2007. "Lampa Lampa porta d'Europa." *La Sicilia*, November 22, 26.

Sherkasi, Muhammed. 1973. "Agricultural Settlement during the Italian Colonial Rule." *Economic Bulletin: Central Bank of Libya* 13: 18–26.

Sigona, Nando. 2003. "How Can a 'Nomad' Be a 'Refugee'? Kosovo Roma and Labelling Policy in Italy." *Sociology* 37 (1): 69–79.

——. 2005. "Locating 'The Gypsy Problem.' The Roma in Italy: Stereotyping, Labelling, and 'Nomad Camps.'" *Journal of Ethnic and Migration Studies* 31 (4): 741–56.

——. 2010. "Gypsies out of Italy! Social Exclusion and Racial Discrimination of Roma and Sinti in Italy." In *Italy Today: The Sick Man of Europe*, edited by Andrea Mammone and Giuseppe Veltri, 143–57. London: Routledge.

——. 2012. "Locating 'The Gypsy Problem.' The Roma in Italy: Stereotyping, Labelling and 'Nomad Camps.'" In *Roma in Europe: Migration, Education, Representation*, edited by Anca Pusca, 71–88. New York: International Debate Education Association.

Simon, Rachel. 1992. *Change within Tradition among Jewish Women in Libya*. Seattle: University of Washington Press.

Smith, Andrea, ed. 2003. *Europe's Invisible Migrants: Consequences of the Colonists' Return*. Amsterdam: Amsterdam University Press.

Smith, Horace. 1818. "Ozymandias." *The Examiner* February 1, 73.

Spackman, Barbara. 2017. *Accidental Orientalists: Modern Italian Travelers in Ottoman Lands*. Liverpool, UK: Liverpool University Press.

Spadaro, Barbara. 2013. *Una colonia italiana: Incontri, memorie e rappresentazioni tra Italia e Libia*. Florence: Le Monnier.

Spivak, Gayatri Chakavorty. 1988. "Can the Subaltern Speak?" In *Marxism and the Interpretation of Culture*, edited by Cary Nelson and Lawrence Grossberg, 271–313. Urbana: University of Illinois Press.

St. John, Ronald Bruce. 2008. *Libya: From Colony to Independence*. Oxford, UK: Oneworld.

Staines, Patrick. 2008. *Essays on Governing Malta (1800–13)*. San Gwann, Malta: Publishers Enterprises Group.

Staniscia, Stefania. 2011. *Islands: Hot Spots of Change*. Barcelona: LISt Lab Laboratorio Internazionale Editoriale.

Starr, Kevin. 2015. *California: A History*. Rev. ed. New York: Modern Library.

Steer, G. L. 1939. *A Date in the Desert*. London: Hodder and Stoughton.

Steimatsky, Noa. 2009. "The Cinecittà Refugee Camp (1945–50)." *October* 128 (Spring): 22–50.

Stermieri, Fabrizio. 2016. "Il villaggio della speranza." *Voce*, February 25. Accessed August 8, 2018. http://voce.it/it/articolo/1/memorie/il-villaggio-della-speranza.

Stewart-Steinberg, Suzanne. 2016. "Grounds for Reclamation: Fascism and Postfascism in the Pontine Marshes." *differences* 27 (1): 94–142.

Stoler, Ann Laura. 2008. "Imperial Debris: Reflections on Ruin and Ruination." *Cultural Anthropology* 23 (2): 191–219.

——. 2016. *Duress: Imperial Durabilities in Our Times*. Durham, NC: Duke University Press.

Stoler, Ann Laura, and Carole McGranahan. 2007. "Introduction." In *Imperial Formations*, edited by Ann Laura Stoler, Carole McGranahan, and Peter C. Perdue, 3–42. Santa Fe, NM: School for Advanced Research Press.

Stone, Dan. 2017. *Concentration Camps: A Short History*. Oxford: Oxford University Press.

Strazzeri, Martina. 2011. "Lampedusa, tagliarsi le vene per non essere rimpatriati." *Frontierenews.it*, June 21. Accessed August 8, 2018. http://frontierenews.it/2011/06/lampedusa-tagliarsi-le-vene-per-non-essere-rimpatriati/.

Stritmatter, Roger, and Lynne Kositsky. 2013. *On the Date, Sources, and Design of Shakespeare's* The Tempest. Jefferson, NC: MacFarland.

Sulpizi, Francesco, and Salaheddin Hasan Sury. 2002. *Primo Convegno su gli esiliati libici nel periodo coloniale: 28–29 ottobre 2000, Isole Tremiti*. Rome: Istituto Italiano per l'Africa e l'Oriente.

——, eds. 2003. *Secondo Convegno su gli esiliati libici nel periodo coloniale: 3–4 novembre 2001, Isole Egadi–Favignana*. Rome: Istituto Italiano per l'Africa e l'Oriente, Centro Libico per gli Studi Storici.

Sury, Salaheddin Hasan, and Giampaolo Malgeri, eds. 2005. *Gli esiliati libici nel periodo coloniale (1911–16): Raccolta documentaria*. Rome: Istituto Italiano per l'Africa e l'Oriente.

Svirsky, Marcelo, and Simone Bignall, eds. 2012. *Agamben and Colonialism*. Edinburgh: Edinburgh University Press.

Teruzzi, Attilio. 1931. *Cirenaica verde*. Milan: Mondadori.

Ticktin, Miriam. 2011. *Casualties of Care: Immigration and the Politics of Humanitarianism in France*. Berkeley: University of California Press.

Tintori, Guido. 2016. "Italian Mobilities and the *Demos*." In *Italian Mobilities*, edited by Ruth Ben-Ghiat and Stephanie Malia Hom, 111–32. London: Routledge.

Touring Club Italiano. 1929. *Guida d'Italia: Possedimenti e colonie*. Milan: Touring Club Italiano.

—— [Consociazione Turistica Italiana]. 1940. *Guida d'Italia: Italia meridionale e insulare, Libia. Guida Breve*. Milan: Touring Club Italiano.

Triandafyllidou, Anna. 2014. "Multi-levelling and Externalizing Migration and Asylum: Lessons from the Southern European Islands." *Island Studies Journal* 9 (1): 7–22.

Triaud, Jean-Louis. 1995. *La légende noire de la Sanûsiyya: Une confrérie musulmane saharienne sous le regard français (1840–1930)*. Vol. 2. Paris: Éditions de la Maison des Sciences de l'Homme.

Triulzi, Alessandro, and Robert Lawrence McKenzie, eds. 2013. *Long Journeys: African Migrants on the Road*. Leiden and Boston: Brill.

Trousset, Pol. 1974. *Recherches sur le limes tripolitanus: Du Chott el-Djerid a la frontière tuniso-libyenne*. Paris: Éditions du Centre National de la Recherche Scientifique.

Turcato, Davide. 2012. *Making Sense of Anarchism: Errico Malatesta's Experiments with Revolution, 1889–1900*. New York: Palgrave Macmillan.

"Turchi: Storie di elicotteri e barche a Lampedusa." 2009. Audio documentary. Reported by Marzia Coronati and Elise Melot. December. Accessed August 8, 2018. http://amisnet.org/agenzia/2009/12/09/turchi-storie-di-elicotteri-e-barche-a-lampedusa/.

Turner, Bryan, and Peter Hamilton, eds. 1994. *Citizenship: Critical Concepts*. Vols. 1 and 2. London: Routledge.

"Un nigeriano rifiuta l'espulsione, incendi e guerriglia al Cie di Ponte Galeria." 2013. *Corriere della Sera*, February 18.

UNHCR (UN Refugee Agency). 2014. "UNHCR Central Mediterranean Sea Initiative (CMSI): EU Solidarity for Rescue-at-Sea and Protection of Refugees and Migrants." December. Accessed August 8, 2018. http://www.unhcr.org/531990199.html.

——. 2018. "Figures at a Glance." August. Accessed August 8, 2018. http://www.unhcr.org/en-us/figures-at-a-glance.html.

Urry, John. 2007. *Mobilities*. Cambridge, UK: Polity.

Vacanze di Guerra: L'odissea dei bambini italiani di Libia. 2010. Film. Directed by Alessandro Rossetto. Rome: Luce.

Valera, Paolo. 1912. "Prigionieri di guerra nell'isola di Ustica." *Avanti!*, January 20, 3.

Valluy, Jérôme, ed. 2005. "Introduction: L'Europe des camps: La mise à l'écart des étrangers." *Cultures & Conflits* 57: 5–11.

Van Baar, Huub. 2015. "The Perpetual Mobile Machine of Forced Mobility: Europe's Roma and the Institutionalization of Rootlessness." In *The Irregularization of Migration in Contemporary Europe: Detention, Deportation, Drowning*, edited by Yolande Jansen, Robin Celikates, and Joost De Bloois, 71–86. New York: Rowman & Littlefield.

Vandewalle, Dirk. 2012. *A History of Modern Libya*. 2nd ed. Cambridge, UK: Cambridge University Press.

Varikas, Eleni. 2007. *Les Rebuts du monde: Figures du paria*. Paris: Stock.

Vassallo Paleologo, Fulvio. 2012. *Diritti sotto sequestro: Dall'emergenza umanitaria allo stato di eccezione*. Arriccia, Italy: Aracne.

Vellani, Ercole. 1931. "Cronache coloniali: Cirenaica. La cattura di Omar el Muktar." *Rivista delle Colonie Italiane* 5, no. 10 (October): 804–6.

Veneziani, Gianluca. 2015. "Se per il fisco italiano, gli esuli istriani sono ancora 'jugoslavi.'" *L'intraprendente: Giornale d'opinione dal Nord*, April 18. Accessed August 8, 2018. http://www.lintraprendente.it/2015/04/se-per-il-fisco -italiano-gli-esuli-istriani-sono-jugoslavi/.

Virgil. *The Aeneid*. Translated by Robert Fitzgerald. New York: Vintage Classics, 1983.

Virilio, Paul. 1975. *L'insecurité du territoire*. Paris: Stock.

Von Henneberg, Krystyna. 1996a. "The Construction of Fascist Libya: Modern Colonial Architecture and Urban Planning in Italian North Africa (1922–43)." PhD diss., University of California Berkeley.

——. 1996b. "Imperial Uncertainties: Architectural Syncretism and Improvisation in Fascist Colonial Libya." *Journal of Contemporary History* 31 (2): 373–95.

Wacher, John. 1995. *The Towns of Roman Britain*. Rev. ed. Abigdon, Oxon, UK: Routledge. Originally published 1975 by B. T. Blasford.

Wacquant, Loïc. 2008. *Urban Outcasts: A Comparative Sociology of Advanced Marginality*. Cambridge, UK: Polity.

Wallerstein, Immanuel. 2011. *The Modern World-System*. Parts I–IV. Berkeley: University of California Press.

Wang, ShiPu. 2018. *Chiura Obata: An American Modern*. Berkeley: University of California Press.

Waters, William. 2010. "Deportation, Expulsion, and the International Police of Aliens." In *The Deportation Regime: Sovereignty, Space, and the Freedom of Movement*, edited by Nicholas De Genova and Nathalie Peutz, 69–100. Durham, NC: Duke University Press.

Weiss-Wendt, Anton, ed. 2013. *The Nazi Genocide of the Roma: Reassessment and Commemoration*. Oxford: Berghahn.

Welch, Rhiannon. 2016a. "Contact, Contagion, Immunization: Gianni Amelio's Lamerica (1994)." In *Italian Mobilities*, edited by Ruth Ben-Ghiat and Stephanie Malia Hom, 68–87. London: Routledge.

——. 2016b. *Vital Subjects: Race and Biopolitics in Italy, 1860–1920*. Liverpool, UK: Liverpool University Press.

Wong, Aliza. 2006. *Race and the Nation in Liberal Italy, 1861–1911: Meridionalism, Empire, and Diaspora*. New York: Palgrave Macmillan.

Woodcock, Shannon. 2012. "Gender as Catalyst for Violence against Roma in Contemporary Italy." In *Roma in Europe: Migration, Education, Representation*, edited by Anca Pusca, 51–70. New York: International Debate Education Association.

Wright, John. 2010. *A History of Libya*. New York: Columbia University Press.

Zaccaria, Paola. 2013. "The Art and Poetics of Translation as Hospitality." In *The Conditions of Hospitality: Ethics, Politics, and Aesthetics on the Threshold of the Possible*, edited by Thomas Claviez, 168–84. New York: Fordham University Press.

Zerafa, Thomas. 2011. "When the British Planned to Make Lampedusa Part of the Maltese Islands." *Times of Malta*, July 17. Accessed August 8, 2018. http://www.timesofmalta.com/articles/view/20110717/life-features/When-the-British-planned-to-make-Lampedusa-part-of-the-Maltese-Islands.375992.

Zerai, Mussie. 2013. "Here's How to Live in Libya: Detention Centers for Refugees and Displaced Persons, Thanks to European Funds!" *Agenzia Habeshia per la Cooperazione allo Sviluppo*, June 5. Accessed August 8, 2018. http://habeshia.blogspot.ch/2013/06/heres-how-to-live-in-libya-detention.html.

Ziniti, Alessandra. 2011a. "Lampedusa, guerriglia urbana con feriti. Il sindaco De Rubeis: Mi difenderò." *La Repubblica*, September 21. Accessed August 8, 2018. http://palermo.repubblica.it/cronaca/2011/09/21/news/lampedusa_guerriglia_urbana_isolani_contro_maghrebini-21989712/.

——. 2011b. "Maroni: Esodo biblico, Ue assente, la Tunisia invia le truppe sulle coste." *La Repubblica*, February 14. Accessed August 8, 2018. palermo.repubblica.it/cronaca/2011/02/14/news/sbarchi_maroni_esodo_biblico-12432273/.

Index

CPSIA information can be obtained
at www.ICGtesting.com
Printed in the USA
FSHW020551310719
60555FS

9 781501 739903